THE SOCIAL THOUGHT
of the World Council
of Churches

THE
SOCIAL
THOUGHT
of the World Council
of Churches

by

EDWARD DUFF, S.J.

LONGMANS, GREEN AND CO
LONDON · NEW YORK · TORONTO

LONGMANS, GREEN AND CO LTD
6 & 7 CLIFFORD STREET LONDON WI
BOSTON HOUSE STRAND STREET CAPE TOWN
531 LITTLE COLLINS STREET MELBOURNE

LONGMANS, GREEN AND CO INC
55 FIFTH AVENUE NEW YORK 3

LONGMANS, GREEN AND CO
20 CRANFIELD ROAD TORONTO 16

ORIENT LONGMANS PRIVATE LTD
CALCUTTA BOMBAY MADRAS
DELHI VIJAYAWADA DACCA

First Published 1956

*Printed in Great Britain by
Jarrold & Sons Ltd, Norwich*

PREFACE

A PROJECT of this kind—to survey the mind of the Ecumenical Community as it judges the contemporary social order—could not be seriously undertaken without the co-operation of officials of the World Council of Churches. At the direction of the General Secretary, Dr. W. A. Visser 't Hooft, the Archives of the Council were made available to the writer with no limitations indicated as to their use. Indeed the only conceivable complaint is that the former Director of the World Council's Study Department, Dr. Nils Ehrenström, never failed to suggest more files to be searched. For, working at the Secretariat at Geneva made it possible to examine the records of the World Council's predecessor, the Universal Christian Council on Life and Work, successive drafts of World Council documents on social questions, the comments by collaborators of the ecumenical effort, the complete file of the Ecumenical Press Service, and the stenographic minutes of the relevant Sections of the Amsterdam and Evanston Assemblies.

The plan of the project and the rationale of the organization of the material of this study are described in the Introduction.

In the course of his work the writer profited from conversations with Professors William Banning, John C. Bennett, Panayotis Bratsiotis, Emil Brunner, V. A. Demant, Werner Kägi, Walter G. Muelder, and Doctors Hans ten Doornkaat, C. L. Patijn and J. C. C. Rupp. These conversations occurred at different stages of the development of the book and of the writer's understanding of the material; at times, then, when many of the questions asked must have seemed ingenuous. From all of these conversations, however, the writer retains memories of active sympathy and unfailing charity.

Of all the officials of the World Council, a special measure of gratitude is reserved for the Reverend Paul Abrecht, Secretary of the Department on Church and Society, and for Mlle Hélène Leckie, the Librarian. The overworked Reverend Paul Abrecht always found time to answer questions. The world of scholarship is admittedly enormously indebted to industrious librarians. Mlle Leckie added personal interest in the project to competent professional service.

Like all other students at the Graduate Institute of International Studies—under whose direction the present study was completed —the writer is bound to express his gratitude to its Secretary, Mme Alice Goebel. The range of interests of Professor Jacques Freymond, Director of the Institute, who guided this dissertation, provided the writer with insights extending beyond the specialized scope of this book.

In acknowledging—and in no routine fashion—the aid of others, the writer would underline the familiar protestation that the conclusions offered are his own. The fact that he is a Catholic priest of the Society of Jesus may suggest a special force to that protestation. It may embellish it with a new interest. Whether it adds anything to the value of the study here offered is for the book itself to demonstrate and for others to say.

EDWARD DUFF, S.J.

Geneva,
December 8, 1954

ACKNOWLEDGEMENTS

We are indebted to Messrs. George Allen & Unwin Ltd. for extracts from *The Christian Faith and the Common Life* by Nils Ehrenström and *The Churches Survey Their Task* edited by J. H. Oldham; The Right Reverend the Lord Bishop of Chichester for an extract from *The Stockholm Conference*; The Student Christian Movement Press Ltd. for material from *The First Assembly of the World Council of Churches* edited by W. A. Visser 't Hooft and *The Church and the Disorder of Society*; and The Student Christian Movement Press Ltd. and Messrs. Harper and Bros. for extracts from *The Kingship of Christ* and *The Evanston Report* by W. A Visser 't Hooft.

TABLE OF CONTENTS

LIST OF ABBREVIATIONS

Amsterdam   W. A. Visser 't Hooft (ed.), *The First Assembly of the World Council of Churches* (New York: Harper & Bros., 1948; London: Student Christian Movement Press, 1949).

Archives   *The Archives of the World Council of Churches,* Geneva, Switzerland.

CDS   *The Church and the Disorder of Society* (New York: Harper & Bros., 1948; London: Student Christian Movement Press, 1948).

CHTC   *The Christian Hope and the Task of the Churches* (an omnibus volume of the survey brochures prepared for the Evanston Assembly), (New York: Harper & Bros., 1954).

Evanston   W. A. Visser 't Hooft (ed.), *The Evanston Report* (New York: Harper & Bros., 1955; London: Student Christian Movement Press, 1955).

EPS   *The Ecumenical Press Service,* issued weekly from Geneva, 1933– . Before January 1947, known as the International Christian Press and Information Service.

ER   *The Ecumenical Review,* published quarterly at Geneva, 1948– .

History   Ruth Rouse and Stephen C. Neill (eds.), *A History of the Ecumenical Movement, 1517–1948* (London: S.P.C.K., 1954; Philadelphia: Westminster Press, 1954).

Oxford   J. H. Oldham (ed.), *The Churches Survey Their Task: The Report of the Conference at Oxford, July 1937, on Church, Community and State* (London: George Allen & Unwin, 1937).

Stockholm   G. K. A. Bell (ed.), *The Stockholm Conference of 1925* (London: Humphrey Milford, 1926).

ORIGINS AND DEVELOPMENT OF THE WORLD COUNCIL OF CHURCHES

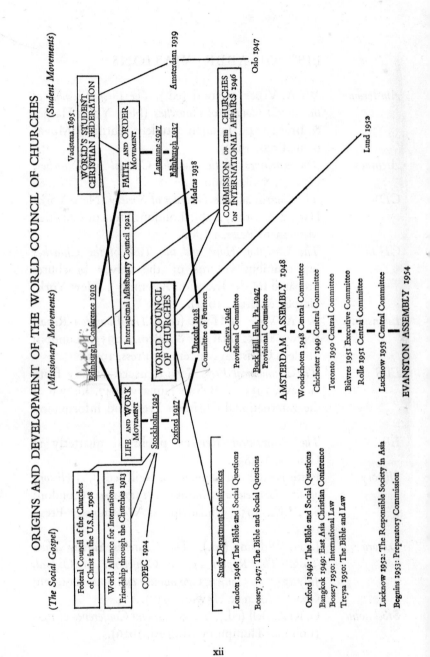

INTRODUCTION

THE present survey is an investigation of the Ecumenical Movement's criticism of the economic order, the political institutions and the international developments of our times. It is not a theological study.

The theological premises and implications of the organized effort to achieve ecclesiastical unity, engaging the hopes of most of the Protestant churches and winning the qualified collaboration of some Orthodox groups, have been examined in an extensive, if somewhat specialized, literature. That ecclesiastical phenomenon is commonly known as the Ecumenical Movement; its historic culmination is the World Council of Churches which was formally constituted on August 23, 1948. In its sifting of the meaning of the Christian religion, the Ecumenical Movement has considered and expressed judgments on many of the social issues of the day. The present study seeks to order these judgments, indicate their inspiration in the common Ecumenical tradition, trace the evolution of this tradition and evaluate its strength. It is an essay, then, in a neglected chapter in the history of social criticism, an effort to organize the evidence of social concern and to analyse the demands for social order on the part of a religious movement of impressive proportions.

The demand for control of economic processes which will serve justice and freedom, for the rule of law in international relations which will assure peace, is voiced in all the languages of the globe and is based on the most diverse claims. The demand, however exploited to political advantage, undoubtedly manifests humanity's common insistence; it is expressed in protests against unemployment, against racial discrimination, against insufficient housing and medical care, against all refusals of national independence, against all invasions of human rights, against the burden

of armaments and the threats of war. There is an increasing
awareness at the same time that the norms needed to assure equal
justice and preserve peace must not be subject to human change,
that the standards required must be sought outside the institutional
mechanisms to be regulated. Norms and standards not of
human contriving nor affected by human caprice belong to
what is popularly called the order of spiritual values. It
is one of the marks of the times that—with whatever sincerity and whatever meaning—such values are being invoked
today.

It has become a commonplace that civilization is in danger
because man's technical skills have outrun his moral controls,
his spiritual development.[1] It is noteworthy that few groups are
as articulate and insistent in making that assertion as the atomic
physicists whose research and technology elaborated the Absolute
Weapon. It is curious but significant that this is so, indicative of
an intellectual revolution that has taken place since Victorian
times when a grandfatherly God was in his heaven and all was
said to be right with the world. More than mere time has intervened between Dr. Thomas H. Huxley's counsel that men of
science should sit down before the facts like little children and
Dr. Harold C. Urey's protestation that he is a 'frightened man'.
Innocence was lost and moral neutrality rejected when the fact
to be contemplated burgeoned into a mushroom-shaped cloud
hanging over Hiroshima. 'The cosmic process has no sort of
relation to moral ends,' declared Professor Huxley. His nephew,
Aldous, living in a generation too sobered by subsequent events
to subscribe to such Olympian shallowness, entitled his effort to
analyse moral relations, *Ends and Means*. The scientists who
converged on Washington from the several sites of the Man-
hattan district in the summer of 1945 were one in demanding
controls not found in the scientific order for the tool they had
perfected. Nuclear energy which taps the forces of the cosmic
process must be promptly related to moral ends, insisted the

[1] Thus, Lord Boyd Orr, sometime Director of the U.N.'s Food and Agricultural
Organization, appeals for a 'new order', since 'nineteenth-century economics and politics
cannot carry twentieth-century science'. *The White Man's Dilemma*, p. 7

Federation of Atomic Scientists: it must be harnessed to serve the purposes of peace exclusively.

A contemporary of the elder Huxley, Thomas H. Buckle, wrote a *History of Civilization*, offering the assurance of happy times to come, since man, a product of nature, was, as engineer, explorer and industrialist, subduing nature. The meaning of history entertained by this prognosis involved nothing more complicated than the future following the past, with the future brighter because indeed it was ahead and man was, most certainly, intelligent. A contemporary of Dr. Urey, Arnold J. Toynbee, has written *A Study of History* as a record of 'God revealing Himself'. The pattern of history, in the Toynbee analysis, is found in a series of Challenges and Responses, with the future always precarious, given man's ambiguous will and the gratuity of God's grace; at present mankind is experiencing one of its recurrent Times of Troubles, since the values which sustained the modern age have been eroded.

The Victorian confidence in the automatic workings of the unsupervised trade mechanism to establish an equilibrium of justice by the balancing off of multiple selfishnesses has only withered flowers to mark its tomb. Another contemporary of the elder Huxley, Charles Dickens, characterized the essential hypocrisy of that gospel of self-interest in the words of one of his greatest characters: 'Everyone for himself and God for all of us, as the elephant said when he danced among the chickens.' In self-defence the dispossessed turned to the State to master the manipulators of the market. Experience has cooled that early revolutionary enthusiasm and expectation. For in due time the hymns of fraternal solidarity were replaced by the war chants of fascism and the humourless *mots d'ordre* on every topic from the new laws of inherited characteristics to the canons of musical criticism, all issuing from the oracles of the successful workers' revolution ensconced beyond human view in the Kremlin. Pierre Joseph Proudhon would have difficulty in greeting Alexei Grigorievitch Stakhanov as a brother in the battle of freedom. The cure for social disaggregation by surrender to the State, the

remedy for the effects of individualism by the therapy of collectivism, has proved hideously costly. The fact should not be
surprising. For collectivism, it has been remarked, is only social
atomism packed tight.

The accelerating pace of technological developments makes
the need of some sort of social control as evident and as necessary
as the light signal which endeavours to guide the increasing
traffic of an increasingly mechanized society. The menace of
modern means of transportation not only illustrates the problem;
it is part of it. Another contemporary of T. H. Huxley, William
Ewart Gladstone, lived long enough to be able to envisage a
railroad trip from Calais to Pekin. He had entered the government, as Mr. Denis Brogan has observed, under Sir Robert
Peel in 1835 when that future boss of the London Bobbies was
recalled from Rome to be Prime Minister, travelling at a rate no
faster than Hadrian who voyaged to Britain 1800 years before.
Had Gladstone in his last days visited the military academy at
Sandhurst he would surely have had pointed out to him a young
cadet, disappointingly slow at mathematics, the son of one of his
political colleagues. The boy, destined after many adventures
to succeed the Grand Old Man as Prime Minister of Great
Britain, was to live to avow that all his waking hours were
tormented by the problem of thermo-nuclear realities, a meaningless term to Gladstone for whose generation atoms recalled at
most the ineffectual philosophy of Democritus.[1] For Sir Winston
Churchill, however, the term portended the possibility of an
Asian (but not necessarily a well-mannered New Zealander)
sketching from the remnants of London Bridge the ruins of
St. Paul's, volatilized in a fashion beyond Macaulay's direst
nightmares. The destruction could come from planes based
on a distant continent travelling faster than the speed of
sound; it might indeed be borne by a missile, piercing the

[1] Mr. Churchill's alarm is understandable in the light of information on the destructive
power of the latest weapon. If the average bomber load in the Second World War is
represented by an object four inches high, the Nagasaki-Hiroshima atomic bomb would
be a 1,666-foot column, the improved, contemporary 'conventional' atom bomb would
measure 4,998 feet, and the thermo-nuclear superbomb, on a similar scale, would call
for a 63-mile-high standard.

stratosphere, launched by dutiful technicians who never saw an Englishman, guided by forces whose intimate nature is still unknown.

Such terrors of technology run wild must be tamed, it is universally agreed. It was mad enough when disease blighted the crop on colonial plantations and temporarily embarrassed some exporters or, at worst, boosted the price of tea. After all, that evil was chargeable to blind nature, and bacteria could be isolated and plants sprayed. The danger, the aggravatingly absurd danger, in a world whose dimensions had shrunk to almost a neighbourhood, is now seen as a product of the perversity of human decisions. An arbitrary tariff policy, adopted without debate by the United States Congress, could close the copper mines of Chile. Mistreatment of native workers in South Africa by high-handed managers could bring on a strike that would ruin the savings of small investors in Scotland. Social unrest in Arabian oil fields could immobilize the autobuses of Stockholm. Doctrinaire fiscal theories could lead to a currency devaluation, an irresolute tax policy to inflation, either producing widespread unemployment affecting ultimately workers in other countries. National selfishness, elaborated into slogans, could strand thousands of refugees homeless on an overpopulated continent while on another continent land without people awaited settlers. Irresponsible statements by political leaders could fan popular impatience into a general war which would arm Brazilians to fight Bulgarians.

The decisions of intractable human wills are conceded a capital importance in the peaceful and equitable management of an interdependent, technological world society. The need of norms of conduct in international affairs and economic policies and the importance of their observance, if only in the interest of human survival, is a growing conviction in all countries. Indeed many serious commentators have not hesitated to speak of a crisis of contemporary civilization in moral terms, ascribing the root of present difficulties to man's refusal to submit to rules not of his own making and indicating the inescapable necessity of a *metanoia*, a profound change of heart, if mankind is to surmount its present problems.

In such a situation the judgment of religious groups is accorded a more attentive hearing. The very survival of organized religion whose disappearance was so confidently prophesied by the more sanguine spokesmen of the gospel of Progress a century ago, indeed its increasing vitality, have engendered at least a grudging respect. The failure of the creeds of secular mysticism is, to be sure, no argument for the validity of the assertions about man's nature and his destiny proclaimed by Christianity; the manifest insufficiency of other creeds to inspire a tolerably human order, and especially the disastrous consequences of political faiths relentlessly pursued, have, however, aroused a new awareness of the possible relevance of traditional religious values. A contemporary religious philosopher has remarked: 'It is not true, as seems sometimes to be said, that without God man cannot organize the world. What is true is that, in the last analysis, without God he can only organize the world against himself.' In thoughtful circles today such a verdict does not evoke the depreciatory dismissal that would have greeted it in even the politer salons a hundred years ago.

This new receptiveness to the social criticism emanating from religious groups is, in part, a result of a new attitude of the Protestant communions particularly, a new accent in their public statements. The churches are by no means content to deplore the faithlessness of the modern world while encouraging the cultivation of private pieties. The Ecumenical Movement in modern Protestantism encompasses two tendencies: a search for the unity of the churches and, simultaneously, for the social consequences of religious truth. The sentimental, essentially subjective, conception of religion as affecting merely personal relations at most and, at its highest, as satisfying private needs, the notion that religion is concerned with the use one made of one's solitude, has given way to a new emphasis on the Christian community and on the responsibilities of the Christian to remake the world closer to the biblical ideals of justice and peace. The two tendencies ultimately took concrete form in two international organizations: the World Conference on Faith and Order, concerned with church unity, and the Universal Christian Conference on Life and Work, instituted to study the social implications of the gospel message. The World Council of Churches was born of the fusion of these two organizations.

The purpose of the present study is to examine one of these twin tendencies in the Ecumenical Community, the tradition represented by the Life and Work Movement (and also by the defunct World Alliance for International Friendship through the Churches) and continued in the World Council of Churches.

To this end it has seemed advisable to begin with an historical sketch of the World Council, its antecedents and development. Since the weight to be attached to pronouncements of the World Council and its subordinate organs demands an understanding of the authority each possesses, it has been necessary to attempt a definition of the nature and function of this instrument of the Ecumenical Community. As a 'fellowship of churches' the World Council includes within its membership different theological traditions importing diverse social outlooks and emphases. The section of the present study called 'The Social Philosophy of the World Council of Churches' endeavours to analyse these emphases and the ecumenical efforts to effect a synthesis of viewpoints on social questions and international affairs in the light of a common biblical inheritance. An analysis of the actual positions adopted on the problems of the day is the burden of the chapter entitled 'The Social Policy of the World Council of Churches', the material being organized, for convenience sake, under the headings of the divisions found in the Report of Section III of the First Assembly of the World Council at Amsterdam in 1948. A final chapter, 'Conclusions', offers an evaluation.

The particular advantage of focusing attention on the World Council of Churches (and the antecedent tradition which it continues) is that there the consensus of the social thinking of the Ecumenical Community and its common contribution to the history of social thought is concentrated. The editor of the

Report of the Oxford Conference of 1937 on Church, Community and State conceded that 'profounder, more penetrating, more illuminating discussions' of the subjects treated might well enough be found elsewhere; he pointed out, however, that the value of the statements issued by this parent organization of the World Council turned precisely on the fact that representatives of diverse theological traditions were prepared to speak 'together'.[1] More definite stands, more cogently argued, on the subjects engaging the World Council's attention may undoubtedly be found in the books of representative modern Protestant thinkers such as Reinhold Niebuhr, Emil Brunner, Karl Barth, Paul Tillich, John C. Bennett, V. A. Demant and Archbishop William Temple. In the World Council pronouncements, however, is found the official mind of the member churches and the common utterance of the diverse theological traditions on the social and international issues of the day.

A few cautions may profitably be suggested to the reader. Only the declarations of the Assemblies of the World Council of Churches, convened every five years or so, and of the Central Committee between Assemblies represent the official position of the Council. Such pronouncements, as will be seen later, do not commit the member churches. Exploring the mind of the Ecumenical Movement, the present study draws upon a mass of documentation of differing degree of authority. In addition to Assembly Reports, 'received and commended to the churches for their serious consideration and appropriate action', there is material from conferences and publications more or less sponsored by the World Council but for which the Council takes no official responsibility; other citations will be observations made by participants in commission meetings and hence, palpably, the private opinions of individuals who, though active in the movement, are in no sense authorized spokesmen for the Council. Such opinions are introduced to show the range of viewpoints in the World Council constituency and to demonstrate the

[1] J. H. Oldham (ed.), *The Churches Survey Their Task* (hereafter referred to as *Oxford*), p. 26.

process of the ecumenical dialogue. The World Council Study Department followed a somewhat similar point of view in preparing for the delegates to the Evanston Assembly a symposium, 'Ecumenical Documents on Church and Society, 1925–1953', compiled from sources beyond the restricted range of official Council pronouncements. Efforts will be made to indicate which positions have an official character as pronouncements of the World Council of Churches. They can be readily identified, being limited to the official Reports of the Amsterdam and Evanston Assemblies and the public statements of the Central Committee. Even these pronouncements have in the last resort authority only in so far as their intrinsic wisdom commends them to the member churches. This problem will be examined in the chapter entitled 'The Nature and Authority of the World Council of Churches'.

Furthermore, while it is the public pronouncements of a World Council Assembly on a controversial issue of the day (such as the statement on Capitalism and Communism of the Amsterdam meeting) which interest the news editors of the world Press, these debates do not necessarily reflect the deepest concerns of the Council. A specific statement on a single theme should not distract attention from the general purpose of the Council which is to mobilize its membership for a whole gamut of responsibilities in the temporal order and, more profoundly still, to encourage unremittingly the union of the churches.

Moreover, while alive to the social consequences of the religious imperative—strikingly so in its work for refugees—the World Council, being 'a fellowship of churches', has objectives and ideals which are not shared by organizations whose goals are exclusively humanitarian. The difference may be sensed in a dictum of Archbishop Temple who presided over the World Council in Process of Formation. 'The right relation between prayer and conduct,' His Grace of Canterbury remarked one time, 'is not that conduct is supremely important and prayer may help it but that prayer is supremely important and conduct tests it.' Archbishop Temple's interest in social problems was

unfeigned; his personal effort to assure a wider recognition of the
claims of social justice was unflagging; being a religious man,
however, his scale of values was fixed by God's revelation and a
spiritual purpose dominated all his activities. Similarly, as a
religious organization, the World Council of Churches has a
perspective other than that of a mere movement for social reform,
and goals greater than the elimination of economic injustice and
the preservation of world peace. It is the social criticism of the
World Council of Churches which falls within the scope of this
study. The writer is fully aware, however, that such an approach
is not an adequate analysis of the total meaning of the organized
form of the Ecumenical Movement. The ecclesiastical significance and theological interests of the World Council have engaged
other pens.

Again, the categories employed in the World Council's social
diagnosis, the language of ecumenical discourse, may present
some passing difficulties for, let us say, the lay reader. It is not
surprising, given its membership, that the phrasing of the World
Council's pronouncements is intransigently biblical. It is unhappily true, nevertheless, that such an idiom, such concepts
even, are not universally and immediately intelligible today.
Pastor Hans Asmussen of the Council of the Evangelical Church
in Germany was conscious of the problem when he explained the
criticisms of the 1945 Stuttgart Declaration acknowledging his
church's share in the guilt of the German people. 'A Christian,'
he remarked, 'speaks a very special language which is not understood by everyone. The discussion, therefore, which took place
in Stuttgart and its results may have the same effect as if two
Germans conversed in the German language in the midst of a
group of Chinese.' The writer has endeavoured on occasion to
translate some of these unfamiliar phrases into terms less elusive
to those unacquainted with the idiom of Protestant theology.
How successful he has been is for others to say. To him, as a
Catholic priest, the theological approach of, say, Lutheranism
or contemporary Barthianism represents a different tradition,
making particular demands upon his understanding. He has,

however, striven—such indeed is the whole purpose of this study—to comprehend clearly and to report faithfully his understanding of the different traditions influencing the common attitudes and general policy of the World Council of Churches on the social problems engaging its attention.

The question naturally arises as to what extent theological traditions actually influence social judgments, whether there are, in fact, grounds for ascribing specific social attitudes to confessional creedal positions. The supposition, if unqualified, can lend itself to oversimplifications, even to contradictions.[1] The personal experience of every individual, the history of his national group, the pattern of prejudices and cultural presuppositions inherited with one's economic status, the consequences for the evangelistic opportunities of his church following on political developments or social change, all these factors (not to speak of more human motives) inevitably colour one's social outlook and condition one's social judgments to a greater or lesser degree.[2]

For example, when a Czech theologian begins his comment on an essay describing political conditions in Central Europe, prepared for a World Council survey on international affairs, with the remark that his country's pre-war foreign policy was wrong because it was not oriented towards the USSR, the reader is justified in surmising that that political assessment is inspired more by Pan-Slavism than by the gospel insights possessed by the

---

[1] On hearing of Pastor Martin Niemöller's offer to fight on the Nazi side during the last war, Karl Barth wrote: 'Do not forget that Niemöller has always been and remains today a good—a too good—German. . . . Do not forget that Niemöller is also a good—a too good—Lutheran. Lutheranism permits and demands the belief that there is a real chasm between the ecclesiastical and the political. At the bottom of this strange act of Niemöller's you will find the Lutheran dualism between the Kingdom of Heaven and the kingdom of the secular powers; between the gospel and the law; between the God revealed in Jesus Christ and God working in nature and through history. . . . There are some German theologians and Christians who are free of the ingredients of this doctrine. They are just a few, you may be sure. But I fear that Niemöller was never one of this small number. He is capable of letting himself be put to death by Hitler.' Cited by F. Ernest Johnson in *The Social Gospel Re-examined*, p. 34. But Barth does not find in Niemöller's Lutheranism an explanation of his neutralism in the face of Soviet Communism, a neutralism, incidentally, which the Swiss theologian endorses.

[2] On this point the chapter, 'The Revolution and the Churches', in Professor Denis Brogan's *The Price of Revolution*, should be read.

Evangelical Church of the Czech Brethren.[1] South African politicians and even pastors may seek to justify a policy of *apartheid* on biblical precedent, but the suspicion lingers that the economics of cheap labour and the very human fear of cultural engulfment in the swelling Negro population are not negligible factors in that policy. An argument can be elaborated[2] attributing parliamentary democracy and religious toleration to a specific confessional tradition, but historians are inclined to yield the palm to the growth of the middle classes, to the spread of a new philosophy (sufficiently hostile to religion, incidentally) on the origin of society and to the need of social equilibrium and civic peace for untrammelled trade.[3] The slogan, 'Christianity is the religion of which Socialism is the practice', had wide resonance in the heyday of religious liberalism in Europe and of the ascendancy of the Social Gospel Movement in America. Today it is probable that the majority opinion in Protestant circles in the United States holds Socialism, even as an economic system, to be 'anti-Christian' and certainly opposed to the religiously inspired 'American way of life'. Anglican theology is adequately expansive but surely the political preferences of the Dean of Canterbury are not derivable from any of the Thirty-Nine Articles of the Church of England no matter how flexibly interpreted. Finally, the theological arguments advanced in West Germany recently against the morality of rearmament cannot be thought wholly uninfluenced by the (wholly understandable) desire of their proponents for the union of that divided nation and their determination to resist what they believe will freeze the present political division.

No, any tracing of specific social judgments from given creedal positions is likely to be overzealous in intention and

[1] Professor Frantisek Bednar on a projected chapter for Volume IV of the Amsterdam Series (*Archives*).

[2] As by James Hastings Nichols in *Democracy and the Churches*.

[3] As conceded by, for example, H. Richard Niebuhr in *The Social Sources of Denominationalism* (p. 41) and C. E. Osborne's *Christian Ideas in Political History* (pp. 154–60). Marc-Edouard Chenevière, in a doctoral thesis presented to the Faculty of Law of the University of Geneva, declared that 'il n'y a aucune parenté spirituelle entre la Réforme et la démocratie moderne'. *La Pensée Politique de Calvin*, p. 9.

probably inaccurate in its result. An official of the World Council of Churches indicated to the writer that in a round-table discussion calling for a concrete solution in the economic order it would be impossible to identify the confessional allegiance of the participants from the conclusions they offered. On the other hand, theological traditions—if they have any vitality or are adequately understood —inevitably manifest themselves in different attitudes towards the social order, in the selection of subjects which are deemed important, and in the manner of approaching social problems. Thus it is not without significance that the effort to write provisions for the legal equality of wives into the UN Human Rights Convention evokes small enthusiasm from representatives of Moslem nations. Again, reliance on human prudence and the deduction of moral norms from rational analysis is considered by many in the World Council constituency as an affront to God's revelation contained in the Bible. Differences of social perspective do exist by reason of wide differences of theological belief.[1] These differences sometimes have repercussions in the political order, inescapably so when they affect the popular understanding of the State.[2] While it may well be impossible to sift the influence of various confessional traditions in judgments on a concrete social question,[3] it is possible to distinguish varying emphases deriving from creedal positions. After all, a parent organization of the World Council edited a symposium on the social ethics of the several confessions. And Ernst Troeltsch is famous as the author of *The Social Teaching of the Christian Churches*.

[1] Prefacing the papers contributed to the ecumenical symposium, *The Christian Faith and the Common Life*, Dr. Nils Ehrenström, sometime Director of the World Council's Study Department, noted: 'The reader will soon become aware of the great and to some extent irreconcilable differences which emerge in these papers; they reflect the tragic divisions in the Body of Christ which also exist in the social realm, divergences which are not only conditioned by legitimate differences of judgment on the actual situation and its demands but also by the central convictions of faith.' p. 9.

[2] Adolf Keller found in the theologies of Calvinism and Lutheranism explanations of different attitudes among German Protestants towards the Nazi régime. Cf. his *Church and State on the European Continent*, especially p. 347. Reinhold Niebuhr argued that Lutheranism prepared the social soil for German Fascism. Cf. his *Christianity and Power Politics*, pp. 49–51.

[3] For example, all the member churches of the World Council are for peace; some, however, advocate renunciation of armed force.

Finally, an organization which publicly tells the world what is wrong with its economic order, which challenges current cultural standards and offers prescriptions for improving international relations may seem, by reason of the sweep of its criticism and the ineffectiveness of its action, solemnly self-important. This study will be reporting the resounding condemnations of forms of economic injustice, for example, issuing from ecumenical gatherings. The walls of Jericho are still standing. The true proportions of the force of ecumenical opinion in modern society are nowhere more accurately recognized than among the officials of the World Council of Churches.

Indeed, one may freely recognize the lack of decisive consequence of religious ideas generally in the shaping of contemporary society. While it is true that theology as an intellectual discipline enjoys more respect than was accorded it a hundred years ago, and though prayer and liturgical practices are not today so cavalierly dismissed as species of self-delusion and organized superstition, the impact of the ideas elaborated by religious groups on existing social institutions and political developments is not very impressive.

There is in some Protestant circles, especially in the United States, a vague fear that the World Council of Churches represents the foreshadowing of a spiritual imperialism, threatening to establish a party-line in economic and, particularly, political questions. The limited resources of the Geneva Secretariat, quite apart from the restrictions of the Constitution of the World Council (not to mention the unresolved tensions within the ecumenical family) makes such a development highly imaginary. Any such alarm should be readily quieted by a candid consideration of the relative impotence of religious forces in the shaping of modern society. Ours has been termed with ample evidence a post-Christian era. The social survey, *English Life and Leisure*, made by B. Seebohm Rowntree and G. R. Lavers in 1951, revealed the practical irrelevance of Christian concepts in the lives of large sections of the British population. Their conclusions were confirmed for France by Dr. Simon Ligier's massive

two-volume inquiry, *L'Adulte des Milieux Ouvriers*, published
the same year. The bustling activity of religious organizations
in the United States may conceal a weakness almost as great.
Scientific research on a national scale is lacking but a survey
made by a team of Columbia University sociologists of the social
attitudes of the citizens of Akron, Ohio, indicated in passing
that religious teachings had small impact on their judgments in
concrete social situations.[1] The officials of the World Council
of Churches would probably subscribe with only minor reservations to the thesis argued by J. V. Langmead Casserley in the
Maurice Lectures of King's College, London, for 1951, published
as *The Retreat from Christianity in the Modern World*. That retreat,
his evidence indicates, has followed two main avenues—into
irreligion and, paradoxically, into 'religion', that is to say, into
political faiths, superstitions of science and cultural absolutes as
substitutes for Christianity.

The delegates to the World Council's First Assembly were
warned against any exaggerated notions of the importance of
their influence. 'Among the outstanding leaders of human
society in recent generations,' Emil Brunner told them, 'we find
few Churchmen; other voices have possessed greater power of
conviction and other minds more prophetic vision.'[2]

All of this is true and perhaps a little too obvious outside
religious circles. What is missed, in consequence, is the evidence
of the increasing vitality of religious thought and its endeavour
to come to grips with the predicament of modern man living in a
society dominated by technics with resulting social complications.
Specialization, not least in the academic disciplines, has shunted
theology to the province of a separate Faculty whose subject-
matter is deemed peripheral to the educated man's main concerns
and of interest only to those who have opted for an honorific
if markedly unremunerative career of uncertain social utility.
The intellectual contribution of religious groups towards the

---

[1] Alfred Winslow Jones (ed.), *Life, Liberty and Property*.

[2] *The Church and the Disorder of Society*, p. 178 (hereafter referred to as *CDS*). The book,
one of four symposia prepared for the four Sections of the Amsterdam Assembly, was
distributed in page proofs to the delegates.

solution of evident difficulties in constructing a truly humane
Temporal City are, as a result, sketchily known in circles where
such ignorance is particularly unfortunate. Such ignorance may
have more serious consequences. As competent an historian of
civilizations as Arnold Toynbee, recalling the Christian origins
of our Western convictions on the dignity of the person and the
sacredness of individual liberty, has expressed his doubts that these
values can endure when the religious roots which have sustained
them find no nourishment in the intellectual diet of modern man.

The suggestion may lend new pertinence to the present study
of the social thought of the World Council of Churches. André
Siegfried believes so. The French economist closes his history
of the social effects of Protestantism with an account of the
growth of the Ecumenical Movement culminating in the formation of the World Council; he notes the persistent difficulties
blocking the road to church unity and hails the common effort
of the member churches for a just social order and a stable
international society; this development, concludes M. Siegfried,
represents 'in the history of Protestantism and indeed of
Christianity in general, an event of capital importance, a manifestation of the aspirations, perhaps of the necessities of our age'.[1]

[1] *Les Forces Religieuses et la Vie Politique*, p. 218.

I

THE HISTORY OF THE
WORLD COUNCIL OF CHURCHES

i. The Origin of the Ecumenical Idea

On August 23, 1948, an event bringing to its culmination a significant movement in modern religious history occurred in Amsterdam. In the Main Hall of the Concertgebouw that Monday morning Pasteur Marc Boegner, President of the French Protestant Federation, proposed a resolution to an international gathering. The motion, as repeated by the Chairman, the Archbishop of Canterbury, Dr. Geoffrey Fisher, stated '. . . that the formation of the World Council of Churches be declared to be and is hereby completed'. It was adopted *nemine contradicente* by 351 delegates from 44 countries representing 147 churches and religious organizations.[1] The action answered an invitation extended ten years earlier by a Committee of Fourteen whose circular letter explained that the proposal to establish 'a consultative Body representing all Churches which accept its basis and approve its aims and to which each should bring its distinctive witness, arises by an inevitable process from the various movements since 1910—and especially those movements commonly called *Life and Work* and *Faith and Order*'.[2]

The vote of the Assembly at Amsterdam brought into being a permanent and official association of a large number of Christian

---

[1] According to Harold Fey, correspondent of the *Christian Century*, non-denominational American Protestant weekly, there were 352 delegates instead of the 450 expected. Only 24 of the 85 seats allotted to Orthodox representatives were filled. *Christian Century*, LXV (October 6, 1948), 40, p. 1030.

[2] *Documents of the World Council of Churches*, p. 9.

churches[1] who consider the Council a fellowship manifesting their unity, a conversation centre for their common search for full, organic union and a mechanism for the co-operative study and solution, in the light of Christian principles, of the pressing problems of contemporary society.

With the creation of the World Council of Churches the Ecumenical Movement took institutional form. Implying universality from its etymological meaning of 'the inhabited world', the Ecumenical Movement has been defined by the committee which prepared the semi-official *History* as covering 'those aspects of Church History concerned: (*a*) with the bringing of individual Christians of different denominations together for purposes of co-operation; (*b*) with the bringing of different Churches as such together for purposes of co-operation; and (*c*) with the bringing of different Churches into union'. The range of such a definition is suggested by a bibliography of more than 2,000 volumes on ecumenicism appearing as early as 1936; it involves an account of the formation of Church federations in different countries,[2] of international confessional associations,[3] of church mergers and of interdenominational youth organizations as well; it includes inevitably an examination of the trends in theological opinion and social philosophy that presaged and facilitated common action. In its account of the World Council of Churches the present study will be content to indicate the influence of missionary and student movements and of the efforts to make religion relevant to social needs, particularly in the

---

[1] Except the Roman Catholic Church, absent by reason of her dogmatic position (*viz.* that unity exists; and she is the centre and source of it) and the Orthodox Churches of the Moscow obedience whose refusal to participate will be discussed later. The Roman Catholic position is set forth in the Encyclical *Mortalium Animos* (1928) and the instruction of the Holy Office, *De Motione Oecumenica* (*Acta Apostolicae Sedis*, XVII, 1950, pp. 142–7). A chapter by the Rev. Oliver S. Tomkins is devoted to the topic in *A History of the Ecumenical Movement, 1517–1948*, edited by Ruth Rouse and Stephen Charles Neill (hereafter referred to as *History*), pp. 677–93.

[2] e.g. The Federal Council of Churches of Christ in America, 1908; the Swiss Protestant Federation and the French Protestant Federation, 1909; the British Council of Churches, 1922.

[3] First Lambeth Conference (representing all the churches of the Anglican Communion), 1867; Presbyterian World Alliance, 1875; Methodist Ecumenical Council, 1881; International Congregational Union, 1891; Baptist World Alliance, 1905; Lutheran World Federation, 1923.

interests of world peace, merely adverting to the quest for Church unity.

1. *The Problem in the Mission Field*

The delegates at the Amsterdam Assembly whose vote had just constituted the World Council of Churches had heard a speaker[1] declare the evening before: 'The Ecumenical Church is a child of the missionary movement.' They had convened as representatives of their respective churches in answer to a Letter of Invitation which had invoked the memory of the Edinburgh Conference of 1910 as an event of crucial importance in ecumenical history;[2] this Conference was the climax of the missionary enterprise of the nineteenth century which gave Protestant Christianity its global extension;[3] moreover it adumbrated the permanent, institutional form the Ecumenical Community would adopt.

Extensive missionary activity in the nineteenth century gave rise to the problem of mutual relations between denominations in the same field and suggested the possibility of common planning at home. The avoidance of sectarian competition supposed a delimitation of territories to be evangelized and an effort to preach 'the essentials of Christianity', forgetting 'the non-essentials' of denominationalism. The new Christians, moreover, manifested an impatience with what they deemed outmoded factional loyalties. The idea of the essential universality of Christianity, they felt, was obscured and even mocked by the multiplicity of ecclesiastical forms. At home the greater efficiency of pooled effort made an irresistible appeal; collaboration in the

[1] The speaker, John A. Mackay, Chairman of the International Missionary Council, explained: 'Churches, whose previous history had been marked by disunity, first began to manifest a spirit of understanding and co-operation upon the missionary frontier. Evangelical fellowship on the missionary road preceded ecclesiastical fellowship in the home sanctuary. Christian Churches which took seriously their missionary obligation and crossed the frontiers of non-Christian lands began to transcend the barriers by which they had been divided in their home countries.'

[2] Significantly, the *History of the Ecumenical Movement* chooses 1910 as the key date in its division of chapters.

[3] In his magistral *History of the Expansion of Christianity*, Kenneth Scott Latourette devotes three volumes (IV, V, VI) to 'The Great Century, 1800–1914'. These were published as a unit.

production of religious literature in the vernacular of the mission countries, common support of educational institutions, exchange of information on methods of evangelism seemed obvious if the forces of Protestant Christianity were to exploit effectively what was felt to be a great opportunity in world history.

The World Missionary Congress which convened in the Assembly Hall of the Church of Scotland on Edinburgh's famous Royal Mile in August 1910 was the seventh and most important of such international encounters called to formulate a common Protestant Christian strategy. Although it was agreed in advance that there should be no discussion involving ecclesiastical or doctrinal differences, the desire for unity expressed itself in a strong statement on the serious hindrance presented by Christian divisions. The delegates, official representatives this time of denominational mission boards, sensed above a programme of functional co-operation the vision of international Christianity. Before adjourning they established a Continuation Committee which during the war years provided crucial assistance to 'orphaned' missions and led in 1921 to the formation of the International Missionary Council[1] which today links more than

[1] The significance of the meeting was described by its Chairman, John R. Mott, in these terms: 'The Edinburgh Conference has familiarized Christians of our day with this idea of looking steadily at the world as a whole, of confronting the world as a unity by the Christian Church as a unity.' Honorary President of the World Council of Churches at the time of his death in 1955, Dr. Mott was so dominant during the formative years of the International Missionary Council and of the World's Student Christian Federation that their early history can largely be written in terms of his personality and activities. It is not without significance that John R. Mott was a Methodist of American pioneer stock; he once explained his life as a response to the challenge of a travelling English Evangelist to 'seek first the Kingdom of God', an appeal which he said 'went straight to the springs of my motive life'. In the judgment of Walter Marshall Horton, when delivering the Hoover Lectures on Christian Unity at the University of Chicago in 1948: 'If we ask what made Edinburgh possible, the first and most far-reaching answer is: *the Evangelical Movement which renewed the life of the British and American churches between 1738* [the date of Wesley's Aldersgate experience] *and 1910.* Like the Continental pietists, their direct forerunners, the Anglo-Saxon evangelicals were not doctrinally indifferent but they thought only a few Christian doctrines really pertained unto salvation: those, namely, which had something to do with that strange warming and changing of the heart known as conversion or regeneration in which they saw the turning point of each man's eternal destiny. "If thy heart is as my heart," said Wesley, "give me thy hand." A deep communion of hearts was one of the fruits of the Evangelical Movement wherever it went, together with a consuming passion for bringing all men everywhere into this same blessed communion.' *Towards a Reborn Church.*

thirty autonomous national councils of various constituencies, thus embodying the idea of federal unity. The IMC, today listed in all documents as 'in association with the World Council of Churches', is thus the direct outgrowth of the 1910 meeting on mission problems.

2. The Influence of Student Groups

At the ancient royal château at Vadstena, Sweden, in August 1895 a group of young people gathered to found the World's Student Christian Federation. Its inspiration was markedly evangelical, its purposes were resolutely missionary.[1] Reviewing its achievements a half-century later, an historian observed: 'The creation of the World's Student Christian Federation was the logical result of the great missionary drive of the century: the Federation is the child of the mission movement.'[2] The religious impulse manifested in the growth of the Young Men's Christian Association, with its emphasis on the evangelization of the laity by the laity, received an additional imperative on American campuses. The new element was an absorbing interest in missions. Paralleling, perhaps, the new national consciousness of the importance of the United States in world affairs (jingoists were making political capital of the supposed responsibilities of 'Manifest Destiny'), these student leaders were possessed by the idea of world evangelism and their part in it. The universities were conceived (as one book on the movement termed them) as 'Strategic Points for the Conquest of the World'. The advantages of uniting Christian student groups in an international organization for common action in the personal and missionary apostolate was evident to these earnest and eminently practical minds.

If the International Christian Student Movement owed its

---

[1] '(1) To unite the associations or organizations of Christian students of the entire world; (2) To gather information on the religious situation of students in all countries; (3) To promote the following activities: (a) to bring students to become disciples of Christ and recognize him as the sole Saviour and God, (b) to deepen the spiritual life of students, and (c) to enlist students for the work of spreading the Kingdom of Christ through the whole world.' Clarence P. Shedd, *Two Centuries of Student Christian Movements*, p. 36.

[2] Suzanne de Diétrich, *Cinquante Ans d'Histoire*, p. 10.

origins to the missionary impulse, the Ecumenical Movement,[1] culminating in the World Council of Churches, is indebted to the Student Christian Movement in a fashion difficult to over-estimate. The generosity and world vision of Protestant youth groups—one[2] in America, for example, adopted the motto, 'The Conversion of the World in this Generation'—supplied in later years the leadership of the ecumenical organizations. An old photograph of the four General Secretaries of the WSCF-sponsored international Christian student relief organization offers striking evidence: Dr. John R. Mott became Honorary President of the World Council, W. A. Visser 't Hooft its General Secretary, Robert C. Mackie Associate General Secretary, and Henri-Louis Henriod served as Warden of the Ecumenical Institute, the study centre conducted by the World Council. William Temple, Archbishop of Canterbury, who presided in May 1938 at the Conference at Utrecht which drafted the Constitution of the World Council of Churches, and served as Chairman of the Council's Provisional Committee, acknowledged that he glimpsed the possibilities inherent in the ecumenical ideal at meetings of the British branch of the WSCF. 'The great spiritual unity created by the Federation,' he wrote, 'appeared as an illustration of what the Church of Christ must become for all its members.'[3] The 1911 Congress of the Federation at Constantinople, which established the inter-confessional character of the organization, served as a bridge for Orthodox participation in ecumenical activities; it also witnessed the entry on the ecumenical scene of an Orthodox Seminary professor, the Reverend Germanos Strenopoulos, subsequently Archbishop of Thyateira and a President of the World Council of Churches. A delegate at the Life and Work Conference at Oxford in 1937, where plans were definitely formulated for the creation of the World Council of Churches, remarked that as she looked about her there was scarcely one of the leaders whom she did not

[1] The word first gained general currency, it is said, in WSCF circles.
[2] The Student Missionary Volunteers.
[3] T. Tatlow, *The Story of the S.C.M. in Great Britain and Ireland*, p. 613, cited in de Diétrich, p. 65.

recognize as a fellow worker whom she had met at some earlier stage of her Student Christian Federation activity.[1] The remark could have been made with even more appositeness at the Amsterdam Assembly.[2]

Although the members of the Student Christian groups were in no sense representing their different communions—the fact probably facilitated the building of friendships among future leaders of the different churches—the experience of the Federation in constructing a union of national associations, fully autonomous but pledged to mutual assistance, undoubtedly influenced the structure of the future World Council.[3] Open to all the intellectual tendencies in the religious world, the Federation experienced the theological debates and spiritual tensions which are part of the continuing life of the Ecumenical Community. *The Student World*, the monthly organ of the Federation, discussed the questions which even today claim a large part of the table of contents of *The Ecumenical Review*, the quarterly of the World Council of Churches. The fact is scarcely surprising: Dr. W. A. Visser 't Hooft edited both publications. Can the Federation be considered the tap-root of the World Council? A participant in a discussion of the projected History of the Ecumenical Movement clearly thought so. He 'urged that the present ecumenical

---

[1] William Adams Brown, *Towards a United Church*, p. 34. The delegate was Miss Ruth Rouse.

[2] As a further illustration of this continuity, it is noted that the hymnal and book of prayers compiled by the WSCF are currently used at WCC meetings. The English publisher for most of the literature on the World Council, moreover, is the SCM Press, owned by the British branch of WSCF.

[3] Among other personalities can be listed Archbishop Söderblom, whose attendance at WSCF international congresses was a prelude to his chairmanship of the Stockholm Conference on Life and Work; Joseph H. Oldham and William Paton, introduced to the mission apostolate through the British unit of the Federation, the first being Organizing Secretary of the Oxford Conference of 1937 and inspirer of the central theme of Amsterdam's Commission III 'The Church and the Disorder of Society', the second being Secretary of the Provisional Committee of the World Council; H. P. van Dusen, Chairman of the World Council's Study Committee; Reinhold Niebuhr and John C. Bennett, Chairman and Secretary respectively of Amsterdam's Commission III—not to speak of those whose part in their national student organizations introduced them to the ecumenical world, such as Hanns Lilje and R. van Thadden of Germany, Josef Hromadka of Czechoslovakia, L. Zander of Russia, Pasteur Pierre Maury of France, Bishop V. S. Azariah of India, etc.

movement be recognized for what it is as growing out of the developments of the Student Christian Movement'.[1]

3. The Social Gospel

Socialism arose during the nineteenth century on the European continent as a political protest against the economic evils resulting from the dominant philosophy of individualism. Religious voices, too, were raised (though somewhat later) expressing indignation over man's refusal to recognize his responsibility to his fellows. In England Methodist lay preachers were in the forefront of the nascent Trade Union movement and in the Church of England personalities such as F. D. Maurice, Charles Kingsley, Scott Holland and Bishops Westcott and Gore were influential in organizations with the significant titles, 'The Christian Social Union', 'The Christian Social League', 'The Guild of St. Matthew' and 'The League of the Kingdom of God'. In France the monthly organ of the Protestant Federation of Social Christianity began to appear in 1887; in Switzerland the name of Ragaz is remembered; in the United States the new accent on the social consequences of the Christian message, first announced after the Civil War by Washington Gladden, was developed by later preachers such as George Herron, Shailer Mathews, Francis Peabody and especially by Walter Rauschenbusch whose thought had an international resonance. Scorning the tacit acceptance of the cruel abuses of industrial capitalism by pulpits concerned only with the middle-class world of piety and private virtues, these prophets proclaimed the need—as the title of one of Rauschenbusch's books stated—of 'Christianizing the Social Order'. The task, it was felt, was no less than the radical remaking of economic institutions according to a programme directly inspired by the gospel and heralded in Christ's teaching of His coming Kingdom. Shailer Mathews of the University of Chicago was not hesitant:

By the Kingdom of God Jesus meant an ideal (though progressively approximated) social order in which the relation of men to God is

---

[1] *Minutes and Reports of the Meeting of the Provisional Committee*, Buck Hill Falls, Penn., April 1947, p. 40. The participant was the Rev. Dr. Floyd Tompkins.

that of sons, and therefore to each other, that of brothers. . . . This ideal is not beyond human attainment but is the natural possibility for man's social capacities and powers.[1]

An expression of the sanguine expectation of that outlook (and evidence of its widespread appeal) was a novel, *In His Steps*, written by a minister, the Reverend Charles Sheldon, and designed to be read from the pulpit.[2] According to the story each member of a fictional congregation pledges himself before every action to consider 'What would Jesus do?' and to act only in the light of the answer. The resolve results in a total transformation of the community.

To assure this remaking of society demanded organization. Accordingly, in December 1908 the overwhelming majority of the Protestant Churches of the evangelical tradition in the United States formed the Federal Council of the Churches of Christ in America 'to secure a larger combined influence for the Churches of Christ in all matters affecting the moral and social condition of the people, so as to promote the application of the law of Christ in every relation of human life'.[3] But the Social Gospel Movement was not merely an American phenomenon. The aspirations it expressed were a major preoccupation of Protestant thought throughout the world.

The realization, induced by the First World War, of the interrelation of nations led the ranks of what was sometimes called 'Applied' or 'Practical' Christianity to join forces for international action. Well before the outbreak of hostilities, British and German clergymen were at work to allay the growing

[1] *The Social Teaching of Jesus*, pp. 54, 77; quoted by J. C. Bennett in *Protestant Thought in the Twentieth Century* (New York: Macmillan, 1951), p. 128.

[2] The novel, appearing in 1898, was translated into twenty-one languages and by 1933 had sold 23 million copies, making it, it is claimed, the world's all-time 'best-seller' after, of course, the Bible.

[3] From the preamble to the Federal Council's Constitution, as quoted in Brown, *op. cit.*, p. 2. Other purposes are listed but a historian of the Council, John A. Hutchinson, asserts that the social application of the gospel was the dominant motive: *We Are Not Divided*, p. 25. See also Charles Howard Hopkins, *The Rise of the Social Gospel in American Protestantism, 1865–1915*. The author calls the Federal Council 'the climax of official recognition of social Christianity' (p. 302). Cf. also the critical but objective study, *The Background of the Social Gospel in America*, by Willem A. Visser 't Hooft.

tension between their countries. On a visit to Berlin for the Kaiser's Jubilee in 1913 the American philanthropist, Andrew Carnegie, learned of the programme and, conceiving of religion as a happy solvent of national enmities, gave $2,000,000 to endow the Church Peace Union, an organization which, as sponsor of the World Alliance for Promoting International Friendship through the Churches, was to play a significant role in the evolution of the Ecumenical Movement towards its culmination in the World Council of Churches.[1] For it was at the meeting of the World Alliance, at Oud Wassenaer near The Hague in October 1919, that the proposals emanating from England, Scandinavia, Switzerland, the United States and even Constantinople for an international meeting of Christian leaders were reduced to a concrete plan.[2] The Universal Christian Conference on Life and Work, parent organization of the World Council of Churches, was the result.

4. The Quest for Christian Reunion

The importance of close collaboration for the success of missionary endeavours was the reason for the calling of the Edinburgh Conference of 1910. Unity of action was the refrain of the meeting and a permanent secretariat was established to assure such unity. The prior agreement to by-pass doctrinal discussions while considering problems of collaboration seemed, however, stultifying to one delegate, the Protestant Episcopal Bishop of the Philippines, Charles H. Brent. Bishop Brent believed: 'It is little short of absurd to try to bring into the Church

---

[1] How pathetically Carnegie had misjudged the gravity of the international situation can be seen from a letter he wrote to the Secretary of the Church Peace Union in February 1914: 'Peace is about a reality now; and before you have gone very long, permanent peace will be established in the world, and then you will find yourselves trustees of a fund and will not know what to do with it.' The letter was read by the recipient (Henry A. Atkinson), reviewing twenty-five years of the history of the World Alliance for Friendship through the Churches at a meeting attended by representatives of twenty-two National Committees in Geneva, August 11-16, 1939. The text is in *Friendship Stands*, Report for the Management Committee of the World Alliance (Geneva, 1939), p. 7; quoted by Ehrenström in *History*, p. 567.

[2] The history is related in *Steps Towards a United Church*, by Charles S. Macfarland, a member of the original Preparatory Committee for the meeting.

of Christ the great nations of the Far East unless we can present an undivided front. For purely practical reasons we feel the necessity of the Church's realization of unity. It must be either that or failure in our vocation.'[1] Above the programme of functional collaboration Bishop Brent envisaged an organic union of the churches.

It was on his initiative that the General Convocation of his Church, meeting in Cincinnati in October of that same year, issued an invitation 'to all Christian Communions throughout the world which confess our Lord Jesus Christ as God and Saviour' to attend a conference to examine 'the questions concerning the faith and constitution of the Church' in the belief that 'the beginnings of unity are to be found in the clear statement and full consideration of those things in which we differ, as well as those things in which we are one'. The dogmatic basis of unity had been devised at an earlier Convention of the same Protestant Episcopal Church in 1888. The Lambeth Quadrilateral, so termed after its adoption by the Anglican Conference of 1920, has four bases: the Bible, the Nicene Creed, the two Sacraments and the Historic Episcopate; it represented an initiative which Bishop Brent resolved to revive and extend. The war postponed definite arrangements for the proposed Conference while at the same time raising fresh problems for religious minds. It was not until the summer of 1927 that the theologians representing their various churches convened at Lausanne the World Conference on Faith and Order for the mutual explanation of their various doctrinal traditions.[2] A Continuing Committee gave permanence to the meeting and arranged for further study in preparation for a second Conference. This was held in Edinburgh in 1937, and

---

[1] Alexander C. Zabriskie, *Bishop Brent*, p. 92.

[2] In the Hoover Lectures on Christian Unity at the University of Chicago, Professor Walter Horton thus describes the theological problem underlying the Lausanne discussions: 'But just how does a church maintain communion with Christ? How does it ascertain whether its present life and teaching are continuous with the life and teaching of the Founder? How can it be sure that its members are properly dependent on the one Head, its branches nourished from the one Taproot, its superstructure properly based on the one Foundation, its flock properly related to the one Shepherd? Here is the great point of divergence between Christian churches.' Horton, *op. cit.*, p. 63. These questions relating to the nature of the Church, continue to be central in Faith and Order study.

authorized its Continuing Committee, under certain conditions, to bring the Faith and Order organization into the proposed World Council of Churches as a permanent commission.

ii. The Life and Work Movement

For the initial meeting of the Universal Christian Conference on Life and Work, five years of preparation were needed before 528 delegates of 31 churches from 38 nations gathered for the service of worship in the Storkyrkan, the Stockholm Cathedral, on August 19, 1925. The delegates had responded to a Letter of Invitation[1] declaring that 'the world's greatest need is the Christian way of life not merely in personal and social behaviour but in public opinion and its outcome in public action', a goal involving the responsibility of 'putting our hearts and our hands into a united effort that God's will may be done on earth as it is in heaven'.[2] It was an ample undertaking expressed in confident language.[3]

[1] The Conference was sponsored by the Federal Council of the Churches of Christ in America, the World Alliance for Promoting International Friendship through the Churches, the British Conference on Christian Politics and Citizenship. The British Conference—COPEC—was sponsored by the Church of England and the British Free Churches and was held at Birmingham, April 5–12, 1924. Its declared basis was 'the conviction that the Christian faith, rightly interpreted and consistently followed, gives the vision and power essential for solving the problems of today, that the social ethics of Christianity have been greatly neglected by Christians with disastrous consequences to the individual and to society, and that it is of first importance that these should be given a clearer and more persistent emphasis'. *Reports* I, p. iv. Reviewing the Conference twenty-three years later, Maurice B. Reckitt could find 'no insights to challenge the attention'. *Maurice to Temple*, p. 172. COPEC was, however, of much the same inspiration and outlook as Stockholm, and its seven volumes of Reports formed part of the preparation for the first Life and Work Conference.

[2] 'To this end', continued the letter, '... we will consider such concrete questions as that of industry and property, in relation to the Kingdom of God; what the Church should teach and do to help to create right relations between the different and at times warring classes and groups in the community; how to promote friendship between the nations and thus lay the only sure foundation upon which permanent international peace can be built'. G. K. A. Bell (ed.), *The Stockholm Conference of 1925* (hereafter referred to as *Stockholm*), p. 18.

[3] Immediately following the opening service, the delegates were received at the Palace by the King of Sweden who assured them that the aim of the Conference was no less important than that of the Council of Nicea. *Stockholm*, p. 46. The purpose of Nicea had been to define the nature of Christ and therefore the essential content of the Christian religion.

The scope of the Conference had been limited to 'united practical action . . . leaving for the time our difference in Faith and Order'.[1] But on what levels of action should Christian forces function? By providing a Christian programme to match the Socialist programme, as one delegate suggested?[2] Or by serving as the 'soul' for the new instruments of international political and social collaboration, as another delegate urged?[3] A sometime Professor of Ethics called attention to the difficulties of applying Christian principles to concrete problems, given the complicated structures of modern social living and the consequent danger either of meaningless generalizations or of unauthoritative private opinions.[4] Was united practical action possible without unity of faith?[5] The current slogan announcing that 'doctrines divide, action unites', was soon seen as no adequate answer to the irrepressible question of the significance, indeed of the need, of theology. The American delegate who remarked: 'All you do in theology is useless for our practical task,' revealed the widespread, probably dominant, instrumental conception of Christianity

---

[1] The determination to avoid theological discussion led the organizers of Stockholm to reject the suggestion that the Conference be held close in time and location to the Conference on Faith and Order. Over the signatures of Archbishop Söderblom, Chairman, and Henry A. Atkinson, General Secretary, a letter was sent on April 14, 1922, to Richard Gardiner, Secretary of the Faith and Order Preparatory Committee, explaining that the International Committee was 'unanimous on the wisdom of keeping the two Conferences entirely distinct . . . Life and Work to confine itself in the main to co-operation for the application of the Spirit and Teaching of Christ to social, national and international relationships while Faith and Order devotes its attention to the ultimate and more remote goal of unity.' Cf. Macfarland, op. cit., p. 111.

[2] Stockholm, p. 56.

[3] Ibid., p. 172.

[4] The Rt. Rev. E. Billing, Bishop of Västerås, Sweden, noted that 'one stands before the painful alternative of either talking in such general terms that such talk altogether loses its point, or [of] losing oneself in technicalities in the widest sense, and thus postulating as a necessary item of faith something which in reality is only a private opinion, or perhaps the creed of a party'. Ibid., p. 194.

[5] Pasteur Wilfred Monod asserted that the methodology of hypotheses was employed at Stockholm: 'Recourse was had to the rule counselled by psychologists and pastors: "act as if . . ." We proceeded as if the Church of Christ on earth presented a single battle-line under a single commander.' The same delegate observed that the Conference distinguished between faith and belief. Since faith, in the Evangelical meaning of the word, is a spiritual attitude, a religious experience, the same 'belief' can express itself in many 'beliefs', he argued. The influence of Ritschl is evident. La Conférence Universelle du Christianisme Pratique, pp. 47, 48.

as providing inspiration for human betterment.[1] Was Christianity profoundly more than a precious solvent of social conflicts, larger in importance than an agent for achieving desirable social reforms—the abolition of prostitution, the control of alcoholism, the cleansing of municipal politics, the humanizing of the penitentiary system, the alleviation of unemployment and the outlawing of war? The continental delegate who remarked that he 'would as soon think of asking his ten-year-old daughter just back from Sunday School for a theological opinion as of asking an American', clearly thought so.[2] To avoid theological discussion it had been decided to confine consideration of the first of the six main subjects of the Conference—The Church's Obligation in view of God's Purpose for the World—to a public presentation by seven spokesmen of different ecclesiastical traditions.

Despite the easy assurance of a French spokesman of the Social Gospel,[3] it was immediately evident that varying theological conceptions conditioned all viewpoints on temporal topics. The preacher at the opening service had proclaimed: 'We believe in the Kingdom of Heaven. We are conspirators for its establishment. That is why we are here. That is the meaning of this Conference.'[4] Two speakers at the opening session had challenged the delegates to make a new social effort 'in order to accelerate the coming of the Kingdom of God', to be rebuffed by a Lutheran Bishop: 'Nothing could be more mistaken or more disastrous than to suppose that we mortal men have to build up God's

---

[1] Adolf Keller, 'Stockholm 1925 in the Light of 1950', *ER* II (Summer 1950), 4, p. 370.

[2] Cf. Willard L. Sperry, *Religion in America*, p. 134.

[3] Pasteur Elie Gounelle: 'This Conference is deeply divided on the question of the meaning to be given to the scriptural idea, which inspires us all, of the Kingdom of God. Some are only willing to see in it a synonym for salvation by grace, or for forgiveness, others see in it a new material social order ruled by God. But whatever our explanation of the Kingdom of God may be, whether spiritual or material, individual or social, is of little account after all. The relations between nations, as a practical matter for all of us who are here, ought to be governed by the laws of this Kingdom.' *Stockholm*, p. 453. The speaker suspected that the German separation of the interior realm of religion from the political and social world, each with its autonomous laws, 'was a refuge for reactionary and militarist workings against the Republic, democracy, socialism and pacificism'. Cf. *La Conférence Universelle du Christianisme Pratique*, p. 108.

[4] *Stockholm*, p. 38. The preacher was the Rt. Rev. Theodore Woods, the Anglican Bishop of Winchester.

Kingdom in the world.'[1] The division of opinion concerned the reason for calling the Conference—to determine the role of religion in social life; it raised the question as to whether there could be a specifically Christian judgment on social problems.[2] The problem was of more than academic interest. 'When pressed to their source the differing attitudes towards Christian duty were seen to be rooted in theological differences', the Chairman of the Life and Work Executive Committee was later to note.[3] Eventually, the problem compelled the setting up of a committee of theologians whose discussions brought the Life and Work movement closer to Faith and Order activities and thus contributed to the future formation of the World Council of Churches.

1. After Stockholm

The Stockholm Conference can be fairly described as an impressive, ten-day public demonstration during which the fact that Christianity has social consequences was asserted in three languages and the complexity of the problems arising from that assertion profitably, if disconcertingly, discovered. A Continuation Committee was named to pursue the objectives of the Conference and to plan for later meetings; it was this Committee which in 1930 transformed itself into a permanent organization with the title, the Universal Christian Council for Life and Work.[4] Led by dedicated

[1] *Ibid.*, p. 76. The speaker was the Rt. Rev. Ludwig Ihmels, Bishop of Saxony, who also said, 'Thus we learn from Holy Scripture that the Church has only one task which is to bear witness to Him who was and is and is to come. . . . We can do nothing, we have nothing, we are nothing.'

[2] The Chairman, Archbishop Nathan Söderblom of Stockholm, in a letter summarizing his impressions two months after the Conference, put his finger on the touchstone of divisions: 'Is the Kingdom of God a force immanent in humanity, a programme to be advanced by energetic and enthusiastic human activity? Or is it a judgment and a salvation wrought by God, working in an inscrutable fashion, through the ages to the fulfilment of history, a specifically divine activity before which we must bow in adoration even though it escapes our poor human comprehension?' *La Conférence Universelle du Christianisme Pratique*, p. 2.

[3] Brown, *op. cit.*, p. 91.

[4] European theologians, prone to consider Americans superficial, could point to arguments such as: 'In our great cities, in four of our commonwealths and in the nation, the Council of Churches is to the religious life what the Chamber of Commerce is to the business life.' Rev. Roy Guild, *Stockholm*, p. 696. Earlier, another American had

pioneers[1] the Life and Work Movement sponsored a short-lived Institute of Social Christianity;[2] a Secretariat at Geneva carried on a programme of ecumenical education and, within the limits of its possibilities, of social action.[3]

explained the value and origin of the Federal Council, observing that 'the woeful waste of energy and substance due to the overlapping of sectarian causes and to competitive churches offended the decided preference which Americans have for efficiency as against traditions. In a country governed by public opinion it is of first-rate consequence that religious propaganda shall be sound, reasonable, well-informed and also well-organized. ... We can obtain a wider hearing for the essentials which underlie denominationalism than for the beliefs peculiar to any single denomination.' Rev. S. Parkes Cadman, *Stockholm*, pp. 669–70.

[1] Dr. Adolf Keller, who directed the Institute and Secretariat, recalled: 'The Stockholm Movement was mostly an army without troops. The ecumenical idea penetrated only with majestic slowness into the rank and file of the Churches.' Keller, *op. cit.* An American member of the World Council's Central Committee has questioned how deeply 'the ecumenical idea' has penetrated the membership of its constituency. Cf. Angus Dun, 'We Intend to Stay Together', *ER* II (Spring 1950), 3, p. 267. Dr. Samuel McCrea Cavert, Associate General Secretary of the World Council, expressed his satisfaction that 'the churches have been represented at Evanston by outstanding national leaders [who] have given convincing evidence that they genuinely believe in an ecumenical advance;' he added, however, 'The World Council must frankly admit that the average church member does not see far beyond his denominational boundary or even his parish.' *EPS*, August 30, 1954.

[2] At Stockholm the Bishop of Västerås had called for the setting up of 'an international, scientific, ethico-sociological institute' where the facts and functioning of contemporary society could be studied and the information and advice made available 'for such communities as labour for the social and moral welfare of humanity'. Pastor Elie Gounelle had urged the establishing of an institute to study particularly the situation of the working class. Cf. *Stockholm*, pp. 193, 172. The World Council of Churches is presumably permanently conscious of the need of such a social research centre.

[3] The key figure was Dr. Adolf Keller whose career as an ecumenical ambassador began in 1919 when he was sent by the Swiss Protestant Federation to the Federal Council of the Churches of Christ in America with a view to establishing what later became the Central Bureau for Inter-Church Aid whose activities were subsumed into the Life and Work orbit. Before its merger with the World Council of Churches in 1945 as its Department of Reconstruction, the Bureau had, over the years, dispensed 12 million Swiss francs in relief work. Ecumenical Summer Schools were organized, a weekly 'International Christian Press and Information Service' (to become later the World Council sponsored 'Ecumenical Press Service') was issued, inquiries were organized on current problems of unemployment, alcoholism, religious persecution in Russia, etc., collaboration was maintained with international organizations, particularly with the International Labour Organization and with the Nansen Committee. Cf. *En marche vers l'unité chrétienne* —Tiré à part du *Christianisme Social*, jan.-fév., 1937. Financial stringency forced the fusion of the administrative headquarters of the Life and Work Movement with the Secretariat of the World Alliance for International Friendship and the suspension of its quarterly periodical, but there is a genetic relationship between the activities of the Geneva Secretariat of those years and much of the work of the present World Council of Churches. Thus, the World Council's Study Department is a direct continuation of the Research Department of the Life and Work Movement.

The 1930's, however, refused to confirm the bright expectations of the post-Versailles world of the Stockholm Conference. A world-wide economic crisis shattered for ever belief in the inherent equilibrium of the mechanisms of industry and trade which would automatically distribute in greater abundance the fruits of an ever-expanding prosperity. The benign harmony of nature, which an easy optimism supposed needed only to be lubricated with the religiously inspired sentiment of goodwill, turned out on closer examination to have uncertain foundations. Psychologists, plumbing the personality, found dark depths, nurturing blind and malign urges. The very structure of matter lost its comforting solidity when mathematics and the microscope combined forces to demonstrate that the familiar atom, building-block of the universe, was compacted of impalpable electrical energy. The security of the Acquisitive Society which had regarded all meta-economic considerations as remnants of unscientific superstition or products of unproductive romanticism, was challenged by political religions which promised the dispossessed, the social outcasts and the rancorously restless, goals for living larger than those conceded to the mythical Economic Man. As the League of Nations revealed its essential impotence to control contemptuous violations of the political *status quo*, there was no safety in recalling the assurance of Woodrow Wilson: 'National purposes have fallen more and more into the background and the common purpose of enlightened mankind has taken their place.' Confronted by a *Volk* in jackboots and *Stahlhelme*, a balance of power, which the American President believed belonged to an era happily 'left behind', was nervously sought.

The Ecumenical Movement was similarly traversed by a ground-swell of protest against its intellectual prepossessions.[1] The rise of 'dialectical theology', which received its name from

[1] At a meeting of the Universal Christian Council of Life and Work in 1933 a German delegate shocked the exponents of the Social Gospel by impugning the Conference of Stockholm which had given birth to the organization. 'Its message is obsolete ... the offspring of the humanitarian ideals of the Enlightenment and the French Revolution. .... The rising Reformation theology today would put a critical question-mark at almost every sentence in it.' No wonder the Chairman saw a 'need for reinforcing the motives which furnish the Movement with its driving power'. Cf. Ehrenström in *History*, p. 560.

Kierkegaard and its impetus from Barth, challenged the identification, widespread in Life and Work circles, of the Kingdom of God with an ideal social order realizable in this world; it scorned the assumption that human behaviour was conditioned essentially by environment rather than by sin; it mocked the bland hope that social ills could be healed by education and mutual understanding.[1]

In Germany especially, the controversy on the theological justification of Christianity had ceased to be an idle academic debate. Members of the 'Confessing Church' were quietly seized and dispatched to concentration camps while 'German Christians', willing to accommodate doctrine to the demands of a victorious ideology, were favoured by a régime which appointed a *Reichsbischof* to prove its regard for religion. The pretension of the modern State to control all the areas of life showed itself in all its malevolence and brutal power where an official ideology reinforced the dictatorship; disturbing tendencies in the same menacing direction, however, were noted in other lands. With belief in society as a *communitas communitatum* irreparably fractured, the integuments of national life were being riveted together by man-made myths.

2. Oxford, 1937

The theme for the scheduled World Conference was not difficult to find: 'Church, Community and State'. In the inter-relation of these social realities, declared the Letter of Explanation to the Churches, 'is focused the great and critical debate between the Christian faith and the secular tendencies of our time. In this struggle the very existence of the Christian Church is at stake.'

To examine the scope and explore the implications of that

[1] Karl Barth has thus described the state of theology after the First World War: 'Dans l'orthodoxie, cristallisation de la doctrine détachée de ses origines; dans le piétisme, fuite dans l'expérience chrétienne confondue à tort avec son origine; dans la philosophie des lumières, réduction de la doctrine, que l'on ne comprend plus, à des maximes morales ou sentimentales; enfin, chez Schleiermacher et chez ses successeurs de droite ou de gauche, réduction de l'expérience chrétienne elle-même à l'expression suprême de l'instinct religieux universel. Telles sont les quatres pierres d'angle de la prison dans laquelle nous étions enfermés.' *Parole de Dieu, Parole Humaine*, pp. 243-4.

'great and critical debate', a series of symposia was organized on different aspects of the central theme, the papers being circulated for comment among a wide range of specialists before being re-edited by the original contributors for publication as background volumes of the Conference.[1] Oxford's Sheldonian theatre was the scene of the second World Conference on Life and Work which opened on July 12, 1937, with 300 delegates, named by more than 120 churches in 45 countries, present. Consultants chosen for their professional competence, youth leaders looking forward to their own international rally in Amsterdam in 1939, and the visitors found the general theme divided into five fields for closer examination.[2] Separate Sections of about eighty members considered (1) The Church and the Community (or, in the wider meaning current in Germany, *das Volk*), (2) The Church and the State, (3) The Economic Order, (4) Education, (5) The World of Nations. There were, to be sure, public meetings as at Stockholm, but the record indicates that Oxford

[1] The General Editor and organizing genius of the Conference was Dr. Joseph H. Oldham, borrowed from the International Missionary Council in 1934, and made Chairman of Life and Work's Research Department. A conference of theologians and jurists, meeting in Paris that same year, produced a symposium, *Die Kirche und das Staatsproblem in der Gegenwart*; with two other ecumenical inquiries directed by the Geneva Secretariat, *Totaler Staat und Christliche Freiheit* and *Kirche, Staat und Mensch: Russisch-Orthodoxe Studien*, edited by Nils Ehrenström. Dr. Oldham enlisted the services of a young Dutch theologian, W. A. Visser 't Hooft, familiar as General Secretary of the WSCF with the various traditions of the ecumenical world, to collaborate with him in producing the basic study on the Oxford theme, *The Church and its Function in Society*. The background volumes were entitled: *Church and Community*; *Church, Community and State in Relation to Education*; *The Universal Church and the World of Nations*; *The Christian Understanding of Man*; *The Kingdom of God and History*; and *The Christian Faith and the Common Life*. The London firm of George Allen & Unwin was publisher for the series.

[2] Dr. Oldham saw the significance of the central theme of the Conference in major terms; its analysis, he believed, would cast light on the basic problem of the hour, the shape and civilization of the future: 'The struggle today concerns those common assumptions regarding the meaning of life without which, in some form, no society can cohere. These vast issues are focused in the relation of the Church to the State and to the community because the non-Christian forces of today are tending more and more to find embodiment in an all-powerful State which is committed to a particular philosophy of life and seeking to organize the whole of life in accordance with a particular doctrine of the end of man's existence and in an all-embracing community of life which claims to be at once the source and the goal of all human activities: a State, that is to say, which aims at being also a Church.' *The Christian Faith and the Common Life*, p. ix.

was more of a working Conference than a demonstration. An impressive amount of preparatory work had been undertaken to present an adequate consensus of opinion of the different ecclesiastical traditions. The voices of German theologians were not heard at Oxford, the Nazi régime having refused passports to the delegates; their thought was available, however, in papers which served as background material for discussions in the Sections. The attendance of distinguished scholars and men of experience in large political affairs guaranteed a note of proportion and actuality in the Conference's pronouncements. The Section on Church and State, for example, was chaired by Max Huber, former President of the World Court and later of the International Red Cross; Alanson B. Houghton, sometime US Ambassador to the Court of St. James, and Francis B. Sayre, Assistant Secretary of State, were among the American members of the same group. The most distinguished authority of the English-speaking world in the field of Political Science, Professor Ernest Barker of Cambridge, participated in the discussions on Church and Community presided over by Sir Walter Moberly, Chairman of England's University Grants Committee. Economists of the standing of John Maud, R. H. Tawney, Sir Josiah Stamp, André Philip and Sir Alfred Zimmern were on hand to share their historical and scientific information with the theologians.

What was the effect of this venture of collaborative thought 'to define the points in the contemporary situation at which the specifically Christian understanding of life is crucially involved'?[1] The Professor of Church History in the University of Chicago, J. H. Nichols, believed that 'the authority of the Oxford Reports was unprecedented, at least in Protestant social ethics, and their competence enabled them to rank with the best of secular thought, a phenomenon scarcely seen since the seventeenth century'.[2] Dr. Visser 't Hooft was later to note that the study volumes, especially, on the Oxford theme served to stimulate thinking in

---

[1] *Oxford*, p. 26. Action would be the test in Dr. Oldham's judgment, action to be measured by the effort to 'evoke and educate a conscience which may help to save society from corruption and decay'. *Ibid*. p. 48.

[2] *Democracy and the Churches*, p. 235.

theological faculties, in forums and among lay groups; direct comment on the reports, solicited from the Churches, was 'disappointingly meagre', he added, attributing the silence to the fact that 'most Churches had as yet no corporate and relevant teaching on the problems of society and felt, therefore, unable to express an official opinion on the findings of Oxford'.[1] Thus, the delegates were divided on the moral permissibility of bearing arms under modern conditions of warfare, though unanimous in seeing it as a fruit and manifestation of sin. The message of the Oxford Conference was under no illusions: it felt obliged to inculcate the unity of Christians in an unbroken fellowship of prayer 'if war breaks out'. Unity in Christ, not as a theme for aspiration but as an actuality already illustrated at Oxford, was the central affirmation of the message. And, reviewing areas of possible Christian action to transform international life, the Conference did not fail to note 'the efforts of those movements which are working for the cause of international understanding through the Churches [and to] rejoice in the decision ... to recommend the creation of a World Council of Churches'.[2]

3. Negotiations with the Faith and Order Movement

The pressure of political developments, plus a general deepening of theological perspective in the Protestant world, had been drawing the Life and Work and the Faith and Order movements closer together. The Christian duty to reform the social order was more and more sensed in Life and Work circles to be that of witness to a single community of the redeemed, existing somehow by divine action. Fascism's contribution to the Ecumenical Movement was a heightening of the realization of that community. Certainly it was not an invisible Church which the rampaging totalitarians were determined to suppress if they could not, preferably, *gleichschalten* it. The Faith and Order Movement from its side could not ignore the theological implications of this sociological phenomenon, this rise of a Counter-Church. Economic factors also played a part in the growing

[1] *The Ten Formative Years*, p. 28.   [2] *Oxford*, p. 187.

desire to pool the two movements of ecumenical significance which perforce depended for financial support on largely the same constituency.

Authorized conversations between the leadership of the two movements resulted in a detailed plan for a World Council of Churches. Before adjourning its two weeks' Conference at Oxford, on July 26, 1937, the Universal Christian Council for Life and Work accepted the proposal that it should surrender its interests to the new, more comprehensive organization. The Conference on Faith and Order, meeting in Edinburgh on August 3–18, attached conditions to its approval of the project, demanding guarantees that the proposed World Council would respect its identity and specifically theological task. A constitution and plans for a provisional organization were drawn up at Utrecht on May 9–12, 1938, by a Committee of Fourteen, named by the two parent movements. No place had been made in the World Council structure for the International Missionary Council, a federation of combined denominational mission boards and national councils, but a Joint Committee was organized to serve as a bridge for the two-way traffic in ecumenical ideas to and from the mission lands.

With a courage that rose above the forebodings of war the Provisional Committee looked forward to August 1941 when the Assembly of the Churches would bring the World Council into existence and discharge them of their responsibility for supervising an organization 'in Process of Formation'. In the event, the Provisional Committee was compelled to supervise the Geneva Secretariat of the organized expression of the Ecumenical Movement, with its title so qualified, for ten years through difficulties unforeseen at the time but with unexpected opportunities for service as well. Decentralization, with offices in London and New York and co-operation supplied by the Northern Ecumenical Institute at Sigtuna, Sweden, made possible a tenuous contact with its war-torn constituency; geography gave Geneva an obvious advantage and the ingenuity and audacity of the headquarters staff ensured that ecumenical thinking, especially on the character of the post-war world, was communicated to both sides of the battle-front. The war-time preoccupations of the Geneva office of the World Council of Churches in Process of Formation were by no means confined to communicating information and inspiration. Pressing practical tasks were undertaken; chaplaincies for prisoners of war were organized, and Bibles and religious reading distributed in camps, while planning went forward on the prodigious problems of emergency aid when the fighting would cease. A department of Reconstruction and Inter-Church Aid, functioning on the principle that 'all Churches which can help shall come to the rescue of all the Churches which need help', was set up and ready from the first moment to co-operate with UNRRA. Supplying temporary prefabricated churches, paper for the production of religious literature, medical care and vacations for ailing church workers, and arranging theological scholarships were its main projects. Its Refugee Commission grew to an enterprise accounting for the largest share of the personnel at the Geneva headquarters. Its activity in co-ordinating the work of denominational relief committees and promoting the settlement of refugees is beyond the scope of this study. Work for refugees continues to be a major part of the activities of the Geneva centre of the World Council.

4. *Preparations for Amsterdam*

The Provisional Committee of the World Council met for the first time after the war at Geneva in February 1946. Reviewing developments and surveying possibilities, the meeting fixed the date of the constituting Assembly, chose for its theme, 'God's Order and Man's Disorder', elected five Presidents representative of different theological and ecclesiastical traditions in the organized Ecumenical Movement,[1] accepted a gift from John D. Rockefeller, Jr., to purchase the Château of Bossey, near Geneva,

[1] The Archbishop of Canterbury, Dr. Geoffrey Fisher; the Archbishop of Uppsala, Dr. Erling Eidem; the Archbishop of Thyateira, Dr. Germanos Strenopoulos; Pasteur Marc Boegner and Dr. John R. Mott.

as an educational centre and conference locale, approved plans looking to consultations with the Russian Church and appointed a delegation to visit the Orthodox Churches of the Middle East.

It was decided that the main theme, 'Man's Disorder and God's Design',[1] would be examined under four aspects each reflecting a facet of the comprehensive bearing and collective interest of the World Council membership and would be discussed separately in sectional gatherings at the Assembly to meet in two years at Amsterdam. 'The Universal Church in God's Design', the topic of Section I, was manifestly a theological inquiry primarily and as such a prolongation of Faith and Order studies. 'The Church's Witness to God's Design', the title of the topic of Section II, was concerned with missionary problems and techniques of contemporary evangelism. The traditional emphasis of Life and Work on social and economic problems predominated in the subject-matter of Section III, 'The Church and the Disorder of Society' and of Section IV, 'The Church and the International Disorder'. Sectional Commissions were organized to prepare a volume on each topic, with contributors to the symposia being asked to keep two emphases in mind—evidence of the rebirth of the Churches and of their growing unity. The preparation for Section IV was entrusted to the newly-formed Commission of the Churches on International Affairs, an agency jointly sponsored by the World Council of Churches and the International Missionary Council to advise the parent bodies of world order issues, to represent them at United Nations and other international organizations, and to clarify the ecumenical conscience on matters involving inter-governmental relations.[2]

---

[1] The social pessimism of the first formulation of the theme, 'God's Order and Man's Disorder', was lightened in a rephrasing adopted at a Study Commission meeting at Cambridge in mid-August.

[2] The creation of the Commission was evidence of the co-operation of the World Council of Churches and the International Missionary Council, formalized by a decision in 1947 to add the phrase 'in association with' each other in every listing of their formal titles and sealed by the indispensable aid rendered by the Missionary Council in arranging for the participation of representatives of the churches in missionary lands at the Amsterdam Assembly of the World Council of Churches.

5. The Participation of the Orthodox Churches

The relations of the Orthodox Churches to the Ecumenical Movement have been ambiguous. The single jarring note in a printed survey of the Oxford and Edinburgh Conferences of 1937 was struck by an Orthodox delegate who complained that his ecclesiastical tradition was discriminated against, its dogmatic positions ignored, its sacramental practice affronted.[1] After some controversy, especially in Greece, in the spring of 1949 over the legitimacy of Orthodox Churches belonging to the World Council,[2] similar disquietude was manifest at the Faith and Order meeting in Lund, Sweden, in mid-August 1952, where Archbishop Athenagoras, spokesman in the West for the Patriarch of Constantinople, explained that the question of participation on the part of the Orthodox Churches, its mode together with a common code of procedure for official delegates, could only be definitively and properly settled by a Pan-Orthodox Council, difficult to assemble under present international conditions.

It cannot be said, however, that the World Council of Churches has been negligent in its efforts to achieve a fuller participation of all of the Orthodox Churches.[3] The first post-war meeting of the Provisional Committee had dispatched a committee to

[1] Professor S. Zankov of the Faculty of Orthodox Theology at the University of Sofia remarked that of the nineteen Reports presented at public and plenary sessions at Oxford, only one was introduced by an Orthodox delegate, that no representative of Orthodoxy was invited to give one of the solemn allocutions of the closing session, that the conception of the Church prevailing was that of liberal Protestantism assembling a League of Churches like the League of Nations, that the united Communion service at Oxford was offensive to the Orthodox delegates since it was the sole official service and arranged without consulting them, that no one noticed their absence, demanded by their religious convictions, from the Communion service. *Cahier du Christianisme Social*, Sept.–Dec. 1937, pp. 288–92.

[2] *EPS*, May 6, May 13, May 27, July 18 and October 21, 1949.

[3] Addressing the Study Department Commission, meeting at Bossey, June 23, 1947, Dr. 't Hooft indicated that 'The Assembly must be of such a nature that the Orthodox must feel not only that the door is open but that we are working in a framework where we have already taken into consideration that they ought to be in, that their place is in the World Council of Churches' (*Archives*). At a meeting of the World Council's Reconstruction Department at St. Cergue, March 12, 1948, Dr. 't Hooft outlined the steps that had been taken to ensure the presence of the Orthodox Churches at Amsterdam, adding: 'World Council of Churches leaders realize that the full participation of the Eastern Orthodox Churches in the World Council is essential if the Council is to be truly ecumenical and world-wide in scope.' *EPS*, March 12, 1948.

visit the Orthodox Churches of the Near East and had approved an approach to the Church of Russia. The correspondence with Moscow that ensued, if indefinite, was sufficiently friendly to justify Dr. Visser 't Hooft's expectations as expressed at the World Conference of Christian Youth at Oslo in late July 1947: 'The Moscow Patriarchate considered that it was not ready this year to send a youth delegation from the USSR. We hope, however, that our fellow Christians from that great country will participate fully in future ecumenical meetings.'[1]

The World Council's General Secretary might have been less sanguine had he remembered the resentment of the Patriarchate of Moscow at the World Council's association with Russian Church *émigrés* and Synods-in-exile which refused it allegiance. He might also have been mindful of the campaign of the Russian Church to achieve hegemony over all ecclesiastical bodies within the Soviet orbit.[2] As late, however, as the special pre-Assembly publicity releases, the Ecumenical Press Service was writing:

No word has yet been received as to whether the Church in Russia will be represented at Amsterdam. It is possible that after the Conference of Orthodox Churches, beginning July 7, which has been called by the Moscow Patriarchate, an official word may be received concerning the participation of the Russian Church in this Assembly of the World Council.[3]

[1] *EPS*, July 1947, p. 196.

[2] Apart from the evidence of violence in the *Anschluss* of the Uniate Churches in the Ukraine and Transylvania, the declaration of the Patriarch Alexei during a visit to Rumania may be noted. Referring to the coming Pan-Orthodox Conference at Moscow, he declared: 'An Orthodox front is a necessity which must be realized. We should be conscious of the great truth that the Orthodox Church is powerful. For this reason, these Eastern Churches will form, without doubt, a front to be overcome by none.' *Ibid.*, June, pp. 18–25, 47. Later, in a letter answering an objection that only the Ecumenical Patriarch of Constantinople can canonically convoke a Council of Bishops, Patriarch Alexei explained: 'Our invitation to our colleagues, the Heads of the Autocephalous Churches, is both natural and lawful, especially under present conditions when not one of the centres of the Eastern Church would be a suitable venue for the holding of such a conference, if only because they do not offer a guarantee of freedom from political pressure for the study of ecclesiastical matters. The only place providing freedom from all foreign interference is the seat of our Patriarchal Throne, since it is situated in a country where the freedom of the Church is assured by law.' *Ibid.*, October 10, 1947.

[3] *Ibid.*, June 18–25, 1948.

The Conference referred to was 'The Meeting of Heads and Representatives of the Autocephalous Orthodox Churches in connection with the Quincentenary Celebrations of the Russian Orthodox Church's Attainment to Autocephalous Status', as the official Report termed the gathering. At the official opening of the celebration in the Sokolniki Cathedral, G. G. Karpov, Chairman of the Committee of the Ministerial Council of the USSR for the Affairs of the Russian Orthodox Church, welcomed the visitors and interpreted the presence in Moscow of the delegates from the other Orthodox Churches as indicating their support of the new social and political Soviet order and their consequent wish to oppose efforts from abroad by countries desirous of undermining its position. *Pravda*—which the month before had disclosed the decision of the Central Committee of the Communist Party of the USSR for an intensification of atheist activity—listed the names of the clerical dignitaries present who had supported the nomination of Patriarch Alexei of Moscow as the one designated to promote a closer union among Orthodox Churches through the world. The same ecclesiastics— the Patriarchs of Georgia, Serbia, Bulgaria and Rumania, representatives of the Patriarch of Alexandria and of the Russian Church in Ethiopia, delegates of the Orthodox Churches in Poland and Czechoslovakia—joined His Beatitude of Moscow in rejecting the invitation to attend the Amsterdam Assembly, terming the World Council 'imperialistic' and describing the Ecumenical Movement as mainly 'political and antidemocratic'.[1] The resolution was a rebuff to Archbishop Germanos, one of the five Presidents of the World Council, who was present at the Conference.

The news reached Geneva by way of a Radio Moscow broadcast on July 23. It was confirmed by an official letter at the time of the Amsterdam Assembly, declining the invitation in view of

[1] During the debate on the Ecumenical Movement at the Pan-Orthodox Conference, one speaker hurled the (fairly improbable) charge of Roman Catholic infiltration of the World Council. This account of the Russian Church's attitude to the Amsterdam Assembly is taken from *EPS*, July 30, 1948, A. De Waymarn's review of the *Official Report* of the Moscow Conference, in *ER* II (Summer 1950), 4, p. 403, and from the *Minutes of the Meeting of the Central Committee of the World Council of Churches, Amsterdam and Woudschoten*, p. 25.

the World Council's 'present tendencies' and forwarding the text of the resolution of the Moscow Conference, eloquent if tendentious explications of the judgment rendered a month earlier. The decisions taken and the Reports adopted by the First Assembly of the World Council failed to ameliorate the condemnation decreed by the leaders of the Russian Orthodox Church. The *Journal of the Moscow Patriarchate* printed the address of Archbishop Hermogenes of Kazan, Rector of the Academy of Theology in Moscow on October 15, 1948, at the opening of the winter semester, accusing the Ecumenical Movement of heresy and imperialist political aims.[1]

The hostility was unmistakable.

iii. THE WORLD COUNCIL IS FORMED AT AMSTERDAM

The First Assembly of the World Council of Churches was at once a personal encounter of religious-minded individuals committed to a spiritual purpose, a demonstration of solidarity of more than 150 churches, the constituting of an organization, and an effort to reach conclusions on common problems by study and discussion. The two weeks of the Amsterdam Assembly included, therefore, services of worship, public meetings featuring formal addresses, examination of and decisions on the Constitution, programme and budget of the Council, and discussions in the four Sections which prepared the Reports to be 'received' at Plenary Sessions to be 'commended to the churches for their serious consideration and appropriate action'.

Since debate in the Sectional Meetings was private, the 200 Press representatives concentrated their attention mainly on the pageantry of the Assembly, augmented by Holland's preparations for the Coronation of Queen Juliana, and on the more dramatic incidents at the public meetings. The spotlight was focused on

---

[1] 'Already before Amsterdam we could regard Life and Work as the logical expression of radical Protestantism with its denial of the divine humanity of Christ, the seven sacraments, the Virgin Mary and the honouring of the saints; moreover, since the Amsterdam Assembly, the Ecumenical Movement has revealed itself as a political party and as confederate of those who would launch a third, bloody war, although that has been masked in Christian phraseology.' *EPS*, October 7, 1949.

Karl Barth solemnly reminding the delegates that their function was not to concoct a facile 'Christian Marshall Plan' nor pretend to be God's administrative technical experts rather than His obedient witnesses. The East-West tension undoubtedly received the main publicity when an American attacked Soviet Communism for its rejection of moral law and its denial of human rights, and a delegate from an Iron Curtain country indicted the moral bankruptcy of the West. The world's divided state would become less sharp, declared John Foster Dulles, 'if those who believe in moral law and human dignity will make it apparent by their works that their political practices are in fact being made to serve their faith'. Speaking from the same platform, Professor Josef L. Hromadka of the John Huss Theological Faculty at Charles University in Prague, saw in Communism, 'although under an atheist form, much of the social impetus of the living Church'.

The Sections had been asked to bring to the Plenary Session an incisive statement of 2,000–2,500 words addressed primarily to the churches and written in a language intelligible to the regular church member; the statements, it was further indicated, should contain three major elements: (a) a limited diagnosis of the situation, (b) an exposition of the Christian position on the issues treated, and (c) recommendations to the churches and to Christians.[1] Inevitably the Reports were the work of energetic drafting committees; nor were they substantially modified during the discussions at the Plenary Sessions.[2]

The reactions to the social pronouncements of Amsterdam

[1] A reporter for the Assembly News, a bulletin issued daily at Amsterdam, remarked: 'Somehow or other, facilities for closer debate must be found in future World Council meetings. Mere "points of view" and "convictions" have been too numerous. But the disciplines of the ecumenical encounter have started.'

[2] Harold Fey, correspondent of the non-denominational Protestant weekly, Christian Century, believed that the Assembly 'partially reversed itself on the most important issue to come before it'. He writes: 'After condemning equally the ideologies of capitalism and communism, it [Amsterdam] sought to placate American opinion by confining its criticism to capitalism of the laissez-faire variety.' He supplies what is obviously an editorial judgment: 'The principal reason for the action was the Assembly's belated recognition that 85 per cent of the World Council's budget is raised in America. The Report of Section III had in effect endorsed "The Middle Way" as the only economic philosophy under which the Christian ends of justice and peace can be achieved in a technological society. News-starved correspondents seized on this action and cabled the entire text

varied with the source of the comment. In Europe, where the mangled and macerated tissues of finance, production and trade necessitated the economic surgery of large-scale nationalization and where the fraternity born of the Resistance movements (joined with the compromised reputation of the middle classes) had given Socialism a new moral authority, the severe strictures of Section III on capitalism occasioned small disquietude. From conservative religious circles in the United States, protest was voiced that the evils attributed to capitalism had been brought under social control, that—in any case—they were not inherent in the system but manifestations of human selfishness.[1] The righteous indignation expressed in some commercial circles challenged, in effect, the justification of any judgment on economic affairs coming from a religious group; ironically, the same circles decry on occasion the absence of leadership by religious forces.[2]

to America. The American reaction was said to be hostile, so World Council officials began to worry over its effect on contributions. President Charles P. Taft of the Federal Council of Churches who was absent when the vote was taken [in plenary session?], returned and proposed to confine the condemnation of capitalism to "the wholly self-regulating, *laissez-faire* theory of capitalism". But the representatives of churches from other parts of the world stand considerably to the left of American church opinion on what it means to apply Christian principles to the economic order. So the Assembly modified the statement, but only by adding "*laissez-faire*".' *Christian Century* LXV (September 22, 1948), 38, p. 980. The Official Report of Amsterdam notes only: 'At a later session the changes proposed by the Drafting Committee were submitted to the Assembly. Attention was called especially to the new formulation concerning the Church's attitude to capitalism and Communism as follows: "The Christian churches should reject the ideologies of both Communism and *laissez-faire* capitalism." These changes were accepted without further discussion.' *The First Assembly of the World Council of Churches*, edited by W. A. Visser 't Hooft (hereafter referred to as *Amsterdam*), p. 87. In a conversation with the author, Professor John C. Bennett who was Secretary of Section III at Amsterdam found the addition of the adjective of verbal significance only since it was *laissez-faire* capitalism which the text of the Report had described and condemned, he pointed out. Cf. also his article, 'Capitalism and Communism at Amsterdam', *Christian Century* LXV (December 15, 1948), 50, pp. 1362ff.

[1] H. Paul Douglass, 'Some American Reactions to Amsterdam', *ER* I (Spring 1949), 3, p. 289.

[2] *Fortune*, a monthly edited for the business community, had editorialized: 'The way out is the sound of a voice, not our voice, but a voice coming from something not ourselves, in the existence of which we cannot disbelieve. It is the earthly task of the pastors to hear this voice, to cause us to hear it and to tell us what it says. If they cannot hear it or if they fail to tell us we, as laymen, are utterly lost. Without it we are no more capable of saving the world than we were capable of creating it in the first place.' XXI (January 1940), p. 27.

The Amsterdam scrutiny of the world situation and its recommendation to improve it was judged of modest value by Kenneth G. Grubb, Chairman of the Commission of the Churches on International Affairs. Sir Kenneth,[1] who, as Chairman of Section IV, had presented the Report to the Assembly, observed at a meeting of the World Council's Central Committee a year later that the document 'did not contain anything striking'.[2] An Indian observer expressed his dissatisfaction with the indefiniteness of the Amsterdam attitudes—and perhaps thereby his misunderstanding of the complex character of the World Council of Churches and its official conception of its function—when he complained that the churches had not taken a stand on the contemporary power conflict in international affairs.[3] A reporter for the *Assembly News* seems to have anticipated such reproaches and, after explaining the inherent difficulty of arriving at an ecumenical consensus, endeavoured to place the significance of the public pronouncements of the Assembly in proper perspective:

> This message cannot be called 'the mind of Christ' nor 'the mind of the Church' nor is it the pontifically inspired utterance of the new World Council. True, it is the World Council speaking at its first Assembly. But in the end it is the word of the delegates, honest, humble men and women—for the most part not better endowed with insight and devout wisdom than their fellows—committed at this crucial time to speak a Christian word to the world. The Amsterdam Assembly's finest message will be the delegates themselves and through them renewed and rededicated Churches.[4]

The World Council, it is worth repeating, is only an instrument of its member churches.

[1] As he is now; he was knighted in 1953.

[2] *Minutes and Reports of the Second Meeting of the Central Committee* (Chichester), p. 81.

[3] 'The question the Younger Churches would like to raise is why the Churches should show such conflicting attitudes in the realm of power politics. The youth of the Younger Churches often feel that the international outlook of the Churches is feeble when compared to the solidarity of Islam or Communism. The approach of the Churches to international affairs appears like a form of pious nihilism full of sentimental aspirations that are not taken seriously.' Chandran Devanesan, 'Post-Amsterdam Thought from a Younger Church', *ER* I (Winter 1949), 2, p. 146.

[4] *EPS*, September 7, 1948.

iv. From Amsterdam to Evanston

The declaration of Amsterdam deemed of largest significance by the leaders of the Ecumenical Movement was the determination proclaimed in the message: 'We intend to stay together.' The practical consequences of that determination occupied the Committees of the Assembly[1] which reviewed the provisional Constitution and made recommendations on structure, policy and administration; its fulfilment was the responsibility of the ninety-member Central Committee, elected to exercise authority between Assemblies in the name of the component churches. The activities of the World Council of Churches, the problems confronting the newly created organization of the Ecumenical Movement, can thus be reviewed by examining the principal subjects on the agenda of the annual meeting of the Central Committee.

1. *Amsterdam-Woudschoten, 1948*

The Central Committee met for the first time immediately after the solemn adjournment of the Assembly at Amsterdam (continuing at nearby Woudschoten) to elect its Executive Committee of twelve, to confirm permanent staff appointments, to approve the rules and composition of departments and committees, to resolve World Council relationships with other ecumenical organizations and to apportion the burdens of budget-raising. In the midst of a discussion of these organizational details an announcement was made foreshadowing a major preoccupation of the World Council in the years ahead: how to remain above the crisis of contemporary history without failing in its mission. It was reported that one of the delegates, missing at Amsterdam, Dr. Lajos Ordass, Bishop of the Lutheran Church of Hungary, had been arrested. In due course Bishop Ordass was sentenced for violating currency laws in distributing foreign relief funds, a conviction that implicated the Lutheran World

---

[1] The Committees were concerned with practical problems of the World Council as an organization (Constitution and Rules and Regulations; Policy; Programme and Administration) and with the 'Concerns of the Churches' (including the life and work of women in the Church, the significance of the laity, and the Christian approach to the Jews).

Federation, an agency sharing office-space and collaborating with the World Council's Department of Inter-Church Aid.[1] In a subsequent spectacle trial in Sofia, a group of local Bulgarian Protestant pastors confessed to espionage on behalf of the British and American Governments. Among the alleged intermediaries were Dr. J. Hutchinson Cockburn, head of the World Council's relief programme, and his assistant, the Reverend Robert Tobias. Public opinion, particularly in England, expressed growing alarm at the trend of developments affecting the freedom of the Churches in Eastern Europe. The Archbishop of Canterbury spoke of

a deadly struggle between the Christian faith and the Christian Church on the one side and on the other a Communism which will not tolerate any form of the Christian Church unless it be subservient to itself and which, as we know from such evidence, even when it tolerates it, only too often takes care by insidious means to frustrate its activity, to sap its life and to cut off from it boys and girls as they grow up.[2]

The determination to escape involvement in the ideological struggle dividing human loyalties in every nation, a struggle symbolized (and over-simplified) by the alternatives 'East versus West', would test the skills of the Council's leadership.

2. Chichester, 1949

In addition to reviewing the operations of the World Council's Secretariat, the Central Committee, meeting at Chichester in mid-July 1949, discussed *in camera* the deteriorating political situation and the possible action open to the Council. The analysis offered by the Secretary-General found, on the whole, no direct persecution of religion in East Europe but pointed to a policy

[1] The Lutheran World Federation had received from the Hungarian Ministry of Finance official approval of the financial arrangement for which Bishop Ordass was condemned. As events proved, the régime was intent on replacing the Bishop by more accommodating ecclesiastical administrators. Evidence of the prior hostility of the Government is clear from the admissions of a secret policeman detailed to follow Bishop Ordass on his last visit to the Geneva Headquarters of the World Council and spy on his activities. The policeman sought political asylum in the West. Cf. J. Hutchinson Cockburn, *Religious Freedom in Eastern Europe*, p. 87.

[2] Presidential address to the Joint Synod of the Convocation of Canterbury. Cf. *EPS*, January 21, 1949.

of regimentation of the churches. Such political control forbade the churches 'to render any public witness except when they are invited to join the official choir of glorification of the new régime'. Lest the effects of such a policy be underestimated, Dr. Visser 't Hooft emphasized that such regimentation 'is more, not less dangerous for the purity of the Church'.[1] At the conclusion of the meeting the Central Committee issued a strong statement condemning (but not identifying) totalitarianism.[2]

3. Toronto, 1950

The world and the organized Ecumenical Movement were confronted with a new crisis in the early summer of 1950, one that would test the durability of the juridical system of collective security while exposing the organization and the functioning of the World Council of Churches to unexpected strains. The United Nations' Security Council had been convoked in emergency session in the last days of June 1950 to consider alarming reports arriving from its observers watching the borders of a nation in the Far East created under its own auspices. The decisive action of armed intervention to repel the aggressor and re-establish peace, authorized by the Security Council, was endorsed by the World Council's Central Committee in a public statement of sizeable consequences:

> An act of aggression has been committed. We, therefore, commend the United Nations, an instrument of world order, for its prompt

[1] Chichester Minutes, p. 65 and ER II (Autumn 1949), I, p. 63.

[2] The discussion of the Central Committee has been summarized and its action explained thus: 'There was a common conviction that the World Council of Churches had no mandate to make a judgment on the merits of the particular economic systems (e.g. capitalism and communism looked at on the economic level) and that the churches could be exploited by quite opposite political interests. Nor was the feeling absent that the Churches were themselves often to blame for failure in the achieving of social justice in different parts of the world where the Christian Gospel had been preached. There was, moreover, a strong sense of the necessity of maintaining fellowship with all the Churches in both East and West and of consideration for the complex and difficult character of the personal problems involved for those who live on a razor's edge. . . . But the Central Committee at Chichester believed the issue to be an issue of conscience. It felt compelled to declare its deliberate condemnation of totalitarian doctrine and totalitarian methods as in fact a denial of absolute moral standards and a moulding of the minds of the young in a pattern utterly opposed to the message of the Gospel.' The Bishop of Chichester, 'The Chichester Meeting', ER II (Autumn 1949), I, p. 37.

decision to meet this aggression and for authorizing a police measure which every member nation should support. At the same time, governments must press individually and through the United Nations for a just settlement and conciliation.[1]

The Central Committee had expressed its mind before. At Chichester it had spoken out against further dismantling of Germany's industrial plant, called for the protection of the Holy Places in Palestine and underlined the obligation of widening the emigration possibilities for the refugees of the world. At Toronto it issued a document of historic importance for the Ecumenical Movement, 'The Church, the Churches and the World Council of Churches', an analysis of its own nature. On the basis of an inquiry by the Commission of the Churches on International Affairs (restricted to Islam and countries where Roman Catholicism is preponderant), entitled 'Religious Freedom and Dominant Faiths', it had condemned limitations of religious liberty. It had, moreover, concerned itself with *apartheid* in South Africa, repeated its opposition to exploitation, discrimination and segregation, and authorized the sending of a multi-racial delegation to render fraternal assistance if the churches of that troubled area could be persuaded to extend an invitation. It had fixed on a theme for the next Assembly—'Jesus Christ as Lord is the only Hope of both the Church and the World'—a topic involving the field of eschatology on which theological attitudes were divided. It was the resolution on Korea, however, adopted unanimously by the Central Committee (save for two abstentions on grounds of pacificism), that caught the world's attention.

The World Council of Churches, despite all its endeavours, was judged to have taken sides in the cold war.[2] The letter of the

[1] *The First Six Years*, p. 119.

[2] General Secretary Dr. W. A. Visser 't Hooft, in a subsequent conference, explained the import of the Toronto resolution under three points: (1) No statement of any World Council of Churches body is a statement on behalf of all member churches; thus, the resolution of the Central Committee can be accepted or rejected by member churches. (2) The Central Committee had followed the decisions of the Amsterdam Assembly concerning the task of the World Council of Churches with respect to the rule of international law; it had implemented the decision that the only organ of international order which is available should uphold the rule of law over against aggression. (3) The World

Commission of the Churches on International Affairs warning
that the Stockholm Peace Appeal was politically motivated
aggravated the accusations. The World Council Resolution on
Korea was included as evidence in an exhibition staged at Yenching
University, Pekin, to demonstrate the alleged use 'American
imperialism' was making of Christian institutions.[1] *Pravda*
publicized on August 5 'An Appeal to the Christians of the
World', signed by the Patriarch of Moscow, the Catholicos of
the Armenian Church, and the Catholicos of Georgia, claiming
that the resolution of the World Congress of the Partisans of
Peace calling for the banning of the atomic bomb 'puts every
one of us under the obligation to lift up his own voice against
the employment of weapons of death'. The Appeal of the
Orthodox Prelates was addressed in part to 'the Protestant world
in the shape of the World Council of Churches' which, it was
asserted, 'would give substance to its condemnation of war-
mongering by supporting the Stockholm Peace Manifesto'.[2]

Council had not identified itself with any bloc of nations against other nations. Cf. *EPS*,
September 8, 1950. Unhappily, at the same time, the Patriarch of Moscow, the Metropolitans of Kiev, Krutiza and Leningrad had protested publicly to the UN Security
Council 'against the American aggression in Korea. In the name of Christ, the Saviour
of the world, it [the Russian Orthodox Church] calls imperatively for a cessation of
violence and bombing, for the withdrawal of foreign troops and for the ending of this
illegal war.' *Ibid.*

[1] Yenching, an institution of higher learning founded and directed by American
Protestant missionary groups, was seized by the Ministry of Education of the People's
Republic of China in February 1951. After visiting the exhibition, Dr. James Endicott,
Chairman of the Canadian Peace Congress, wrote: 'The final painful humiliation for me,
a missionary, was to see the *Ecumenical Review* of the World Council of Churches on
display. There were big red circles around pages 62 and 63 showing the Western Christian
support for MacArthur's mass slaughter of the Korean people and the denunciation of
the Stockholm Appeal to ban the atom bomb. Chinese students at Yenching and everywhere else are entitled to draw the most serious conclusions about the nature of the
tie-up between Western Christianity and Western imperialism from the matter contained
in this *Ecumenical Review* of the World Council of Churches. The only thing left for the
World Council of Churches to discredit itself completely in the eyes of all Asia and to
give final proof of the exposure of imperialism under the cloak of religion is for it to
deny or keep silent about the present large-scale American germ warfare against the
Chinese [sic] people.' *China Monthly Review*, June 1952, p. 547.

[2] Quoted in *EPS*, September 1, 1950. Earlier, Archbishop Luka of Crimea—in civilian
life, Professor Voino-Yasenetsky, winner of a Stalin Prize in 1945—appealed in the
Journal of the Moscow Patriarchate to Christians in 'Anglo-Saxon countries [to thwart] the
bloody plans of their militarists'. Quoted in *EPS*, April 23, 1948.

Despite the insistence of the East Asia Christian Conference, sponsored by the World Council and convened at Bangkok in December 1949, that 'it is not the challenge of any ideology but the knowledge of the love of God in Christ for men that is the basis of the Church's social and political concern', a Moscow periodical branded the meeting as 'a mobilization of reactionary forces to combat the nationalist movement towards the freedom of the peoples of Asia' and attacked the World Council as the 'foe of democracy'.[1]

By way of explicating its attitude the World Council, after its Executive Committee meeting at Bièvres, France, January 30–February 1, 1951, dispatched a letter to its member churches decrying the war psychosis of the hour, deploring the international and social perils of rearmament, demanding that every chance for negotiations between the belligerents be seized, recommending universal economic co-operation and urging all to pray for peace. The letter reasserted the World Council's 'independence of all secular power', its effort 'on a basis of open brotherly conversation between the Churches to give a genuine Christian answer to the crucial questions of the present situation', and specified that 'the task of the Church today is to raise its voice in the first place in defence of the men and women for whom Christ died and who, in their material or spiritual insecurity, are the real victims of the great conflicts of our time'.[2]

4. Rolle, 1951

The storm over the Korea resolution had not blown out when the Central Committee convened at Rolle, Switzerland, on

---

[1] 'For a number of years measures have been in progress in the USA for forming from the Christian Churches a single religious centre for the fight against communism and democracy. As is known, the Vatican, the obedient tool in the hands of world reaction, the universal bulwark of obscurantism, keeps only the Catholic Church united. Now American imperialism is setting up a world centre for religion to embrace all the Churches. It was for the furthering of this conception that the so-called World Council of Churches, which directs in particular the activities of the Protestant Churches, was started.' *Literaturnaya Gazeta* of March 18, 1950. Quoted in *EPS*, March 31.

[2] The quotations are from the General Secretary's summary of the principal emphases (and, probably, intentions) of the Bièvres document. Cf. *Minutes and Reports of the Fourth Meeting of the Central Committee* (Rolle), p. 58.

August 4, 1951, for its Fourth Meeting.[1] Indeed the storm was only an episode in a continuing situation challenging human loyalties. While the Amsterdam Assembly was in session, cargo planes were supplying the blockaded city of Berlin. The division of the world deepened steadily and menacingly. The formal constitution of two governments in Germany, the progressive sovietization of East Europe, the organization of the North Atlantic Treaty defence, the stalemate in the United Nations, the installation of a People's Democracy in China, the possession of the atom bomb by both East and West, and, finally, the invasion of South Korea, all were phases and factors of that divided world. Since history is inescapable, the World Council of Churches was part of that world. It was earnestly endeavouring to discover its practical role in it, a task made complex by the very nature of the Council and the involvement of some of its constituency.

The Rolle meeting had before it two assigned themes for consideration. The first subject of discussion resulted in a Statement, 'The Calling of the Church to Mission and to Unity', suggesting implications for the future structure and relationship of the International Missionary Council and the World Council of Churches. The second theme, 'The World Council of Churches in Times of Tension', was discussed in closed meetings. The subject concerned the plight of religious groups in East Europe, the situation in China of the World Council's member churches 'with their complete acceptance of the Government's leadership and control' and their decision 'to sever all connection with

[1] Bishop Albert Bereczky of the Reformed Church of the Danubian District of Hungary resigned from the Central Committee and the Commission of the Churches on International Affairs, claiming to see a pro-Western orientation of the World Council in its implied criticism of the Partisans of Peace and its failure to note the protests of Lutheran and Reformed Churches in Hungary against the Toronto Resolution as well as their condemnation of German (presumably West German) remilitarization and their demand for the recognition of the People's Democratic Republic of China. Rolle *Minutes*, p. 55. Professor Josef L. Hromadka, of the Evangelical Church of the Czech Brethren, wrote: 'In a tragically decisive moment of world history, the World Council of Churches identified itself (under most dubious circumstances) with one group of great powers, backed its military might and encouraged all UN members to participate in it. Something terrible happened.' 'A Voice from the Other Side', *Christianity and Crisis* XI (March 19, 1951), 4, p. 28. Professor Hromadka is presently a member of the Central Committee.

Christian missions from the West',[1] and the problems occasioned by the social revolutions, the insistent nationalism, and the revival of ancient, dormant religions in South-east Asia.

To be unwillingly involved in the implications of the cold and not-so-cold war was undoubtedly annoying to World Council officials. The activities of the Secretariat, its departments and commissions, were adequately absorbing without the distracting agitation of secular ideological issues. Though the International Refugee Organization was expiring, the problems of the world's homeless remained a responsibility of the Department of Inter-Church Aid and Service to Refugees. In co-operation with other ecumenical organizations the Youth Department was planning a Youth Conference in South-east Asia. The project of a semi-official history of the Ecumenical Movement was advancing slowly. The Commission on the Life and Work of Women in the Churches had organized itself. The Ecumenical Institute at Celigny was conducting its courses, gathering groups from different professions to examine their vocational problems in the light of the Gospel. Indeed, plans had been approved to create a Graduate School of Ecumenical Studies at Bossey, affiliated with the Faculty of Theology of the University of Geneva. A wide range of theological thinking has been organized to survey systematically the full scope of the Assembly Theme of Christian Hope. 'To promote co-operation in study' had been defined as one of the functions of the World Council. The Study Department was endeavouring to overcome the 'disquieting apathy and unconcern'[2] of the member churches towards the common

---

[1] Rolle *Minutes*, p. 69. Dr. T. C. Chao resigned as a President of the World Council in a letter terming the Toronto Resolution 'much like the voice of Wall Street' and protesting the impossibility of being a loyal citizen of the People's Republic of China and an official of the World Council of Churches. *Ibid.*, p. 55. Dr. Chao was subsequently reported to have been arrested and removed from the campus of Yenching University in Peking, where he had been Dean of the School of Religion, because his 'confession' failed to measure up to the rigid requirements of the 'ideological remoulding' movement sponsored by the Chinese Government. *New York Times*, May 25, 1952, p. 2 (European edition). Miss Sarah Chakko of India was elected to succeed Dr. Chao as President. Archbishop Athenagoras, Exarch in the West of the Patriarch of Constantinople, replaced his predecessor, Archbishop Germanos, deceased.

[2] Rolle *Minutes*, p. 97.

enterprise; it was circulating reports, organizing conferences, encouraging the formation of national study commissions. It had lent its good offices in the creation and servicing of the unofficial Ecumenical Commission on European Co-operation, subsequently known as the Committee on the Christian Responsibility for European Co-operation.[1] Within the capacities of a full-time staff of two—divided, moreover, by the Atlantic Ocean—the Commission of the Churches on International Affairs pursued its mission of expressing the ecumenical outlook on the international scene. The influence of the CCIA in some situations was illustrated later when the Director was dispatched during the US State Department's efforts to arrange a cease-fire in Korea, to interpret to President Syngman Rhee the widespread desire for peace in America and Europe.

5. Lucknow, 1953

The Central Committee, long desirous of making the ecumenical actuality visible in the Far East, sat in Lucknow, India, December 31–January 8, 1953. Its principal business was preparation for the Second Assembly, scheduled to take place in the United States, thus honouring a commitment made at the Utrecht meeting in 1938, and now fixed at Evanston, Illinois.

To make available to those planning for the discussions at Evanston information on the conditions in Asia, as interpreted according to the convictions and concerns of Christians on that side of the world, a four-day Ecumenical Study Conference was arranged immediately before the meeting of the Central Committee.[2] The fruit of the Study Conference appears in the letter addressed from Lucknow by the Central Committee to its member churches underlining the responsibility created for the churches by the situation in Asia. The poverty and social disorganization there, it was indicated, call for action by churches in more developed countries on behalf of government-sponsored

---

[1] Cf. Paul Abrecht, 'The Churches and European Unity', ER IV (April 1952), 3, pp. 296 ff.
[2] The papers and discussions were published under the title, *Christ—the Hope of Asia*.

Technical Assistance Programmes. The national revolutions in Asia impose upon the churches there an obligation to make their life 'a witness to social justice and political freedom', since the Christian understanding of man, it was pointed out, is directly relevant to the search for new foundations of society. Distressed at the 'widespread sense of frustration over the increasing bitterness which affects relations between powers', the Central Committee in a letter to the President of the UN General Assembly urged that, since the immediate object for which the United Nations intervened had been fulfilled, the unification and independence of Korea should be pursued by 'negotiated settlements'. It was the method which the World Council's Executive Committee was to recommend a year later in a letter to the four Foreign Ministers meeting in Berlin in February 1954 to discuss the unification of Germany and a peace treaty for Austria.[1]

The World Council was even more mindful of the scandal of the division of the churches, the specific concern of the Faith and Order Commission of the Council. At its Third World Conference at Lund, Sweden, August 15–28, 1952, the 225 delegates from 114 churches agreed: 'We have now reached a crucial point in our ecumenical discussions.' They noted, moreover, that their future tasks involved more than the traditional presentation and comparison of their separate religious convictions, that there is 'need for co-operative, creative study of issues which affect varying interpretations of the unity and disunity of Christians'.[2] One of these issues includes the influence of non-theological factors which hinder or assist the unity of the Church. A letter of the British Scripture scholar, Professor C. H. Dodd, to the Commission was the catalyst opening this new field of study. Professor Dodd invited a frank investigation of the part which 'unavowed motivation', attitudes based on confessional loyalties, and denominational traditions with their peculiar social and political predilections, play in the expression

---

[1] The letters are in *The First Six Years*, pp. 133–6.
[2] *Ibid.*, p. 26.

of specifically theological opinions on Church unity.[1] The Lund Conference was the last meeting before Faith and Order, in the interests of a more complete integration into the organizational structure of the World Council, surrendered its semi-autonomy as a Commission, becoming a Department in the Division of Studies paralleling the Department on Church and Society.

v. The Second Assembly at Evanston

Northwestern University in the Chicago suburb of Evanston, Illinois, is, like many American institutions of higher learning, the outgrowth of the determination of pioneers to provide future ministers for the community and to guarantee that the youth of the nation would have a religiously oriented education. Founded just over a hundred years ago in what was then frontier country by Methodist preachers, a religious group whose activity has always been strongly marked by missionary zeal, impatience of denominational differences and intense concentration on social reform,[2] its evangelical origins, its extensive Lake-shore campus, amply furnished with halls and meeting-rooms, its location in the centre of the American continent, all recommended it as the scene of the Second Assembly of the World Council of Churches. For the last seventeen days of August 1954, delegates of 132 of the 163 member communions of the Council gathered there for prayer, common counsel and planning for the future of the organized instrument of the Ecumenical Movement.

[1] Professor Dodd wrote: 'At Amsterdam the delegates from behind the Iron Curtain were insisting that the ecclesiastical questions that occupy us must not be treated in abstraction from what is going on in the political and social spheres. Quite clearly they thought that it did not matter very much whether the sacraments should be safeguarded by apostolic succession or whether the Church is an "event" created daily and hourly by the Word of God; what mattered was that Christianity should find ways of embodying itself in the new Communist or "proletarian" society as it did in the feudal and bourgeois societies of the past. If it does so, then as a matter of fact, of course, fresh "confessional" divergences will arise. That is why, I think, it would be salutary to bring into the open those social and political matters which I am sure constantly weigh with us, though they may not be avowed.' 'Unavowed Motives in Ecumenical Discourse', ER II (Autumn 1949), 1, p. 56.

[2] Northwestern's first Dean of Women was Frances Willard who founded the Women's Christian Temperance Union, an organization influential in obtaining the enactment of national prohibition legislation. Even today alcoholic drinks are not sold in Evanston.

Divided into fifteen groups considering the theme of Christian Hope and subsequently into six sections studying subjects of ecumenical interest,[1] the delegates found it almost impossible to follow the Assembly as a whole.[2] They knew that the international situation had deteriorated since their meeting at Amsterdam. The Report of the UN Disarmament Sub-Commission, published on July 29, acknowledging the continuing impasse, was a reminder that the menace of war, its terrors magnified by newly-developed thermo-nuclear weapons, had not abated. Nevertheless, with the assurance of Christ's promises, the Message of the Evanston Assembly proclaimed: 'we can face the powers of evil and the threat of death with a good courage'. The Assembly was reluctantly compelled to acknowledge its inability to solve satisfactorily the question of the meaning of hope, in effect to relate proximate goals and ultimate ends.[3]

With the liberty allowed in ecumenical discourse, differences of opinion on other subjects were voiced. Mr. Charles Taft boldly extolled American society and its free-enterprise system as 'at its best, a product of Christian principles', while for Professor Josef Hromadka the danger is that the Church will identify itself with human absolutes or find absolute evil in any secular institution, a danger seemingly successfully escaped in Czechoslovakia by his own church. In the judgment of Dr. Benjamin Mays, racial segregation stood condemned by the gospel; Dr. Ben Marais of South Africa saw in the scriptural episode of the Tower of Babel the beginning of *apartheid* and concluded: 'It is clear that God willed the existence of separate nations and that

[1] Faith and Order: 'Our Oneness in Christ and our Disunity as Churches'; Evangelism: 'The Mission of the Church to those outside her Life'; Social Questions: 'The Responsible Society in a World Perspective'; Inter-group Relations: 'The Church amid Racial and Ethnic Tensions'; The Laity: 'The Christian in his Vocation'; International Affairs: 'Christians in the Struggle for World Community'.

[2] The proceedings appeared as *The Evanston Report*, edited by W. A. Visser 't Hooft (hereafter referred to as *Evanston*). Popular interpretations include: James Hastings Nichols, *Evanston: an Interpretation*; Cecil Northcott, *Evanston World Assembly*; and H. G. G. Herklots, *Looking at Evanston*.

[3] *Evanston*, p. 70. The Report of the Advisory Committee on the Main Theme was forwarded to the member churches 'for their study, prayer and encouragement'. The Orthodox participants disassociated themselves from the Statement.

He wills to perpetuate the divisions into races and nations.' To an Evangelical pastor from the Soviet Zone of Germany, Dr. Guenter Jacob, the question of being a believing Christian or a Communist was 'an either-or proposition'; Dr. János Péter of Hungary held that one can be both. Such opinions are, to be sure, merely views held within the World Council. The positions the World Council 'commended to the Churches for study and appropriate action', as well as the authority of its judgments, will be considered later in this study.

If there was not the atmosphere of new beginnings at Evanston as at Amsterdam, there were elements that made the meeting memorable. There was the articulateness of the delegates from Africa and Asia, a constant reminder (despite the absence of the churches of China) of the awakening of the hundreds of millions of people of those continents and of their demand for recognition. The President of the United States and the Secretary-General of the United Nations journeyed to Evanston to address Plenary Meetings of the Second Assembly, evidence that the Council and the idea it represented commanded the attention of secular authorities. There was the interest of the organs of public information represented by the presence of 646 correspondents, radio and television newscasters, proof that millions of people in many lands were waiting to learn what was being said and done at Evanston. The pronouncement of the Assembly on social questions was felt by some commentators to represent a 'swing to the right' in the World Council's attitude. A more equitable judgment would suggest that the Report on the Responsible Society was the result of fuller information of the state of the world, a wider experience in ecumenical dialogue and more leisurely preparation than had been true of the comparable Amsterdam document.

Because it was the Second Assembly there was a certain factualness about the Evanston meeting. The Council was no longer an experiment: indeed it had been functioning long enough to warrant a survey by a committee which had suggested certain changes in structure and administration in the interests of greater efficiency. The representatives of the member churches and the officials of the Council had come to know one another well by reason of regular encounters at meetings of the Central Committee and in the course of mutual efforts in aid of refugees. A certain camaraderie had grown up in the Ecumenical Community. The questions to be discussed were inevitable facets of familiar problems offering small prospect of imminent solution. The world had not changed much, certainly not for the better, in the six years since Amsterdam, and the differences of theological position in the World Council constituency, based as they are on strongly held convictions, were not easily to be bridged or dissolved.[1]

The delegates who returned home from Evanston had the mandate to make effective the Assembly's recommendations in the life of their separate communions. They had consulted together about the Council which at Amsterdam they had 'covenanted together' to form. Despite the concurrent growth of confessional solidarity—the international associations of the Presbyterians, Anglicans, Disciples of Christ, Lutherans and Methodists had convened in America before the Evanston Assembly—the Council after six years was undoubtedly a stronger, more articulate organization. The Churches which had resolved to stay together were resolved to go forward together to a future hidden from human sight.

[1] Chosen to fill the largely honorific posts on the Council's presidium on a basis of confessional and geographical representation were: Professor John Baillie of the Church of Scotland; Bishop Sante Uberto Barberi, missionary leader for the Argentine, Uruguay and Bolivia of the Central Conference of the US Methodist Church; Bishop Otto Dibelius of the Evangelical Union Church of Berlin-Brandenburg; the Most Reverend Mar Thoma Juhanon, Metropolitan of the Syrian Reformed Church of St. Thomas of Malabar, South India; Archbishop Michael, spiritual Chief of the Greek Orthodox of North and South America acknowledging jurisdiction of the Ecumenical Patriarch; and the Right Reverend Henry Knox Sherrill, Presiding Bishop of the Protestant Episcopal Church of the United States. Bishop G. K. A. Bell of Chichester, England, was elected an Honorary President.

II

THE NATURE AND AUTHORITY OF THE WORLD COUNCIL OF CHURCHES

WHAT had been brought into being by the resolution voted *nemine contradicente* in Amsterdam's Concertgebouw on August 23, 1948? 'A fellowship of churches which accept our Lord Jesus Christ as God and Saviour', declared the Constitution of the now officially constituted World Council of Churches. But what precisely is 'a fellowship of churches'?

The plan for the projected World Council which was laid before the Conferences at Oxford and Edinburgh in 1937 seems to have envisaged no more than a new organization which, in the interests of greater efficiency, would couple the movements of Life and Work and Faith and Order and secure for the interests they represented the official recognition and support of the churches. The latter feature contained implications that were possibly unsuspected at the time. For the churches to enter into official association with one another, to declare (as they did at Amsterdam) that their mutual relations expressed an extant unity, a unity they pledged to perpetuate, raised questions concerning the character of that unity and demanded serious examination of the nature of the World Council of Churches.

A federation of churches co-operating for determined goals presents no particular problem of analysis: such organizations exist as Christian Councils or Federations of Churches in nearly every country. The commitment, however, whereby some 150 churches 'covenanted together to constitute this World Council of Churches', seemingly produced something more than the familiar church federation. How describe the result? How define the nature of a 'fellowship' of churches holding divergent views on the basis of ecclesiastical unity but seeking to express a unity they had experienced? The Archbishop of Uppsala remarked later: 'If the Amsterdam delegates had been consistent, they should have separated with an anathema. But, thank God, they expressed their firm determination to stay together in spite of differences which might seem almost fundamental.'[1] They not only resolved 'to stay together' in an organized fellowship but determined to 'move forward towards the manifestation of the One, Holy Church' when the justification for the World Council of Churches—'an emergency solution'—presumably will have happily ceased.[2] To be sure, there was at Amsterdam little of the easy optimism which, Archbishop Yngve Brilioth told the delegates, characterized the pre-Lausanne hopes of the Faith and Order movement: 'the ideal of a united Church is a tangible possibility to whose realization in the not too distant future we may look forward'. On the other hand, however distant that future now appeared, however realistic was the recognition of the difficulties involved, the formation of the World Council of Churches represented an official commitment of its member churches 'to express that unity in Christ already given to us and to prepare the way for a much fuller and much deeper expression of that unity'.[3]

A new fact had come into being in the field of ecumenics but no categories exist in ecumenical discourse to describe it.

It was not long after the Amsterdam Assembly that the need for attempting such a description forced itself upon the World Council. The demand for clarification of the implications of membership was first voiced in the Orthodox Church of Greece, disturbed, in part, by Karl Barth's comment that 'not one of the Churches represented at the Assembly had confronted the others with the claim of being the infallible Church, the sole source of

---

[1] *ER* III (April 1951), 3, p. 250.
[2] From an address, 'The Task of the World Council of Churches', a Report presented to the Assembly on behalf of the Provisional Committee by the General Secretary. *Amsterdam*, p. 29.
[3] *Ibid.*

salvation'.[1] The uncertainty of the relations of the member churches to one another in a fellowship of unity was not confined to the Orthodox. The question required more definite answers on the nature of the organization expressing that unity; plans were set on foot to provide at least a provisional response.

It was no easy task. There was, to begin with, no historical precedent to evoke nor even an agreed vocabulary of terms.[2] Some ecumenical experts held that success was impossible, this being an effort to define the ineffable. Thus Professor L. A. Zander of the Russian Orthodox Institute of Paris argued that the Ecumenical Movement—including its organized expression, the World Council of Churches—functions on a level beyond rational description.[3] And the Archbishop of Uppsala saw the World Council as 'a form of Christian community which cannot be defined because its essence is dynamic, because it is continually transcending the limits of its previous and present existence'.[4] The problem of defining the relations of the churches to one another within the organization of the World Council (thus

[1] *Réforme*, October 23, 1948 as quoted in *EPS*, October 29, 1948.

[2] A former Associate General Secretary of the World Council, Bishop Stephen C. Neill, observes in a recent book: 'The word *Church* appears to be commonly used in modern speech in no less than six different senses.' *The Christian Society*, p. 296. Discussing the resulting problems of orthography, the editors of *Christendom*, the forerunner of the World Council's *Ecumenical Review*, acknowledged their realization of 'perpetual inconsistency' in the use of upper or lower case initial for the term: 'To capitalize or not to capitalize are the only option which English usage allows. But the meanings of "church" are multiple. A correspondent points out that at least a dozen meanings have been recognized in various *Christendom* articles and challenges us to be explicit in the future as to what meaning is intended in any context. He suggests we attach a subscript to every use of the word—church$_1$, church$_2$ and so on—so that everyone will know exactly what is being talked about.' *Christendom* VIII (Autumn, 1943), 4, p. xiii. The present writer has encountered the same problem. He has followed the orthography of the World Council documents.

[3] 'It especially belongs to that sphere of religious experience in which dogmas are seen to be the rationalized schemata of super-rational truth. Accordingly, for the dogmatic consciousness ecumenism is a paradox (easily converted by its opponents into sheer absurdity), an antinomy (regarded by many as simply a contradiction), an object of faith and inspiration explainable but not defined by reason.' 'The Problems of Ecumenicism', WCC Study Department Document 48E/708A (mimeographed). Professor Zander wrote that 'from a dogmatic point of view ecumenicism itself may be defined as the intercommunion of Christians who regard one another as heretics'.

[4] *ER* III (April 1951), 3, p. 251.

clarifying its nature) was complicated by the fact that the member churches themselves have refrained from giving detailed and precise definitions of the nature of the Church.[1]

How then achieve a definition which would take into account the various ecclesiologies of its member churches, ecclesiologies ranging from the ironical conception of the Church not as 'an organic historical entity but a social contract and Rousseau and Hobbes are its prophets'[2] to the affirmation of the Church as a thoroughly concrete, historical entity uniquely identified with a single ecclesiastical communion?[3] How, in fact, talk about the World Council of Churches without using the language, the categories and expressions of one or other particular conception of the Church not necessarily acceptable to all the member churches?[4] How, finally, summarize a situation that was basically built on a paradox: an agreement on the sovereign importance of church unity by member churches holding conflicting views on the mode of ultimate unity,[5] an agreement that the divisions between existing churches (with which the World Council deals

[1] 'It is a conspicuous lack in American Christianity that the Church remains so vague a concept. There is no clear idea among us as to what the nature of the Church is, or as to the criteria by which its functions may be determined.' F. Ernest Johnson in *The Social Gospel Re-examined*, p. 121. Dr. Johnson was Director of the Department of Social Research of the Federal Council of the Churches of Christ in America.

[2] C. C. Morrison in *Christendom* II (Spring, 1947), 2, p. 283, as quoted by J. Robert Nelson, *The Realm of Redemption*, p. 191.

[3] 'The Orthodox Church claims to be *the* Church. . . . She is aware of the identity of her teaching with the Apostolic message and the tradition of the ancient Church. . . . She finds herself in an unbroken succession or tradition of faith. Her ministry also stands in right and unbroken succession of orders. She is aware of having been the same since the beginning. And for that reason she recognizes herself, in this distorted Christendom of ours, as being the only guardian of the primitive Faith and Order—in other words, as being the Church.' Father George Florovsky, 'The Doctrine of the Church and the Ecumenical Problem', *ER* II (Winter 1950), 2, p. 153. Professor Florovsky was a member of the Committee which composed the Statement, 'The Church, the Churches and the World Council of Churches' (cf. *infra*).

[4] Thus the Survey prepared for the Faith and Order Section of the Evanston Assembly speaks of 'the One Holy, Catholic and Apostolic Church . . . [as] actually fragmented into exclusive and mutually suspicious bodies called confessions, denominations or sects', a conception certainly unacceptable to the Orthodox, to advocates of the Branch Theory of the Church and even to believers in the adequacy of national churches. *The Christian Hope and the Task of the Churches* (hereafter referred to as *CHTC*), p. 3.

[5] A substantial part of the World Council's membership, holding that Christian unity already exists in a common loyalty to a common Lord, seek no organic unity.

provisionally) contradict the very nature of the Church, accompanied by divergent opinions on the nature of the Church?

There were some who thought that any attempt by the World Council at self-analysis was premature, any interpretation of its own theological implications was impossible. It was the need of explaining the possible coexistence of mutually opposed theologies of the Church in a common fellowship that made the effort imperative. A draft paper was prepared by the General Secretary who had devoted considerable thought to the question over the years; the draft was revised and reduced in length by a committee of theologians, whose version furnished the basis of a two-day debate by the Council's Central Committee, meeting at Toronto, Canada, July 9–15, 1950. The result was a seven-page statement, 'The Church, the Churches and the World Council of Churches', commended 'for study and comment in the churches'.[1] The phrase implies that the Statement is not an 'official document' of the World Council. It was used, however, as the foundation for the discussions on 'Our Oneness in Christ and our Disunity as Churches' in the Survey prepared for the Faith and Order Section of the Evanston Assembly; it represents the World Council's current understanding of its own nature, and its current formulation of the ecclesiological implications of its own existence. Though it is a somewhat technical document, composed by theologians for consideration by ecclesiastical leaders, the Statement must be employed in any exposition of the nature and authority of the World Council of Churches.

1. *Negative Disclaimers*

By way of clarification the Statement begins by a series of negations, making five assertions of what the Council is *not*. The assertions of the Statement will be set out in italics.

(1) *The World Council of Churches is not and must never become a super-Church.* To dispel a persistent misunderstanding the

---

[1] *Minutes and Reports of the Third Meeting of the Central Committee* (Toronto), pp. 84–90; and *ER* III (October 1950), 1, pp. 47–53. Also found in *The First Six Years, 1948–54*, pp. 113–19.

Statement repeats anew that every member church retains the constitutional right to ratify or reject utterances or actions of the Council, since the Council is incapable in principle of legislating or acting for its member churches. This clear assertion emphasizes the instrumental character of the Council, its aspect of being an agent of the collaborating churches. The point is underscored in the flat declaration that the Council 'is not the World Church. It is not the Una Sancta of which the creeds speak.'[1]

To dispel any lingering disquietude the Evanston Assembly, through the Report of its Faith and Order Section, repeated: 'The World Council of Churches is not a Super-Church.'

(2) *The purpose of the World Council of Churches is not to negotiate unions between Churches, which can only be done by the Churches themselves acting on their own initiative, but to bring the Churches into living contact with each other and to promote the study and discussion of the issues of Church unity.* Though 'the Council exists to break the deadlock between the Churches', no member church need fear that it will be pressed to take a decision against its own conviction or desire, promises the Statement.

A publication of a former Associate General Secretary of the World Council, Bishop Stephen C. Neill, reports thirteen achievements of complete organic union of denominations in the last fifteen years, two agreements for unconditional intercommunion and two for limited intercommunion, sixteen progressing negotiations with a view to organic union, seven

---

[1] To avoid just such misunderstanding a phrase in Amsterdam's Section III draft Report was changed to the plural (i.e. 'The Christian church*es* . . .') during a discussion at a plenary meeting. *Amsterdam*, p. 87. A certain ambiguity arises, however, from a view prominent in World Council circles and seemingly held by the General Secretary that God uses the World Council as the Una Sancta on occasions or that the Una Sancta becomes transitorily incarnate in certain ecumenical encounters. Thus: 'If then the World Council cannot pretend to represent the *Una Sancta*, it can and must affirm that in it and by it—when it pleases God—the *Una Sancta* is made manifest.' W. A. Visser 't Hooft, 'Le Conseil Oecuménique des Eglises' in *Hommage et Reconnaissance*, Recueil de travaux publiés à l'occasion du soixantième anniversaire de Karl Barth (Neuchâtel: Delachaux & Niestlé, 1946), p. 138. Cf. also *The Universal Church in God's Design* (New York: Harper & Bros., 1948), p. 185. In his Report to the Evanston Assembly the General Secretary reverted to the same theme, terming the World Council 'an instrument at the service of the churches to assist them in their common task to manifest the true nature of the Church'.

with the goal of some other kind of closer fellowship, and six which are temporarily suspended or are abandoned.[1] In none of these negotiations has the World Council been broker or lent its good offices. As a place of ecumenical encounter, however, it hopes to serve as an occasion at least of conversations looking towards the coalescence of the churches. Furthermore, by its mere existence as a fellowship of churches which have 'covenanted together to constitute this World Council of Churches', it represents the 'holy dissatisfaction' of the member churches with their existing disunity and a commitment to search for greater unity. 'Entrance into the World Council,' the General Secretary has written, 'presupposes willingness to manifest together with other churches that measure of unity which is now granted to the churches in the Council and to strive with them for the manifestation of the full unity of the Church of Christ.'[2] At the Evanston Assembly the General Secretary returned to the same point, declaring that the World Council should seek to 'create the conditions in which the churches come to know each other, enter into searching conversations with each other and learn from each other, so that the walls of partition become transparent and finally disappear altogether'. Not that the Council itself can or should promote unions between churches, Dr. Visser 't Hooft noted: 'But the Council can and must work to create a situation in which there is so much in common between the churches that there is no adequate reason for them to remain separate from each other.'

This assumption encountered opposition on the part of the Orthodox at Evanston. Their delegation entered a formal demurrer to the World Council's approach to the problem of church unity.

As chief of the delegation, Archbishop Michael of the Greek Orthodox Archdiocese of North and South America, one of the new Presidents of the Council, read a separate statement rejecting the Faith and Order Report and repeating that the Orthodox

---

[1] *Towards Church Union, 1937–1952.*
[2] *The Universal Church in God's Design*, p. 191.

Church alone offers the key to unity.[1] A retiring President of the Council, Pasteur Marc Boegner, found the Orthodox statement 'an unheard-of shock',[2] but two newly elected Presidents, Bishop Henry Knox Sherrill and Professor John Baillie, indicated that the declaration 'came as no surprise'. Professor John Baillie explained: 'We have long understood that we can only keep the Orthodox within the World Council if we allow them to express their dissent on this point. They want to stay in and we want to keep them in.'

(3) *The World Council cannot and should not be based on any one particular conception of the Church. It does not prejudge the ecclesiological problem.* It is significant that nowhere in the Statement, 'The Church, the Churches and the World Council of Churches', is the term 'the Church' defined.[3] Is it an abstraction or an entity, an idea (in the platonic sense) or a fact in the historical order with a continuity in time? Is it a common verbal cover for the sum total of Christians, a concrete society of restricted membership or a grouping awaiting future events (whether beyond human history or in time) before defining itself adequately? Such questions are for the individual member churches to settle. It is of the nature of the World Council that such divergences exist within its constituency. Indeed, the flip comment of an American news weekly that the Amsterdam Assembly could not define what it meant by 'the Church' was an absurd show of professional

---

[1] 'The whole approach [of the Faith and Order Report] to the problem of reunion is entirely unacceptable from the standpoint of the Orthodox Church. . . . From the Orthodox viewpoint, reunion of Christendom, with which the World Council of Churches is concerned, can be achieved solely on the basis of the total, dogmatic Faith of the early, undivided Church, without either subtraction or alteration. . . . The Episcopal Succession from the Apostles constitutes an historical reality in the life and structure of the Church and one of the presuppositions of her unity through the ages. The unity of the Church is preserved through the unity of the Episcopate. . . . In conclusion, we are bound to declare our profound conviction that the Holy Orthodox Church alone has preserved in full and intact "the faith once delivered unto the saints".' *Evanston*, pp. 93–5.

[2] *Le Figaro*, September 9, 1943, p. 1.

[3] For the first time apparently in World Council literature, the preparatory volume for the Faith and Order Section of the Evanston Assembly, 'Our Oneness in Christ and Our Disunity as Churches', explains in a footnote: 'Throughout this survey the word "Church" is used, not only in reference to the One, Holy, Catholic and Apostolic Church, but also to those numerous bodies which are associated to form the World Council of Churches.' No distinction of meaning was subsequently attempted in any given context.

incompetence. As even a casual journalist might have surmised, if there was common agreement on the meaning of the word there would be no need for the plural—'Churches'—in the title. Nor, in fact, would there be reason for the continued existence of the Council itself.

'There is room and space in the World Council,' the Toronto Statement explained, 'for the ecclesiology of every Church which is ready to participate in the ecumenical conversation and which takes its stand on the Basis of the Council, which is "a fellowship of churches which accept our Lord Jesus Christ as God and Saviour".' The Statement acknowledges that at times the utterances of the Council may seem to be couched in the language of some particular theological tradition but insists that there is not and cannot be an official ecclesiology. The assurance was probably intended to allay any uneasiness occasioned by the phrase 'the Church in the Churches' employed on occasion by the General Secretary, and to clarify any uncertainty arising from the description of the Council by the Chairman of the Provisional Committee as 'a method, thanks to which the Universal Church has at its disposal a means to manifest itself in a more permanent and effective manner than has been the case in the last four, yes, the last eight centuries'.[1] Such views, in the light of the Toronto Statement, are to be considered personal and no more representative nor authoritative than any other ecclesiology within the World Council membership.[2]

(4) *Membership in the World Council of Churches does not imply that a Church treats its own conception of the Church as merely*

---

[1] Archbishop William Temple, addressing the delegates of the Faith and Order Conference at Edinburgh in 1937 on the projected World Council. Leonard Hodgson (ed.), *The Second World Conference on Faith and Order*, p. 20.

[2] However, Professor Henry P. Van Dusen, President of Union Theological Seminary and Chairman of the World Council's Study Department Commission, commenting on the Toronto Statement, asserted that 'the document reflects the traditional Continental Reformed viewpoint, modified but not radically recast by the two other principal ecclesiastical outlooks in the Ecumenical Movement . . . it is all too patently oriented towards those of somewhat extreme "Catholic" conviction who look upon the World Council with misgiving if not positive distrust'. *ER* III (April 1951), 3, p. 253. Dr. Van Dusen felt that the statement did not take the ecclesiology of the Free Churches sufficiently into account.

relative. Under this point, the liberty of each ecclesiastical communion within the World Council to maintain its own views on the nature of the Church was repeated—including the freedom to deny the adequacy of other member churches, a controversial and obviously sensitive topic developed further in the Statement.[1]

(5) *Membership in the World Council does not imply the acceptance of a specific doctrine concerning the nature of Church unity.* Just as there is no official World Council position on the nature of the Church neither is there one on the nature of church unity, although in 'covenanting together' to form the Council the member churches have pledged themselves to strive to achieve a larger unity. Within its constituency are churches intransigent in their demand for an ultimate organic, dogmatic and sacramental unity, while others, as the Toronto Statement noted, 'hold that visible unity is unessential or even undesirable'. All views on unity are legitimate, provided that the churches concerned are prepared for sincere collaboration, using the World Council as a provisional instrument for a consideration of 'divisions between existing churches which ought not to be because they contradict the very nature of the Church'. 'The whole point of the ecumenical conversation,' the Statement declared, 'is precisely that all these conceptions enter into dynamic relations with each other.'

2. *Positive Convictions*

The Toronto Statement, 'The Church, the Churches and the World Council of Churches', continued by setting down eight

[1] This point would seem to have been implicitly challenged by the Swiss Protestant Church Federation in its approval of the Toronto Statement. The Faith and Order Commission's Survey, published in preparation for the Evanston Assembly, reports that the Swiss reply pointed out 'that the word "church" as applied to member constituents of the Council does not refer to either meaning of the word *ekklesia* in the New Testament, but to organizational entities of a particular tradition or confession'. *CHTC*, p. 15. The comment seems to repeat the misapprehension of Karl Barth that none of the churches at Amsterdam claimed to be *the* Church. Apart from the Orthodox, who have hardly been reticent in asserting an historical identity with the *ekklesia* of the New Testament, the conference of the Anglican bishops, meeting at Lambeth in 1948, declared that 'the Anglican Communion is not a sect. It is a part of the Church Catholic.' Accounts of the Churches' understanding of themselves will be found in *The Nature of the Church*, edited by R. Newton Flew.

'positive assumptions' which underlie the World Council of Churches and the ecclesiological implications of membership in it.

(1) *The member Churches of the Council believe that conversation, co-operation and common witness of the Churches must be based on the common recognition that Christ is the Divine Head of the Body.* In language echoing the Basis of the World Council, the first assumption argues that a common acceptance of 'our Lord Jesus Christ as God and Saviour ... compels all those who acknowledge Him to enter into real and close relationships with each other—even though they differ in many important points'.[1] The point was developed in the course of considering requests to clarify or amplify the Basis as enunciated in the Constitution. The analysis of the problem by a committee of three theologians, appointed by the Central Committee, resulted in a decision to leave the language of the Basis untouched, a recommendation approved by the Evanston Assembly. The Basis, argued the Committee, performs three functions:

(*a*) It indicates the nature of the fellowship which the churches in the Council seek to establish among themselves, 'a fellowship of a unique character. ... The churches enter into relation with

[1] In an account of the nature of the World Council of Churches, it is apposite to point out that the Explanatory Memorandum, written by Archbishop William Temple, which was sent along with the proposed Constitution and Letter of Invitation to the Churches in 1938, indicated that the Basis is to be taken as an affirmation of faith not as a creedal test and that the Council does not concern itself with the fashion in which these affirmations are interpreted in the different Churches (cf. *Documents of the World Council*, p. 16). Fifteen years later the General Secretary expressed a preference that the Basis—first formulated by the Young Men's Christian Association, meeting in Paris in 1855—should not be pressed to greater precision. Cf. *Minutes and Reports of the Fifth Meeting of the Central Committee* (Lucknow), p. 50. Interpretation of the affirmation of faith by the member churches leaves to the decision of the individual denomination questions such as whether 'acceptance of our Lord Jesus Christ' necessarily supposes baptism (it doesn't in the Salvation Army or the Society of Friends) or whether 'as God and Saviour' is to be taken literally (it is not by the Remonstrantse Broederschap—the Arminian Church—of Holland). Moreover, as Professor L. A. Zander pointed out in arguing against laying down a dogmatic criterion, since it is the churches which subscribe to the Basis, it is possible for a liberal theologian (one who does not believe in the divinity of Christ, for example) to participate in World Council activities if he happens to belong to a church that has no binding confession of faith, while another theologian, of more orthodox opinions, would be debarred if his church had formulated its doctrinal liberalism. *Op. cit.*, p. 5.

each other because there is a unity given once for all in the person and work of their common Lord and because the Living Lord gathers His people together.'

(b) It provides the orientation point for the work which the World Council undertakes, a point of reference for ecumenical conversations, an ultimate norm and standard for the activities of the Council.

(c) It indicates the range of fellowship which the churches in the Council seek to establish, the criterion which must be met by a church which desires to join the Council. In presenting the 'Draft Statement on the purposes and function of the Basis' to the Evanston Assembly, the Central Committee noted that the fundamental affirmation of Christian belief as incorporated into the Constitution 'is therefore less than a confession and more than a mere formula of agreement'. The question 'as to whether any particular church is in fact taking the Basis seriously', was, however, judged to be beyond the competence of the World Council.[1]

(2) *The member Churches of the World Council believe on the basis of the New Testament that the Church of Christ is one.* The second assumption is shared by all the member churches, although some attribute the oneness to the acceptance of a common doctrine and authority and to an historical continuity from an original church founded by Christ, while others find the oneness in 'a universal spiritual fellowship'. In the presence of the 'holy dissatisfaction with the present situation felt by men and women in many Churches' and in view of the divergence of opinion on whether the oneness of the Church of Christ already exists inchoately, is to be recovered, or is to be achieved in the future, the Toronto Statement concluded: 'The Churches realize that it is a matter of simple Christian duty for each Church to do its utmost for the manifestation of the Church in its oneness and to work and pray that Christ's purpose for His Church be fulfilled.'

(3) *The member Churches recognize that the membership of the Church of Christ is more inclusive than the membership of their own*

---

[1] Evanston *Assembly Work Book*, pp. 51–3; and *The First Six Years*, pp. 9–10.

Church body. They seek, therefore, to enter into living contact with those outside their own ranks who confess to the Lordship of Christ. The Churches are agreed that by virtue of baptism and faith all individual Christians pertain somehow to the Church of Christ; they are in disagreement on whether corporate groups of Christians, called 'churches', pertain to the Church of Christ as parts of a whole; they are agreed that, since membership in the Church of Christ is not restricted to the Christians[1] of a given ecclesiastical communion, the Churches should abandon their former isolation and seek fellowship in the Ecumenical Movement with all united in Christ; they are in disagreement on the consequences of their agreement.

Because all Christians are somehow one in Christ, are they all, therefore, perforce one in the Church of Christ? The possibility of a distinction is a matter of disagreement and the divergence of views on the point touch the fundamental problem of the nature of the World Council. The problem was faced at Toronto in discussions which, according to the General Secretary, supplied 'moments of anxiety when it seemed that the World Council had come to a real crisis in its history'.[2] For at issue was the question: 'Do we *want* the kind of World Council in which some of the member churches deny that other member churches are in a full and true sense churches?'[3] The answer was affirmative and, despite the cost to very human emotions in accepting a situation which allows the member churches to make such denials of one another, the crisis was surmounted. The discussion, concluded Dr. Visser 't Hooft, resulted in 'a deeper understanding both of the very real differences which exist between the member Churches of the Council in their conception of the Church and also of the not less real work of the Holy Spirit by which these Churches are brought into fellowship with each other'. It was better, in the judgment of the Russian Orthodox member of the

[1] But the World Council is by definition a fellowship of churches not of individual Christians.

[2] *ER* III (October 1950), 1, p. 77.

[3] The phrasing is that of the Rev. Oliver S. Tomkins, then Associate General Secretary of the World Council, in the *Christian Century* LXVII (August 9, 1950), 32, p. 944.

Central Committee, to have doctrinal controversy than vague agreement. The differences frankly faced were acknowledged in the next 'assumption' which declared:

(4) *The member Churches of the World Council consider the relationship of other Churches to the Holy Catholic Church which the Creeds profess as a subject for mutual consideration.*[1] *Nevertheless, membership does not imply that each Church must regard the other member Churches as Churches in the true and full sense of the word.* Is it possible to maintain a 'fellowship of churches' which accords to some the right to deem the deepest convictions of others presumptuous delusions? The issue—notwithstanding all good-will and fraternal feeling—was as stark as that. And it was—despite all aspirations towards the unity that is 'Christ's purpose for his Church'—inescapable. A member of the Central Committee is reported to have declared with profound emotion that, if the substance of this assumption were removed, 'he would have to say good-bye after thirty years of devoted service in the ecumenical cause; neither he nor his church would be any more wanted'.[2] A spokesman for another theological tradition subsequently raised the question whether 'Churches which do not and cannot recognize other member Churches as

---

[1] Is there a point beyond which there is no further ground for 'mutual consideration'? Dr. Leonard Hodgson, former Theological Secretary of the Faith and Order Commission, seemed to suggest as much in his lecture, 'The Task of the Third World Conference', at Lund in 1952, when he spoke of a 'chasm' in the divergent answers to the question 'whether we believe it to be God's will that the Church should be an earthly body with a continuing history in space and time. If any man thinks that the only continuity and unity required is that of the risen, ascended Lord, Jesus Christ, the same yesterday, today and for ever, that He embodies Himself as and when He will in this or that group of men and women as corporately they make the response of faith, so that the same group can at different times be and not be the Church according to the presence or absence of faith—if any man thinks this, I do not see how there can be any reconciliation of that belief with the conviction that there must be some kind of historical unity and continuity of the earthly body.' Oliver S. Tomkins (ed.), *The Third World Conference on Faith and Order, Lund, 1952*, p. 115. The dichotomy is expressed also in terms of authority in the Report of the American Theological Committee, presented by Professor Clarence T. Craig and published in *The Nature of the Church*, edited by R. Newton Flew, pp. 242-3. The crucial question is phrased in these words: 'Is it possible for a number of Christians (laymen) to organise themselves into a local church which will be an authentic part of the whole Church?' *Ibid.*, pp. 243-4.

[2] Related by O. S. Tomkins in the *Christian Century*, *op. cit.*, p. 945. Dr. Tomkins was present at the Toronto discussion.

really part of the Church, should have joined? Should they remain?'[1]

The Toronto discussion demonstrated that no ecclesiology, no matter how exclusive or exigent, is to be anathematized, that no Church willing to participate in the ecumenical dialogue is to be excluded from the Council. 'There is a place in the World Council,' said the Statement, 'both for those Churches which recognize other Churches as Churches in the full and true sense and for those which do not,' for, despite differences of faith and order, 'they recognize one another as serving the One Lord and they wish to explore their differences in mutual respect, trusting that they may be thus led by the Holy Spirit to manifest their unity in Christ.'

(5) *The member Churches of the World Council recognize in other Churches elements of the true Church. They consider that this mutual recognition obliges them to enter into a serious conversation with each other in the hope that these elements of truth will lead to the recognition of the full truth and to unity based on the full truth.* 'These elements,' noted the Statement, '. . . are a fact of real promise and provide an opportunity to strive by frank and brotherly intercourse for the realization of a fuller unity.'

(6) *The member Churches of the Council are willing to consult together in seeking to learn of the Lord Jesus what witness He would have them bear to the world in His name.* In default of discussion elsewhere in the Statement, it must be assumed (although the paragraph of explanation is ambiguous) that this point concerns the possibility of common pronouncements on the social consequences of the Christian religion by the member churches of the World Council.

The Constitution of the Council defines the fellowship in terms of its functions, the first of which are listed as:

  i. To carry on the work of the two world movements for Faith and Order and for Life and Work.
  ii. To facilitate common action by the Churches.

---

[1] C. T. Craig in *ER* III (April 1951), 3, p. 218.

This may well have been the aspect of the nature of the Council which the Archbishop of Canterbury, one of its six Presidents, had in mind when he assured a meeting of the British Council of Churches in Ireland nearly two years after the Toronto Statement:

> The World Council has no creed of its own. A Church, a denomination, a sect has some credal basis which expresses its fundamental belief. . . . But the World Council is not a Church at all and it explicitly disavows any pretensions to be one. . . . It is supposed that the Basis 'our Lord Jesus Christ as God and Saviour' sufficiently expresses this Least Common Multiple of Christian co-operation.[1]

'The World Council of Churches,' said the Call to the Amsterdam Assembly, 'is itself both a declaration of the spiritual unity of its member churches and a means through which they may express that unity in action.'[2] 'To promote this unity and to serve them (the churches) as an organ whereby they may bear witness together to their common faith and co-operate in matters requiring united action' was the formulation of this function issued by the Provisional Committee.[3]

Reservations on the part of the Orthodox

Certainly the Orthodox Churches have persistently viewed the Ecumenical Movement primarily as a collaborative effort in the area of social and moral action. Indeed the official title in Greek for the World Council of Churches is somewhat ambiguous. It is taken from the 'Message to all Churches of Christ everywhere', issued by the locum tenens of the Patriarchal Ecumenical throne and eleven Metropolitans in January 1920, calling for the creation of a League of Churches—*Koinonia ton Ekklesion* (in the context of the recently established League of Nations: *Koinonia ton Ethnon*)—for co-operative action on practical points of common policy by the Churches and against the moral evils threatening Christendom.[4] The point of view

---

[1] *EPS*, May 9, 1952.   [2] Buck Hill Falls *Minutes*, p. 85.   [3] *Ibid.*, p. 90.
[4] G. K. A. Bell (ed.), *Documents on Christian Unity* (First Series), pp. 44–8.

was made even clearer by the twenty-two Orthodox delegates at the Lausanne Conference on Faith and Order in 1927 when they abstained from voting on the final proposals, the Metropolitan Germanos, a future President of the World Council, explaining in their name that 'the mind of the Orthodox Church is that reunion can take place only on the basis of the common faith and confession of the ancient, undivided Church of the seven Ecumenical Councils and of the first eight centuries'. They subscribed to the position of the Patriarch's Message of 1920, in the light of which they concluded: 'We desire to declare that in our judgment the most which we can do now is to enter into co-operation with other Churches in the social and moral sphere on the basis of Christian love.'[1] As at Lausanne, Dr. Germanos, Metropolitan of Thyateira, author of the 1920 'Message', read at the 1937 Edinburgh Faith and Order Conference a declaration expressing the belief of the Orthodox delegates that the 'solid basis' of discussions on Church unity must be 'the dogmatic teaching of the ancient Church as it is found in the Holy Scriptures, the Creed, the decisions of the Ecumenical Synods and the whole life of the undivided Church'.[2]

The delegation appointed by the Provisional Committee of the World Council to visit the Churches of the Near East in the interest of the Amsterdam Assembly encountered (and seemingly accepted) an interpretation of the Council as an interdenominational agency for social action.[3] As a result of the resolutions adopted by the Conference of Representatives of the Autocephalous Orthodox Churches held at Moscow, July 8–18, 1948, only the Greek-speaking Churches, the Orthodox in the United States and the Russian Exarchate in Western Europe under the

---

[1] *Faith and Order*, Proceedings of the Lausanne Conference, pp. 384–5.

[2] Leonard Hodgson (ed.), *The Second World Conference on Faith and Order*, p. 156.

[3] The agreed statement issued at Constantinople, February 17, 1947, reads: 'The Delegation representing the World Council of Churches has been received at the Phanar by the Holy and Sacred Synod of the Ecumenical Patriarchate and has held conversations with the Patriarch and Synodical Committee of the World Churches Movement. As a result of the meetings, the Holy and Sacred Synod and the Ecumenical Throne reaffirm in principle their co-operation with the Movement which seeks to achieve Christian co-operation in all good works.' Buck Hill Falls *Minutes*, p. 109.

jurisdiction of the Ecumenical Patriarch were represented at Amsterdam.[1] Speaking on their behalf, Archbishop Germanos felt obliged to make a special cautionary statement to the Assembly promising further Orthodox reflections on World Council activities.[2] One such judgment was expressed by the Ecumenical Patriarchate of Constantinople of which Archbishop Germanos had been for many years Exarch in the West with headquarters in London. In an encyclical letter of January 31, 1952, addressed to the Patriarchs and Heads of the Autocephalous Orthodox Churches, his Beatitude Athenagoras of Constantinople interpreted the World Council as an ecclesiastical instrument for common action and a useful agency through which the religious truths of Orthodoxy can be imparted to 'the heterodox' and Western techniques of church organization learned.[3]

At the Evanston Assembly the Metropolitan Gennadios of Heliopolis explained the purpose and spirit of Orthodox participation in ecumenical gatherings: it is the frank proclamation of the Orthodox faith and the refusal to consider either the belief or the ecclesiastical constitution of the undivided Church over a thousand-year period a subject for review or discussion. The Orthodox groups participating in the Ecumenical Movement,

[1] Nicholas Zernov, 'The Eastern Churches and the Ecumenical Movement', in History, p. 667. In addition to these twenty official delegates there were twenty other Orthodox from the United States and from a section of the Russian Church in Exile present at Amsterdam as 'observers' or youth visitors or members of the staff.

[2] 'We welcome, nevertheless, this occasion to express the general feeling of the Orthodox delegation that, owing to conditions now prevailing in our churches, we have not had sufficient time for the preparation for this Conference and, therefore, we must base ourselves especially upon the consideration of our churches which in due time will express themselves about the World Council of Churches and its aspirations.' Amsterdam, p. 220.

[3] 'It is, therefore, quite clear that the principal aim of the [World] Council is a practical one and that its task is pleasing to God as an attempt and a manifestation of a noble desire that the churches of Christ should face together the great problems of humanity. Because this is the aim of the World Council and also because the Orthodox Church in her past participation in the pan-Christian movement has sought to make known and impart to the heterodox the riches of her faith, worship and order and her religious and ascetic experience, as well as to inform herself about their new methods and their conceptions of church life and activity (things of great value that the Orthodox Church could not possess and foster on account of the particular conditions in which she lived), we consider that in many ways the future participation and co-operation of the Orthodox Church with the World Council of Churches is necessary.' ER v (January 1953), 2, pp. 167–9.

then, have always made clear their understanding of a restrictive conception of the World Council's function; they would limit it, seemingly, to a collaboration of the churches for the practical purpose of improving social conditions.

Other elements in the ecumenical constituency felt that this function of bearing a common witness before the world should be kept paramount. After the Lund Conference of Faith and Order in August 1952, where the General Secretary of the World Council urged that the object of visible Church unity should have a central place in the deliberation of future Assemblies, the editorial voice of the Social Gospel emphasis in France found the whole trend in the Council a disturbing distraction from the proper concerns of the Ecumenical Movement: '*Le Christianisme Social*, troubled by the tragic developments in the world, had put more hope in the Life and Work Movement than in the Faith and Order Movement. Now that they are united, may theological imperialism never absorb and destroy interest in human problems.'[1] A devoted collaborator of the World Council, Professor Walter Horton, had expressed the hope—even after Amsterdam—that the Life and Work movement might be able to maintain a separate identity. He listed the principal reason in italics: '*to keep the liberal consensus from breaking up*', explaining that many extreme liberals (the Czechoslovak National Church, for example), active in Life and Work, do not subscribe to the theology of the World Council Basis.[2]

Does the bearing of a common witness before the world by the member churches suppose not merely a consensus of purpose, programme and objectives in the temporal order but a further and deeper spiritual unity, a visible, institutional oneness? Does co-operation for common action call for the spiritual solidarity of a single Church (however achieved)? Well before the World Council was constituted, an American ecumenical leader, Dr. Samuel McCrea Cavert, Chairman of the Committee on Arrangements for the Amsterdam Assembly, prophesied that priority

[1] Pierre Poujol in the issue of Oct.-Nov. (Nos. 10–11), 1952, p. 577.
[2] *Towards a Reborn Church*, p. 18.

would have to be accorded to the search for unity among the member churches if only in the interests of the effectiveness of the Council's work in the world.[1] In any case, the protestation of some of the pioneers of the Life and Work movement that 'doctrines divide, action unites', the premise of the Stockholm Conference that it was possible to concentrate on 'united practical action . . . leaving for the time our differences in Faith and Order', appeared abysmally innocent as the organized Ecumenical Movement acquired more experience and the 'holy dissatisfaction' with present divisions manifested itself more and more imperiously in the member churches.

This common witness before the world to a common Lord, the subject of consultation of the member churches, is described in the sixth 'assumption' of the Toronto Statement as 'God's gracious gift' enabling them to manifest 'something of the unity, the purpose of which is precisely "that the world may believe" and that they may "testify that the Father has sent the Son to be the Saviour of the World"'. Is it here being suggested that the World Council's analyses of social disorder and its programme of practical charity, its aid to refugees, for example, are a form of evangelism?

The question is occasioned by the ambiguity of the paragraph of explanation (written, to be sure, by theologians) and by the absence of discussion in World Council literature on the place of study of social questions or of co-operation with international

---

[1] 'Perhaps the crucial question has to do with the character and essential genius of the World Council itself during the earlier years of its organized life. Is it to be primarily concerned with the relations of the Churches to each other or is its major emphasis to be on the relations of the Church to the world at large? . . . But the painful question arises whether the Churches have attained sufficient unity among themselves to enable them to speak to the world in a way which will cause the world to listen. Until they can demonstrate in their relations with each other the power of the moral and spiritual standards which they recommend to the nations, can they expect the world to give heed? . . . The Churches cannot wait to speak until their own internal problems have been fully solved, yet they cannot speak convincingly until those problems have been solved. The World Council must therefore develop the two lines of responsibility at the same time. But for the sake of having a voice that will carry moral authority the primary emphasis must be laid to the Churches' achieving unity among themselves which will afford hope that through Christ the unity of mankind is possible.' Epilogue in William Adams Brown, *Towards a United Church*, p. 200–1.

organizations. Are social order and international peace goods worth working for by the Christian for their own sake? Has the Temporal City a certain autonomy that should be respected in all efforts to keep its foundations in a constant state of repair and its ramparts in a constant state of readiness? Or must all work for the common good, all public service which the Greeks called *leitourgia*, be undertaken primarily to lead co-workers to participate in the Liturgy of the Churches? The questions concern the Social Philosophy of the World Council and cover points seemingly not yet studied in the Council's constituency.

(7) *A further practical implication of common membership in the World Council is that the members should recognize their solidarity with each other, render assistance to each other in case of need, and refrain from such actions as are incompatible with brotherly relationships.* Frank affirmation of convictions, despite differences, and mutual aid, particularly in times of need and persecution, are suppositions of the solidarity expressed by membership in the Council, the Toronto Statement declared. However, 'actions incompatible with brotherly relationships towards other member Churches defeat the very purpose for which the Council has been created'. Presumably, proselytism is here meant and implicitly condemned.[1]

(8) *The member Churches enter into spiritual relationships through which they seek to learn from each other and to give help to each other in order that the Body of Christ may be built up and that the life of the Churches may be renewed.* 'The World Council of Churches,' noted the Report of the Amsterdam Assembly's Section I, 'has come into existence because we have already recognised a responsibility to one another's churches in our Lord Jesus Christ. . . . Before God, we are responsible for one another.'[2] The Toronto Statement points out that a mutual exchange of thought and experience is an obligation arising from the spiritual

---

[1] However, the Survey prepared for the Faith and Order Section of the Evanston Assembly noted: 'While many will agree that membership in the Council clearly means not to reject another member church by anathema or by the making of proselytes, the question remains an open one for others, subject to careful scrutiny in particular areas and with respect to particular circumstances of religious life.' *CHTC*, p. 46. The Evanston Assembly set up a continuing study of proselytizing.

[2] *Amsterdam*, p. 57.

relationship that is the result of the churches 'covenanting together' to constitute the World Council.

Apart from the responsibilities resulting from the spiritual relationships of the member churches in the World Council, what in their essence are these spiritual relationships? To ask the question is to seek anew to define, under a different guise, the nature of the World Council and to encounter afresh the inherent paradox of the ecumenical entity.[1] The World Council certainly sees itself as something of immensely more spiritual significance than an agency 'breathing the atmosphere not of undenominationalism but of interdenominationalism', as one commentator on the Toronto Statement described it.[2] It has been suggested that the empirical reality which emerged from the decision taken by the member churches at Amsterdam on August 23, 1948, bears some comparison to the Evangelische Kirche in Deutschland, founded at Eisenach earlier the same year. The efforts at self-analysis of these two expressions of ecumenicism, as well as the controversies thereby provoked, have sufficient parallel to justify a short excursus into the recent religious history of modern Germany.

When Hitler came to power there existed (in addition to the United Church in Old Prussia, an alliance of diverse Evangelical denominations) a federation of Lutheran and Reformed churches dating from 1922, an association which left the interior structure and creedal position of the two ecclesiastical communions untouched. Announcing its purpose of 'deconfessionalizing public life', the Nazi State in 1933 ordered the formation of a unified Evangelical Church. For religion, too, was to be centralized, organized, rationalized in accordance with the régime's policy

---

[1] 'The nature of the World Council of Churches cannot be stated simply without stating it wrongly. It can only be stated as a paradox. State the paradox wrongly and you are left with a contradiction.... The paradox may be stated thus: "The World Council is a fellowship of churches which, accepting our Lord Jesus Christ as God and Saviour, is united in believing that he wills, in some sense, a great unity for his church, but is divided in understanding the nature of that unity. This paradox becomes a contradiction if the differences in understanding the nature of the unity of the church go so deep that they destroy the grounds of fellowship."' Oliver S. Tomkins, *Christian Century*, *op. cit.*, p. 944.

[2] Professor William Robinson, *ER* III (April 1951), 3, p. 256.

of *Gleichschaltung*. Invoking the *Führerprinzip*, the Third Reich gave this unitary Evangelical Church a single superior in the person of a *Reichsbischof*. Resistance to this perversion of religion was expressed by groups from Lutheran, Reformed and United communions who formed the Confessional Church (*Bekenntniss-kirche*) which gathered in a synod at Barmen in 1934 and issued its celebrated Declaration as testimony of a common Protestant heritage. Defying the pretensions of totalitarianism, the Barmen Declaration proclaimed the imprescriptible rights of Christ and the freedom of the Church, a community not constituted by the *Diktat* of any human authority but created by the Holy Spirit and maintained by the preaching of the Gospel and the administration of the Sacraments, a community which is only 'the Church' to the degree in which it confesses and proclaims the Word of God. The influence of the dialectical theology of Karl Barth on the Declaration of Barmen was unmistakable.

The prophetic affirmation of faith of Barmen clarified the issue against the collaborating 'German Christians'. It also occasioned a re-examination of the theology of the Lutheran and Reformed traditions especially concerning the nature of the Church, the doctrine of the Lord's Supper and the authority of the ecclesiastical hierarchy. Prominent in the resistance of the Evangelical churches to Nazism were the Brotherhood Councils (*Bruderräte*) of the United Church of Prussia, groups principally of Calvinist orientation whose best-known spokesman was Pastor Martin Niemöller. The Brotherhood Councils considered the Barmen Declaration the Charter of a Church (though such an interpretation was excluded by the document itself) and held that the common convictions shared by all members of the different Evangelical traditions were more important than their doctrinal divergences. Emphasizing the fact rather than the content of belief, they found the core of Christianity in the act of faith where God reveals his presence to the believer, the Church being the place where the divine initiative in the form of preaching and sacraments manifests itself.

On the other hand, Lutheran opinion, particularly in the

Landeskirchen, emphasized the content rather than the act of faith and held that the Church can only exist where there is an acceptance of basic articles of belief, as expressed in the historic formularies of the Reformation era, and an authoritative teaching on the Lord's Supper. The tension between these two traditions produced a crisis in the Confessional Church and a schism at the Synod of Oeynhausen. The tensions continue within the Evangelical Church in Germany, constituted at Eisenach in 1948, and embracing three ecclesiastical communions differing in organization and cult, in their conceptions of the nature of the Church and on other points of theology involving baptism and marriage. Lutheran groups tend to consider the EKiD a simple *Bund*,[1] a federation of churches. A few days before the Eisenach meeting establishing the EKiD, they had formed the United Evangelical Lutheran Church in Germany (VELKD), an entity which, they deem, has the essential marks of the Church. Germans of Calvinist orientation, on the other hand, tend to identify the EKiD with the Church. The World Council at Amsterdam listed it as a Church.[2]

The value of the comparison with the EKiD lies in the existence of opinion that the World Council manifests dynamically some characteristics of essential 'Churchness'.[3] Although the Toronto Statement repeats the Amsterdam affirmation that the Council is not a super-Church, adding the explicit disavowal that it is not 'the Una Sancta of which the Creeds speak', the spiritual relations between the member churches which it represents are

---

[1] A footnote in *History* (p. 467) indicates the relevance of comparing the EKiD and the WCC: 'How, then, is the word *Bund* to be interpreted? Is it *union, federation, confederation* or *fellowship*? It is precisely on this point that different views are held in the Church itself; and any account of it which goes beyond citing, *in German*, its official documents is exposed to criticism from one side or another.'

[2] *Amsterdam* (p. 233) also records the Swiss Protestant Church Federation among the 'Churches represented at the Assembly'.

[3] Even before the member churches officially committed themselves at Amsterdam 'to stay together', the view that the Ecumenical Movement represented a spiritual reality organically related to the One Church was voiced, as in these words from a Report of the 1937 Oxford Conference of Life and Work: 'We speak as Christians; that is . . . as members of the many particular Churches—congregational, denominational, national, free, or established, or other forms of the Christian society, in which the life of the one Church finds varying expression.' *Oxford*, pp. 77–8.

felt to constitute some sort of spiritual entity, currently escaping satisfactory definition, but destined to develop, perhaps by the transformation, chrysalis-fashion, of its present organization, revealing a more unified Christian community. The Survey prepared for the Faith and Order Section of the Evanston Assembly closes its discussion on 'What May the Council Become?' with the judgment:

> Since the purpose of the Council is not to be a federation nor to become a World-Church by synthetically appropriating the diverse doctrines and polities of member churches, it must always look forward to its own decrease so that the manifestation of the oneness of the Church may increase.[1]

'For the Council,' the Toronto Statement noted, 'exists to break the deadlock between the Churches.' As the conversations between the churches develop and as the churches enter into closer contact with each other, they will no doubt have to face new decisions and problems.

3. Unity and Autonomy

The authors of the Toronto Statement were confident that: 'None of these positive assumptions, implied in the existence of the World Council, is in conflict with the teachings of the member Churches.' The eight responses received from the 160 member churches[2] indicate that the confidence of the Central Committee was justified. However, though it made no reference to the Toronto Statement, the 1952 encyclical letter of the Patriarch of Constantinople defining the purpose of the World Council as primarily practical[3] and counselling against participation in Faith and Order discussions, 'since this Commission of the

---

[1] *CHTC*, p. 48.   [2] *Ibid.*, pp. 15–16.

[3] The point of view of the Oriental Churches must be difficult for the World Council officials to comprehend on occasion. Thus the Consultation of the representatives of the Autocephalous Orthodox Churches, held at Moscow in July 1948, opposed participation in the World Council because it was concentrating on social problems to the neglect of the search for dogmatic unity. The resolution adopted declared: 'The direction of the efforts of the ecumenical movement into the channels of social and political life, and towards the creation of an "Ecumenical Church" as an influential international force,

Council seeks to promote the union of the Churches', must be considered an implicit reservation on the exposition of the ecclesiological significance of the World Council contained in the 1950 document. At the Lund Faith and Order Conference in August 1952 the Patriarch's representative in the West, Archbishop Athenagoras, Metropolitan of Thyateira, proffered the excuses of the Greek Church for its absence and explained the mode of participation of the Orthodox delegates in future meetings of the World Council.[1]

The confidence of the Central Committee that the Toronto Statement conflicted with the teaching of none of the member churches was largely founded on the reassurance of the autonomy of each ecclesiastical communion within the Council. Indeed the Amsterdam Assembly resolution on 'The Authority of the Council' was reprinted as the Introduction to the Toronto Statement, renewing the description of the World Council as 'an instrument' of the member churches, expressly prevented by its Constitution from usurping any of the functions which already belong to its constituent churches or from legislating for them or from controlling them in any fashion. Concerning decisions looking to a larger unity, 'the churches remain wholly

---

appears to us to be a falling into the temptation rejected by Christ in the wilderness. . . . During the last ten years (1937–48) the question of the reunion of the Churches on a basis of dogma and doctrine has no longer been discussed. This has been put back to a secondary and educational rôle, directed to the use of future generations. This being so, the contemporary ecumenical movement no longer attempts to secure the reunion of the Churches by spiritual ways and means.' *The Acts of the Consultation of the heads and representatives of the Autocephalous Orthodox Churches* (Moscow, 1949), II, pp. 435–6 as quoted by Zernov (*loc. cit.*) who adds: 'It was on the strength of these conclusions that the Moscow Consultation decided to refrain from participation in the ecumenical movement as at present constituted.' Present at the Moscow meeting were representatives of the Church of Greece and Archbishop Germanos, Exarch of the Patriarchate of Constantinople, destined to become a President of the World Council of Churches.

[1] Orthodox theologians will be allowed at future Conferences 'to make only positive and definite statements about our faith without being involved in sterile disputes or voting for resolutions . . . which cannot be settled in this way'. Delegates 'will be ready to give information on questions relative to the teaching of our Church but not to express their opinions or even the opinion of our Church on the teaching of your Churches. We do not come to criticise other Churches but to help them, to illumine their mind in a brotherly manner by informing them about the teaching of the One, Holy, Catholic and Apostolic Church which is the Greek Orthodox Church, unchanged since the apostolic era.' O. S. Tomkins (ed.), *The Third World Conference on Faith and Order*, pp. 125–6.

free', the Central Committee repeated in 1950, 'in the action which, on the basis of their convictions and in the light of their ecumenical contacts, they will or will not take'.

Whatever authority the World Council possesses as an organizational entity, therefore, resides in the Assembly of official delegates of the constituent churches and, between Assemblies, in the Central Committee elected by them, whose members in turn represent specific ecclesiastical groups. None of the World Council's executive departments is endowed with a super-confessional personality. 'Each individual represents a voice *in* the Council,' remarked the General Secretary, 'rather than the voice *of* the Council.'[1] Rule IX of the Constitution circumscribes the manner in which public statements may be issued by an organ of the Council and emphasizes the full freedom of the member churches to accept, ignore or reject the positions taken. To indicate that the Assembly, the centre of authority in the Council, is essentially an agency of the churches which have 'covenanted together', Reports presented are 'received' (not 'adopted') and, with the consent of the official delegates of the member communions, 'commended to the churches for their serious consideration and appropriate action'. The Resolution of the Central Committee in 1950 approving the armed inter-vention of the United Nations in Korea committed none of the churches nor all of them, it was carefully explained later. A Committee on Structure and Functioning, after an examination of the Secretariat, recommended that all documents should bear a clear indication of their degree of authority. Reports of conferences sponsored by the Ecumenical Institute at Bossey on contemporary social problems, for example, should indicate that the conclusions reached are not necessarily World Council judgments.[2]

At a later point in this study, attention will be devoted to the difficulty of obtaining an ecumenical consensus and the circum-stances conditioning the formulating of clear pronouncements

---

[1] W. A. Visser 't Hooft in *Hommage et Reconnaissance*, p. 20.
[2] Lucknow *Minutes*, p. 86.

on social and international issues. The problem derives largely from the ambiguous nature of the World Council which has been described as a chemical solution in suspension whose elements still escape adequate analysis. Seeing itself as more than a mere association of churches, this matrix of a continuing ecumenical dialogue, whose subject and purpose is church unity, disavows any independent jurisdiction over those engaged in the fraternal discussion or control over the trend of their talk. The resulting tension is intrinsic to a Council representing a search for unity by constituents maintaining full autonomy of decision. The Executive Committee adverted to this problem in a letter addressed to the member churches after the Central Committee had adopted the controversial Resolution on Korea:

> The chief task of the World Council of Churches is to maintain and develop the fellowship between the Christian Churches. But we recognize that the World Council has also the important task of giving concrete witness to the Lordship of Christ and to the implications of His Lordship for national and international life. We were all the time conscious of these two obligations which, things being as they are, often enter into conflict.[1]

In the frequently repeated phrase of Archbishop Temple any authority of the Council among its constituent members consists 'in the weight it carries with the Churches by its own wisdom'.[2] 'For,' concluded the Toronto Statement, 'the Council exists to serve the Churches as they prepare to meet their Lord who knows only one flock.'

It is the decisions of the participating ecclesiastical communions which will shape the future of the fellowship created at Amsterdam in 1948 and, in so doing, clarify the nature and authority of the World Council of Churches.

[1] *ER* III (April 1951), 3, p. 267.
[2] In the 'Explanatory Memorandum' which accompanied the Letter of Invitation to the Churches to join the Council. *Documents of the World Council of Churches*, p. 16.

III

THE SOCIAL PHILOSOPHY OF THE WORLD COUNCIL OF CHURCHES

i. INTRODUCTION

'THE World Council of Churches has come into being at a moment of peril for all mankind which is without precedent in the whole of human history.'[1] In public pronouncements, particularly at the Amsterdam Assembly, the Council has analysed the deep disorder characteristic of contemporary society and the world of nations; it has suggested a general strategy (and proclaimed a Christian mandate) for achieving a more equitable social order, one closer to the exigencies of the Christian vision of the world. What are the sources of the Council's social analyses, the bases of its judgments on human institutions, the criteria of its recommendations? What—in the most general sense of the term—is the social philosophy of the World Council of Churches?[2] Such an inquiry, suggesting at first sight a task of

[1] Henry P. Van Dusen in the General Introduction to the Amsterdam Assembly Series of volumes (New York: Harper & Bros., 1948).

[2] The inquiry is legitimate and has been of continuing interest to Life and Work and the World Council. As early as 1932 Life and Work's Research Section sponsored a conference on 'Church, Creed and Social Morality' and published in 1935 a symposium 'Une Enquête sur l'Ethique Sociale des Eglises'. A search for a social philosophy is certainly implied in the background questions suggested by Dr. Nils Ehrenström, sometime Director of the World Council's Study Department, to the collaborators of one of the Oxford Conference preparatory volumes: 'How far are the various spheres of the common life, like the family, economics, the state and the world order, to be regarded as manifestations of the will of God? Has God a purpose for the ordering of these spheres as well as for the action of Christians in these spheres? Is a distinctively Christian judgment on the structure of society possible, or does this apply only to the motives of persons acting within this structure? If God has a purpose for the ordering of the common life, what are the sources and grounds of the Christian's knowledge of that purpose, and in what respects does the Christian differ from the non-Christian in his understanding of this purpose? Has the Church as a corporate body a specific capacity for understanding and

90

synopsis if not synthesis, yields no simple summary. The search for a comprehensive and coherent answer to the question must take into account the history and nature of the World Council.

It must not be forgotten that it was only with the formation of the World Council at Amsterdam in 1948 that the member churches formally committed themselves to engage in the ecumenical dialogue. Previous conferences, such as those of Stockholm and Oxford, for example, had been the outcome of the enthusiasm of interested individuals, authorized to represent their churches but without responsibility beyond their personal loyalty to an ideal for the outcome of any continuing project. It is no reflection on the faithfulness of these pioneers to observe that, quite apart from national and denominational differences, geographical distances and the length of time between meetings made the pursuit of a common ground of social analysis difficult. In the twelve years between Stockholm and Oxford a certain ecumenical amnesia was inevitable. It is reported that not one of the thirty-five delegates lodged in one of Oxford's colleges for the 1937 Conference had ever heard of Archbishop Nathan Söderblom before his memory was invoked on the opening day. Yet Söderblom was the dominant figure at the previous Conference at Stockholm and the first President of the Continuation Committee which evolved into the Universal Christian Council for Life and Work. He had died just six years earlier. The Amsterdam Assembly paid reverence to the leaders of the Ecumenical Movement who had helped to draft the provisional

interpreting God's purpose for society? How far are human existence and behaviour conditioned by sub-personal factors, and how far are these factors controllable by human thought and will? Are the various spheres of human life in society subject to relatively independent and diverse laws of their own, and if so, what is the nature and what are the limits of that autonomy? May there be a difference in the will of God for a Christian concerning his action as a private person and his action in his official and public capacity? Can the Christian commandment of love be realized in all spheres of life? If not, what are the limits of such realization and what alternative principles are applicable and binding (e.g. justice and loyalty)?' Cf. Introduction to *Christian Faith and the Common Life*, pp. 10–11. The Provisional Committee of the World Council directed the Study Department in preparation for the Amsterdam Assembly and particularly for the work of Sections III and IV to undertake an inquiry on 'the Biblical Authority for the Church's Social and Political Message today', a continuing project that has included conferences on the foundations of International Law and the basis of human justice.

constitution of the World Council at Utrecht in 1938 and had not lived to see the completion of the enterprise they had envisaged. For the younger delegates the names were undoubtedly personalities of ecclesiastical history. Even today the World Council, as an instrument of the member churches for common tasks, is obviously dependent on the amount of interest a given project engenders among the confessional groups.

The Study Department, moreover, is not supposed to contrive a social philosophy for the World Council. Its exclusive function is to stimulate ecumenical thinking and provide an exchange of views. The fulfilment of that function is affected by differing interests in the member churches, by a dependence on the co-operation of collaborators, frequently fully-occupied professors, and currently by the ideological division of the world. As the Director of the Study Department reported at the Lucknow Meeting of the Central Committee: 'In spite of the best of intentions, in spite of all efforts to redress the imbalance, we must admit that it [the study programme] is still predominantly Western in outlook and execution.'[1]

A further factor complicating the elaboration of a common social philosophy, a common basis of social criticism, derives from the very nature of the World Council which is an association of distinct ecclesiastical entities each having its proper ethical inspiration and emphasis. The General Secretary high-lighted the problems occasioned by this fact when discussing the authority of the World Council to make public pronouncements on current issues.[2]

---

[1] Lucknow *Minutes*, p. 52.

[2] 'The particular churches speak on the basis of their confessions and (or) their confessional theologies. Their witness is an application of all that their members have heard and learned in their common effort to live by the revelation of God in Jesus Christ. Within these churches there may be considerable divergences and tensions but there are nevertheless common "traditions" which enable each of them to speak in one voice. Now the World Council has no such background. It has nothing but its basis, which is interpreted in different ways. It has no common spiritual language. The meaning of witness and confession is understood differently by different churches. And while they are all at one in recognizing the authority of Holy Scripture, there are deep divergences between them as to the actual significance of that authority for the life of the Church.' W. A. Visser 't Hooft, 'The Significance of the World Council of Churches', *The Universal Church in God's Design*, p. 189.

A study of the social philosophy of the World Council of Churches promises no facile answers.

ii. 'OUR DEEPEST DIFFERENCE'

The differences of approach among the World Council's member churches in the field of ethics are not unrelated to the differences in the field of theology which manifest themselves in ecumenical discussions on church union. There are, in fact, two main currents of thought concerning the conception and content of a social philosophy in the World Council constituency as there are two principal points of view in the understanding and methodology of the Ecumenical Community on questions of Faith and Order. The First Assembly recognized this latter fact and attributed to the two divergent positions 'our deepest difference'. It assigned to each a descriptive term which by reason of its ecclesiastical ambiguity is not very apposite in the present context.[1] The language of the Amsterdam Report can be employed, however, in acknowledging that in questions of social philosophy also, the two categories each represent 'a whole corporate tradition of the understanding of Christian faith and life'; and to indicate that in ethics as in ecclesiology the two conceptions 'are inconsistent with each other'.[2]

As captions for these two categories which include divergent points of view on the basis of human justice and the method of appraising social institutions, recourse will be had to a distinction introduced into ecumenical discourse at the time of the Oxford Conference. In a background volume for that 1937 gathering of the World Council's predecessor, the Universal Christian Council for Life and Work, the Organizing Secretary, Dr. Joseph H. Oldham, spoke of an 'ethic of ends' and an 'ethic of inspiration'.[3] It was the second of these approaches that Dr. Oldham favoured as essential if 'the Church [is] to take its part in the creation of a new world'.

---

[1] Cf. Appendix.   [2] *Amsterdam*, p. 52.
[3] W. A. Visser 't Hooft and J. H. Oldham, *The Church and its Function in Society*, pp. 234 ff.

As described by Dr. Oldham, 'the ethic of inspiration' insists that the fundamental and characteristic Christian moral attitude is not obedience to fixed norms or to a moral code but a living response to a living person, a fellowship with God who is sovereignly free and whose Will is sought for a present personal decision. Archbishop Temple once evidenced this outlook in declaring that revelation is not truth about God but the living God Himself. An 'ethic of ends', on the other hand, is based on an idea of the proper ordering of society and its parts whose overall purposes and particular functions are discoverable by a rational examination of their nature and operations. Such a system of ethics presents, if you will, a static conception in the sense that any analysis brings the actuality of a myriad of economic trans-actions and personal encounters to a halt in the mind and fixes their ideal relationships; for an 'ethic of ends' supposes a meaning-ful universe and, in the light of that general conception of teleology, assigns goals for economic and political institutions, appraises programmes, projects the direction of corrective legislation and commands personal action according to norms derived from a fixed hierarchy of values.

The conflict between these two approaches to social morality is another phase of the debate between the advocates of the Natural Law versus the Bible alone as the criterion of judgment on social problems. As in all debates, differences are magnified and purely debating points made by each side. Some of the language of the Amsterdam Report on Social Questions suggests a complete reliance on an 'ethic of inspiration'.[1] On the other hand, the delineation of the Responsible Society, adumbrated at Amsterdam and depicted in larger detail at Evanston, supposes an 'ethic of ends', a settled conception of the objective kind of social order meeting Christian requirements.

The Secretary of the Section on Social Questions at the Second Assembly reported 'a growing ecumenical consensus about the

[1] e.g. '... preaching of Christian truth in ways that illuminate the historical conditions. ... The Church ... inspires its members to ask in a new way what their Christian re-sponsibility is.' Declarations by the Church in 'the form of warnings against concrete forms of injustice' evoke the idea of 'prophetic utterances'. *Amsterdam*, pp. 81–2.

basis of Christian social concern' as embodied in the inquiry 'for want of a better word ... called the Responsible Society'. The value of the study project is said to lie in the fact that 'it suggests the positive social goals towards which Christians should work and it provides ethical criteria to help Christians in their efforts to reshape the existing social order'.[1] 'Positive social goals' presuppose a discoverable hierarchy of values; 'ethical criteria' are objective norms of moral judgment; both are essential elements of a social philosophy of the 'ethic of ends' category. However, the author, who is the Secretary of the World Council's Department on Church and Society, believes that the ethical approach based on 'positive social goals' and 'ethical criteria' is compatible with the ethical emphasis rejecting 'fixed norms' and relying on 'a living response to a Person'.

If such compatibility is possible and the continuance of the two ethical emphases is a permanent fact of ecumenical discourse, the author's conclusion is inescapable: 'There is not and probably will not be *full* agreement about the principles and standards which should be used by Christians to guide their thinking about social problems.' The observation would seem to warrant the verdict that the possession of a coherent social philosophy is beyond the expectation of the Ecumenical Community, a situation jeopardizing the justification of the present study and enfeebling the possibility of the elaboration by the World Council of Churches of any consistent social policy. On the other hand, the 'deepest difference', though theological in origin, is also immensely worth investigating as it shows itself in the approach to social ethics and the formulation of social policies. It must be repeated, however, that the essential differences between 'an ethic of inspiration' and 'an ethic of ends' are theological, for the divergences repose on conflicting conceptions of human nature, and therefore on varying judgments on man's spiritual possibilities, the mode of his apprehension of truth, natural and divine, his relationship to his Maker and to Jesus Christ, the bond of his union with his fellows, the value of human effort, the

[1] Paul Abrecht, 'Christian Action in Society', *ER* II (Winter 1950), 2, p. 143.

purpose of society, the origin and object of the State—in short, all the areas of human intercourse and community action that are the proper concern of a social philosophy.[1] The present work, as the Preface noted, is not a theological study. Nevertheless, it will be possible to examine the ethical attitudes present in the World Council constituency and their manifestations in the field of social policy without making an overt or, certainly, any extended excursus into the field of dogmatics. Some of the theological roots of the conflict between an 'ethic of ends' and an 'ethic of inspiration' will be indicated in an Appendix.

iii. The Sources of Social Criticism

The sources of the truth on which to base judgments of political trends and social institutions, the foundation of any commendatory or condemnatory verdicts, is a crucial question in the construction of a social philosophy. On this point the differences between the 'ethic of ends' emphasis and the 'ethic of inspiration' emphasis in the churches constituting the World Council assert themselves.

It is impossible to estimate how widespread, even among the heirs of pietism, is the confidence in a meta-rational, quasi-aesthetic capacity for sensing moral goodness, described in a volume prepared in connexion with the Oxford Life and Work Conference of 1937.[2] For practical purposes, however, the membership of the World Council divides on the key question of the Natural Law as an expression of the divine Will for human conduct, on the capacity of reason as an adequate mode of apprehending moral truth. The difference of opinion rests ultimately, to be sure, on conflicting theological appraisals of human nature. They are, therefore, radical; and they are important, for they concern

---

[1] This has been demonstrated in the case of Barth, Brunner and Niebuhr as leaders of the New Reformation Theology by Theodore Alexander Gill in a University of Zürich dissertation published as *Recent Protestant Political Theory*.

[2] 'How does, or should, the Christian reach a judgment upon any moral question? . . . He develops a moral sensitivity or tact which has at least something of the distinctively Christ-style or Christ-mind in it. . . . Somewhere in all moral decision the Christian has to come to rest in immediate intuition of this sort.' Professor Herbert Henry Farmer in *Christian Faith and the Common Life*, pp. 158–9.

the problem of the relation of the Christian faith to the social order which the World Council avers is part of its responsibility. The Christian religion, by definition, is concerned with the ultimate issues of human existence. Economic processes and political programmes are concerned, comparatively speaking, with proximate issues. What is the connexion between the two? To confuse them, to deny the importance of keeping ultimates and proximates separate, is to turn religion into sociology or, conversely, political science into biblical talmudism. How is the Christian to use the insights of his faith to guide him in making judgments on temporal affairs?

1. *The Natural Law*

The advocates of an 'ethic of ends' based on the Natural Law deduce their moral judgments from their conception of the nature of man-in-himself. Such an analysis provides, moreover, an understanding of the nature and purposes of society and its political agency, the State. The defenders of an 'ethic of inspiration' rely on their perception of the Word of God in the reverent reading of the Bible. Neither group seems to have successfully enlightened, much less convinced, the other in the matter of the bases of its ethical approach to social questions.

Admittedly the word 'natural' in the phrase 'the Natural Law' occasions confusions. It is frequently mistaken for 'normal', as when unpleasant conduct is explained as being 'only natural', a manifestation of the limitations and frailty of human nature as encountered every day in community life. Again, 'natural' becomes confused with 'normal' (meaning average) when supposedly proper norms of behaviour are predicated on statistical evidence of their usual non-observance. A further ambiguity derives from the common acceptation of 'law' as an enactment, a decree of some human authority which, being of human creation, is subject to modification. In the Ecumenical Community there are reservations regarding the Natural Law, quite apart from explicit theological objections, reservations resulting from the confusion of a principle with a code and from the false supposition that the Natural Law is a species of calcified legalism 'with fixed and specific content'.[1]

The Law of Nature is not a code nor an enactment made by man. Fundamentally it is a statement of the facts of human nature as such. And the essential statement of the facts of human nature as such is this: man is a psycho-physical being, an animal capable of rational thought, endowed with an eternal destiny by reason of his spiritual nature. Further consideration of human nature as such reveals that man is fashioned for association with his fellows,[2] in other words, to live in society whose general purposes are clear from the needs of man as such (and are furnished only by communal life) and whose attributes, including authority, are consequences of its purposes. The facts of human nature as such declare that man must act in accordance with his nature if he is to achieve his destiny, a necessity resulting from his dependence on his Creator. The Christian knows, moreover, that man cannot achieve his destiny without redemption nor, for that matter, conduct himself morally without the Grace of God.

The obligation imposed by the Natural Law manifests itself in the judgments of conscience which is nothing other than human reason operating in the field of behaviour and dictating actions to be done because they are in accord with human nature as such or to be shunned because opposed. Basically, the Natural Law is the objective order of things which the human intelligence can discern and to which it recognizes it must make personal actions and social structures conform. To employ a familiar example to indicate how an inspection of the nature of an entity reveals the law of its proper operations: a razor, once recognized as such, is not used to hack through an iron bar. It would be unnatural to use it so, just as it is unnatural to keep (or to try to keep) a cat in a pond, or, conversely, a fish in a cage. The nature of things is permanent. Twice two is four because of the nature

---

[1] For example by Reinhold Niebuhr in *CDS*, p. 19.

[2] In Aristotle's familiar phrase, Ἄνθρωπος φύσει πολιτικὸν ζῷον, 'Man is by nature a social being', one destined for community living. *Politics*, I, ii, 9.

of numbers. Because of the constancy of human nature as such, the Natural Law can be described as an objective statement of the essential human situation.

The Natural Law is also a term used to denote the universally admitted general principles of moral conduct such as 'oaths are to be kept'.[1] The fact that such principles are universally acknowledged does not constitute the Natural Law; it is, rather, an indication of a universal capacity of reason to judge some actions improper because at variance with human nature as such. Hence the phrase, 'an unnatural mother' ascribed to a parent seriously neglecting her children, or the condemnation as 'unnatural' of confessions extorted by torture or by psychological manipulation of the victim.

It is freely conceded that the human intelligence, while capable of arriving at the general moral truths flowing from an understanding of human nature as such, will be less certain and less accurate in deducing further conclusions deriving from these immediately evident general principles, hence the need of the intellectual virtue of prudence in making ethical analyses and the role of positive civil legislation to specify and apply the principles of the Natural Law. Moreover, every Christian believes that the limitations of imperfect human moral knowledge has been supplemented and perfected by God's special revelations, notably by the gospel of Jesus Christ, and that grace is necessary to observe the prescriptions of even the Natural Law in its entirety.

[1] Thus Richard Hooker, sixteenth-century Anglican divine: 'The general principles [of the Natural Law] are such as it is not easy to find men ignorant of them. Law rational, therefore, which men commonly use to call the Law of Nature, meaning thereby the Law which human nature knoweth itself in reason universally bound unto, which also for that cause may be termed most fitly the Law of Reason; this Law, I say, comprehendeth all those things which men by the light of their natural understanding evidently know, or at least may know, to be beseeming or unbeseeming, virtuous or vicious, good or evil for them to do.' *Ecclesiastical Polity*, I, viii, 9, as quoted by Alan Richardson and Wolfgang Schweitzer (eds.), *Biblical Authority for Today*, p. 116. Frequently quoted is Gladstone's reference to 'the higher ground of natural justice, that justice which binds man to man; which is older than Christianity, because it was in the world before Christianity; which is broader than Christianity, because it extends to the world beyond Christianity; and which underlies Christianity, for Christianity itself appeals to it'. Cited by C. E. Osborne, *Christian Ideas in Political History*, p. 68.

Such conceptions, it may be noted, were dominant when the Common Law of England was born; the consequences of the common conviction of a 'Law behind the law' influenced the political institutions of the English-speaking world; that heritage undoubtedly conditions in greater or lesser degree the viewpoint on social ethics of the membership of the World Council of Churches in the Anglo-Saxon world. As Pollock and Maitland observed in their classical *History of English Law*, the twelfth-century jurists at Westminster 'were penning writs that would run in the name of kingless commonwealths on the other side of the Atlantic Ocean'. That such commonwealths are kingless is wholly incidental to the spirit of the Common Law whose founders had spurned the prestige of the *Corpus Juris Civilis* of Roman Law with its voluntaristic principle, 'Quod Principi placuit legis habet vigorem',[1] to declare in the words of one of the first formulators of the new legal system, Henry of Bracton: 'The King is under God and the law, because the law makes the King. There is no King where Will and not Law is the principle of his rule.' For, as a later document of the same tradition, the American Declaration of Independence, declared, 'the Laws of Nature and of Nature's God' judge political régimes, men being endowed with certain inalienable rights by their Creator. Right reason is deemed to be both the instrument and the criterion for determining justice in society.

2. *Biblical Insights*

The whole viewpoint of the 'ethic of ends', or the Natural Law approach, supposes in men a capacity to apprehend the general pattern of correct personal moral existence and of a just social organization. The whole viewpoint of the 'ethic of inspiration', or the New Reformation Theology approach, rejects any continuity between man's sin-wrecked powers and the fulfilment of his ultimate responsibilities, between the puny constructions of human endeavour and the transcendent realm of the divine, between rational knowledge of present duty and

[1] 'The will of the Prince gives law its force.'

the proper ordering of society on the one hand and the truths conveyed through the Word of God on the other.[1]

The two viewpoints express the 'deepest differences' on the subject of social philosophy in the ecumenical community. Opening the war-time Conference on 'The Life of the Church and the Order of Society', Archbishop William Temple, Chairman of the World Council of Churches, found the differences of crucial importance and opted for the Natural Law as the single conceivable basis of social criticism.[2] Delivering the Stone Lectures of 1948 at Princeton University on 'Recent Trends in European Theology', Dr. W. A. Visser 't Hooft, General Secretary of the World Council, formally rejected the basis proposed by Archbishop Temple, preferring instead the 'ethic of inspiration' approach to social questions.[3] Dr. Visser 't Hooft is satisfied that the Bible alone furnishes not only an adequate ground for apprehending social obligations but supplies as well, at least in outline, the content of the principles necessary for human conduct, for appraising the proper functioning of society

[1] 'It is only by means of the contradiction between two ideas—God and man, grace and responsibility, holiness and love—that we can apprehend the contradictory truth that the eternal God enters time, or that the sinful man is declared just. Dialectical theology is the mode of thinking which defends this paradoxical character, belonging to faith-knowledge, from the non-paradoxical speculation of reason and vindicates it as against the other.' Emil Brunner, *The Theology of Crisis* (London and New York: Scribner's Sons, 1929), p. 7, as quoted in Gill, *op. cit.*, p. 58.

[2] 'We approach our task as Anglicans, that is, as heirs of the whole richness of Catholic tradition and also of the special insights of the Reformation. And here a great choice must be made: Do we or do we not follow the Reformers in their rejection of all Natural Theology? It comes as a surprise to most British theologians, when they are first introduced to continental controversies, to discover that this is the main point of division between Catholics and Protestants: not Eucharistic doctrine, not even Papal supremacy, but the possibility or impossibility of Natural Theology. For the Reformers pressed the doctrine of the Fall of Man to a point where the human reason is regarded as incapable of apprehending any divine truth. If we adopt that position, there is not much more to be said.' *Malvern, 1941*, pp. 12–13.

[3] 'It is often taken for granted that the only possible basis for Christian action in the realm of State and society is some form of natural theology. Thus Archbishop Temple said . . . that the decision against natural theology leads straight to the complete separation of the spheres of Church and State for in that case the Church is concerned wholly and solely with the work of grace and it has no right to approve or disapprove of the action of the State. But with all due respect to Archbishop Temple's insight we must say that this is a false alternative. It is possible to take one's stand on the Bible alone.' *The Kingship of Christ*, p. 140.

and judging the decisions of the State. The World Council's General Secretary concedes that to make the Bible an apt instrument of social criticism is a task still to be achieved.[1]

This rejection of the social philosophy of the Natural Law, or moral evaluations based on the conclusions of reason, is founded on radical theological grounds in an indictment that summarizes the objections shared by a majority, probably, of the constituency of the World Council. Acceptance of a rational norm of social ethics is a limitation of the sovereignty of Christ in Dr. Visser 't Hooft's view: 'for the enthronement of reason means the enthronement of man who becomes his own lawgiver'; Natural Law ethics is, moreover, 'the law of the old Adam, [it lacks] the eschatological perspective which is distinctive of Christian ethics, [it] tends to comfortable compromises instead of dynamic witness'.[2]

Such an ethical orientation is an evocation of Calvin's teaching on the Kingship of Christ—with reservations on its implications of a theocratic State—and rests uniquely on the revelation of God in Christ apprehended in a reverent and intelligent reading of the Bible. In such a situation the spirit of Christ—'which by nature is a continuous, dynamic event'[3]—is imparted to the believer enabling him to make practical decisions of obedience to the divine Will in the concrete circumstances of daily life. A German scholar, Werner Wiesner, writing in an ecumenical symposium, stated this ethical foundation as the person of Jesus Christ in an essay on 'The Law of Nature and Social Institutions'.[4] The result is an ethical attitude rather than a system, the confrontation

---

[1] 'In this respect the Bible is still very largely a closed book. We have only the vaguest ideas about its message concerning the abiding realities of social and political life. We operate with a few obvious texts or a few general principles but we know next to nothing about the Biblical witness with regard to such basic elements of our common life as property, justice, work, soil, money. . . . Just as we need a Biblical theology, so we need a Biblical social ethics.' *The Kingship of Christ*, p. 144.

[2] *Ibid.*, p. 141.

[3] H. Kraemer in *Contributions to a Christian Social Ethic*, p. 21.

[4] 'The bases of law are not any principles which can be separated from the holiness of God, but God's own holy Person. But this appears to us only where it has become flesh in Jesus Christ. So that the ultimate authority and criterion of law are not to be derived from some consciousness of rights implanted in reason but only from the revelation of God in the flesh.' *Christian Faith and the Common Life*, p. 129.

of the individual by the expectations of his Lord, personally experienced, rather than the availability of a pattern by which he may measure approximations to ideal justice. Dr. Hendrik Kraemer, then Director of the World Council's Ecumenical Institute, emphasized this result and indicated the ground of this ethical attitude in his Bossey Conferences on 'The Bible and Social Ethics' as nullifying all systems of ethics.[1]

This ethical attitude is capable of waiting patiently, confident of a divine directive.[2] It faces the reality of sin and regards civil rights as deriving from the action of Christ in history. It would see human pride lurking in the protestation that 'all men are created equal, that they are endowed by their Creator with certain unalienable Rights, that among these are Life, Liberty and the pursuit of Happiness'. That such truths are considered 'self-evident' would be judged an indication of man's incorrigible capacity for self-deception. Such an ethical attitude invites, to be sure, severe strictures from Anglican advocates of the Natural Law, as an abandonment of the gift of reason.[3] The reply would explain that the Bible is not considered an automatic vending machine proffering ready-made solutions to contemporary social problems, but that it offers the earnest inquirer a general

---

[1] 'Christian living on the individual plane and on the social plane in the light of the dealing and will of God whose ways and thoughts are always higher than ours, can never be stabilized in any historical or theoretical system, the splendid theocratic laws of the Old Testament included. There may be systems of philosophical ethics: there can never be a system of Christian ethics, at least if it is true to its nature. That would mean to forget and deny that God is an active God whose love, holiness and justice transcend all possible standards. All legalism and moralism stand condemned under the judgment of the ever-dynamic and ever-new dimension of God's activity.' *Ibid.*, p. 25.

[2] In his Annual Report for 1952 the World Council's General Secretary regretted that 'our fellowship is not at present giving clear and definite guidance to its members and to the world concerning the way out of the present impasse (i.e. the East-West conflict). This is of course due to the circumstance that our Churches live in different worlds and have very widely different views on the international situation. Many of these Churches are themselves divided on important questions of international affairs. We should not be ashamed if we fail to find common answers and solutions. We must wait until He gives us the word to speak.' Lucknow *Minutes*, p. 74.

[3] 'God's Word is addressed to our reason. It is not given to us to enable us to lay reason aside in attempting to solve our scientific, historical, social, political, economic and technological problems. Hence we are not to look in the Bible for economic laws, practical programmes and constitutions, social policies or even for solutions of our practical moral problems.' Alan Richardson in *Biblical Authority for Today*, p. 119.

orientation (which admittedly has not yet been sufficiently explored for guidance in social problems) rather than a blue-print of an ideal economic or political order.

By common agreement the most striking contemporary example of the employment of the Bible as the exclusive source of ethical standards and of the application of the doctrine of the Kingship of Christ as a criterion for judging social institutions is found in an essay of Karl Barth, 'The Christian Community and the Civil Community'.[1] The Swiss theologian constructs his conclusions by the argument from analogy: he infers the nature and functions of the State, for example, from the nature and mission of the Church, the terms of human justice from the divine movement of justification, the character of civil liberty from the spiritual freedom of redeemed individuals. It is an immensely interesting essay and would seem to represent a relaxation of Barth's rigorous insistence that the divine order is so trans-cendental as to have no human parallel.

The argument, of course, provides a methodology of social criticism available only to the Christian and offers no suggestions on how the non-believer or pagan is to make moral judgments— or whence, indeed, issue his civil rights. The role of the citizen who happens not to be a Christian has not captured the serious attention of the scholars who find the content of social ethics exclusively in the Bible. The Barthian position concedes, more-over, only a narrow and negative function to the State, one principally founded on its obligations to assure freedom of the gospel, a curious conclusion since in politics Barth is a Socialist. It occasions statements that seem to confuse realities commonly supposed to have different meanings. Thus, during a Central Committee discussion on religious persecution in Eastern Europe, Dr. Martin Niemöller remarked: 'We should seek religious liberty as it is observed elsewhere but let our brethren know that they already *have* religious liberty because Christ has set them free.'[2]

[1] In *Against the Stream*, pp. 13–50. Also published separately as *Christengemeinde und Bürgergemeinde* (Zollikon-Zürich: Evangelischer Verlag, 1946) and *Communauté Chrétienne et Communauté Civile* (Geneva: Editions Roulet, 1952).

[2] Chichester *Minutes*, p. 12. Emphasis in the original.

Nor does the ethical attitude inculcated by exclusive reliance on the Bible solve, for example, the problem that vexed Dr. Walter Simons, President of Germany's Supreme Court. At Stockholm he explained his plight: his Christian conscience was illumined by the biblical injunction of love for one's enemies but the State had posted him 'to sit in judgment on crimes committed by my brethren and to mete out punishment on them'.[1]

The differences of the two ethical approaches are indeed deep.

iv. THE SCOPE OF SOCIAL CRITICISM

It was objected at a plenary session of the First Assembly of the World Council of Churches that the paragraphs on the Responsible Society contained in the Report of the Section on Social Questions, while undoubtedly affirmations of unimpugnable wisdom, were disconcertingly indefinite both as to the mechanisms for the social control of economic activities implied and the concrete action, asserted as incumbent on the individual Christian, envisaged. The short and inconclusive discussion touched the problem of the scope of social criticism, the range and level of judgment the World Council should exercise in its comments on economic life and political trends, and the character of the guidance which it could reasonably be expected to furnish its constituency.

A veteran of the Ecumenical Movement, Pasteur Paul Conord, had earlier raised the question when forwarding his requested criticism on the draft chapter diagnosing contemporary social ills for the Amsterdam background volume. Given the dominance of technics in modern society, he asked, should the Church (a) decide if technological developments are good or bad in themselves,[2] (b) promulgate detailed regulations governing, for example, the hours and conditions of labour, trade-quotas and the limitation of certain industries, or (c) limit itself to affirming general principles leaving to interested parties the job of drawing

---

[1] *Stockholm*, pp. 290–1.

[2] 'If we decide that technics are bad in themselves,' remarked Pasteur Conord, 'then it's 'back to Gandhi'' for us.' *Archives*.

concrete conclusions? Pasteur Conord held that ecclesiastics had no competence to pronounce on precise problems requiring technical knowledge; he believed that the policy of affirming general principles which would tend to heighten the sense of personal responsibility to God and one's fellows might seem insufficient but it was, in his opinion, the only realistic approach.

But the policy of asserting general principles is not universally accepted in World Council circles, as was shown by the difference of opinion between Dr. Patijn and Professor Bennett when they came to discuss the chapter 'The Strategy of the Church' in the same volume. The Dutch Government official was well aware that 'the Church's task *vis-à-vis* the community in its social and political life is an indirect one'. He believed, however, that the Church's responsibility required that 'the full weight of prophetic judgment [be] thrown into the balance at the heart of the real difficulties and at the right moment, with the greatest possible knowledge of the facts'.[1] Dr. Patijn recognized the economic disorder of our society as 'a structural one' and believed that the Church should not default on its responsibility of giving guidance because of the technical issues involved 'since in the most important institutional problems of our day ethical issues are interwoven with the technical aspect'. Stands could be taken on burning, concrete, living problems, he was convinced, if there was collaboration and interaction in the institutional Church, the clergy contributing 'the light of revelation, the appeal to faith and spiritual courage, the laymen their expertness and open-mindedness to fact'.

This impatience with abstract solutions led Professor Bennett (whose teaching had been cited by Patijn) to object that less than justice had been accorded to the place of proximate norms or 'middle axioms' in the programme of the criticism of social questions by the churches. Middle axioms (the term came into use at the time of the Oxford Conference) are 'those goals for

---

[1] 'It is useless . . . to proclaim theories about the true natural order for economic or international life since no one in real difficulty will get help from mere abstractions. . . . The social problem is not capable of solution in abstract terms but is involved in the conditions of living of our present society.' *CDS*, pp. 161, 165.

society which are more specific than universal Christian principles and less specific than concrete institutions or programmes of action', Professor Bennett explained. As examples he cited two convictions: that the Church should seek to overcome involuntary racial segregation, and that it should seek the development of an organized world community to overcome the anarchy of inter-national life.[1] How these objectives would be achieved, what institutions would be the instruments of the desired change, would be left to technical experts as being beyond the mandate and, presumably, the competence of the churches.

The policy of middle axioms would not seem to satisfy Dr. Patijn's demand for practical ethical guidance. It is all very well, he would say,[2] to declare that families should have habitations compatible with human dignity, but does justice authorize, in the circumstances of the post-war world, governmental control of building materials to prevent the construction of luxury homes? What is the ethical answer to a proposal of State subsidy for low-rental housing for the economically disadvantaged? Since overcoming involuntary racial segregation is a moral objective, are not the *means* to be employed of ethical significance sufficient to claim the attention of the churches? Surely revolution to attain such a goal would be judged ethically reprehensible. Would sanctions against discrimination in employment practices, on the other hand, be judged ethically good? Are there, in fact, middle axioms indicating the ethical propriety of compulsion and the scope of the State? To set down an obligation of working for the development of an organized world community as a proximate norm of Christian judgment is plainly inadequate; such a declaration blandly ignores the actually existing United Nations and unhelpfully withholds an explicit answer to the practical question of the proper ethical attitude Christians should adopt towards that concrete organization. As a matter of fact, the Central Committee of the World Council of Churches was

---

[1] *Ibid.*, p. 159.

[2] Obviously I am continuing the debate based on a footnote explanation of Professor Bennett and am thus suggesting Dr. Patijn's rebuttal, interpreting his position as disclosed in the volume and in meetings of World Council commissions on Social Questions.

later, by its 1950 Resolution on Korea, to endorse not merely the United Nations as an institution but the use of arms under UN auspices to repress aggression.

But Dr. Patijn has another objection to the promulgation of general principles as the proper expression of the policy of the churches in judging social questions. It is an objection widely held in the Ecumenical Community and influences the World Council's attitude on economic and political institutions. Whence come these general principles to be proclaimed? he asked. From human wisdom, from the natural law, from theological constructions like the orders of creation and corporate groups, from a mélange of liberal philosophy and the unacknowledged intrusion of national aspirations and class interests? Under the guise of general principles the pretensions of human reason obscure the light of revealed truth, he objected, and biblical counsel, disassociated from its concrete significance expressed in concrete circumstances, is transformed into a dead language using the adages of worldly wisdom. The objection raises anew the question of an 'ethic of inspiration' or an 'ethic of ends'.

The quasi-tactical question of the proper level of the churches' judgments, then, leads back to the unsettled question of the sources of a social philosophy or even the possibility of one. 'To know what tasks the State has to perform, we have to know what justice is, the relation between the State and law, etc.,' remarked Professor Jacques Ellul during the discussions of Commission III in preparation for the First Assembly. Such knowledge was not to be achieved by a study of human nature and its exigencies, he was sure.[1] This assertion that the norms of justice, the roots of law, the goals of society and the function of the State are hidden from sin-darkened human reason and disclosed only to the grace-aided searcher of the scriptures had been preceded by a curt and somewhat cryptic remark of another

[1] 'I do not see how we can base ethics on the order of creation because creation has been perverted by the Fall, bringing total separation of man from God and condemning him to death. I think we can conceive of a Christian ethics based on a more or less stable law founded on the discernment of spirits in the light of the march of the world towards the Kingdom of God.' *Archives.*

participant in the discussion. 'The Church,' observed Dr. J. H. Oldham, 'should not pronounce on matters that belong to the sphere of rational judgment,' answering a request that his chapter on the effects of technics should include some practical suggestions on their social control.

Another point of view within the Ecumenical Community, one more common in Anglo-Saxon countries, was expressed by an American collaborator, for whom justice is 'written into the structure of the world' whose nature and purpose, seriously examined, indicates the existence of a moral order binding on all men. Professor Walter Horton, who spent a year at the World Council's Secretariat assisting in the study preparations for the Amsterdam Assembly, called attention to a pronouncement of several churches in the United States which based its proposals for peace and international order on the Natural Law approach.[1] Such a viewpoint assumes that institutional mechanisms to ameliorate contemporary social disorders can and should be constructed or modified (and certainly judged) in the light of the most reasoned understanding of the needs of the commonwealth, institutions which will be imperfect as all human things are imperfect, and undoubtedly tentative and experimental, given the complexity and gravity of the difficulties to be overcome.

These differences of opinion on the scope of social criticism, it must be remembered, are debated by participants in the ecumenical dialogue who are convinced of the social responsibility of the churches. Anyone conceiving of religion as an escape-hatch from temporal involvement into an after-world of untroubled salvation would scarcely be interested in the Ecumenical Movement; in any case, such a person, if he found himself at Amsterdam

---

[1] 'The Delaware (1942) Report on the Basis of a Just and Durable Peace begins with a reference to a moral law which is "fundamental and eternal". This order of law is a part of God's design which is not revoked or destroyed by the higher order of Grace. We are saved by Grace but not in defiance of law.' *Archives*. In the formulation of this description of a just international order, sponsored by the Federal Council of Churches, Mr. John Foster Dulles played a leading role as both a prominent Presbyterian layman and an eminent jurist. The political philosophy of the document is familiar in a nation which explained its Declaration of Independence as being a logical conclusion of 'the Laws of Nature and of Nature's God'.

in 1948 or at Evanston in 1954 as a delegate to the Assembly, would presumably not have elected the Section concerned with cultural, economic and political problems as the centre of his activity. The World Council, moreover, owes its existence in part to a reaction against the individualism and isolationism that characterized an earlier viewpoint of its member churches. The problem is admittedly one awaiting further thought and, perhaps, experimentation. The answers involve inevitable considerations of the social function of the churches and of the World Council of Churches. For, as the First Assembly asserted, one of the pressing needs of the times is 'to find ways of realizing personal responsibility for collective action in the large aggregations of power in modern society'. It is 'a task', the Report conceded, 'which has not yet been undertaken seriously'.[1]

v. The Roots of Law and Justice

The World Council of Churches is permanently mindful of the importance of a common, coherent basis for its social pronouncements. Stimulating an ecumenical dialogue that would engender a consensus on the fundamental criteria of social criticism has been a continuing responsibility of the Study Department. Since all the member churches are agreed that the Bible contains God's message to men, the Sacred Scriptures have served as the starting-point and centre of this study. Its results have been so far inconclusive.

1. *The Appeal to the Bible*

As early as 1945 an inquiry on the 'Biblical Authority for the Church's Social and Political Message Today' was gotten under way. Originally planned to result in a volume providing a common platform for the judgments on economic institutions and international affairs to be made by the Amsterdam Assembly, the project proved more knotty than the Provisional Committee

---

[1] *Amsterdam*, p. 75.

(which had ordered the symposium) suspected. The first conference of biblical scholars gathered in London in mid-August
1946, to examine the basic questions involved in the inquiry.
The conflict between the advocates of the Natural Law and the
defenders of 'The Bible alone' viewpoint was clear. The subsequent conference, convened at Bossey in early January 1947,
devoted itself to discovering some definite hermeneutical
principles by which to pass from the Bible's message to the social
and political questions of the day.

A new difference appeared at this second meeting when Karl
Barth and Anders Nygren encountered one another: the Swiss
and Swedish theologians personified the Reformed and Lutheran
traditions and served as spokesmen respectively for the doctrine
of the Lordship of Christ and that of the Two Realms. The
differences derived from something profoundly deeper than
confessional loyalties; the argument was by no means an academic
controversy over theological terms. The Barthian view proclaims
Christ's sovereignty over all the area of human activities; it
spurns all distinctions between ethics and dogmatics; it recognizes
a single standard for the moral evaluation of social institutions
as well as of individual behaviour—the Gospel; it knows only
one norm of moral truth—God's Word in Christ. Social and
political life also must be made to manifest, therefore, their
subjection to Christ's Lordship as the supreme and single rule of
goodness, albeit the Christian will be always mindful of the tran-
sitory nature of this world and of its incorrigible opposition
to its true Lord Whose power, now hidden, will be revealed in
glory at His triumphal return. For Nygren, too, as a Christian
theologian, this present world is under God's domination but
He rules it by His Law; Christ's Kingdom, the realm of the
Gospel, belongs to the Age that is to come. Social and political
life, according to this Lutheran view, is controlled by God's
creative and sustaining activity in the interval between the
First and the Final Advent of Christ. They are ruled by
the Creator's ordinances among which must be listed human
laws and the authority of the State; the secular realm is

not to be measured by the exalted demands of the Gospel; it has its day and, by God's permission and for His purposes, a relative autonomy until Christ's return brings in the New Age.[1]

Thus the Bossey Conference raised the question of the *situs* of the biblical basis of the Church's Social and Political Message Today. Was it to be found in the Gospel alone or partly in the Law and partly in the Gospel? Moreover the question, 'What is the Kingdom of God?' that had troubled Stockholm arose again, this time posed in rigorously theological terms. Does the Kingdom of Christ already exist? Can it be achieved in larger measure by social institutions submitting to the sovereignty of their Lord? Or is the Kingdom of God a condition to be disclosed in the New Age subsequent to Christ's return in glory? Confessional teachings are obviously reflected in differing interpretations of the Bible.[2] The dogmatic considerations that dominated the Bossey Conference ultimately concerned differing conceptions of the biblical teaching on the Last Things, on the relations of this world to the next, their continuity or opposition, the interpenetration of their common divine authority, the proper moral attitude of the Christian whose creed includes a belief in Christ's return. Your ethics, it was evident, did indeed depend on your

[1] This Lutheran ethic emphasized, especially in the 1930's, a doctrine of *Ordnungen*, particular forms of social organization conceived to possess a certain intrinsic moral authority, juxtaposed to that of the Bible, because God employs them for His creative and preserving activity in this present world. These 'social orders', having been given a limited autonomy, serve as subordinate sources of moral 'values', as normative indications of moral rectitude. They include the nation, the family, marriage, the State, the economic system, even the trade union. When the concept was extended to include the race, the indigenous culture of a *Volk*, its collective destiny, the peculiar genius of its legal system, it is evident how readily this philosophy lent itself to the manipulations of the National Socialist propagandists with the result that the religion of the 'German Christians' was fundamentally a worship of the sum-total of the racial characteristics of the *Volk*.

[2] A commentator on the Bossey Conference concluded: '(a) If we are dealing with the social and political message of the Bible, dogmatic considerations cannot be excluded; (b) every participant in ecumenical discussions and indeed every ordinary reader of the Bible brings with him certain presuppositions which have made possible for him an understanding of the Bible. . . . The conclusion is evident that we understand the Bible in different ways and that, therefore, to proceed to a common interpretation of the Bible is far from easy.' Wolfgang Schweitzer, 'The Bible and the Church's Message to the World', *ER* II (Winter 1950), 2, p. 128.

eschatology.[1] The editor of the Report on the two conferences noted that 'five different views were expressed concerning the basis of Christian ethics'; he acknowledged that meagre results were achieved.[2] No mention was made of the Bible study project during the Amsterdam debates.

A subsequent gathering of twenty theologians from ten denominations of eight nations, meeting at Wadham College, Oxford, June 28–July 6, 1949, resulted in a symposium that in title fulfilled the 1946 mandate.[3] The problem of discovering a coherent social philosophy or theology, based on the Bible, admittedly still remained.[4] The inquiry was continued at a conference on 'The Biblical Doctrine of Law and Justice' sponsored by the World Council Study Department and held at Treysa, Germany, in early August 1950.

The 'Common Convictions', subscribed to by this group of thirty scholars, accepted the Bible as the single source of moral truth and intransigently asserted the impossibility of separating even the concept of human justice from the process of Redemption whereby man's essential spiritual condition and communion with his Creator was determined:

> Our knowledge of the nature, the origin, the validity and the function of human justice arises from our faith in the Gospel of Jesus Christ. Therefore a right understanding of human justice is possible only where the righteousness of God revealed in Jesus Christ is accepted by man in faith.[5]

[1] As the World Council's General Secretary asserted, lecturing on 'Recent European Theology' at Princeton University: 'We can truthfully say to each other: "Tell me what your eschatology is and I will tell you what your attitude is in relation to Church, state and society." From the first beginnings of the modern Ecumenical Movement until our own day this is the underlying theme to which we are forced back again and again.' W. A. Visser 't Hooft, *The Kingship of Christ*, p. 83.

[2] *From the Bible to the Modern World*, p. 100. 'There was at the end of the Conference as at the beginning considerable divergence between the participants. The authority of the Bible was variously defined and the method of applying the Bible to social and political questions (directly, indirectly, etc.) was variously conceived. This is a problem which must be reckoned with in ecumenical discussions and messages.' *Ibid.*, p. 38.

[3] *Biblical Authority for Today*, edited by Alan Richardson and Wolfgang Schweitzer.

[4] For example, the conclusion: 'It is agreed that in applying the biblical message to our day, interpreters diverge because of differing doctrinal and ecclesiastical traditions, differing ethical, political and cultural outlooks, differing geographical and sociological situations, differing temperaments and gifts.' *Ibid.*, p. 243.

[5] *The Treysa Conference*, p. 47.

There were, in addition, two sets of 'differing convictions' framed, each conditioned by either the doctrine of the Two Realms or that of the Kingdom of Christ, thus continuing, in effect, the debate opened at Bossey by Anders Nygren and Karl Barth.[1]

The inquiry on the social relevance of the Bible and its use in appraising concrete issues of justice among men and nations is one that cannot indefinitely be filed away as incomplete. No mere subject for a common-room causerie among theologians and scripture scholars, it is immediately connected with the desire, frequently expressed at ecumenical gatherings, for a coherent, commonly accepted foundation—a philosophy, if you will—on which to base World Council pronouncements on economic and political questions. There are, to be sure, few in the World Council constituency who regard the Bible as a superior sort of Koran, listing the detailed prescriptions for a divinely ordered temporal theocracy or as a convenient manual supplying ready answers to complicated problems of equitable trade relations between nations. Such fundamentalism is associated rather with the small but determined groups—notably the International Council of Christian Churches—which attack the World Council for its alleged slighting of biblical truth.[2] The demand, however, voiced continually in ecumenical assemblies for a specifically Christian view of the State, of armed service in time of war, of the development of economically backward countries, still awaits clearer indication of the concrete source and scope of the Christian view of such temporal topics. A plenary meeting at Evanston, for example, was furnished with a justification of contemporary patterns of racial segregation in South Africa, not as applications of biblical insights but of biblical ordinances.

---

[1] Is it an indication of 'non-theological factors' in ecumenical discourse that in a conference held in Germany the majority opinion reflected a Lutheran emphasis?

[2] Thus, the Rev. Carl McIntyre, President of the International Council: 'We have a general thesis. This thesis is that the Bible teaches private enterprise and the capitalistic system, not as a by-product or as some side-line but as the very foundation structure of society itself in which men are to live and render an account of themselves to God.' *The Rise of the Tyrant*, p. xiii.

2. *Law between Nations*

A discussion on the nature of human justice and the foundations of law—in effect, a consideration of the norm of social morality—was occasioned by another Bossey Conference with a substantially different context: an examination of the basis of international order, strained to the breaking-point by East-West tension and seriously troubled by wholesale violations of human rights including religious persecution. The same differences of opinion on the source of moral knowledge and the criteria of moral appraisals are to be noted: (*a*) a consistently Christological ethic, measuring all things uniquely by the Person and Message of Jesus, (*b*) the biblical doctrine of the Orders of Creation within which human law has its place and by whose revealed content it must be judged, and (*c*) the Natural Law approach, wherein reason discovers in the structure of created things the rules of their proper functioning.

The Conference, which addressed itself to the general topic 'The Church and International Law', owed its convening to a proposal made by Bishop Eivind Berggrav, Primate of Norway's Lutheran Church, at the 1949 meeting of the World Council's Central Committee. The worsening of the prospects for peace, the plight of the veto-stalled United Nations, the violations of religious freedom especially in Eastern Europe, suggested to this resolute foe of the Nazi tyranny the necessity of a profound study of the significance of law in international affairs. The question had been raised earlier in ecumenical circles, notably by Baron van Asbeck, Professor of International Law at the University of Leyden, in an essay contributed to the background volume for the Amsterdam Assembly.[1] The Conference, composed of twenty experts, lawyers, men engaged in political affairs, and theologians, spent a week at Bossey in mid-April 1950, meeting under the joint sponsorship of the Commission of the Churches for International Affairs, the World Council's Study Department and the

---

[1] 'The Church must proclaim that the state is not an end in itself, nor does it establish its own law, but it is God's instrument for the establishment and maintenance of a legal order in this world, a legal order both for *national* and for *international* life.' *The Church and the International Disorder*, p. 69.

Ecumenical Institute. The Central Committee had directed a study of the following subjects: '(a) The present position as regards the investigation of the problem of Natural Law and its significance for international affairs today. (b) The Christian understanding of law and justice. (c) The relation in which the Christian view of law stands to the view based on the Natural Law and the connections existing between them.'[1]

The Committee, unhappily for our present purposes, chose to broaden the scope of its discussion. Its Report was edited under the following heads:

I. The responsibility of the Church in regard to international affairs.

II. Ways to the Christian understanding of international law:
  (a) Law and justice in general, including the question of Natural Law;
  (b) International law in general;
  (c) International law and State sovereignty;
  (d) International law and man's person.

III. The task of the Church:
  (a) Responsibility and guilt of the Church;
  (b) Permanent essentials;
  (c) Present duties.[2]

Despite the distinguished presence of Dr. Max Huber, former President of the Hague Court of International Justice, the Conference may have felt a lack of enthusiasm for any concentration on the Natural Law. Apart from an English disciple of Arnold Toynbee and a New Zealander who, judging from the official *Minutes*, was silent during the discussions, the participants were all from the Continent (about equally divided between the Lutheran and the Reformed traditions),[3] a provenance which could not be expected to acquaint them with the Common Law tradition of the British Commonwealth and the United States, a legal system of Natural Law origin.

---

[1] Chichester *Minutes*, p. 86.   [2] *Report* to the Central Committee. *Archives*, p. 2.
[3] One participant—Dr. E. J. Colombos—listed himself as a member of both the Orthodox Church and the Church of England.

The findings of the Conference on a wide range of topics in the field of international relations have no appositeness for our present inquiry. The summary treatment of the essential subject assigned for study by the Central Committee was suggested by the *rapporteur* as indicating the need of further study which might reconcile conflicting dogmatic positions.[1] The discussion of the Report by the Central Committee at its Toronto meeting was perfunctory, confused and certainly inconclusive. The Evanston Assembly's Section on International Affairs was confronted anew with the question when it considered the continuing problem of the 'common foundation of moral principles' whose absence was said to inhibit the growth of a genuine world community. Still unresolved in World Council discussions are questions regarding the roots of law governing relations between men and the norms of justice guiding their conduct.

vi. THE PATTERN OF CHRISTIAN SOCIETY

An environment in which a Christian can live out the implications of his religion fruitfully: such, in summary, is the social order envisaged by the World Council of Churches and under study in its continuing inquiry on 'The Responsible Society'.

This concept, which serves as 'a criterion by which we judge all existing social orders and at the same time a standard to guide us in the specific choices we have to make', was first formulated at the Amsterdam Assembly of the World Council in words incorporated verbatim into a Report of the Second Assembly:

> A responsible society is one where freedom is the freedom of men who acknowledge responsibility to justice and public order and where those who hold political authority or economic power are

---

[1] 'The diversity of views on the theological foundation of law, as it emerged in the discussion of this question, need not give rise to disquiet. Rather, we should note with gratitude that consciousness of the Church's responsibility in the field of law and theological reflection on the question of law, have everywhere taken on a new lease of life.... The diversity of views prevailing on important questions of the foundations of law means that we must go into the matter further....' H. H. Walz (ed.), 'The Church and International Law: Covering Memorandum to the Central Committee', May 30, 1950, unpublished. *Archives*, p. 6.

responsible for its exercise to God and to the people whose welfare is affected by it.[1]

The core of such a concept is the Christian notion of man.

The Amsterdam argument suggests the following summary: Man, as God's free creature, has an intrinsic dignity, forbidding him to be used as a means to any other purpose, political or economic, and an essential responsibility, reposing on his duties to God and his neighbour and involving the work of salvation. The kind of society, therefore, properly corresponding to the responsible nature of man must have a government subject to popular control, criticism and, if necessary, peaceful change; its economic institutions must be subject to the requirements of justice and yield equal opportunities; its centres of power must be subject to law and tradition and should be widely distributed through the entire community. Freedom of conscience and religious practice, freedom of personal participation in community decisions and freedom of access to truth and the propagation of individual opinions are necessary characteristics and conditions.

The idea of a Responsible Society, the Second Assembly stressed, should be realized in small groups as well as in large. The family was the primary instance of the first type mentioned and the disruption of family life was deplored.[2] The existence of other communities was indicated: the Christian congregation, people co-operating in the same work or the same factory, youth and, in some parts of the world, the village community or tribal groups. It was not clear whether membership in such groups

---

[1] *Amsterdam*, p. 77 and *Evanston*, p. 113. The author of the paragraph was Sir Walter Moberly, a distinguished English educator.

[2] The Index of the source-book prepared as background for the World Council's inquiry on the Responsible Society has no entry under the word 'family', indicating that the subject has not so far been of immediate concern in ecumenical encounters. It is difficult, therefore, to know the place accorded the family, its nature, origin and function in ecumenical thought. A passing reference from a Study Conference on the Church and the Problem of Social Order, held at Regensdorf in March 1933 under the auspices of the Universal Christian Council of Life and Work, states that 'the institutions of the family and the Church [are] directly ordained of God'. John W. Turnbull (ed.), *Ecumenical Documents on Church and Society*, p. 44.

was considered optional, the result of a personal decision (such as joining a sports club) or whether it was a consequence of an impulse implanted in human nature. The bonds of cohesion of such subordinate groupings, if they are other than self-interest, were not explained.

What was suggested, however, was the function or at least the value of such smaller forms of community as are found (to use examples from the Amsterdam Report) 'in local government, within industrial organizations, including trade unions, through the development of public corporations and through voluntary associations'. Such groupings serve as a counterbalance to the State in cultural, political and economic fields and in fostering the growth of the Responsible Society.[1]

It will be profitable to examine more closely some aspects of this concept of the Responsible Society.

1. *The State*

None but the most egregious romantic, however, could believe that the fundamental decisions dictated in the interests of economic stability in the post-war world could be made by any other than the political authority of the different nations. Merely to review some of the measures adopted to get production under way after the economic dislocations of the war or to facilitate the transition to a peace-time economy evokes the fact of the State and its crucial role in an industrial society where the principle of the division of labour imports the destruction of the economic self-sufficiency of family units. Currency stabilization, credit controls, export subsidies, agricultural marketing plans, Government loans, tax concessions, tariff adjustments were employed in greater or lesser degree in every country. Legislation and State subvention were required to expand educational opportunities, including training the unemployed in new skills. Governments were obliged to intervene and codify new patterns of industrial relations for the protection of the public interest.

[1] 'By such means it is possible to prevent an undue centralisation of power in modern technically organised communities and thus escape the perils of tyranny while avoiding the dangers of anarchy.' *Amsterdam*, p. 77.

The most striking instance of the possibility of voluntary action on a large scale in modern history was the success of private religious organizations, the World Council of Churches prominent among them, in finding homes and jobs across the seas for Europe's Displaced Persons but, here again, the very size of the refugee problem and the large sums required to collect, catalogue, care for and ultimately transport some of Europe's homeless called for action by interested Governments. Any serious consideration of economic and political institutions in the modern world involves a consideration of the nature and the function of the State.

On this subject unhappily there is a lack of consensus of opinion in the Ecumenical Community, the diversity of view being founded not merely on universal human differences of political preference, the conservative temperament eternally confronting the instinctive liberal (as illustrated in Anglo-Saxon politics), but resulting rather from conflicting theological conceptions of God's dealings with men.[1] Theological literature in England and the United States reveals small interest and scantier worry on the problem of the nature of the State. Despite disappointing evidences of the growth of reactionary social ideas in the American Protestant community as reported in the pre-Evanston Survey, religious groups in the United States (and in England) almost universally conceive of the State as a natural and necessary political instrument to protect and advance the temporal peace and prosperity of society. No hesitation is felt on theological grounds in conceding a positive function to the State; 'to promote the general welfare', in the words of the United States' Constitution. Continental theology, on the other hand,

---

[1] 'When we turn to Continental Protestantism and inquire into its conception of the State, at first sight such a question seems meaningless. The wealth and variety of the conceptions of the State within all the Churches and Christian bodies which bear the name "Protestant" is so varied and so confusing that it is impossible to give an adequate answer to this question. These conceptions ring all the changes that can possibly be imagined on the idea of the State; they range from the idealist's depreciation of the State or the anarchist's absolute denial, up to the most extreme form of the conservative deification of the State; yet each in turn justifies his point of view by appealing to the principles of Protestantism.' Nils Ehrenström, *Christian Faith and the Modern State*, p. 98. See also Adolf Keller's *Church and State on the European Continent*.

with its more pessimistic view of human nature generally conceives of the State in negative terms as a dike against anarchy, as an instrument to save man from the socially disruptive effects of his own selfishness, as the essentially coercive co-ordinator whereby a tolerable existence of sinful man in a sinful world is made possible. This negative view of the State has been heightened by the theological revival in recent times calling for a return to the insights of the Reformation; its influence in World Council circles has certainly echoed an Augustinian accent, recalling memories of the great African thinker's description of the State as a *magnum latrocinium*.[1]

In the judgment of the sometime Director of the World Council's Study Department, 'the theological argument which regards the State mainly as a protection against social chaos and the fear of anarchy has been a large factor in the tendency to interpret the ordering function of the State in terms of the social and economic *status quo*',[2] a verdict that could only be adequately appraised by a census of the political positions adopted by the partisans of such a theological emphasis. Karl Barth, for example, displays no uneasiness over the radical transformations of society in East Europe. Generally speaking, it is obvious that the theological outlook which condemns all human aspirations, activities and organizations as spiritually insignificant cannot be expected to concern itself very seriously with attempts to ameliorate by means of economic and political

---

[1] Thus, Emil Brunner: 'That the Christian affirms the necessity for the State is a correlate of his knowledge of Original Sin.' *Der Staat als Problem der Kirche*, p. 12. Again, 'The existence of the State is justified solely and entirely by the fact of sin; that is, the State is a means of counteracting the destructive influence of sin upon life and society, by means of coercion, in order that it may provide the basis for a life which is at least in some measure human.' *Die Kirche und das Staatsproblem*, p. 12. And Max Huber, distinguished jurist and layman: 'Every State represents human sin on the large scale; in history, in the growth of every State, the most brutal, anti-divine forces have taken a share to an extent unheard of in individual life save in that of some prominent criminals. In the State we human beings see our sin magnified a thousand times. The State is the product of collective sin.' *Staatenpolitik und Evangelium*, p. 11. Quoted in Ehrenström, *op. cit.*, p. 193. During the Sectional meeting at Evanston, the Secretary's Minutes reveal, a delegate from Canada insisted that the nature of the State must be discussed by the Drafting Committee. His own views were clear from his reference to the State as 'a monster'.

[2] Ehrenström, *op. cit.*, p. 219.

institutions the social disorder which it regards as inevitable and irremediable.

The World Council's Second Assembly repeated the conviction of previous ecumenical meetings that no one form of government has a universal claim on Christians; it reaffirmed the declaration that the State is not the source of social justice, but seemingly was newly prepared to accord the State a positive function when it declared that the government 'must be the guardian [of social justice], ready if necessary to accept responsibility to counteract depression or inflation and to relieve the impact of unemployment, industrial injury, low wages, and unfavourable working conditions, sickness, and old age'. Alongside the action of the State there was assigned to 'the non-governmental sectors in economic life ... employers and employees in all their varied organizations' the task of being 'the guardian of responsible private action in society'.[1]

The distinction of function suggests a growing consciousness in World Council circles that the State is not coextensive with society, an awareness hinted in a phrase of the memorandum prepared for the Evanston Section on Social Questions. Noting that 'there is no single criterion by which we can determine exactly how far the State should go in extending its functions in the economic sphere', the document observed in passing that the government is 'a trustee for the society as a whole'.[2] Has society as a whole responsibilities for the social order, particularly in the economic sphere, other than those within the jurisdiction of the State? The question has not yet been explicitly raised in discussions on the Responsible Society but is certainly implicit in the goals indicated for the Responsible Society.[3]

---

[1] *Evanston*, p. 116.   [2] *ER* VI (October 1953), I, p. 83.

[3] Professor William Banning asserted in a paper entitled 'The Changes in Society and State and the Church's Call for a Responsible Society', prepared by the Commission of Social Affairs of the Dutch Ecumenical Council and made available by the World Council's Study Department: 'Any campaign for a responsible society must include the proper recompense for work, social security, the combating of unemployment, satisfactory human relations within the individual business, the removal of mistrust in industrial enterprises, the call of responsibility in and for work and labour and an active cultural policy' (p. 7). Many of these objectives are beyond the competence of the State, some fall obviously within the jurisdiction of other 'forms of association'. How, for example, can the State 'remove mistrust in industrial relations' or assure the 'intelligent use of leisure

2. *Property*

An even greater imprecision than is found in World Council discussions on the nature and functions of the State occurs in the summary treatment of the place of property, both as a moral right and a social reality, in a more just social order. Advocates of socialization were reminded in a Report of the First Assembly that property is not the root cause of human evil, the defenders of the existing property system were warned that ownership is not an unconditioned right and the Church, it was explained, cannot resolve the debate between the two contestants. This almost Olympian attitude is particularly disappointing since it concerns a subject which the Oxford Conference of 1937, Amsterdam's predecessor as the ecumenical encounter considering social questions, had declared to be of practical importance.[1] Unhappily the question has not appeared on the agenda of subsequent World Council meetings nor do the Minutes of the Sections on Social Questions at Amsterdam or Evanston reveal any consideration of the topic, much less debate on it. The omission is more regrettable in the light of Oxford's admission that the question was not merely a fruitful subject for study by the Ecumenical Community but a topic that had been neglected.

Amsterdam's Section III addressed itself to the depersonalizing effects of a society dominated by technics. This type of society, it was indicated, is characterized by huge concentrations of economic and political power against which the individual is

time'? The questions reveal what a fruitful concept is that of the Responsible Society, how it provokes discussion (and, conceivably, stimulates personal initiative) in working out relative fields of responsibility in a Responsible Society. Where, to raise a topic not yet considered by the World Council, rests the primary responsibility in the area of culture and, to be more precise, in the matter of education? Would the Evanston Assembly endorse, as satisfying the role of the State in a Christianly-orientated society, the following judgment: 'It is the government's responsibility in a free society to create an environment in which individual enterprise can work constructively to serve the ends of economic progress'? The definition of jurisdiction is from President Eisenhower's 1954 Economic Message to Congress.

[1] 'This is a sphere in which Christian teaching on ends and principles in relation to economic life could have immediate results if it were translated into actual economic decisions.' The topic, Oxford indicated: 'should be given close attention by any agencies for further study which may be established in the future [i.e. by the World Council of Churches whose formation had been approved at Oxford]'. *Oxford*, p. 117.

almost defenceless and by the proletarianization of the industrial worker who may almost be defined as a tool-tender of someone else's machine. Oxford had hoped that later ecumenical thought would have some suggestions on how the reality of the principle of private property could be reformulated in a day of the anonymous corporation and the assembly line and translated into concrete economic and political institutions. Such institutions, as a curb on the reckless employment of power and as an instrument for the moral enfranchisement of the proletariat, might well be considered important elements in 'the Responsible Society'.[1]

The Oxford Conference had offered some interesting leads for such an inquiry. The institution of property was mentioned in connexion with one of the five middle axioms, ends or standards applicable to the testing of any economic situation, which declared: 'The resources of the earth, such as the soil and mineral wealth, should be recognized as gifts of God to the whole human race, and used with due and balanced consideration for the needs of the present and future generations.'[2] The institution of ownership was conceived to be a mechanism, resulting from social experience, designed to serve these needs. The social character of property was strongly emphasized, the right itself being described as 'relative and contingent'—relative, presumably, to the purposes which established and justify it, and contingent on the superior claims of the community. The existing system of ownership was found defective both because of 'the largely non-moral processes by which [it] has been developed' and

[1] Emil Brunner argues the thesis, 'Without private property there is no freedom', in his *Justice and the Social Order*, pp. 54 ff. 80 ff. Reinhold Niebuhr has pointed out: 'The obvious facts about property which both liberal and Marxist theories have obscured are: that all property is power; that some forms of economic power are intrinsically more ordinate than others and therefore more defensible, but that no sharp line can be drawn between what is ordinate and what is inordinate; that property is not the only form of economic power, and that the destruction of private property does not therefore guarantee the equalization of economic power in a community; that inordinate power tempts its holders to abuse it, which means to use it for their own ends; that the economic, as well as the political, process requires the best possible distribution of power for the sake of justice, and the best possible management of this equilibrium for the sake of order.' *The Children of Light and the Children of Darkness*, p. 83.

[2] *Oxford, ibid.*

because of the unsatisfactory distribution of actual property. Coming to the key question of contemporary society, the Oxford Conference underlined the crucial importance of distinguishing various forms of property. The problem is a complicated one. There are, for example, decisive differences in the personal relationships of the small farmer to his freehold, the independent retailer to his shop and the shareholder to the modern corporation. The deed to the family farm, the receipted bill of sale for the shop's fixtures and goods, and the shares possessed by one of the 1,100,000 stockholders of the American Telephone and Telegraph Company each represent a certificate of ownership. The reality of possession, the power of control which the three types of papers (recognized in civil law as forms of ownership) denote are, however, enormously different and the social consequences of crucial importance, as the Oxford Conference pointed out.[1]

Subsequent ecumenical thinking has shown small interest in pursuing the problem, has not subjected the existing régime of ownership to further moral scrutiny nor seriously considered possible adaptions of present institutions of property better calculated to control concentrations of economic power. Institutional methods of distributing property by, say, policies of progressive taxation or profit sharing, have not been among the World Council's social inquiries, possibly because of the limitations of the Study Department's resources, possibly because they have been judged too specific or technical in content[2] but possibly, too, because of a difference of opinion in the Ecumenical Community on the importance and even the possibility of widely dispersed ownership.

[1] 'All property which represents social power stands in special need of moral scrutiny, since power to determine the lives of others is the crucial point in any scheme of justice. . . . Industrial property in particular encourages the concentration of power; for it gives the owner control over both the place and the instruments of labour and thus leaves the worker powerless, so far as property relations are concerned, allowing him only the organized strength of his union and his political franchise to set against the power of ownership.' *Ibid.* pp. 118–19.

[2] Yet the question of Technical Assistance to Underdeveloped Countries is a current object of study by the World Council.

3. *Further Implications and Problems*

As the World Council's study on the Responsible Society has progressed, it has been characterized by an increasing attention to the stubborn facts of the economic process and a growing respect for personal initiative as essential for the health of society. The importance of productivity and efficiency in industry as well as the necessity of a just distribution of the fruits of the machine have been recognized.[1] Rejecting the 'no enemies to the left' outlook of some Socialists, emphasis has been put on economic flexibility, on the significance of the private sector of the economy, on adaptable and decentralized action by the State, even on the place of the enterprising, energetic, expert business man. If indications of the specific economic and political institutions of the desired social order have not emerged, the inquiry has introduced into the ecumenical dialogue some fresh elements, while posing several questions still to be answered.

The whole direction of the social order envisaged is towards decentralization. It is more than arguable[2] that society today is not disorganized but overorganized unto the destruction of community. By 'community' is meant here that state of social life in which the meaning and purpose of existence are intimately interwoven into the institutions by which the essential functions of life are fulfilled. When farming or working or loving or serving are recognized as related to the ultimate meaning and purpose of existence, then all the routine activities of life are enriched and men generally have what Le Play called 'social peace', the satisfaction of community. This relationship can best be achieved, without any doubt, in smaller groups, but only so long as the small group fulfils the essential function of its existence. Once the small group's purpose has been removed, it fails to be significant and any attempt to relate the meaning of personal

---

[1] The importance of productivity is seen in the following fact: 20,000 workers at the factory in Wolfsburg, Germany, produce 750 Volkswagen automobiles each day; 51,000 are employed at the Renault works at Billancourt, France, to produce the same number of vehicles. *Le Figaro*, December 11, 1953.

[2] For example by Robert A. Nisbet in *The Quest for Community*, whose argument is sketched above.

living to it becomes a sterile sentimentalism. In stressing the importance of curbs on State action and in suggesting that centres of economic and political decision be returned to subordinate groups, the World Council seeks to build healthy social tissues. The writings of Mumford and Röpke indicate that modern technology can be directed to the functional independence of small groups as easily as it has been directed towards their repression.

The emphasis on the principle of subsidiarity in the Responsible Society inquiry is endlessly suggestive and includes on the political level all the principles of federalism. 'Moreover, the renewing of personal life through the corporate life of small groups', as the Evanston Assembly recommended, the finding of personal fulfilment through fellowship, implies inevitably a recognition of differing functions in society and, in consequence, a certain hierarchy, not of dignity, but of authority, an idea which challenges the social egalitarianism widespread enough in World Council circles, a carry-over doubtless from the exuberance of the days of Christian Socialism.

One element in all thinking on the social order, however, seems to have escaped the attention of the World Council constituency, that of motivation. Glancing references, too scanty to be judged a fixed point of view, give the impression sometimes that efforts to build the Temporal City are no more than forms of evangelism by way of attracting passers-by into the temple of the true God. Christianity, it is repeated, must supply the spiritual dynamic for social living, but how this is to be done is never indicated beyond (one can suppose) the force of example of an honest life. Christianity, one reads regularly in World Council pronouncements, cannot be identified with any economic system or political order. Yet, on the other hand, the members of the Ecumenical Community are constantly exhorted to make their faith count in the contemporary world.

Would the position taken by another inter-confessional body, the Federal Council of the Churches of Christ in the United States, be thought too controversial or simplicist by the World Council? That American religious organization in its *Social Creed of the*

Churches of 1932 declared that Christianity brings to the social order, not a set of particular ideas, but the motivation engendered by the ideals and goals of faith.[1] Such an attitude, of course, concedes a limited and subordinate autonomy to the temporal order and means abandoning the one-dimensioned vision of the unique City submitting itself to its heavenly King.

The social order which the World Council envisages is manifestly still to be elaborated. Under the caption, 'The Responsible Society', however, it has projected the general criteria for the economic and political institutions which the Christian must labour to construct in a world in which he is, to be sure, only a pilgrim but in whose activities he is inescapably involved.

vii. THE CONTRIBUTION OF THE ORTHODOX CHURCHES

In a study of the social philosophy of the World Council of Churches, should the Orthodox Churches be listed as proponents of an 'ethic of ends' or of an 'ethic of inspiration'?[2] Despite the different theological foundations of the two competing ethical attitudes and the constant emphasis of Orthodox participants on the primacy of dogmatics in ecumenical discourse, the question has small appositeness. The reason is simple and derives more from historical experience than theological premises: the Orthodox Churches have not seriously nor systematically concerned themselves with social or political questions as problems for the Christian mind as well as tasks for Christian charity.

Despite Orthodox insistence in regarding the World Council exclusively as an instrument for the collaboration of the churches in practical and social questions, despite an occasional complaint that Orthodoxy is not adequately represented on World Council

[1] 'The teachings of Christ which bear on economics are not expressed in technical terms but deal primarily with motives and human values for social intercourse.' Quoted by Charles S. Macfarland, *Christian Unity in Practice and Prophecy*, p. 295.

[2] The view of Professor P. Bratsiotis, in the World Council symposium on 'The Biblical Authority for the Church's Social and Political Message Today', that Orthodoxy recognizes the Natural Law, believes that the Bible, expounded and supplemented by Apostolic tradition, yields new and profounder insights and that faith in Christ ought to inspire and govern the attitude of the Church in social and political matters, would certainly place the Orthodox Churches in the 'ethic of ends' category of approach to social questions. Cf. *Biblical Authority for Today*, pp. 27 ff.

committees and in its administration,[1] Orthodox groups who do participate in World Council activities seem to have no specific contribution to make to the effort to analyse and resolve the 'peril for all mankind which is without precedent in the whole of human history'—to employ the language of the Amsterdam Message. During that Assembly the Metropolitan Chrysostom of Philippi and Neapolis gave an address on 'The Christian Witness in Social and National Life' at a public meeting on August 30. Invoking the benefits Christianity had bestowed on Western civilization, His Beatitude confined himself to a plea for personal spiritual reformation.[2] What these spiritually renewed individuals are to do about international and domestic problems, His Beatitude did not indicate; in what direction their principles would lead them in economic amelioration and political decisions, he did not hint. Exclusively spiritual cures for institutional disorder would seem as inadequate a solution as superficial social palliatives. Possibly the Orthodox speaker was addressing himself more to the obligation of evangelizing the world (the scope of Section II at Amsterdam) than diagnosing the ills of contemporary society and suggesting helpful lines of social stability (the field of Section III). If so, he was not the only commentator whose apostolic zeal or pastoral responsibility led him to confuse the *status quaestionis*.

There is no intention here of deprecating the social consequences of Orthodoxy's constant inculcation of the spirit of charity. The autocephalous churches have, moreover, maintained national traditions under alien occupation, served as the cohesive force of ancient aspirations and, notably in the cases of Greece and

---

[1] e.g. I. Karmiris, 'The Orthodox Catholic Church and her Relations with Other Churches and with the World Council of Churches.' WCC Study Department Document 49E/607A, p. 26. There was no Orthodox representative on the Study Commissions for Amsterdam's Sections III and IV, none on the Preparatory Commission for Evanston's Section on 'The Responsible Society', one only, Dr. Charles Malik, for the Section on International Affairs; and his was, in effect, a purely honorary nomination.

[2] 'The reformation of society must therefore begin by the renewal of individuals and especially by the renewal of those who are responsible for preaching the message of salvation to men and accomplishing God's design on earth. I hope, therefore, with all my heart that the Ecumenical Movement may receive the seal of God's blessing and may bear many spiritual fruits in society.' Text (mimeographed) in *Archives*.

Bulgaria, stimulated the movement for national liberation. These achievements are celebrated by the Bishop of Novi-Sad, Yugoslavia, in his essay, 'The Social Ethics of Orthodox Christianity'. Significantly, however, the Bishop introduces his study with the admission: 'So far as I know, there is no system of social ethics in the Orthodox Church: at least there is none which has exercised any influence for centuries.'[1]

The situation is the result of the primarily speculative character of Eastern theology, of the other-worldly temper of Orthodox spirituality; it is the product, too, of the peculiar historical experience of the Eastern Churches. The theological interest of the Oriental Church has traditionally centred on the mysteries of the inner life of the divinity rather than the problems of the order of creation, particularly the ambiguities of the human predicament. Orthodox spirituality, stemming largely from the monasteries, has counselled a fellowship of poverty and love and a flight from sin—this last involving, at least by implication, a turning away from the self-condemned 'world' of cities with their superficial pleasures, the State with its pomp and military power, and the civil life of trade with its conniving and heartlessness, the arena of bad people absorbed in the things of time. Mundane affairs are apparently judged to be outside the warming ambit of holiness whose cultivation demands a withdrawal, preferably in the form of flight from the contamination of earthly interests, and apparently presupposes, in consequence, an abandonment of any effort to establish justice among sinful men. History has exploited as well as nurtured this preference for passivity in Orthodox spirituality. The Christian Ruler with the divine mandate to protect the Church becomes the Tsar, the symbol of sanctified power, with jurisdiction over ecclesiastical affairs.

In a survey of theological opinions on the nature of the State, made in preparation for the 1937 Oxford Conference of Life and Work, no effort was made to outline the doctrinal presuppositions of Orthodox political thought. The author explained the omission by appealing to his lack of personal knowledge of

[1] In *Une Enquête sur l'Ethique Sociale des Eglises*, p. 25.

Orthodox churches themselves and by pointing to 'the doctrinal formlessness of Orthodoxy'.[1] This last criticism refers undoubtedly not merely to the cosmic vision of Orthodox theology and the mystical preoccupation of its spirituality but especially to its tendency to identify the Church with the religious destiny of the nation. The tendency is especially acute in the idea of the messianic mission of 'Holy Russia' with the Tsar, an Old Testament King *redivivus* leading his people, charged to Christianize the world, and, through the Holy Synod, guiding the Church, whose preaching and Liturgy provide the spiritual symbolism and supernatural alimentation for the nation's divine destiny. Even the radical, pre-revolutionary opposition to what was considered the sterile ritualism of Russian Orthodoxy, the underground religion of the *Raskol*, the Schism, made its protest in the name of the spiritual mission of the Russian nation. Professor Adolf Keller, who believes that the *Raskol* helped to prepare the ground for political nihilism and ultimately for Bolshevism, describes the movement as 'an enthusiastic, ascetic and chiliastic mysticism . . . the religion of simple and oppressed minds and glowing hearts, capable of apocalyptic visions and ready for the Day of Judgment, a new earth and a new heaven'.[2] Generous-minded if anti-intellectual, another emotional effort to return to the simple brotherhood of primitive Christianity, the *Raskol* was, nevertheless, intransigently nationalist. Its complaint against Tsarism was the régime's betrayal of the mission of 'Holy Russia' to the materialism of Western civilization; its strictures on the Orthodox Church included the accusation of betraying Christ to 'the world'. Even the anti-institutional movement in Orthodoxy—and the *Raskol* dated from the seventeenth century—tended to identify the Church with the nation.

The Patriarch Nicodim of Bucharest may well have experienced a definite disquiet during the official visit of the new Praesidium of the Rumanian People's Republic on January 1, 1948. Expressing greetings for the New Year, Premier Peter Groza observed:

---

[1] Nils Ehrenström, *Christian Faith and the Modern State*, p. 67.
[2] *Church and State on the European Continent*, p. 67.

The Church is an institution with permanent usefulness in the life of the people. It is part of the State itself, keeping pace with the spirit of the times. The Orthodox Christian Church, having always understood this, will surely understand it this time.[1]

There was an unconcealed menace in the context of the language of the Premier of the new Communist government but the sentiments expressed were unexceptional. They might even be termed traditional. One can easily imagine Pobiedonostzev, Pro-curator General of the Holy Synod, employing identical phrases in an address to the Patriarch of Moscow fifty years earlier.[2]

The character of its theological preoccupations, the temper of its spirituality and the consequences of its historical identification with the State have poorly equipped Orthodoxy for fruitful

[1] *EPS*, January 30, 1948.

[2] It is possible to see in this historical heritage (rather than in perhaps more obvious explanations) the grounds for the present attitude of officials of the Russian Orthodox Church towards the Soviet Government. Is this what the Rev. Francis House, subsequently Associate General Secretary of the World Council, had in mind when he remarked on his return from a war-time visit to Moscow: 'The Church is as free and as self-governing as at any time in Russian history'? *EPS*, October 1944. The Patriarch Alexei included in the volume of his published speeches and addresses his remark to a representative of *Izvestia*: 'In the war years the Russian Church demonstrated before the whole world its complete solidarity with the country, serving it, and thus doing as the Government does: the Church helps the Government and does its bidding.' His Beatitude noted that he customarily closes his Pastoral Letters with the admonition: 'Let us intensify our intercession for the God-protected and powerful Russian State, headed by its wise leader, whom Divine Providence has appointed to guide our country upon the path of glory and well-being.' *EPS*, June 3, 1949. In the spring of 1948 the Patriarch of Moscow granted an interview to a Reuter's correspondent who asked his 'opinion of Stalin as head of the Soviet people'. The reply declared: 'In this form your question has nothing to do with the position of the Church.' To the question, 'Is there any conflict between the theory and practice of Communism on the one hand and religious beliefs on the other?' His Beatitude answered: 'The question is not clear. The Orthodox Church is not in conflict with anybody within the Soviet State.' *Les Nouvelles Russes*, May 21, 1948, quoted in *EPS*, May 28, 1948. A year later a special Supplement of the *Journal of the Moscow Patriarchate* (No. 4, 1949) reprinted the replies of Alexei to Reuter's correspondent, Donald Dulles, dated August 1 and occasioned by the action of the Patriarch of Con-stantinople in excommunicating any Greek Orthodox supporting Communism. His Beatitude of Moscow called the decision 'a radical contradiction of the fundamental principles underlying the Orthodox Christian creed'. To the question, 'Is there, in your view, a conflict between loyalty to the Soviet State and loyalty to the Russian Church?' the Patriarch of Moscow replied: 'To this question there is only one possible answer: Not only is there no conflict but there never could be one, if our faithful people hold by the true meaning of the Gospel's commandments and the Apostles' legacies to posterity.' *EPS*, September 9, 1949.

collaboration in the task of constructing a social philosophy to serve as an agreed basis for appraising our economic institutions by the World Council of Churches. The ancient Churches of the East have great and abiding glories to boast—a realization of the primacy of doctrine, a Liturgy centring on the transcendent significance of the Resurrection, an unaffected piety, a spirit of personal philanthropy—but an interest in the social consequences of Christianity does not seem to be among their gifts. 'In Orthodox Russia there have never been any important organizations or movements of social Christianity', is the summary judgment of Professor G. P. Fedotov.[1] The experience of Orthodoxy in Russia is paralleled by that of the other autocephalous churches in this regard; the reasons are the same. 'Redemption had a cosmic meaning; but it meant little for daily life, for the solution of social problems.'[2]

As a result, the Orthodox participants at World Council Assemblies have played no discoverable part in the formulation of the Reports on social questions. At Amsterdam and again at Evanston a single representative of Orthodoxy was assigned to the Drafting Committee preparing such a Report. In each instance the delegate chosen was a member of the Church of Greece, intellectually the most active of the Orthodox churches. The Secretary's Minutes fail, however, to offer any evidence of intervention in the Sectional discussions. Part of the difficulty is possibly attributable to lack of fluency in English on the part of Eastern participants. Lack of widespread interest in social questions (and consequently the absence of study) on the part of the Orthodox world is the decisive factor.[3] In ecumenical gatherings the Orthodox participants clearly consider dogmatic questions their speciality and their responsibility. Such, in fact, is the credit claimed for his confessional group by Dr. Nicolas Zernov in his exposition of 'The Scope and Significance of Eastern

---

[1] 'The Church and Social Justice', WCC Study Department Document 50E/609A, p. 15 (mimeographed). [2] Keller, *op. cit.*, p. 76.

[3] Unhappily, the projected volume of Orthodox thinking on the Amsterdam topics was never compiled. The only organized examination of social questions in the Orthodox world, known to the writer, is a study-circle which meets at the University of Athens under the direction of Dr. Panayotis Bratsiotis, Professor of Old Testament exegesis.

Participation in the Ecumenical Movement', contributed to the *History of the Ecumenical Movement, 1517–1948.*[1]

viii. ESCHATOLOGY AND ETHICS

Christianity is not a philosophy but it involves a philosophy of history. It offers a conception of the significance of human life and the value of time based on the belief that the present historical order will reach its end and culmination in a series of events originating beyond this natural universe; these culminating events will bring in the fulfilment of human history. The events terminating the present historical order are known in the Christian tradition as the *eschata*, the Last Things, and the interpretation of their implications is called 'eschatology'. It is the conviction of the World Council that eschatology offers a fruitful field of study for a fresh realization of the bearing of the Christian faith on the religious needs of modern man, that it alone offers a solid ground for a fully human life and for an ethical attitude centred on the Bible. That the theological premises and ethical consequences in the existential order of eschatology are being plumbed by the World Council of Churches is another fruit of the movement for a return to the Reformation in the Ecumenical Community.[2]

1. *The Meaning of History*

It is commonly forgotten how unique the Christian philosophy of history is. The universe represented for the ancient Greeks a

---

[1] 'Their [the Orthodox] chief contribution, however, was in those spheres of Christian life and worship where the Protestant West had been in the past particularly suspicious of the East; for example, in the emphasis on the Eucharist, and on veneration of the saints, and in insistence on the necessity of recognizing the significance of the Blessed Virgin Mary in the work of reconciliation.' p. 673.

[2] 'Thirty years ago, if someone had asked what the relevance of eschatology was for social ethics, he would have received a rather knowing smile and a retort that Christianity had fortunately gone *beyond* eschatology *into* the field of social ethics. Christians had ceased to wait for the coming of the Kingdom of God and were concerned for improving the world and human society and for bringing them up to a certain standard. The fact is that such a development did occur in Christian thinking but it was a sign of the secularization of both the Gospel and the Church. Today we need to move in the opposite direction, away from the social ethics which has its roots in a socially autonomous, idealistic or humanistic outlook, away even from a "Christian sociology" back into the realm of eschatology.' Heinz Dietrich Wendland, 'The Relevance of Eschatology for Social Ethics', *ER* v (July 1953), 4, p. 364.

cosmic order constantly renewed in regular phases. Human existence was caught up in this regular scheme of nature: there was no escaping the sorrowful wheel, whence the inexplicable tragedy of life barely concealed under the blithe spirit of Attic humanism. The Stoic conception of changeless fate, moving in cycles like the spheres of the heavens, explains in good part the annoyance of the Roman philosopher, Celsus, against the Christians. A civilization exalting the high dignity (and moral necessity) of a passive acceptance of, and accommodation to, an implacably fixed order of nature could not but be shocked at the seemingly anarchistic announcement that God had abandoned His transcendence to play a part in human history. For many an Oriental, existence is the expression of an ultimate reality without purpose or activity, and life is an illusion to be escaped in a Nirvana attained by willing not to will, an asceticism opposite in practice but not unrelated in philosophical premises to contemporary Sartrian existentialism counselling maturity through disillusionment in the encounter with nothingness.

The conviction that the universe is self-explanatory, that mankind will realize all its possibilities within the historical order has underlain the dominant philosophy of the modern era. That conviction has been elaborated in theories whose utopian optimism would have astonished the sanguine Democritus and the complacent Lucretius, and whose essentially religious character often mocked the noisy atheism of their advocates. For all these theories, of differing provenance, strive alike to appraise the meaning of history and the significance of life. The various scientific disciplines, formulating the laws of growth in the material universe, bred a bastard belief that began with a naïve act of faith in the existence of a parallel law of development in human history, operating by a process related to nothing beyond itself[1] and whose meaning is synonymous with the fact of movement, by definition, beneficent and infallible. The

[1] Thus John Dewey: 'Since in reality there is nothing to which growth is relative save more growth, there is nothing to which education is subordinate save more education. . . . The criterion of the value of school education is the extent in which it creates a desire for continued growth.' *Democracy and Education*, pp. 60–2.

movement was instinctive, irreversible and infallible.[1] Time would see its fulfilment.

Despite the disillusionment succeeding the easy optimism of the Victorian Age, the human spirit is irrepressible in its longings, a fact of no small theological significance. Contemporary history, in consequence, offers a spate of movements promising liberation from personal limitations in the service of a cause. These grounds for hope, by-products or deviates frequently of the Christian tradition, have one thing in common: the fulfilment of human expectations within the historical order.

2. *The World Council turns to Eschatology*

To stimulate ecumenical thought on the unique character of the Christian faith, particularly its relevance for daily living, the World Council of Churches decided that the main theme of its Second Assembly should explore the realm of eschatology. The choice indicated the desire to concentrate on Bible-centred topics in ecumenical thought; it revealed also the influence of the movement for a return to Reformation insights in World Council circles.[2] A committee of thirty-five theologians of different denominations and schools of thought was appointed to prepare a document on 'Christ—the Hope of the World'. Somewhat revised after examination by the Central Committee in 1952, the Report was presented to the Evanston delegates to serve as the basis for the Assembly's first ten days of common study.

[1] Quintessentially expressed by Herbert Spencer: 'Progress is not an accident but a necessity. What we call evil and immorality must disappear. It is certain that man must become perfect. The ultimate development of the ideal man is certain—as certain as any conclusion in which we place implicit faith; for instance, that all men will die. . . . Always towards perfection is the mighty movement—towards complete development and a more unmixed good.' Quoted by D. C. Somervell, *English Thought in the 19th Century*, p. 164.

[2] 'In early Calvinism, the eschatological point of view is simply dominant. All the individual doctrines are related to eschatology. It is there that the dynamic element of early Calvinism resides. It is from that source, too, that the faith and life of the community and above all the activity of the State derive their provisional character. The present is in expectation of what is to come of the future life. This is the ferment which penetrated the thought and soul of Calvin.' Peter Barth in *Une Enquête sur l'Ethique Sociale des Eglises*, p. 37.

Because of the importance of the subject-matter in the evolution of the social thought of the World Council, the Report is worth close examination. It opens with an analysis of five of the more representative of current substitute-religions under the caption, 'The Hopes of our Time'. They can be summarized in this fashion.[1]

(a) *Democratic Humanism* was judged more an ethical than a political concept. From its Christian origin it draws its recognition of the worth of the human person, the fundamental equality of all men and their essential solidarity; from other cultural and philosophical movements has come its faith, 'faith in the capacity of education or technology to solve all human problems, belief in inevitable progress and above all disregard or denial of God's sovereignty over the world with a consequent failure to see the imperfect, precarious and transient character of all human achievements'. It is the creed of Democratic Humanism that 'man is master of his own destiny and can achieve a perfect society'. Hope need not reach beyond the improving of human existence, for relying on his innate powers man can achieve the good life for himself and his community.

(b) *Scientific Humanism* likewise expresses complete confidence in man. Encouraged by the accomplishments of the scientific method in both the theoretical understanding of nature and the betterment of the human lot, it prizes that methodology as the source of total truth and the sole key to the satisfaction of the needs of mankind. Science, applied to human affairs, offers the illusion of hope for humanity cherished by many outside the ranks of the scientists.

(c) *Marxism* was described as at once a philosophy of history, a practical programme of action and a powerful secular religion. As a philosophy, 'it teaches that man has no fixed nature but is constantly being made and remade in history, which in turn by social action he helps to make'. The Marxist reading of history is fundamentally optimistic, promising the victims of racial discrimination, the peasant scratching at his thin soil, the workman

[1] Included in *CHTC*. Also issued separately as a booklet.

oppressed by a feeling of anonymity, and the scientist revolted by the destructive use made of his knowledge, that they can fulfil their messianic task for all mankind by bringing about the inevitable revolution under the leadership of a disciplined Communist Party, one with allies across all national frontiers.

(*d*) *Nationalism and the Renaissance of Ancient Religions.* Since the last war, and particularly in Asia and Africa, a revolution that is social, political and religious is in progress. For countless millions, history, formerly a wearisome repetition of unvarying events, has become suddenly alive and controllable, an area of combat in the pursuit of political liberation and economic subsistence. 'There is a new confidence among the adherents of Buddhism, Hinduism and Islam that their several religions hold the answer to the ills of the world.'

(*e*) *The Hope of the Hopeless.* Atheistic existentialists have in many countries elevated their frank acceptance of the essential absurdity of human existence into a new absolute, providing the only security open to the honest man. The individual, it is protested, is 'completely alone, surrounded only by meaninglessness, so that if his life is to have any value, he must create such meanings and value for himself, not forgetting that death puts an end to all'. Countless millions, moreover, with no philosophical pretensions, have found the experiences of life so bitter and disillusioning that they refuse to be distracted from the tragedy of existence by the mirages of political nostrums or promises of social amelioration. They have found a certain assurance in sounding the depths of despair and surviving the 'encounter with nothingness', a certain courage in the renunciation of all expectations.

All of these contemporary secularist philosophies of history join ancient Greek, Stoic and Oriental thought in agreeing that human existence is a phenomenon, specialized doubtless, but essentially contiguous to all other events in a time-bound universe of nature, that its significance cannot be sought therefore beyond the limits of history, that history is a drama played before changing audiences with constantly shifting participants but always under a proscenium opening only on to a new epoch of time, the whole framed by the finite.

One Oriental people, however, was convinced that history moved towards a sudden, decisive change, that the change would be wrought from outside the universe, from beyond the limits of time (though occurring in the historical order), that human existence found its meaning and mankind its hope in view of that expectation. Whatever the interpretation of the coming change held by the Jewish people at different periods, it is the conviction of Christians that that event took place in a backward province of the Roman Empire under the Procurator, Pontius Pilate. Such a conviction creates a distinct philosophy of history. For Christianity—not the sentimental perversion of it whose total content is universal benevolence—is unique because of its assertion that history takes its meaning from the implications of that event. In the language of the World Council Report:

> Our hope is grounded in one great Event, comprising the incarnation, ministry, death and resurrection of Jesus Christ. In this Event the purpose of God for man, foreshadowed in His dealings with Israel and declared by the prophets, found fulfilment, and His Kingdom was inaugurated on earth, to be consummated hereafter.[1]

By this event the world has been reconstituted and the human situation redefined. The intrusion of God into the historical process adds a new dimension to the interpretation of life. 'His coming fulfilled the hope of earlier times—and transformed it. He brought to men a new birth into a new life, a new community and a new hope.'

The Christian philosophy of history includes, moreover, the belief that He whose coming gave meaning to history and a new situation to each person, will return to close the course of history and fulfil the destiny of individuals. There is an *omega* as well as an *alpha* to history, for history has a point. That expectation is the ground of hope which specifies and illumines the Christian philosophy of history. It implies as well a certain tension

[1] *CHTC*, p. 14.

measuring the worth of time and pointing imperiously to the culmination.[1]

3. The Variety of Christian Eschatology

'In the beginning was the Word'—a purpose existing outside time directs the course of history; 'the Word was made flesh'— that purpose, personified in Jesus Christ, entered the human scene at a given moment of time; 'and He will come again to judge the living and the dead'—time will be terminated and the transient Temporal City, the stage of history, transformed on His regal return to share His triumph with His expectant followers: these are the pillars of the Christian philosophy of history. The Report of the Advisory Commission on the Evanston Theme indicated the implications of this philosophy for the believer who faces a double temptation:

> In his longing for the heavenly city with all its blessedness he may pass by his fellow-man, fallen among thieves, and leave him by the road side. . . . He may so confine his attention to the possibilities of this present world as to forget that the whole world lies under judgment.[2]

The danger is double: daunted by the apparently unconquered power of evil, the believer may despair of this world and fix his whole attention on that which is to come; assured by his sharing in Christ's risen power, he may forget that what is here given is only a foretaste and confuse man's achievements with God's Kingdom. Since the Christian hope 'is anchored in a Kingdom that both has come and is coming', the life of the believer has a double orientation.

The differing social attitudes deriving from eschatology will depend on the selective emphasis placed by the individual conscience on one of three formulations of fundamental Christian belief: (1) Jesus Christ *came*, (2) He *has come*, (3) He *will come* again. The second version of the Report of the Advisory

---

[1] Cf., for a primitive Christian expression of this conviction, 2 Peter iii. 8–10.
[2] *CHTC*, p. 8.

Commission suggested the same distinction in pointing out that Christian hope must be 'anchored in God Who comes to us in Jesus Christ, and looking at once to what He has done, what He is doing now and what He will do for His people and His world, in completion of His saving work'. Of course, a balanced Christian philosophy of history, an integrated Christian outlook, will keep all these emphases in equilibrium, but that is a considerable achievement of spiritual serenity and certainly a major task of theological synthesis. Given the partial character of personal moral insight and the limitations of any theological synthesis, one or other of the emphases will dominate the religious attitude of the individual and the explanations of the theologian.

Since Christianity is concerned with the 'Kingdom of God' announced by Jesus Christ, these same emphases will manifest themselves in the conviction that the Kingdom—the realm of justice and peace and love—(1) is already realized or (2) is realizable or (3) will be realized beyond history. These emphases, social consequences of various eschatological perspectives, will be (need one repeat?) attitudes rather than systems. For the eschatological outlook is based primarily on biblical considerations which seek to confront the individual with the essential elements of a permanent, personal crisis. Ethics, even social ethics, is conceived as operative in concrete decisions rather than elaborated from a series of principles. Finally, these differing emphases supply varying grounds for the virtue of hope, and changing connotations of the invocation, 'Thy Kingdom Come!' To the extent that the sifting of these emphases is more a matter of logical distinction than of firm theological differentiation, the classification of their consequences will be arbitrary, even adventitious. It must be recognized, however, that the differences frequently run deeper than mere meter-readings of religious psychology or the contrasting temper of schools of spirituality, and involve fundamental, dogmatic divergences.

(a) A one-sided concentration on the benefits bestowed by Christ—the emphasis expressed in the phrase, 'He *came*'—produces an ethical escapism, a spiritual smugness, a religious isolationism.

Confident of possessing the secret of salvation and the resources for enduring evil, confident that human culture is fundamentally ephemeral and the world evanescent, this sort of Christian awaits almost apathetically the close of the drama of history whose outcome is predetermined and, therefore, not interesting. Such religious individualism restricts the relevance of the Gospel to the transcendental sphere alone and reduces the idea of the Kingdom of God to the fact of personal immortality.[1] Ethical irrelevance and social pessimism are its consequences. This emphasis, confining the jurisdiction of Christ to the spiritual concerns of individual souls and isolating the interests of the Kingdom from the ways of the world, is traditionally considered a consequence of Luther's teaching. Though a prominent Lutheran theologian[2] argues that such a distortion can only be attributed to unenlightened followers of the sixteenth-century reformer, it is not without significance that there exists no Evangelical periodical devoted to social questions in Germany or Scandinavia. Moreover, a German member of the World Council's Commission of the Churches on International Affairs, Professor Rudolf Smend, felt compelled to list as an obstacle to his country's active interest in the work of the Commission, 'our heavy burden of theology'.[3]

(b) The opposite extreme of emphasis which considers the Kingdom of God a wholly future condition to be ushered in by the imminent return of Christ, is an aberration recurring with curious regularity in exotic sects throughout the history of

---

[1] In the opinion of an American historian of religion, H. Richard Niebuhr, this essentially other-worldly faith, which 'condemns every aspect of the present world, including culture, religious strivings and every attempt at an amelioration of social evils as the expression of a depraved and lost will, has been resurrected today by the crisis theology of Germany'. *The Social Sources of Denominationalism*, p. 275.

[2] E. Berggrav, *Der Staat und der Mensch*, pp. 365 ff.

[3] 'For far too long German theology (especially of late Lutheranism which has been so much misunderstood) has refused to co-operate in working out a Christian ethic for public life, on the pretext that the Kingdom of God has nothing to do with the political orders of this world. Through this refusal German theology has left a free field open to all the demons of power-politics and created the foundations of that political helplessness and uncritical loyalty of the German people without which the Third Reich and its uncontested duration would have been unthinkable.' *Göttinger Universitäts-Zeitung*, December 20, 1946, as quoted in *EPS*, January 1947, p. 13.

Christianity. These world-forsaking millenarians sharply separate the glorious future from the squalid present and, by a pedantic literalism in their reading of prophecies, feel liberated from temporal involvements. Anarchism, sometimes in the harmless form of abandonment of all possessions in organized flight from the cities, sometimes in the more direct fashion of social revolt, characterizes this social attitude. Apocalypticism, it need scarcely be said, has no adherents in World Council circles.

That millenarianism represents the primitive Christian conception was the claim of a school of Bible critics at the beginning of the century among whom Albert Schweitzer is the most celebrated name. Considering Christ a visionary, bemused by His belief in the imminent end of the world, these writers held that only a few central ideas can be salvaged from the Gospels. The rest, they insisted, is vitiated by the error of judgment of Jesus who propagated an 'interim ethic' to tide people over the short time remaining before human history was concluded in cosmic catastrophe. A contributor[1] to the symposium sponsored by the World Council, 'The Biblical Authority for the Church's Social and Political Message Today', agreed that the judgments expressed in the New Testament were conditioned by the expectation of the early end of the world, thus limiting its usefulness as a source of social guidance, for 'to make a social and political programme in the expectation that what has not happened in 1900 years will surely happen in our time is criminal dereliction of Christian responsibility'. It is perhaps characteristic that the author believed that the Church 'has no obligation to work for the transformation of social institutions. Its sole task is to call men to their true citizenship in the age to come. Absorption in social tasks of the present age only diverts from the real objective.'[2] That the writer was at his death in 1953 Vice-Chairman of the Commission on Faith and Order illustrates possibly the tension in the World Council structure, predicted by Dr. Cavert,[3] between the two functions, ecclesiastical unity

---

[1] Professor Clarence Tucker Craig.   [2] *Biblical Authority for Today*, pp. 42–3.
[3] Cf. *supra*, p. 81 n.

and social reform, between the tendencies represented by the parent organizations, Life and Work and Faith and Order. For the millenarian the Kingdom of God is a spiritual conception, a wholly future situation which will be realized outside time.

(c) For those whose ethical attitude reflects an exaggerated emphasis suggested by the phrase 'He *has* come', the Kingdom is a form of social organization to be realized in history by human efforts. When President Charles W. Eliot of Harvard gave his memorable address to the University Divinity School in 1909 on 'The Religion of the Future', he invoked no visions of the New Age when all the former things of the historical order will have passed away. The 'Religion of the Future', this Christian educator argued with unconscious irony, should concern itself with the needs of the present, with public baths, playgrounds, wider and cleaner streets and better dwellings.[1] Christianity is thus reduced to an aspect of Civics. A climax to the human drama with a divine judgment closing the temporal sequence is shadowy (when not merely symbolic) in the thought supporting this ethical attitude. The Last Things are interpreted, by a transposition manifesting biological observation rather than theological insight, as a stage in the perfection of society, ever evolving but obeying always inherent and necessary laws of development.[2] Religious socialism is a common political expression of this ethical attitude; it tends to identify reform legislation and international organizations with God's will; rising literacy rates, the growth of trade union membership and voting rights for women, along with the improvement of medical care, provide it with grounds for hope. However attractive its sympathies and

---

[1] The next time a President of Harvard addressed the University Divinity School was in 1953. Dr. Nathan Pusey, adverting to his famous predecessor's views, remarked: 'This faith will no longer do.... It is leadership in religious knowledge and even more in religious experience of which we now have a most gaping need.' 'A Religion For Now', *Harper's*, December 1953, p. 20.

[2] An American exponent of the 'Social Gospel', Harry F. Ward, announced that: 'The new social order will be based not on fighting but on fraternity . . . not simply because the co-operative fraternal life is the highest ideal of human living but because the spirit and method of co-operation is the scientific law of human progress.' *The New Social Order* (New York: Macmillan, 1919), p. 104, as quoted by Reinhold Niebuhr in *Faith and History*, p. 236.

admirable its public activities, it must be acknowledged that this emphasis annuls the essential tension of the Christian faith introduced by the reality of the eschatological events: it neglects the power of evil in history and seems sanguinely to expect (judging at least from its optimistic prophecies) the salvation of society to be achieved by human efforts and within history.

(d) The main theme of the Evanston Assembly—'Christ—the Hope of the World'—implied that an eschatology which harmonizes in a balanced view the full scope of the Gospel message can alone lead men past the mirages of the demonic utopias of the day to meaningful living in modern society and can furnish a secure hope which will at once shed light on the perplexities of evil and impel Christians to play a responsible role in human affairs.

4. Eschatological Synthesis

In the perspective of such a balanced eschatology, the Report of the Advisory Committee indicated, God's purpose has declared itself in history through Christ, liberating men from their self-centredness, their isolation, even from the curse of death, fashioning thereby a new beginning for humanity, a new meaning for history, both to be fulfilled beyond time. His victory is already achieved, His Lordship is already established, but both are hidden in the ambiguities of history and apprehended only by faith, giving the Christian a participation in that victory and a knowledge of the laws of the Kingdom of God Whose sovereignty is untouched by social disorder, unaffected by human treachery. Sharing the victory of Christ does not spare either the individual or the Christian Community misunderstanding and even persecution at the hands of a world which crucified its Lord. Nor does the existence of the Kingdom of God, already planted in time, guarantee social justice and international harmony. Though He presently reigns in history and is progressively transforming the world, accessible always to believers who attend to His Word, God's purpose as personified in Christ will be consummated only at his triumphant return, an event ending the sequence of past-present-future, fulfilling the expectation of faith and completing the mission of the world to serve as the stage whereon was played the divine drama of God's mysterious plan in history.

Such a perspective catches up all the positive values of contemporary secular utopias and integrates them in the fuller dimensions provided by the comprehensive Christian philosophy of history. Further, it imposes on Christians, the Advisory Commission argues, the obligation of correcting the faulty perspective of contemporary secularist hopes. Christians must purge democratic societies of false assumptions and unjustified illusions. They may welcome the sober scientist as a colleague in many common tasks, thanking God for his human compassion and disinterested service, but they must declare openly that the hope that man can shoulder the burdens of the world is an illusion that leads men through anxiety to despair; for God's sovereignty and man's sinfulness are permanent realities and out of good intentions evil as well as good arises to thwart personal endeavours and to plunge men into tyrannies and wars, civil chaos and social despair. They must uncompromisingly affirm the contemporary demand for economic and social justice, without vindictiveness or partisanship, acknowledging the responsibility of Christians, by act or by default, for the situation exploited by Communists, but they must remind Marxists that the denial of God's sovereignty over human history opens the way to the idolizing of the Party or the economic system, and that the sanguine expectation of the abolition of strife and self-seeking through economic levelling is belied by the facts of human nature and mocked by actual Marxist practice. They must strive to understand the faith and hope by which so many millions in Asia and Africa are seeking to shape their national and personal lives, and must welcome the struggle of those of other faiths to achieve social righteousness and the common good of their peoples; Christians must, in consequence, relate their preaching of the gospel in Asia and Africa to the immediate tasks demanded by Christ's coming. And for those who have renounced all hope in a stark affirmation of the absurdity of existence, Christians must bring an ungrudging sympathy and the assurance that there is One Who understands them better than they understand themselves.

Invoking the principle of analogy employed by Barth, the Report notes as the fruits of Christ's mission and as characteristics of his Kingdom, peace, righteousness, justice, freedom, life, truth, and indicates that these imply certain corresponding objectives for the Christian task in the world—the abolition of war, the just ordering of society, the suppression of unjust discrimination of class and race, the correction of political and economic oppression, the furnishing of adequate food in under-developed areas, the spread of human knowledge. Obviously, such a transfer is available only to someone accepting the Christian faith. Nor does the Report seek to create anything beyond an ethical attitude.

5. *The Unresolved Tension*

A common ethical attitude, a single perspective for judging social problems, proved unattainable at Evanston. The implications of eschatology, as adumbrated in the Report of the Advisory Committee, were the subject of what the Statement forwarding the document to the member churches called 'sharp differences in theological viewpoint'. Deeper than the dissatisfaction expressed over the absence of 'buoyancy' in the Report, its neglect of the action of the Holy Spirit, its denigration of human achievements wrought under the inspiration of hope, its opposition of the Church to the world, its omission of the role of Israel in the Christian conception of the end of history, was the divergence of viewpoint among the delegates on the consequences of the twin assertions of traditional Christian belief: 'He has come' and 'He will come again'. The contrast, if not conflict, appeared at the opening Plenary Session when two theologians presented to the Assembly the Main Theme of Christian Hope, which was to be the subject of study. Professor Edmund Schlink, Rector of the University of Heidelberg, conceded that hope imports 'an active

concern in the right ordering of society', but he was certain
that

> If in our thinking about this subject we place the emphasis on the
> preservation of this threatened world, then we shall miss the point
> of our Assembly theme completely. If we expect Christ to insure
> this world so that men may continue undisturbed their pursuit of
> liberty, may carry on their business, and seek an improvement in
> their standard of living, then Christ is not the hope of the world,
> but rather the end of all the world's hopes. . . . We have only to tell
> the world who its Lord already is. It is not up to us to save men.[1]

For Professor Robert Calhoun of Yale University who followed,
theology, particularly as preached in the American environment,
furnishes a 'word for this world', a word of present practical
relevance for a world always in need of renewal. In such a
conception, the Christian gospel is

> a truly historical word rooted in actual existence and demanding
> present day-by-day response, not a remote ideal nor a way of escape.
> It affirms also, in strenuous if not always well-directed action as well
> as in spoken and written language, the Reformers' insistence that
> this world must be transformed according to the will of God, our
> Creator and Redeemer. Its most characteristic prayer is: 'Thy
> kingdom come, thy will be done on earth.' Its characteristic hope
> looks for the ever clearer manifestation of God's sovereignty and
> the power of His promises in human history.[2]

The Second Assembly of the World Council of Churches declared:
'We are not agreed on the relationship between the Christian's
hope here and now, and his ultimate hope.'[3]

The search for a standard for measuring social problems through
the insights offered by eschatology will continue in the Ecumenical Community, since the Advisory Committee's Report was
forwarded to the member churches 'for their study, prayer and
encouragement'. The theme suggested by the phrase of the
Nicene Creed, 'And He will come again to judge the living and
the dead', proved as fruitful in discussion but as unamenable to

---

[1] H. G. G. Herklots, *Looking at Evanston*, pp. 28–9.   [2] *Ibid.*, p. 31.   [3] *Evanston*, p. 70.

final conclusions as had the term 'the Kingdom of God' at Stockholm.[1]

ix. PERSONALITIES AND PRINCIPLES

To estimate with any accuracy the influence of any specific individual thinker on the anonymous Reports officially issued by the World Council as expressing its corporate mind is manifestly impossible. It would be, in effect, to endeavour to graph in terms of personalities the prevailing forces in the Ecumenical Community. Time alone gives the historian the proper perspective for such a task. Nor for our present purpose is such a study indicated: it is the official mind and public speech of the World Council—by definition a fellowship of churches—which is under examination. For an understanding, however, of the dominant attitudes and the direction of thinking on social questions in the World Council a knowledge of the works and activities of certain thinkers is undoubtedly valuable. Happily several of these men have already been the subject of books and monographs.[2]

1. *The Legacy of the Nineteenth Century*

The significance of the radical shift in Protestant theological orientation, associated with the name of Karl Barth, can only be appreciated against the bequest of the previous century which saw forms of Christianity as competing codifications of the religious experience of the nations expressing itself in varying formulas as the group adjusts itself to new conditions. The fashionable conception was compounded of a heritage of German Idealism, the philosophy of Progress, the messianism of Socialist

[1] When, at the close of the Stockholm Conference, the question of a Continuation Committee was being discussed, Licentiate Erich Stange observed: 'In this Conference there has been voiced a double-sided conception of the Kingdom of God, which no one with the catchwords, pessimistic, optimistic, individualistic or social, can dispose of, but which touches deeply on the ultimate purpose of the Gospel. We are glad of the frankness of our discussion. But we have perhaps missed on the whole the real root of the question. Here it seems to me the decisive task for the continuation of the Conference lies.' *Stockholm*, p. 705.

[2] Notably by T. A. Gill, *Recent Protestant Political Theory*, studying Barth, Brunner and Niebuhr.

movements and the vogue of Positivism as expressed in Utilitarianism of British origin and Pragmatism of American provenance. The stern moralism stemming from Kant's teaching was small substitute for its radical attack on the intellectual and historical foundations of the Christian religion. The Kantian act of faith, a postulate of Practical Reason to explain the relation of happiness and morality, was transmuted by Schleiermacher into a certitude accompanying a feeling, a feeling of contact with the Divine Cosmos.

Schleiermacher's influence was pervasive and dominant.[1] The doctrine of the immanence of God in man disintegrated the traditional affirmations of the Christian creeds. The appeal to emotional experience as the basis of faith led to attempts to find the essential 'meaning' of Christianity—as distinguished from historical 'accretions' and cultural 'mutations'—in its social utility. The result was an ethical theism as in Ritschl, content with the self-evident 'values' for significant living offered by the person and teachings of Christ, or a sociologism as in Troeltsch, justifying religion by its relation to community needs. Christianity 'de-Orientalized' was scarcely distinguishable from enlightened common sense emotionally surcharged with a sentiment of fraternity.

Such a mood invited the title 'Protestantism moves towards Humanism and Collectivism' in a chapter of a scholarly history of ideas in the United States.[2] In its cruder forms such thinking has few contemporary champions. On both sides of the Atlantic a new soberness, induced by events as well as by the neo-orthodox movement in theology, has cauterized much of the ebullience of that sentimental social ethic. In some quarters, to be sure, it has its advocates who have not been absent from World Council meetings, individuals who (not unlike the 'German Christians' of the Nazi era) claim to discover religious elements in secular revolutionary movements. Their efforts

---

[1] Professor Jacques Courvoisier of the University of Geneva has observed that Schleiermacher's thought became 'la colonne vertébrale du protestantisme'. *Brève Histoire du Protestantisme*, p. 97.

[2] Ralph Henry Gabriel, *The Course of American Democratic Thought*, pp. 308–31.

appear to confuse Christianity with Sociology and end, in conspicuous instances, in politicizing religion, finding a new gospel of salvation in the aspirations of the proletariat. The conversion to this new gospel has not been difficult.[1]

Schleiermacher had insisted that 'the Reformation must continue'. The developments in the churches of the Reformed tradition in the 'thirties took a direction quite contrary to that envisaged by the philosopher of religious experience. On the Continent it took the form of a mighty protest against all efforts to derive Christian truths from an analysis of human aspirations, however noble, and a return to the biblical emphasis of the Reformation on the absolute sovereignty of God and the essential impotence of moral effort to achieve salvation.[2] The prophet of the revolution in theology was Karl Barth, though he became more of a symbol for a movement than a master of docile disciples.[3]

In the field of the missionary enterprise of the Ecumenical Community, as in that of social reform, the same reaction to the instrumental conception of Christianity manifested itself. The relation of Christianity to the other world-religions, in effect, the question of the function of Christian missions, was the issue. A Rockefeller-endowed survey, chaired by Harvard's distinguished philosopher, Professor W. E. Hocking, concluded that Christianity is merely the highest of the High Religions, a stage in the universal quest for 'righteousness', a precious component of the religion of the future that will represent the 'New Testament of every existing Faith' and serve as the soul of a coming common world culture. The Report, *Rethinking Missions*:

[1] Cf., for example, Leonard M. Outerbridge, *The Lost Churches of China*.

[2] The emphasis of Pascal is also echoed: 'La foi chrétienne ne va principalement qu'à établir ces deux choses, la corruption de la nature et la rédemption de Jésus Christ.' *Pensées* No. 1.

[3] The movement in Europe is described by Professor Emil Brunner in the chapter he contributed to the *Festschrift* honouring William Adams Brown, President of the Union Theological Seminary, *The Church Through Half a Century*, edited by H. P. Van Dusen and S. McC. Cavert. Its repercussions in the United States are indicated in the symposium, *Protestant Thought in the Twentieth Century*, edited by Arnold S. Nash, *passim*—since all the disciplines in the field of theological studies are examined in separate chapters. A more popular presentation of the content and the influence of the revolution in theological emphasis is Dr. Adolf Keller's *Karl Barth and Christian Unity*.

A Layman's Inquiry After One Hundred Years, concluded that the missionary effort, therefore, should welcome the values of other faiths, contribute the spiritual resources of Western civilization through education and medical clinics, rather than by evangelization, serving always the emerging world culture. The answer appeared in another book, *The Christian Message in a Non-Christian World*, prepared for the Madras Conference of the International Missionary Council by Dr. Hendrik Kraemer, subsequently Director of the World Council's Ecumenical Institute. This disciple of Barth insisted that Christianity is not a product of the evolution of human values but the affirmation of the effects of historical events, not so much a religion as a revelation unpossessed and unattainable by humanity until communicated by God through Christ and disseminated to the nations by missionaries.[1]

2. *Karl Barth*

As a specialist in dogmatics the Basle theologian has not concerned himself with the World Council's analyses of social and political problems. At the Amsterdam Assembly he chose to participate in the session of the Committee discussing the role of women in the Church; he was not present at Evanston. Barth's unremitting insistence, however, that Christianity is not a movement of social reform but a settling of accounts between sinful man and his Maker has played a decisive, if negative, part in the outlook of the World Council even on social questions. His theological emphasis and not least the appeal and force of his character have been a constant reminder that political pre-occupations have their place, but a subordinate place, in the Christian vision of the world. Freely invoked, particularly in

[1] The former ideas 'of recommending Christianity as the bringer of enlightenment and freedom, as a capital national and social tonic to make powerful nations, as the infallible guide to progress, has come to naught. . . . Sharing religious experiences, even service to men, "christianizing" the social, economic and political order, though necessarily included in the living act of manifold missionary expression, cannot be the real motive and ultimate purpose. The real motive and ultimate purpose are not founded in anything that man or civilizations or societies call for. As Kagawa has said, the starting-point of missions is the divine commission to proclaim the Lordship of Christ over all life.' *The Christian Message in a Non-Christian World*, pp. 59–60.

circles on the Continent (including East Europe), his message is commonly translated as a warning against confusing the gospel with any existing social structures. His constant admonition against identifying the Kingdom of God with political programmes and economic expedients, however, are regularly repeated in World Council discussions on social topics. On the other hand, his message has not helped appreciably in the difficult task of indicating which precisely are the things that belong to Caesar and which to God nor in discovering to what positive tasks the State should address itself.

Barth himself as a young man had shared the idealism of liberal Christianity. A former pupil of Harnack, he had served on the staff of a liberal review, *Die Christliche Welt*, before accepting a pastorate in a tiny Swiss village. His weekly pulpit obligation brought to light the thinness of the doctrinal assumptions of his teachers and confronted him with an imperiously felt personal need to think through the foundations of the Christian faith. Almost a century before, a young Dane had struggled with the meaning of Christianity and had opted for an uncompromising position which Barth was to make influential in a 'Time of Troubles'. Søren Kierkegaard confided to his diary:

> I have often said that Christianity can be presented in two ways: either in the interest of man (an extenuating adjustment) or in the interest of God (true Christianity). . . . Christianity is not a little moralizing and a few articles of faith; Christianity is the reckoning between God and the world. And now, long after Christianity has, as it is expressed, conquered and deposited a culture, Christianity and the world are so mixed up that the question must be expressed once again in a new potency: is Christianity of God or of man? . . . My very humble work is: to make people aware. I admit that I dare do nothing more—yet I am a cry of alarm.[1]

Kierkegaard had insisted that between man's purposes in history and God's purposes in eternity there is 'an infinite qualitative difference'. Barth agreed, proclaiming the total liberty of God whose message transcends all the categories of human reason

[1] *Journals*, edited by Alexander Dru (Oxford: Humphrey Milford, 1939), No. 1192.

and whose nature is discoverable neither by earnest introspection nor by measuring humanity's achievements but only by listening to His Word.

Beginning with the publication of his *Commentary on the Epistle to the Romans* in 1918, Barth's influence spread rapidly, growing as he occupied successively Professorships at Göttingen, Münster and Bonn and spoke out boldly against Nazism. God, he proclaimed, is *ganz anders*: the ultimate blasphemy is the arrogant assumption that He stands in need of human defenders, that the triumph of His Will awaits the perfectioning of human systems. It is by faith not works that the sinful individual is saved, he repeated in tones recalling Calvin and Luther; one can speak of saving society only by listing the incidental effect of the activity of the community of those who heed God's Word. Not by elaborating systems of ethics but by a total surrender to His Lordship does the Christian play his appointed part in a world where all is relative.

He insisted that he was not himself 'a Barthian' and it is true that many who rallied to his lead calling for a return to the fundamental principles of the Reform did not follow him in all his dogmatic positions; others had marked reservations on what they judged the defeatism of his ethical teaching.[1] In various accents the Barthian emphasis was sounded by Oscar Cullmann, Rudolf Bultmann, Emil Brunner, Paul Tillich, and across the ocean by Reinhold Niebuhr, the leader of 'the shift to the Left politically and to the Right theologically' in American Protestantism.[2] Barth's thought developed, became more organic and

---

[1] 'But the Christian faith, which can easily degenerate into a too simple moralism, may also degenerate into a too simple determinism when the divine grace is regarded as a way of escape from, rather than a source of engagement with, the anxieties, perplexities, sins and pretensions of human existence.' Reinhold Niebuhr, 'We are Men, not God,' *Christian Century* LXV (October 27, 1948), 43, p. 1140.

[2] The publication of Niebuhr's *Moral Man and Immoral Society* in 1932 marked a turning-point, unsuspected at the time, in American Protestant thought. When *Time* magazine, publishing its Silver Jubilee issue, wished to survey the change in the American scene over twenty-five years, it devoted its cover-story to Niebuhr. Niebuhr's thought is popularly presented by an English admirer, D. R. Davies, in *Reinhold Niebuhr, Prophet from America*; a good idea of the movement of neo-Protestantism in all its phases connected with his name and influence can be gathered in reading John A. Hutchinson (ed.) *Christian Faith and Social Action*.

(though he would perhaps resent the term) more humane over the years. His original impact was that of a prophet and he acknowledges his surprise at the widespread reception that greeted his ideas: 'When I look backwards on the road I have travelled, I seem to be like a man who was climbing the bell-tower of a church in the darkness. Instead of grasping the railing, he caught hold of the bell rope. To his great astonishment, the great bell began to toll and the whole world heard its pealing.'[1]

3. Brunner and Temple

A more comprehensive consideration of the social philosophies influential in the World Council's constituency would surely include analysis of Emil Brunner's *Gerechtigkeit*. Calvinist and humanist at once, Brunner's thought is marked by a sturdy sense of realism, a generous openness to truth wherever found and an impressive knowledge of history. Reference might perhaps be made to the doctrine of Christian Sociology elaborated by Anglican writers like Maurice B. Reckitt and V. A. Demant. The decline of influence of this school may be judged from the disappearance of the British review, *Christendom*, and the concentration of ecumenical circles in England on the practical programme proposed by the Labour Party after the war. Such Anglican thinkers as Reckitt and Demant find fruitful social implications in the central dogma of the Incarnation: In Christ human and divine natures are joined in one Person, thus offering a pattern for resolving the tension between the personality and the community; His action, incorporating redeemed humanity into a new Society of which He is the Head, confers on the Christian community the authority of declaring from its intrinsic principles the proper ends of economic activity, social institutions and international relations, and of announcing that its members are pledged to these goals and no others.

In addition to those of the *Christendom* group, two other

[1] *Prolégomènes à la Dogmatique*, as quoted by W. A. Visser 't Hooft, *Introduction à Karl Barth*, p. 5.

Englishmen must be included. Joseph H. Oldham, who contributed so much to the Oxford Conference of 1937 and to the Study preparations for the Amsterdam Assembly, was interested more in the cultural problems of modern society than in its economic institutions. Infirmities and advancing age prevented him from developing for the Evanston Assembly a theme of characteristic interest, the philosophy of work with all its attendant problems of making daily occupations meaningful in an industrialized age. If the reproach of a certain literary academism could be made against Oldham, of an enthusiasm for the prevailing preoccupations of the critics of contemporary culture, the same could not be said of William Temple, Archbishop of Canterbury, and at his death Chairman of the Provisional Committee of the World Council of Churches. A skilled organizer and gifted presiding officer, Archbishop Temple was a student of social philosophy who did not hesitate to make applications to existing conditions. He inspired the war-time Malvern Conference which debated a basic revision of England's economic institutions. His best-selling 1942 'Penguin', *Christianity and Social Order*, concluded with a concrete programme of national legislation, premised by the assertion: 'Our aim must be to plan efficiently for the maximum of freedom.' His untimely death deprived the World Council not only of a thinker with a genuine interest in the problems of social justice, but one with an understanding of the Natural Law system of social thought and an appetite for facts as the necessary preliminary to any viable solution.

4. Niebuhr and Bennett

Certainly ample place would have to be made for the contributions of Reinhold Niebuhr whose thought has formed the younger generation of Americans active in the World Council's social inquiries and whose influence on Europeans is considerable.[1] Indeed one might illustrate the evolution of religious thought in

[1] Thus, Dr. C. L. Patijn, Chief of the office of Economic Affairs of Holland's Ministry of Foreign Affairs, Chairman of the Section on political and economic questions at both the Amsterdam and the Evanston Assemblies, told the author that in social theory he favours Niebuhr.

the United States by recalling that the five Americans invited to give the Gifford Lectures at the University of Edinburgh—founded in the last century to defend the proofs for the existence of God—have been William James, Josiah Royce, John Dewey, William E. Hocking and Reinhold Niebuhr.[1] The first four could certainly not be suspected of accepting any traditional Christian affirmations. It was Reinhold Niebuhr who marked the return towards orthodoxy in American theology. Niebuhr is against abstract and general programmes of ethics as inapplicable to the ambiguous character of man's life in modern society. He counsels the acceptance of approximations of justice that take into account the fallibility of human knowledge and the more than dubious purity of human intentions. The law of love is, to be sure, the ultimate standard of moral rectitude but, by itself, it results in an idealistic ethic with small relevance for the implacable involvements of modern life. The law of self-love, on the other hand, is a permanent and persistent factor of history, marring the desired harmony of man's social relationships. It remains, nevertheless, a power to be acknowledged, accepted, 'used, beguiled, harnessed and deflected for the ultimate end of establishing the highest and most inclusive possible community of justice and order'.[2]

One of Niebuhr's closest associates, his successor at Columbia University's Union Theological School, is John C. Bennett, whose association with the organized Ecumenical Community's study of social questions dates from the Oxford Conference of 1937 when, as a young professor, he was charged with the responsibilities of research preparations in the United States. Secretary of Section III at Amsterdam, he was so identified with the work of the Evanston Section on the Responsible Society that the right-wing Press, disliking his political liberalism and economic preferences, warned against 'Bennettism', undoubtedly to the huge amusement of an essentially modest man. Professor Bennett's predilection is for a mixed economy, a Third Way,

---

[1] David Wesley Soper, *Major Voices in American Theology*, p. 46.
[2] *Christian Faith and Social Action*, p. 241.

which in practice would resemble the social policies he finds represented in the British Labour Party. In social thought he favours the use of 'middle axioms', universally accepted moral truths, as providing the starting-point for deductions in discussions of questions of justice. His social philosophy is adumbrated in a series of public lectures published under the title, *Christian Ethics and Social Policy*.

5. Two Basic Principles of Ecumenical Social Philosophy

From a consideration of these several philosophical and theological approaches, from an examination of the different confessional emphases extant in the World Council's constituency, is it possible to discover any common principles supporting its declarations on social problems?

A recent survey of theological trends counts five operative ethical traditions. The author is convinced, however, that these various traditions converge on 'two complementary principles which follow directly from the attempt to see human life in the light of Christ', the personal principle and the social principle.[1]

These two principles certainly underlie all the analyses and motivate all the judgments in the World Council's pronouncements on economic conditions and international relations. Behind the divergences of social philosophies in the World Council constituency there is a common and insistent emphasis: human society is responsible to rules it has not made, it moves towards goals given to it from without and is judged by norms it cannot change.

---

[1] 'One is the personal principle. This means the supreme evaluation which Christian faith puts upon personal existence. Every person is created for a life of dignity and fellowship in the grace of God's eternal purpose. . . . The social principle means that persons are created "members one of another" as the New Testament says. We exist in a social relationship with God, our Creator, and we are created for and in a community of life with one another. It is especially important to see that these two principles, the personal and the social, belong absolutely together.' Daniel Day Williams, *Interpreting Theology, 1918–1952*, pp. 69–70.

IV

THE SOCIAL POLICY OF THE
WORLD COUNCIL OF CHURCHES

i. INTRODUCTION

THE human race is accustomed to being told by religious authorities that the world is in a bad way. Decrying the trend of the times is commonly considered by modern man as a professional preoccupation of ecclesiastics. In the summer of 1948, however, there was no thoughtful person prepared to dispute the judgment: 'The world today is experiencing a social crisis of unparalleled proportions.' The pronouncement which opened the Amsterdam Assembly's Report on 'The Church and the Disorder of Society' seemed almost platitudinous. In such straits, with such mute awareness of something radically wrong with the world, there was reasonable hope that even the non-religious observer would lend courteous attention to the analysis of social ills offered by the World Council of Churches.

1. Preparations for Amsterdam

It will be useful, before scrutinizing the positions on social and international problems taken by the World Council, to examine the process whereby these judgments were formulated. In fact it was to a most general audience that the Amsterdam Assembly's Section III addressed its Report, diagnosing the errors and indicating its recommendations for social reconstruction and regeneration.[1] The phrasing of the Report was the responsibility

---

[1] In presenting *The Message of the Assembly* at a plenary meeting on September 3, Bishop Berggrav explained that it was 'more like a pastoral letter to fellow-Christians' and distinguished it from the Reports of the Sections which contained what the Assembly had to say to the world. *Amsterdam*, p. 44.

of a Drafting Committee of eleven men, drawn from a Section composed of some eighty delegates who met six times. With quite minor modifications by the membership of the Section, the text was phrased by a Drafting Committee almost exactly divided between laymen and ordained ecclesiastics. Represented on the Committee were four members of churches of the Reformed tradition, three from the Anglican tradition, two from Free Churches, a Lutheran and an Orthodox; five from continental Europe, three from the USA, two from England and an Indian.[1]

The Report, the fruit of three years of ecumenical conversation, was substantially written before the Assembly convened. It was, in fact, largely a summary of a symposium of essays distributed to Sectional delegates in page-proofs, a volume whose lines of major emphasis had been settled at a meeting of the World Council's Study Commission at Cambridge, England, in August 1946, and progressively defined at two subsequent meetings held in June 1947 and August 1948, and through extensive correspondence by those primarily charged to write the final Report.

From the outset it had been decided that the diagnosis of the disorder of society would centre on two crystallizing ideas: '(a) the breakdown of personal relationships and the disintegration of family life, etc., as being the ultimate factor in the disintegration of society, and (b) the pervasive influence of the machine with its implications for good or ill.'[2] The responsibility of the churches for the disorder of society was to be frankly acknowledged and unabashedly detailed as resulting from the irrelevance of their

[1] The Drafting Committee was composed of: (Chairman) Dr. Constantijn L. Patijn (Dutch Reformed Church), (Secretary) Professor John C. Bennett (Congregational-Christian Churches of USA), Professor Emil Brunner (Swiss Protestant Federation), Canon V. A. Demant (Church of England), Sir Walter Moberly (Church of England), Professor Demetrios Moraitis (Church of Greece), Professor Barnabas Nagy (Reformed Church of Hungary), Professor Reinhold Niebuhr (Evangelical and Reformed Church), Mr. George V. Job (Church of South India), Professor Constantin von Dietze (Evangelical Church in Germany), Mr. Charles P. Taft (Protestant Episcopal Church, USA).

[2] Dr. Nils Ehrenström at Bossey, June 24, 1947. *Archives*. The studies of Professor David Riesman of the University of Chicago on the causes and manifestations of social change make a concentration on technics appear somewhat narrow. Cf. his *The Lonely Crowd, Faces in the Crowd* and *Individualism Reconsidered*.

theological teaching and the apathy or involvement of their institutional behaviour. It was finally felt apposite to call attention to promising developments, new beginnings of the relations of churches of different lands to contemporary society. This early conception of the scope of the future Assembly's Section on economic, political and cultural disorder was maintained through successive rearrangements of the material of the background volume and despite inevitable disappointments. Thus it proved impossible to obtain reports on the situation in the Soviet Union or Eastern Europe, though provision had been made for contributions on Russia, Poland and Czechoslovakia. The chapter analysing the social ills of Africa did not arrive. Conflicting explanations of the disturbed Asian scene suggested the solution of providing two accounts. The diagnoses of European and American contemporary civilizations, originally planned as the work of groups on each continent, were ultimately written in each case by a single author. An essay of impressive length, analysing the impact of technics on social living, was found to contain a pregnant adumbration of the outline of a social order satisfying Christian requirements and was, accordingly, divided into two chapters. All of this material was subjected to close scrutiny and repeated discussion through the circulation of the papers to interested individuals in the Ecumenical Community and at two full-scale meetings of the Study Commission in the three years before the Assembly convened. The majority of the members of the future Drafting Committee of Amsterdam's Section III participated in these discussions and were in a position to incorporate the common conception of the disorder of contemporary society and its remedy in the language of the Report. Indeed the authors of the paragraphs in the Report covering particular topics were in most cases those who had discussed the same themes in the symposium.

The eighty delegates to the Amsterdam Assembly who had asked to be assigned to the Section discussing 'The Church and the Disorder of Society', had for their guidance a background volume containing the following chapters:

1. An Introduction, written by Reinhold Niebuhr, delineating the social confusion of the times and the relation of the Christian Church to the crisis of our age.

2. 'Technics and Civilization', a chapter by J. H. Oldham outlining the effects of the machine and the scientific method on modern society, and the points of conflict with the Christian conception of man and his destiny.

3. 'The Situation in Europe', by Jacques Ellul.

4. 'The Situation in Asia—I', by M. Searle Bates.

5. 'The Situation in Asia—II', by M. M. Thomas.

6. 'The Situation in USA', by Reinhold Niebuhr.

7. 'Personal Relations in a Technical Society', an outline by Kathleen Bliss of how modern conditions affect the relations between the sexes, between generations, between neighbours.

8. 'The Involvement of the Church', by John C. Bennett.

9. 'New Beginnings in the Relations of the Church with Society', a report of Christian-inspired experiments of social transformation compiled by E. C. Urwin.

10. 'A Responsible Society', by J. H. Oldham.

11. 'The Strategy of the Church', chiefly an exposition of the economic and political problems to be faced, by C. L. Patijn.

12. 'And Now?', a conclusion by Emil Brunner.

The Report, produced by the Drafting Committee, approved by Section III and 'received unanimously by the Assembly and commended to the churches for their serious consideration and appropriate action' was a statement of six divisions, twenty-nine paragraphs in all. The divisions were:

1. 'The Disorder of Society', composed by Reinhold Niebuhr with a paragraph on the involvement of the churches by John C. Bennett.

2. 'Economic and Political Organization', drafted by C. L. Patijn, apart from a paragraph asserting the incapacity of the Church to arbitrate the debate on whether socialism is a solution or a menace, written by Reinhold Niebuhr.

3. 'The Responsible Society', the definition being that of Sir Walter Moberly with other paragraphs by C. L. Patijn.

4. 'Communism and Capitalism', six paragraphs written by John Bennett with suggestions from Professor Nagy and Dr. Patijn.

5. 'The Social Function of the Church', the language being Professor Bennett's save for a paragraph on Christian political parties by Dr. Patijn.

6. 'Conclusion', a final paragraph composed by Professor Bennett.

The authors of the Report were, it is evident, the principal collaborators in the preparatory study (apart from Oldham whose health was impaired) and the dominant minds of the Study Commission of Section III. They had moved past the generous generalities of the Stockholm Conference of 1925 which concluded that the problems it has considered in 'our friendly discussions'

> are so grave that they cannot be solved by individual effort alone, but that the community must accept responsibility for them, and must exercise such social control over individual action as in each instance may be necessary for the common good.[1]

The Amsterdam authors were the heirs of the Oxford Conference of 1937 which conceived of the Church as an organized community with a corporate responsibility and a specific function in the field of economic activity and political life.[2]

The Oxford emphasis had called for competent study and research in the economic sphere, laity and clergy co-operating in an effort of analysis; it had concluded that to change the economic order 'Christians must be prepared to take sides and participate in political and other forms of group action.' The Amsterdam studies had disengaged a fruitful idea, that of the Responsible Society, one calculated to catalyse positive and practical suggestions in line with the 'new creative solutions' called for in the Section III Report, economic and political arrangements which would harmonize the competing and often conflicting claims of justice and freedom.

---

[1] *Stockholm*, p. 712.

[2] 'The Christian message should deal with ends, in the sense of long-range goals, standards, and principles, in the light of which every concrete situation, and every proposal for improving it, must be tested. . . . [It] should throw a searchlight on the actual facts of the existing situation, and in particular reveal the human consequences of present forms of economic behaviour. . . . [It] should make clear the obstacles to economic justice in the human heart, and especially those that are present in the hearts of people within the Church.' *Oxford*, p. 90.

2. *Preparations for Evanston*

After the Amsterdam Assembly the Chairman of the Study Department felt that 'we are not lacking in theory, in the articulation of fundamental principles'. The time had come, he told the World Council's Central Committee in 1949, to redress the balance in emphasis between theory and practice. Accordingly, an inquiry, 'Christian Action in Society', containing two themes, 'The Responsible Society' and 'The Meaning of Work', was set on foot. The Secretary of the World Council's Department on Church and Society acknowledged that the project doubtless seemed pretentious.[1]

Ultimately at Evanston the 'Meaning of Work' theme, broadened to a consideration of the essential significance of all so-called 'secular' occupations and professions, occupied a Section entitled 'The Laity—the Christian in his Vocation'. Concrete social issues were assigned to the Section 'The Responsible Society in a World Perspective', charged to pursue the line of approach opened at Amsterdam. In a preliminary outline of the subject-matter of the Section the issues were listed under six headings: (*a*) The Role of the State in Economic Life and its Limits; (*b*) The Place of the Worker in Modern Industry and the Role of Organized Labour in Modern Society; (*c*) The Place of the Business Man in Modern Society; (*d*) The Economic and Social Development of the Under-developed Countries; (*e*) The Economic Responsibilities of the West; (*f*) The Responsibility of the Member-Churches in Relation to the Challenge of Communism.

As background for the discussions of the Assembly Sections at Evanston, a series of booklets was edited. The sixty-five-page

[1] 'To many realistic people it may seem paradoxical that the churches of the World Council should launch a new inquiry on Christian Action in Society at a time when the likelihood of any effective action appears so uncertain.... The great complexity of economic and social life today, the comprehensive character of the problems which confront men and which frequently seem beyond human control, and the strength of the forces of evil makes the possibility of significant improvements in community life seem slighter than ever before. In addition, the atmosphere of ill-will, suspicion and hatred which pervades the whole world has resulted in a feeling of despair about social change, especially in the West.' Paul Abrecht in *ER* II (Winter 1950), 2, p. 141.

summary, reporting recent thought and activity of the churches in the social field, prepared for the Section on 'The Responsible Society', was reviewed by its Preparatory Commission in draft form during the planning meetings at Begnins, August 11–19, 1953, and put in definitive form by the Study Department's permanent staff in nearby Geneva.[1] Compiled from descriptions of facts and trends supplied by ecumenical groups in different countries,[2] the Survey note that profound social changes present the Ecumenical Community with the need of fresh analyses as well as new tasks and opportunities. *Laissez-faire* capitalism, it was observed, is being replaced by the social welfare State while socialism on the other hand is reconsidering its basic principles. A fundamental rethinking of the goals of political and economic life was said to be occurring with the debate moving from the sterilities of comparing 'isms' to the more fruitful examination of actual social change, its causes and consequences. Moreover, the current argument in the Ecumenical Community was described as being not so much 'as in the past *whether* the Church has a responsibility in society but *what* precisely that responsibility is and *how* it can be realized'. The duty of Christians to seek what Amsterdam called 'new, creative solutions' to contemporary economic and political problems, to work for the construction of the Responsible Society, was not contested by any sizeable segment of the Ecumenical Community. Nevertheless, the Evanston Survey reported, 'there is also great apathy and indifference in the Church concerning social issues'. Tentative explanation of this situation was found in three factors: (*a*) the lack of a vital faith providing fresh theological insights illuminating the human predicament today and engendering a new determination to struggle for the renewal of society; (*b*) the new social situation in most countries, making outmoded familiar analyses in terms of 'isms' and presenting new problems for Christian social thought; (*c*) the world dimensions of social problems, implying a bewildering variety and an enormous

[1] And included in the book, *The Christian Hope and the Task of the Churches.*

[2] These reports are scheduled for publication in a symposium tentatively entitled, *National Developments in Christian Social Thinking.*

disparity in the problems confronting the Ecumenical Community, a complexity that discourages effort.

The changed situation suggested to the editors of the Survey four contemporary tasks which the churches everywhere must undertake: (a) the development of common convictions regarding the structure of political and economic life, the elaboration of a common ethos, the construction of a social philosophy, whatever its basis, which will provide criteria for judging contemporary social problems; (b) a re-examination of strategy to discover how the social function of the churches can most effectively be achieved; (c) the exposition of the basis of Christian hope, giving meaning to the world's search for more freedom, security, justice and the social and economic institutions for realizing them; (d) an emphasis on the responsibility of the churches to the economically and technically underdeveloped countries experiencing a social revolution.

The Preparatory Commission for Evanston's Section on the Responsible Society met twice before the Assembly, the session of August 1953 producing a memorandum to promote discussion on the topic in the churches. The delegates and consultants of the Section, numbering nearly one hundred, when they began their consideration of the subject at Evanston, expressed the conviction that an important subject had been neglected in the memorandum and working paper: the place of the family in the Responsible Society. The selection of the theme of the family by the 1953 German *Kirchentag* had given the subject new prominence in the Ecumenical Community.

To be sure, a wide range of subjects was broached at the Section meetings, manifesting the preoccupation of the delegates with the issues especially affecting their particular homelands and indicating their political orientation and ethical attitudes. It was the task of the Drafting Committee to harmonize these views and interests in a document which, as the expression of the consensus of the Section, could be submitted to the Assembly to be received as an official Report of the Second Assembly of the World Council of Churches and commended to the member churches for their study and appropriate action. The Secretary's Minutes indicate that the Drafting Committee was composed of nineteen members (including one woman), five from the United States and Canada, three from Asia, the rest Europeans; according to confessional allegiance the Committee was composed of five members from Reformed churches, five from the Free Church or United Church tradition, four Lutherans, four from the Anglican Communion and one Orthodox.[1]

3. *The Issues at Evanston*

The Drafting Committee was mindful of its mandate to indicate the relevance of the Main Theme of Christian Hope to its conclusions and did so in a brief introduction of affirmation that avoided the division of theological opinion on the implications of eschatology. An effort was made to clarify and deepen the term 'the Responsible Society' which was defined as a 'criterion' of judgment but was frequently used as synonymous with the satisfactory concrete social order which the Christian must work to achieve. Doctrinaire debates over social and political categories were recognized as fruitless in view of the changes in economic organization in different countries. These changes, it was noted, occasioned new problems involving the interplay of government, private enterprise and organized groups. In consequence the nature and function of the contemporary State was re-examined and, with the developments and dangers since the Oxford Conference of 1937 in mind, new judgments were framed. Conceding the importance of managerial skills and aware of the

---

[1] Members were: Professor John C. Bennett, USA, Congregational; Rev. Dr. Eugene C. Blake, USA, Presbyterian; Professor Panayotis Bratsiotis, Greece, Church of Greece; Rev. Joshua R. Chandran, India, Church of South India; Mrs. Kiyo Takeda Chou, Japan, Church of Christ; Rev. S. B. Coles, Canada, Presbyterian; Professor Dr. Egbert de Vries, The Netherlands, Protestant Church in Indonesia; Mrs. Rosamond Fisher, UK, Church of England; Rev. Canon Hugh G. G. Herklots, UK, Church of England; Mr. Peter K. Ledig, Germany, Evangelical; Dean Walter G. Muelder, USA, Methodist; Mr. Denys L. Munby, UK, Episcopal Church of Scotland; Dr. Constantijn Patijn, The Netherlands, Dutch Reformed; Bishop János Péter, Hungary, Reformed Church of Hungary; Bishop Enrique C. Sobrepena, Philippines, United Church of Christ; Professor Neils H. Soe, Denmark, Lutheran; Mr. Charles P. Taft, USA, Protestant Episcopal; Professor Constantin Von Dietze, Germany, Evangelical.

place of production as well as distribution in any economic system, the Section was, nevertheless, uneasy about some phases of modern social organization: its appeal to the acquisitive spirit, its great contrasts between rich and poor, its rivalry of occupational pressure groups neglectful of the common good, and its national particularism forgetful of the effects of domestic trade policies on other countries, particularly underdeveloped areas.

The question of the tensions resulting from the conflicts between communist and non-communist societies was considered by Evanston's Section III, not as an issue of international order but as a problem of the immediate duties of the Christian living in either type of society. The subject, relates the editor of the official edition of the Evanston Reports, 'provoked remarkably little debate and agreement was readily reached'.[1] The Section concluded its Report with a consideration of the problems of economically underdeveloped regions which demand international action and involve the interest of all the churches. Choosing the points raised at the Lucknow Ecumenical Study Conference of December 1952, the Evanston Report called attention to the need of developing viable political institutions corresponding to Asian and African traditions and capable of controlling the needed social and economic revolution in progress; land reform and rural development were underscored as of capital importance; the need of a balanced industrial development to raise standards of living was signalized; population pressure on resources was listed as a burning question; the responsibility of interdependence, with new national States proud of their sovereignty and needed foreign capital hesitant to invest without specific guarantees, was deemed a theme for definition and

[1] The four points of agreement were indicated as: '(a) To reaffirm the statement of Amsterdam about the points of conflict between Christian faith and totalitarian communism; (b) to call attention to the strong appeal of communism in particular areas of Asia, Latin America, Africa and Europe where there is a deep desire for social justice; (c) to stress the dangers of an attitude of hysterical fear of communism and of overemphasizing the military aspect in the defence against communist power; (d) to emphasize the need for Christians in communist and non-communist countries to hold each other in special brotherly concern and prayer across all barriers.' *Evanston Speaks*, p. 44.

general acceptance, if bitterness and frustration are to be avoided in the advance of underdeveloped regions.

A single item in the Report on the Responsible Society was changed after its presentation to the full Assembly. By a narrow vote the Evanston delegates preferred to specify, among the points in need of social change, 'a stronger regard for equity in the distribution of wealth and income'. With whatever implications of political preferences and predilections, the Drafting Committee had opted for a larger measure of 'equality'.

Early reaction to the Evanston Report on Social Questions indicated that it was considered a 'balanced and unpartisan judgment'.[1] It was undoubtedly planned as such. While the importance of the family was stressed, caution was expressed against family egotism hindering social responsibility. The need of State initiative and international organization in the development of economic life was recognized, but warning was issued against the union of political and economic power producing an all-controlling State. Former criticism of monopolistic and irresponsible business practices was not withdrawn but contributions of the skilled executive and the incentives for responsible initiative and hard work provided by the business system and resulting in economic progress were freely conceded. Trade unions and professional associations were welcomed but their responsibility to the whole of society was emphasized. The double danger of communism and anti-communism was underscored and the complex problems of competing interests in the social revolutions of the underdeveloped countries were indicated.

The delegates to Evanston and their fellow church-members who studied the fruits of the discussions of the Second Assembly of the World Council of Churches on the political and economic issues of the hour should have had no illusions that the construction of the Responsible Society was a simple task. Indeed they were warned: 'In all these fields, the real dangers are complacency, lack of imagination and the dull sense of hopelessness that settles upon those of little faith.'

[1] For example, the editorial in the *Christian Century* LXXI (September 22, 1954), 38, pp. 1132 ff.

ii. The Disorder of Society

'One social era is passing away and a new one is being born'; with these words the delegates to the World Council's Second Assembly were alerted in a preparatory study.[1] The causes of this 'vast social upheaval' and its particular manifestations were not of essential concern to the Evanston Assembly as they had been at Amsterdam. Evanston, it might be said, proposed to deal with the issues in the political and economic realms rather than with the ills besetting the world. Its declared interest was with the new tasks and opportunities for Christian witness in the social order. The approach was possibly more profitable. However, the analysis by the organized Ecumenical Community in 1948 of what it termed the 'social crisis of unparalleled proportions' has at the very least an historical interest, and yields profitable insights of the points of view then current in the World Council constituency.

1. The Amsterdam Diagnosis: Moral Inertia in the Machine Age

The Amsterdam Assembly's Section III found that the deepest cause of contemporary social disorder 'is the refusal of men to see and admit that their responsibility to God stands over and above their loyalty to any earthly community and their obedience to any worldly power'. The Christian faith, the Report declared, provided at once a personal certainty sufficient to surmount all temptations to apathy, irresponsibility and despair and a divine command 'to overcome the specific disorders which aggravate the perennial evil in human society'. Two chief factors contributing to the contemporary crisis were indicated. Attention was first called to the vast concentrations of economic and political power which magnify individual and group greed, pride and cruelty and by their sheer inertia diminish the ability of modern man to act as a moral and accountable being. The dominance of

[1] *CHTC*, p. 3. The marks of this social change were noted as 'the decline of old social and economic ideologies and institutions, the social effects of continued rapid technical change, the complete shake-up of old patterns of life in Asia, Africa and Latin America, the increasing economic and political interdependence of nations and the effects of the continuing struggle between communist and non-communist countries'. *Ibid.*

technics was signalized as another factor. While relieving men and women of much drudgery and poverty, providing channels of communication between distant peoples and improving the physical health of mankind, technological developments were found to be accompanied by a mechanization of life, an unbalanced economy, the wasting of natural resources, war, and 'the undermining of the natural foundations of society in family, neighbourhood and craft'. Technology, however, it was believed, can be controlled and 'the Christian Church has an urgent responsibility today to help men to achieve fuller personal life within the technical society'. The fulfilment of that responsibility, in the judgment of the Amsterdam Report, will be reparation for past failings. For, despite the presence of Christians in movements of social reform, the churches must plead guilty, it was conceded, of having favoured the privileged classes, of having concentrated on purely spiritual or individualistic interpretations of the Gospel or of having missed the meaning of rising social forces and, in consequence, 'they have been unprepared to deal creatively with new problems as they have arisen in technical civilization'.

In attributing contemporary social disorder to the religious apostasy of Western civilization, the Amsterdam Report had ignored the warning of the Chairman of the Section's Study Commission. In his introductory chapter of diagnosis in the background volume, Reinhold Niebuhr had written that such an interpretation assumed 'that it is possible to define the order of God in detailed and specific laws and rules of justice', an arrogant absurdity since 'God's order can never be identified with some specific form of social organisation'.[1] In Dr. Niebuhr's judgment we are experiencing the inevitable consequences of the failure to adapt institutions to changing economic conditions. Industrialism, he argued, destroyed the organic and traditional forms of society and, as the instrument of imperialism, planted the seeds

[1] CDS, p. 14. Another contributor to the preparatory volume, Professor Jacques Ellul, argued at a meeting of the Section III Preparatory Commission that the diagnosis should start from God's given order, since 'the present desperate situation of the world brought us to see more clearly the concrete topical relevance of that order of God which is revealed in the Scriptures'. Archives.

of conflict in the international field. The conflict between the proletariat and the middle classes, the absence of real community, are manifestations of modern man's inability to achieve tolerable justice and basic security in a civilization created by technological developments. Society, in short, has not learned to live with its own inventions and aspirations. The churches share the culpability for our present plight, for 'Historic Christianity failed to implement the moral imperatives of the love commandment under the new conditions of a technical age.'[1] As a result, political religions have arisen offering rationalizations of society's predicament and solutions of man's personal problems of insecurity and insignificance, solutions which have only aggravated the problems.

The debate on the underlying causes of contemporary social ills was never joined at Amsterdam nor in the preparatory conferences of Section III. Because of a paucity of resources and time (and, doubtless, to avoid controversy), it had early been decided to omit any explicit historical inquiry into the forces shaping Western civilization. How decisively secularism determined the trend of modern history, how it arose, what are its characteristic manifestations and consequences were not explored. A summary religious judgment was expressed.

The two ideas which were chosen as a focus for the diagnosis of the ills of modern society—the breakdown of personal relationships and the disintegration of family life, and the pervasive influence of the machine for good or ill—were subsequently termed indifferently 'factors', 'characteristics', 'occasions', 'forms', and even 'negative causes'. At bottom, the subject preoccupying Amsterdam's thinking on cultural, political and ecumenical affairs was the consequences of modern industrialism.[2]

[1] *Op. cit.*, p. 20. The inherent difficulties are examined later in the section, 'Corporate Christian Influence on Society'.

[2] Commentators to whom the preliminary text of the preparatory volume was submitted pointed out other elements, mentioning the enormous increase in population in modern times, the effect of migrations, the change in the average age-level, the intrusion of the irrational in the field of philosophy, the prevalence of education which ignores values; the general lines of the diagnosis were accepted without reservation, however, and pessimistic conclusions conceded.

The description of the advent and effects of technology, written for the background volume by Dr. J. H. Oldham, owed much to the thought of Lewis Mumford.[1] 'Science and technics,' it was argued, 'had their origin in man's legitimate desire to understand the world, to control it for his own purposes, to add to his knowledge, wealth and power.'[2] The results were deemed to be on the whole negative, technical skills having outdistanced man's social capacities. Man, it was judged, is being conditioned by his environment and his environment is susceptible to manipulation by newly discovered social techniques. 'Science has become an instrument of power, and the disinterestedness of the thinker and the spirit of contemplation of former times have given place increasingly to the drive of the organizer and promoter.'[3] The temper of the technological era was found to be in conflict with Christianity on several scores, basically because it is an expression of a two-dimensional universe within whose assumptions no answers can be found for the meaning of life, a question supposing 'belief in a spiritual reality transcending the world of time and space with which science and technics are concerned'. The challenge to such assumptions, the clearing of the intellectual climate breeding false values, Dr. Oldham concluded, calls for a change in the deep-rooted attitudes to life, a genuine *metanoia* which should commence among Christians first.

The effect of technology on personal living was outlined by Mrs. Kathleen Bliss for the background volume in a chapter sketching the changing relations between the sexes, the generations and neighbours brought about by the division of labour, the manpower demands and the standardization of time schedules of the industrialized age. Technical society was deemed to have

---

[1] A British commentator, a layman, declared himself bluntly 'out of sympathy with the whole line and character of the chapter', terming it an 'amalgam of the work of "clever" publicists and armchair theorists, the type of people who can produce "striking" arguments as to how things might (theoretically) happen but who never bother to ask themselves whether they do, in fact, happen that way'. The critic concluded that it would be 'perilous' to put such analysis 'before the academic ecclesiastics who are likely to be at Amsterdam'. *Archives.*

[2] *CDS*, p. 43.   [3] *Ibid.*

created 'impersonal categories, groupings and interests under the names "capital", "labour", "consumers", and the like, and threatens to fall apart into self-interested groups which the State must attempt to hold together'.[1] How a sense of common membership can be instilled in modern society, an impersonal association of complicated, interdependent parts, so that the riches of community life can become a living reality to the ordinary man was felt to be the great question. Since the chapter was concerned with analysis, no answers were offered.

The differing modes in which the disorder of contemporary society manifested itself in various parts of the world was the subject of separate studies made for the volume prepared for the guidance of the delegates to the Assembly's Section III. The situation in Europe was described by Jacques Ellul, Professor in the Faculty of Law, Bordeaux, in unrelieved terms of gloom.[2] Presumably aided by other collaborators, Professor Ellul concluded that 'the last traces of European civilization are disappearing',[3] its spiritual foundations are being rejected, its traditional values are proving themselves impotent to guide and co-ordinate the dominant forces which are evolving in anarchy out of human control. These forces were listed as the inhuman power of the State,[4] the primacy of production,[5] the extreme

[1] CDS, p. 90.

[2] An Indian commentator wrote with evident satisfaction that reading Professor Ellul's paper 'was like reading Mahatma Gandhi'. Archives.

[3] Oral observation of Professor Ellul at the meeting of Commission III, Bossey, June 26, 1947. The Professor's pessimism was thoroughgoing: he objected during the discussion to the judgment that the machine is neutral, that its effects for good or ill depend on the use made of it, arguing that, since the Fall, man is not free to choose between good or evil in the use of the machine and can use it only for evil purposes. The world, moreover, is the domain of Satan under the Lordship of Christ. Ibid.

[4] 'More than in the rest of the world (even in Russia) it seems that the dominant element in Europe is the State.' '. . . everyone in Europe assumes that the State provides the solution for all problems. This is true even of democrats and liberals: what they want is a different kind of State, but they do not want to change the nature of the State in its technical form (police, finance) which actually determines everything else.' CDS, p. 53.

[5] 'It does not occur to anyone to challenge the idea that man exists in order to produce more and more . . . if we wish to make a serious analysis of our economic difficulties and of the breakdown of humanist civilisation, we must bear in mind that one of its essential causes is this assumption that "production must come first". I do not mean that "over-production" is the cause of the crisis. It has nothing to do with it.' Ibid., p. 54.

development of technics,[1] and war.[2] As a result, the European has become a mass-man, living in a totalitarian society 'even if no explicitly totalitarian doctrine is invoked'. The diagnosis discerned no signs of health anywhere,[3] save in the realization of the Church's mission to the world among a 'remnant' preserved by God.

To diagnose under the title 'The Situation in Asia' the disorder experienced by half the world's population, a concentrated mass of people of diverse cultural patterns inhabiting the immense plains and teeming islands of the Far East, is an effort of comprehension displaying no small courage. Such an analysis must cover with valid generalizations the hill primitives of Thailand and the industrial workers of Japan, the Pakistani Moslem and the Chinese Stalinist, the Borneo animist and the Indian intellectual. The contradictory comments made, not least by Asians, on the summary prepared for the Amsterdam volume by Dr. M. S. Bates, Professor of History at the University of Nanking, a modest scholar well aware of the complexities of the theme assigned to him, might well suggest a certain tentativeness to lay political observers as they interpret current developments in the Far East. In the opinion of Dr. Bates, 'The issues of modern industry and its urban life are faced directly by only small minorities of the Asiatic peoples, except in Japan', since 'the great masses of Asia live by agriculture'. This multitudinous agricultural proletariat the missionary educator saw sunk in a materialism more primitive and more prevalent than the materialism of the machine in the Ruhr or at Pittsburgh, a materialism of 'mass hunger and the insecure toil of human backs', for 'population crowds upon subsistence with unrelenting pressure'. This vast human mass is in ferment undergoing radical political reorganization while former

---

[1] 'Europe as a whole no longer believes in these technics—and no longer has the strength nor the spiritual elevation nor the social organization required to enable it to control the technical instruments which it is being induced to employ. Thus Europe is being led to follow a path which is no longer its own.' Ibid., p. 55.

[2] 'European society is entirely built up on a war basis (in this direction Europe has gone farther than the rest of the world which is moving in the same direction).' Ibid.

[3] Ibid., pp. 61–71.

imperialism retreats. The reorganization is accompanied by cruelty and despotism.[1]

Nationalism was judged the fuel of this ferment in Asia and industrialization the means inflexibly pursued by its determined organizers: 'They want to increase the tangible strength of their respective States as against Western political and economic control and by imitation of Western States.' For these determined leaders of an assertive nationalism, the Soviet system was said to offer an idealized stereotype of success against outside enemies, of the conquest of illiteracy and racial discrimination, of the triumph over landlordism, colonialism and economic exploitation of others, of the victory of modern technology at the service of a directing intelligence.[2] Sovietism, however, is the inspiration and the exemplar, not the controlling force, in the judgment of this experienced American observer writing in 1947: 'It must be reiterated that in Asia even communism does not rival nationalism, still driven by the impetus of protest and fresh ambition, the greatest single emotion socially effective.'[3] Under the shock of awakened nationalism the conservative religious cultures of Asia are faltering and Dr. Bates could not surmise how successfully they will make the painful adaption to the emerging civilization. Certainly, he felt, the insignificant Christian minority in Asia— 30 millions in a mass of 1,110 millions—can scarcely have a direct influence on the outcome.

The Asian critics of Dr. Bates's chapter, particularly the Indians, found his analysis superficial but their comments tended to confirm his judgment on nationalism as the primary factor in Far Eastern developments and the organization of the masses as the preoccupation of Asiatics.[4]

[1] 'Asia has no established tradition of individual or group rights guaranteed against arbitrary authority, no sound basis for democratic organisation on a national scale, despite recent imitation of Western liberal forms in the Philippines and elsewhere.' CDS, p. 64.

[2] 'To the Asiatic who finds in the ways of past or present no possible escape from individual or national poverty, Russia offers a sharp, confident analysis of the hell he is in, a social saviour with all the plausible advantages of omnipotent system.' Ibid., p. 65.

[3] Ibid., p. 66.

[4] Typical comments: 'The proletarian movement has already achieved marvellous results in abolishing slums, the joint control of industry, the sharing of profits and in shifting industrial enterprise from the hands of the shareholders to the national

To balance the viewpoint of a Western scholar, the editors of the background volume for the Amsterdam Assembly decided to invite an Indian to furnish another analysis of 'The Situation in Asia'.[1] The chapter written by M. M. Thomas, then a secretary at the World's Student Christian Federation headquarters in Geneva, is mainly an exposition of the Christian responsibility for Asia's future and a prescription of the proper tactic to follow.[2] Denying the existence of overpopulation as a factor,[3] Mr. Thomas deemed the disorders of the Far East only an extension of the evils of Western industrialism in its imperialist manifestation: 'Asia has in large measure become the "agricultural farm" of the West, producing raw materials for the machines in the West, and absorbing their finished goods.' Rural poverty was seen as the result of the colonial policy of Western industrial nations, and Asian nationalism the inevitable protest. None of the forces active on the Asian scene except Christianity, however, was thought capable of contributing to the emerging civilization the essential ingredient, the idea of responsible personality. The obligation on Asian Christians, then, is particularly heavy. In Mr. Thomas's view the implications of that obligation are also

plane.' '. . . The disorder is a result of Western policies. Progress will come out of the ferment, e.g. labour unions. . . .' '. . . It is my considered judgment that Asia is a potential field for socialism either under the auspices of nationalism or in spite of it. The masses everywhere, whether in the West or East, are for One World under a single government and the greatest hindrance to the formation of a world state does not, perhaps, come from Soviet Russia but it does come from the power-seeking politicians of the West and the economic control the West rightly or unjustly has maintained over decades.' '. . . The core of the problem is the struggle for justice, equality and freedom—all else is subordinate. . . .' '. . . Western imperialism is not retracting but only changing tactics and hands.' '. . . So far as Asia is concerned these revolutionary Communist Parties are the one bulwark of liberal ideas and liberal values. . . .' 'All modern governments are dictatorial, Constitutions are an eye-wash and the world is run by a dictatorial party or dictators with a pompous show of popular consent.' '. . . In India women participate in public life which is not so in United States.' *Archives*. Only India and China, it must be added, supplied spokesmen.

[1] Ironically, a group of ten Asians who read the chapter in Geneva found it deficient in objectivity though conceding that it represented 'a very common Asiatic attitude'. The author was described as 'a Western man talking to the West'. *Ibid*. The problems of the World Council's Study Department in finding collaborators who are at once representative, objective and authentic are manifestly not meagre.

[2] In *CDS*, pp. 71–9.

[3] Both Chinese and Indian commentators were insistent that population pressure was not the root cause of poverty, one claiming that 'Asiatics have increased 30 per cent in the last 300 years, Europeans, excluding the Irish, 300 per cent'. *Archives*.

clear: it requires Asians to share in the struggle against the West
so that responsible governments and tolerable conditions of
existence for the peoples may be achieved.[1]

Only three pages were required to present the diagnosis of
social disorder in the United States in the chapter of the background volume prepared for the Amsterdam delegates. In the
view of the author, Reinhold Niebuhr: 'Since America belongs
in general to the European world in terms of both its culture and
the economic and political institutions of its civilization, there is
no need for a separate full discussion of the American situation.'[2]
Dr. Niebuhr noted some differences: 'the stronger hold which
the creeds of older classical liberalism have upon political and
economic theory in America than in Europe', the absence of
Marxist convictions in the trade union movement, the greater
wealth which 'makes it less necessary, or at least makes it seem to
be less necessary, to establish the kind of controls by which
European nations seek to extend or to restore justice';[3] and the

---

[1] Mr. Thomas was nothing if not concrete: 'In certain countries like Indonesia and
Indo-China it means active participation in armed conflict against the Western European
powers; in the rest of Asia the war is no less real though not so open. . . . Many Christians,
like the writer himself, see in the united front and the coalition programmes of the Asian
nationalism of the Left, the only sane *political way* out of civil war, communal riots,
political domination and intolerable living conditions of the mass of the people.' CDS,
pp. 78–9.

[2] Was Dr. Niebuhr being disingenuous here? Several of his colleagues on Amsterdam's
Preparatory Commission III at least doubted that Europe and the United States constituted a common civilization. It was the argument of Professor Ellul some fifteen pages
earlier in the symposium that 'the situation of the European man is desperate' in part
because of the menace of the values represented by American society.

[3] The American business man would say that this is an *ignoratio elenchi*, that it supposes
that the kinds of controls imposed by European governments are necessary or desirable
in the United States. A World Council collaborator, evidently from American business
circles, commented with scarcely concealed hostility: 'As Mr. Niebuhr's Socialist leanings
are not deducible from theological principles or dogmas, it is only fair to ask where they
come from and if he speaks on the subject with any particular authority by virtue of his
theological attainments. There is a tendency, I believe, for theologians to put laymen at a
disadvantage by assuming a moral superiority over them. This leads them to pontificate
on mundane matters on which they are no wiser than the average citizen. I suspect that
Professor Niebuhr has the impression that his views on Socialism and Capitalism somehow
gain weight because of his distinction as a theologian and that he is not averse to selling a
mundane bill of goods on transcendental grounds. I respect an honest Socialist. Moreover, I have no objection to an argument over the merits of socialism, if my opponent is
prepared to debate the issue on the level of common sense. But, frankly, I find nothing in
Professor Niebuhr's paper concrete enough to sink my teeth into or even to support a

higher degree of social freedom and fluidity. Dr. Niebuhr disbelieved, however, that American experience had made any unique discoveries.[1] It was conceded that the great productive power of America may ease or even obscure for decades the inherent problems created by a technical society, but, Dr. Niebuhr reaffirmed, the basic situation is the same throughout the world and the task of creating community in modern industrial civilization is similar, 'whatever may be the superficial differences on this or that continent'.

The overall diagnosis of the disorder of society presented in the Section III reports resulted in a sombre picture, relieved only by the declaration of the assurance of Christians 'of the final victory over all sin and death through Christ'. The prognosis was indefinite, the Report contenting itself with the statement that 'no inescapable necessity' prejudiced the future, and invoking the responsibility of the Church to rescue men from the tyranny of technology and help them to achieve a fuller personal life. In undertaking such an enterprise the churches were reminded of their past failures and asked not to forget 'to what extent they themselves have contributed to the very evils which they are tempted to blame wholly on the secularization of society'. The indictment was phrased for the Report by Professor John C. Bennett who had contributed an acute analysis[2] of the concrete involvement of religious groups in the current practices of the contemporary social order for a background volume of the

legitimate controversy. If he is disaffected with modern capitalism, including the American variety, as he obviously is, that is his affair. All of us criticize it in some respects and most of us are keenly aware that it needs improvement. But should a spokesman for the Protestant Churches of America raise the flag of socialism without first validating his stand by reasoned argument?' *Archives.*

[1] 'It is probably true, however, that the conditions which created a peculiar American political philosophy have a rather short-range efficacy, and that in time America will have to learn that the maintenance of both freedom and order, of both liberty and equality, is just as difficult as the European nations have found it to be.' *CDS*, p. 82. The year of the Evanston Assembly, two internationally renowned economists and students of cultural change disputed the judgment that the American system was only superficially different. Adolf A. Berle, Jr., published *The Twentieth Century Capitalist Revolution* and Professor William E. Rappard offered his analysis, *A Quoi Tient la Supériorité Economique des Etats Unis?*

[2] 'The Causes of Social Evil', in *Christian Faith and the Common Life*, pp. 175 ff.

Oxford Conference of 1937 and who edited suggestions of several collaborators for a chapter in the Amsterdam series of preparatory studies, indicating how frequently the churches have served as instruments of national, class and racial policies, unfaithful to their professed principles in their investment and hiring practices.

It will be evident that the diagnosis of the disorder of contemporary society found in the Amsterdam Report represents a synthesis of the attitudes of volunteers drawn from the ecumenical constituency. In the nature of things it was a judgment on the times by religious-minded men whose opinions derive more directly from theology than from economic analysis, sociological surveys or historical research.[1] The method has manifest limitations. Indeed the World Council Study Department recognizes 'how inadequately equipped the churches still are when it comes to investigating and realistically assessing facts and trends in their own situation'. That realization was a result of a year-long programme of fact-finding and of consultation with denominational and interdenominational agencies and individual correspondents throughout the world in an endeavour to prepare material for the Evanston Assembly.

2. The Evanston Diagnosis: New Arenas of Social Conflict

Polled five years after the Amsterdam Assembly, the World Council constituency supplied material for a survey of ecumenical opinion which was a more measured, more comprehensive and, it might be added, less pessimistic outline of 'The World Social Revolution' in progress. The brochure recognized 'the basic changes which have taken place in recent decades', reaffirmed a

---

[1] This is not an occupational hazard peculiar to ecclesiastics. Intellectuals (who must call for help to change a tyre on a motor-car) are prone to praise the Chaplin film, *Modern Times*, as an accurate picture of the helpless industrial worker caught in the meshes of the devouring monster, the machine, forgetting that Edwin Markham's poetic reflections on the vacuous, brutalized 'Man with the Hoe' were provoked on seeing Millet's painting of a peasant. The vogue of Robert Jungk's description of American society as dominated by soulless technocrats, *Le Futur a déjà Commencé*, is a case in point. The supposition that it is somehow ennobling to pick cotton by hand but depersonalizing to tend harvesting machines indicates an intrusion of Romanticism in unsuspected quarters. How the present population of the world, which has more than doubled in less than a century, can be fed and clothed without the aid of modern industry is never suggested.

belief in continuing social reform, indicated the global dimensions of economic problems, underlined the inadequacy of analysis in terms of 'isms' and ideologies, and modestly conceded that the complexity of the problems had occasioned among the churches an uncertainty of the precise nature of their social responsibility and the concrete means of exercising it.[1]

First among the significant changes on which the survey volume focused attention was what it termed 'the decline of classical Capitalism'. The editors did not mean to suggest that privately owned commercial and financial institutions are disappearing. Their intention was to underline the fact that the specifically nineteenth-century creed and organization known as Economic Liberalism has been domesticated, that belief in the automatic working of a free market as the mechanism to establish justice has been largely discredited, that the independence of economic activity from social, particularly governmental, control has been successfully challenged. Recalling the dangers connected with capitalism listed by the 1937 Oxford Conference, the Evanston preparatory study noted: 'There are areas of the world where these criticisms still apply but in many countries these specific social evils have been substantially alleviated through social reform.' Whatever the names, generally themes of partisan controversy, associated with the political instruments of these movements of social reform, they have all combated the defenders of the autonomy of economic practices and have successfully achieved legal recognition of some common goals.[2]

[1] CHTC, pp. 3–10.

[2] In the language of a recent report of the Social Commission of the Dutch Ecumenical Council: 'If we look back on the history of the last half-century in the West, the institution we now call the welfare state is seen to be dominated above all by (a) the protection of the weak by authority; (b) the campaign to achieve a juster social order; (c) an effort to do away with the causes of the defects in the economic structure.' Quoted in CHTC, p. 34. Addressing the Economic Club of Detroit, Professor Arthur F. Burns, Chairman of the US President's Council of Economic Advisers, explained: 'Today it is no longer a matter of serious controversy whether the Government should play a positive role in helping to maintain a high level of economic activity. What we debate nowadays is not the need of controlling business cycles but rather the nature of government action, its timing and its extent.' New York Times, October 19, 1954.

Indeed the very success of these social reform movements presents the churches with awkward questions of future policy. The Survey report from the United States observed that political and social developments in that country have realized most of the hopes represented by 'The Social Ideals of the Churches', the celebrated document, twice revised by the Federal Council of Churches. The changes brought about in England in recent years, noted the Survey's chapter 'Trends in Great Britain', and the 'general acceptance by society of the ends which Christians had set before themselves', has led to uncertainty and doubt as to what the future of the social teaching of the churches should be. In post-war Germany, it was pointed out, Christian opinion concedes that the debate on 'capitalism versus socialism' is *passé* and that the immediate problem concerns the finding of the right combination of freedom and control in economic life.

Closely related to the decline of *laissez-faire* capitalism both as a philosophy and a fact, in the opinion of the editors of the Evanston survey volume, has been the 'de-Marxizing' of Socialism. Reviewing a number of declarations of representative Socialist groups, they felt that recent events, particularly the events of two world wars and the encounter with totalitarian governments, has cauterized the optimistic assumption of the inevitability of progress produced by economically determined laws of history and has caused the progressive abandonment of doctrinaire materialism in Socialist thinking. This recognition of the perils of seeking justice through collectivism, this new emphasis on the importance of freedom for the individual, this new openness to the spiritual values of the person found in contemporary Socialist literature was deemed to offer new opportunities for the churches as they think out the possibilities of democratic planning.[1]

---

[1] Were the editors too sanguine or, perhaps, too selective in neglecting Socialist opinion in Latin countries? While they were reading proof-sheets of the survey volume, an important by-election took place in France's Department of Seine-et-Oise with the European Defence Community, approved at the Brussels meeting of Socialist Parties, as the declared primary issue. Though all the candidates had agreed in advance to withdraw

The pre-Evanston Survey found the spiritual situation in Europe 'partly static and partly dynamic' (in the words of Dr. Visser 't Hooft) and pointed to the painful efforts being made, despite the devastation wrought by the war and the cost of the rearmament programme, to deal with unemployment, housing and the rights of workers in industry, to construct supranational agencies of economic and political co-operation and to make the adjustments resulting from the separation of Eastern and Western Europe.[1]

The analysis of Asian problems was free of all political partisanship; it agreed, nevertheless, that Asian society—and indeed all the underdeveloped countries of the world—was undergoing a radical change

> by movements for political independence and self-determination in economic matters, by industrialization and the organization of economic and social life on functional rather than on traditional lines, by the spread of new convictions about the nature of the universe and the meaning of human life and by the revolt against enslaving and exploiting institutions.[2]

New forms of social organization were emerging, heavy with promise and menace, whose lineaments no man could clearly foresee.

Finally, the Survey noted among recent social changes the growing economic interdependence of all countries, so that the welfare of the entire human race falls within the range of social policy. 'Success in the creation of new societies in Asia, Africa, the Middle East and Latin America is vital for the welfare of the world', is a judgment indicating the importance the editors attached to the breadth of understanding required by the needs of our times.

from the final ballot in favour of the one who obtained the highest votes in the preliminary election against the Communist Party candidate, André Stil, the editor of L'Humanité, the Socialist Party candidate persisted in the race when a member of the Mouvement Républicain Populaire topped the list of 'national' candidates. The single reason the Socialist gave for not withdrawing was that 'les électeurs laïques' had to be represented in the election.

[1] CHTC, pp. 28–41.
[2] Ibid., p. 41.

3. The Difference in Diagnosis

The diagnosis prepared for the Second Assembly, it will be noticed, was quite summary, scarcely more than a necessary preliminary to outlining the positive tasks of the Section—to think through some of the implications of the topic, 'The Responsible Society in a World Perspective'. If the generally pessimistic tone of the pre-Amsterdam volume is missing, several reasons may be suggested for its absence. Amsterdam's Section III was concerned by definition with disorders, and a negative task induces almost inevitably a negative viewpoint. Furthermore, whatever be the theoretical view of the industrial civilization of the West and its effects on the human personality, it has shown a vitality, unsuspected perhaps in 1948. European production since that year has laboriously gained and exceeded pre-war levels and the United States economy, the exemplar when not the stereotype of that civilization, has manifested a durability and a resilience that has surprised many a prophet of doom.

It may not be without significance that the more impersonal yet less theoretical Evanston preparatory material was edited by the World Council's Study Department. A broader, more balanced judgment can be expected in a synthesis of many reports than in a symposium of what are, perforce, the viewpoints of individuals.[1] The Geneva Secretariat has before it, moreover, as an example of a serious research project of economic realities and their political and social consequences, the six-volume series on *Christian Ethics and Economic Life*, recently published in the United States. Undertaken in 1949 with the aid of a grant from the Rockefeller Foundation and sponsored by the Department of Churches and Economic Life of the National Council of Churches, the project benefited from the talents and research of professional economists, theologians and authoritative spokesmen of all the essential segments of the American economy. Finally,

---

[1] Contacts with East Europe having become more and more tenuous since the Amsterdam Assembly, only scanty information on conditions in what has been called 'The Dark Side of the Moon' was available for the pre-Evanston Survey. No representatives from that area appeared at the two-week study session of the 'Responsible Society' Preparatory Commission, held in Begnins in August 1953 to approve definitely a statement for the Section.

the location of the World Council's Study Department may well have contributed a larger serenity to the pre-Evanston Survey. It is difficult to sustain for long a metaphysical *angoisse* or brood overmuch about modern man, chained to a pitiless monster of a machine or enslaved by the ogre of the totalitarian State, when living in the midst of Switzerland's sturdy, diversified economy, protected by its political traditions of personal independence.

iii. THE ECONOMIC AND POLITICAL ORGANIZATION OF SOCIETY

In the course of the editorial work of preparing the analysis of the disorders of society for the Amsterdam background volume, one of the contributors, Dr. J. H. Oldham, suggested a question of capital importance. 'Given the conditions of a technical society,' he asked, 'what are the political and economic arrangements which Christians ought to favour for the preservation of the human values involved in the Christian conception of man and what action (if any) can or ought the Church to take to further such arrangements?' 'Political and economic arrangements' are a paraphrase for what sociologists and political scientists call 'institutions', and variously define as 'the established forms or conditions of procedure characteristic of group activity' (MacIver), or 'the social structure and machinery through which human society organizes, directs and executes the multifarious activities required to satisfy human needs' (Barnes).

Unfortunately, Dr. Oldham's question was not seriously pursued at either Commission or Sectional meetings to the point of defining the institutions required. Among the reasons for this was probably the traditional determination of the Ecumenical Movement not to identify Christianity with any particular political or economic system, the diversity of theological views in the World Council constituency on the nature and scope of the State and the absence of technically equipped participants in the discussions.[1] As a result, it is particularly the paragraphs entitled

[1] The only trained economist present at the meeting (June 25, 1947) of Preparatory Commission III, Dr. C. L. Patijn, introduced a note of the concrete during a discussion

'Economic and Political Organization' of Amsterdam's Section III Report that justify the judgment of Professor J. M. Clark of Columbia University that the Assembly's declaration on economic problems 'was significant, but more in terms of general attitudes than specific issues', a verdict endorsed by the Memorandum of the Preparatory Commission for the Evanston Assembly on 'The Responsible Society', meeting at Begnins, Switzerland, in mid-August 1953.[1]

1. Social Mechanisms

The question of attitudes towards specific social institutions is one on which the mind of the Ecumenical Movement is seemingly still in gestation. Whatever vagueness may have bemused the delegates to the Stockholm Conference of 1925, they shared the sanguine expectation of the times that with more good will mankind would continue to march towards ever-expanding prosperity and securer peace. The Oxford Conference of 1937, on the other hand, knew that there exists a permanent problem of social mechanisms channelling economic activity and organizing political life. Technics, it was pointed out, have increased prodigiously man's power so that the means of abolishing the kind of poverty which cripples the human personality are already available.[2] A change of heart, a new spiritual orientation, it was acknowledged, is a palpable necessity, but the principle of personal charity, it was argued, cannot dispense with the complex and mundane tasks of the social order nor does a warm heart substitute for the cold duty of thinking through the institutional forms that best express and maintain in equilibrium the manifold demands of social justice.[3] Convened eleven years later, the Amsterdam Assembly was likewise aware of the pressing,

on the menace of the State by pointing out that only *governments* could administer the Marshall Plan, then under consideration as a means of overcoming the financial breakdown in Europe by the co-operation of different nations. *Archives.*

[1] *ER* VI (October 1953), 1, p. 77.   [2] *Oxford,* p. 103.

[3] 'Christianity becomes socially futile if it does not recognize that love must will justice and that the Christian is under an obligation to secure the best possible social and economic structure, in so far as such structure is determined by human decisions.' *Ibid.*, p. 95. The phrasing suggests Reinhold Niebuhr as the author.

world-wide 'need for stability in the value of money, for creation of capital and for incentives in production'; it recognized that 'coherent and purposeful ordering of society has now become a major necessity', since—as Section III insisted—'justice demands that economic activities be subordinated to social ends'.[1]

Because economic activity had not been subordinated to social ends, it was averred, the disorders earlier diagnosed had arisen. Technological efficiency was becoming an end in itself, imperilling the essential dignity of the person: 'vast millions of people [are] exposed to insecurity, hunger and frustration by periodic inflation and depression', collected 'into great industrial cities' and deprived of 'those forms of human association in which men can grow most fully as persons'. These conditions—economic insecurity, herd existence, housing unfit for human occupancy, loss of a sense of responsibility—are the elements of proletarianization.[2] The situation is scarcely of recent date. In 1859 John Stuart Mill was writing in his celebrated essay, On Liberty: 'At present individuals are lost in the crowd. . . . The only power deserving of the name is that of masses and of governments while they make themselves the organ of the tendencies and instincts of masses.'

How temper the depersonalizing dangers of a technical society? How emancipate the workers from their proletarian status? How achieve the subordination of economic activities to social ends?

2. In Search of Stability and Freedom

The Report of Amsterdam's Section III protested its incompetence to sit in judgment on arguments for socializing the means of production as the solution of the problem or to appraise

---

[1] Amsterdam, pp. 76–7.

[2] Wilhelm Röpke describes the condition (and hints at its causes) as 'nothing less than that human beings have got into a highly dangerous sociological and anthropological state which is characterised by lack of property, lack of reserves of every kind (including the ties of family and neighbourhood), by economic servitude, uprooting, massed living quarters, militarisation of work, by estrangement from nature and by the mechanisation of productive activity; in short, by a general devitalisation and loss of personality'. Civitas Humana, p. 140.

the assertion that such a course leads to the omnicompetent State. It contented itself with pointing out to the advocates of socialization that 'in the light of the Christian understanding of man . . . the institution of property is not the root of the corruption of human nature' and reminding the defenders of the present property system that the claims of justice condition the rights of ownership and limit its exercise according to moral requirements. The needs of the community as a whole, it was insisted, should prevail over economic processes and property rights, persons being more important than purely technical considerations; all institutional forms, in consequence, must make provision for a satisfying life for 'little men in big societies'. Planning was deemed imperative but economic initiative should not be smothered by bureaucratic control.[1] The unspecified complexus of institutions and insights which would offer protection against the twin perils of tyranny and anarchy was happily termed 'The Responsible Society'.

Continuing study of the meaning and implications of the Responsible Society is leading the World Council of Churches towards a precision of its attitude on the institutional reforms needed to achieve an approximate and tolerable justice in human society. Evanston's Section on Social Questions conceded that, at least in the political realm, equity demands permanent and flexible structures.[2]

The Report was explicit on some of the characteristics and purposes of these institutions.[3] For the future of underdeveloped areas it was certain that 'political institutions must be developed'

---

[1] 'To achieve religious, cultural, economic, social and other ends it is of vital importance that society should have a rich variety of smaller forms of community, in local government, within industrial organizations, including trade unions, through the development of public corporations and through voluntary associations.' *Amsterdam*, p. 77.

[2] 'Justice requires the development of political institutions which are humane as they touch the lives of people, which provide protection by law against the arbitrary use of power and which encourage responsible participation by all citizens.' *Evanston*, p. 115.

[3] '(a) Every person should be protected against arbitrary arrest or other interference with elementary human rights; (b) Every person should have the right to express his religious, moral and political convictions. This is especially important for those who belong to minorities; (c) Channels of political action must be developed by which the people can without recourse to violence change their governments; (d) Forms of association within

to effect necessary social and economic reforms. In the economic order the mind of the World Council is not yet formed as it is, for example, on international relations. It recognizes a Christian duty to support the United Nations but is silent on a possible Christian obligation to join a labour union or professional association. It announces responsibilities for concrete programmes of technical assistance to backward areas but has not pronounced on the current claims of labour to a share in the prerogatives of management.

It is positive on the juridical foundations of international co-operation but open-minded on the basis of the ownership of the means of production. It is decisive on the individual's right to religious freedom against encroachment from any quarter but mute on the same individual's right to private property against unwarranted and unrecompensed confiscation. The mechanism of UN Peace Commission teams is commended as a valuable instrument for international order but the mechanism of the market-place as the instrument for establishing prices awaits analysis and an ultimate verdict.

3. Further Problems

Concrete issues of social justice in economic practice will undoubtedly come in for progressively greater scrutiny as the continuing inquiry on the Responsible Society goes forward. The World Council certainly believes that material goods should be available in greater abundance to supply human needs. Evanston, for example, observed that medical care should be extended. But the complicated question of a just equilibrium of wages and prices enters even in that problem in the specialized welfare field; for, in addition to the training of additional professional personnel, more facilities must be created, modern equipment manufactured, hospitals, rest homes and health centres constructed. If such goods and services are to be furnished, the nation's earnings must rise; if they are to be bought, the

society which have their own foundations and principles should be respected, and not controlled in their inner life, by the State. Churches, families and universities are dissimilar examples of this non-political type of association.' *Ibid.*, pp. 115–16.

consumer's income must be increased. An unwise increase in wages in one segment of the economy will mean higher prices which will induce unemployment. Labour costs must go down while labour's income increases if society is going to be able to afford the things that social justice postulates. A more efficient organization of the economy and a greater mechanization will increase output; increased productivity, in other words, is needed for increased production. Increased production is the way in which real wages can be augmented and prices brought down.

Another issue which the World Council will inevitably encounter as it explores the concept of the Responsible Society is the justice of the fiscal policies pursued by Governments, the institution by which the political agency of the community assesses the financial burden of public services. What proportion of such revenue should be raised by direct and what by indirect taxation, what proportion from corporation profits and individual incomes and what from concealed imposts on the purchase of necessary services and consumption if equity is to be served?

The subject of political and economic institutions concerns the social philosophy or the 'common convictions' of the World Council of Churches. For the question is another phase of the problem of the bond between the proximate and the ultimate issues of human existence, of the relationship between religious essentials and temporal importants, between dogmatic absolutes and social contingencies. Is there no connexion nor continuity between them? Is theology so transcendent that it has no need (nor capacity) to be realized in concrete historical institutions? Are there no judgments to be made on systems proposing to order man's life in community, no principles which can be invoked as criteria for moral appraisals of the social forms of political and economic organization? Or is the Christian, unconcerned about temporal structures and liberated from moral systems, to judge merely his present and individual duty in society in the light of insights communicated to him in prayer and the reverent reading of the Word of God? The problem, at bottom one of theology, is not irrelevant to the work of the World

Council's Department on Church and Society. The relation of the Responsible Society to the Christian Hope is of no minor importance, it is clear.

The problem is not yet resolved in the Ecumenical Community and, in consequence, the World Council's approach to the question of political and economic institutions is tentative and imprecise. During a meeting of Evanston's Section on Social Questions, a delegate—George Thomas of the United States—insisted that the discussion must concentrate on institutions. Addressing a plenary session of the Assembly, the Reverend D. T. Niles of South India indicated a preference for the personal (and, perforce, individualistic) approach.[1] As the meaning of the Responsible Society is examined further, ultimate questions of social philosophy—its scope and bases as well as the proper function of social order—will confront the constituency of the World Council of Churches more imperiously still.

iv. THE RESPONSIBLE SOCIETY

At a meeting of the Preparatory Commission a year before the Amsterdam Assembly, the draft chapters of the projected background volume were being examined. A member[2] of the group concerned with social questions had read a sentence from a manuscript under discussion: 'The solution of the problem of power in the totalitarian state is to concentrate economic and political power in the same hands,' and had asked: 'What is *our* solution?' The concept of the Responsible Society was the answer to that challenge. It stands as a symbol of the social arrangement maintaining in dynamic equilibrium freedom and order, liberty and justice while barring the road to tyranny and anarchy.

---

[1] 'It is a question wrongly put when it is asked, "What is the Christian solution which the Church can offer to this or that problem?" For the task of the Church is not to offer Christian solutions to specific problems but to incarnate the Word in every human situation.' Quoted by Cecil Northcott, *Evanston World Assembly*, p. 24. The speaker was not referring, to be sure, to the institutional reform of society but the critique he voiced is apposite in this context.

[2] *Archives.* Dr. C. L. Patijn, Chairman of Section III at Amsterdam. The meeting was held at Bossey, June 25, 1947.

It has proved a serviceable term, supplying a substitute for the conflicting categories of 'capitalism' and 'communism'. For Anglo-Saxons the phrase 'the Responsible Society' recalls the heritage of the Common Law where men are not instruments of group purposes but principals, able to deal justly with their fellows without hindrance; for the continentals, who would accord only a negative function to the State as a dike against sin, it shifts the focus of debate; for those rejecting socially coercive measures as violating the spirit of the suffering Christ, it evokes the possibility of 'new and creative solutions'; for all who are preoccupied by the problem of the control of depersonalizing technics, it presents a summons to build new social tissue, more abiding personal relations; for those disturbed by the unresolved theocratic implications in the revival of Calvinist theology, it offers the reassuring distinction between society and the State; for those alarmed by the extension of the Welfare State, it offers a feasible alternative—personal and group initiative.

The term, 'Responsible Society', declared the Evanston Assembly, 'is not an alternative social or political system, but a criterion by which we judge all existing social orders and at the same time a standard to guide us in the specific choices we have to make.'[1] The observation is undoubtedly to be understood as a rephrasing of the familiar ecumenical protestation that there is no identifiable 'Christian' economic or political order. Surely it cannot be intended to mean that the term is an abstraction without verifiable applications; for the same document several paragraphs later argues that the Responsible Society must be embodied in political institutions and specifies their functions and characteristics. The Amsterdam Assembly, which introduced the phrase, referred to the Responsible Society as a goal for which all the churches in all lands should work. The Secretary of Section III, at a conference for reporters in August 1948, pointed out that in the nature of the case an ecumenical document cannot be precise in suggesting the next steps that would be relevant to serve such different societies as those in Britain, America, India

[1] *Evanston*, p. 113.

and Hungary; he acknowledged, however, that the post-war programme of the British Labour Party was one form of the attempt to make concrete the complexus of moral insights, economic reforms and political orientation subsumed under the term.[1] Since the social goals proposed for the Responsible Society are admittedly beyond achieving or even seriously discussing in the communist-controlled areas of some of the member churches of the World Council, it has obviously appeared more realistic and expedient to emphasize the function of the phrase as a norm and standard.[2]

By way of examining the bearing of the concept, it will be profitable to review the history of the inquiry on the Responsible Society as it has progressed in the World Council Study Department programme.

1. *The Preliminary Outline*

The Secretary's Minutes of Amsterdam's Section III surprisingly reveal no explicit discussion of the idea that was the theme of a long chapter in the preparatory volume given to each delegate. Written by J. H. Oldham, its argument postulated a crisis of man, maladapted to the exigencies of the new world of technics, and a crisis of culture with traditional associations breaking down and the authority of ancient values disappearing. A new social environment must be constructed to sustain personal living in an age of technics, it was contended, a mission implying four major tasks for the Church. To the expounding of these tasks Dr. Oldham brought his genuine conviction of the importance

[1] John C. Bennett in the *Christian Century* LXV (December 15, 1948), 50, p. 1364. Professor Bennett continued: 'I think it is only fair to the Report to say that the general direction in which it points might in some places appear to be a modified capitalism and in other places a modified socialism.'

[2] A memorandum, 'The Responsible Society in a World Perspective', prepared at a meeting of the Preparatory Commission for the Evanston Assembly held at Begnins, Switzerland, August 11–19, 1953, noted: 'We recognize that the concept "responsible society" is not applicable to societies where Christians and other responsible citizens are deprived of the possibility of exercising effective influence over political authority and economic power, as in other lands. It may offer for such persons a criterion for judging the society in which they live. It cannot act as a constructive goal towards which they may work immediately, though they may wish Godspeed to those who find this possible.' *ER* VI (October 1953), 1, p. 76.

of lay action and group experimentation, a wide range of reading and a somewhat professorial confidence in the acumen of his favourite critics of contemporary society.

The Oldham agenda for the Church in the construction of the Responsible Society lacks a clarification of terms which he introduced in the Oxford Conference discussions. It is not evident whether the tasks outlined are assigned to 'organized Christianity', the sum of all the separate Christian individuals of the different denominations, or to the ecclesiastical authorities and official organs of the different denominations. Some of the lines of action suppose the initiative of citizens who are Christians, other suggestions call for new emphases in preaching or official guidance by ecclesiastical bodies. The term, 'the Church', has a double sense, therefore, and from it is asked assistance in the cultural, economic and political areas for the creation of a decent social order. Thus:

(a) A new social awareness must be created, Oldham argued, by inspiring small groups of persons to enter into associations where the common object will be sought in a spirit of mutual sharing and support. Under God's grace, such associations will mature the richer Christian personalities needed for the reforming and reinvigorating of modern mass society; they will, in addition, furnish the pattern of private initiative and communal service capable of supplanting some of the functions currently assumed by the all-provident State. This needed social consciousness will be greatly aided by the sense of solidarity resulting from the experience of communal worship.

(b) A theology of work must be developed. Modern man must recover a sense of the significance of his occupational activity, a conviction that he is contributing something by his hands or head to the purpose of the world, a satisfaction in contemplating a connexion between his vocation and the Christian obligation to love and serve God. The problem is aggravated by modern methods of production which allegedly destroy all pride of creative craftsmanship, reducing the worker to an animated automaton tending a monstrous machine whose functioning is beyond his understanding and whose product is 'untouched by human hands'. 'We have either to translate *"laborare est orare"* into modern English and mould our civilisation upon it, or else acknowledge as pretentious survivals every remaining bastion of the Christian culture.'[1]

(*c*) A morality for group living which will guide collective decisions in the economic and political spheres must be given content. For modern man, for all his boasted freedom of thought and opinion, finds himself commonly compelled to do what society does. The collective character of much of modern life with its political parties, trade unions, employers' and professional associations, restricts the freedom of the individual to take independent decisions and reduces his power to influence effectively positions taken by the group. The situation engenders moral perplexities, the individual seeing small connexion between Christian morality as ordinarily presented and the pressing problems of his daily life. Ethical guidance for group living and a moral strategy and tactics for the Christian minority inevitably involved in the complex movement of a secular society must be devised. For such a charge, clerical professors of Social Ethics, general formularies and theoretical discussions have limited usefulness, it was asserted. The experience of those involved in the complexities of modern society must be considered. Nor will counselling the ordinary human virtues of honesty, industry and decency suffice. There are situations, and Christian living in a secular world is one of them, where the natural virtues (as Nurse Edith Cavell remarked of patriotism) are 'not enough'.

(*d*) There are inescapable political tasks, as well. Contemporary social problems are so complicated, overwhelming and stubborn, that there is a temptation for the Christian to abandon the field, taking refuge in the lazy belief that religion has nothing to do with the market-place but is the use one makes of one's solitude. 'There is,' remarked Dr. Oldham, 'a pietistic as well as a liberal *laissez-faire*. However pious the intention, it is a denial of God's

[1] *CDS*, p. 131.

reign in the world, of the Lordship of Christ over history.'[1] This intellectual absenteeism and moral abstentionism have deprived modern civilization of ingredients essential to social cohesiveness and left a vacuum to be filled by doctrines—and policies—of naked power.[2]

Primary among the political tasks Dr. Oldham saw confronting the Church was that of clarifying the issues involved in 'the tension between the western democracies and Soviet Russia and its satellites'. The essential question, in Oldham's judgment, turns not on political or economic systems but on the struggle between totalitarianism and the ideas of a free society,[3] a contest being waged in greater or lesser degree in every nation. For the creation of that Free Society,[4] that fit arrangement of all the proper social elements, the Christian must labour for the effective honouring of several essential conditions. There must be freedom of conscience, freedom to seek and speak the truth, freedom of dissent; there must be a prizing of personal relations above mere collective contacts; there must be a careful limitation of power and a dispersal of its control, an independence in the religious, cultural, political and economic activities of the community; there must be a just distribution of the material rewards of industrial production; finally there must be genuine political freedom based on popular sovereignty.

It will be clear how Oldham's contribution shaped the

---

[1] CDS, p. 138.

[2] 'It may be regarded as axiomatic that the less a community is held together by cohesive forces in the texture of its life, the more must it be held together by power.' Reinhold Niebuhr, The Children of Light and the Children of Darkness, p. 114. Niebuhr notes only two minimal forces of cohesion in the international community: 'a common over-tone of universality in its moral ideals, and the fear of anarchy. The fear of anarchy will undoubtedly be the more potent of these two; but this fear is certainly not as powerful as the fear of a common and a concrete foe.' Ibid., p. 115. Another theologian notes: 'The greater the decline in the moral vigour of society, the more tasks the State must take upon itself, and the greater the expansion of the element of compulsion in justice, the nearer the approach to the totalitarian State.' Emil Brunner, Justice and the Social Order, p. 182.

[3] 'It is necessary to distinguish between communism as a political and economic system and as a totalitarian control of life. From the former there may be much to be learnt; with the latter Christians can make no compromise.' CDS, p. 139.

[4] The term 'the Responsible Society' was substituted for 'the Free Society' to avoid confusion with the political systems of modern Western democracies. Röpke uses the term 'Civitas Humana', Lippman 'the Good Society', Popper 'the Open Society'.

definition of Amsterdam's Section III Report. On the topic of popular sovereignty, moreover, he had expressed a growing consensus of the Ecumenical Community.[1]

2. *Fuller Exposition*

Subsumed under the general caption 'Christian Action in Society', the ideas broached by Oldham were developed by the World Council's Study Department which has endeavoured to expand them by posing some of the practical questions his socio-philosophical principles evoke. Four projects were undertaken to examine various phases of the implications of the Responsible Society; papers on these topics were circulated and study conferences arranged. The topics were identified in the Study Department's Report of its activities as entitled: (*a*) Moral Problems in Economic and Political Life Today; (*b*) The Responsible Society and European Problems; (*c*) The Witness of Christians in Communist Countries; and (*d*) The Responsibility of Christians for the Social Problems of the Underdeveloped Countries.[2] In more proximate preparations for Evanston, moreover, the Study Department issued a Memorandum on the Responsible Society which was reviewed in the summer of 1953 by the Preparatory Commission for the Section on Social Questions.[3]

The Memorandum proposed to set forth in constructive terms possible answers to some of the questions that had been raised by the changes in political and economic life. Concerning political structures, the Evanston background document added the note of 'the rule of law . . . to protect the rights of individual citizens and of minorities'. A warning against making the state co-extensive with the nation or with society was sounded and the

---

[1] Memorable is Niebuhr's epigram: 'Man's capacity for justice makes democracy possible; but man's inclination to injustice makes democracy necessary.' Despite his celebrated insistence on the total transcendence of Christianity, Karl Barth believes: 'When I consider the deepest and most central content of the New Testament exhortation, I should say that we are justified, from the point of view of exegesis, in regarding the "democratic conception of the State" as a justifiable expansion of the thought of the New Testament.' *Church and State*, p. 80. Cf. also John C. Bennett, *Christian Ethics and Social Policy*, pp. 85 ff.

[2] *The First Six Years*, p. 32.   [3] The text is in *ER* VI (October 1953), I, pp. 73–90.

existence of subordinate, semi-autonomous forms of association was indicated without further description of their role. 'The Church, the family and the university' are the examples given. The importance of the principle of voluntarism, of the possibility of popular community action, of the opportunities for the exercise of professional responsibility is included in germ in this warning against the politicizing of life. The principle of the competence and liability of these 'forms of association' has possible application to the economic field as well, where trade unions and employers' organizations surely fulfil the description given and might, in consequence, be given legal functions to perform. The possibility of peaceful political change, the Preparatory Commission believed, requires effective popular participation in political parties and the establishment of machinery for the progressive transfer of sovereignty to colonial peoples, within the structure of international law, in recognition of their right to national freedom and social justice.

In the economic realm the concept of the Responsible Society supplied, in the view of the Preparatory Commission, 'no single criterion by which we can determine exactly how far the state should go in extending its functions'. Among the necessary functions listed are the prevention of serious depression or inflation, the relief of the consequences of unemployment, sickness, industrial injury and old age. Furthermore, the State, as the trustee of society, is assigned the duty of policing private-interest groups. For while the State may grow to be the enemy of freedom, it was held to be the only instrument by which real freedom for large sections of the population is made possible.

It had been almost customary in some church circles to condemn the profit-motive as 'unchristian'. The pre-Evanston Memorandum declared simply and realistically: 'An economic system exists for the maximum production of goods and services at lowest cost to meet consumers' needs', and noted that such an objective raises complicated problems of priorities whose possibilities can only be assessed in the light of technical knowledge illumined by Christian insights. An example was given of a government policy of full employment with resulting risk of inflation. Factors determining the just distribution of wealth were recognized as multiple, a proper reward for incentive being acknowledged as having its proper place, though the imperilling of political institutions and the destruction of the possibility of true fellowship—between nations as well as between individuals—was noted as the inevitable consequences of great contrasts between rich and poor.

The Memorandum underlined the need of flexibility and adaption in economic relations, supported necessary State intervention in the economic process while maintaining the importance of the private sector of the economy. Some countries, it was pointed out, need 'entrepreneurs to be adventurous and to take risks so as to bring about technical and economic innovations'; in others 'socially responsible management' is called for.[1] Agriculture in some countries needs modernization of its equipment and Government-guaranteed price-supports against disastrous fluctuation both of climate and of supply and demand. And the consumer must be protected against exploitation. 'Rules of the game' must be developed if all sectors of the population—producers and consumers, employers and labour, agriculture and industry—are to enjoy a common prosperity, economic freedom is to be preserved and the abuses of economic power controlled. An interesting development of the application of 'guaranteed rules of the game' concerns the participation of labour in the management of enterprises whether the arrangement be called joint production committees, industrial councils, comités d'entreprise, or Mitbestimmung. In the view of the Preparatory Commission the churches should welcome this development which, at the same time, calls for the spirit of responsibility and more factual knowledge.[2] Finally, since economic activity

---

[1] And some countries need both, it might be added.

[2] The Chairman of Amsterdam's Section III, Dr. C. L. Patijn, a professional economist and an official of a government which has legally established employer-worker committees, saw 'no hope' in such councils of collaboration since 'they would shift the burden of price increases on to the consumer'. CDS, p. 167.

today has world-wide repercussions, the trade policies of some countries and the emigration possibilities of others have moral import. International co-operation and integration, along with assistance to underdeveloped countries, were deemed moral imperatives in the light of the insights and goals of the Responsible Society.

Indeed the Memorandum of the Preparatory Commission invited the churches to study a programme of a concentrated series of specific problems connected with the underdeveloped countries, problems that can only be considered and coped with by international action. Listed, with some of their ethical and economic implications, were the complex issues of (1) proper political institutions, (2) land reform and rural development, (3) industrialization, (4) population pressures, (5) responsibilities attendant on independence, (6) the competition of communism, religious nationalism and the need of Western understanding.

3. *Towards Definition*

The Preparatory Commission's Memorandum served as the frame and supplied most of the ideas for the Section Report at Evanston. The fact was inevitable: a group of a hundred people of differing interests and confessional allegiances, coming from different countries and meeting together only a few times, can scarcely be expected to compound an original and comprehensive declaration. Moreover, as Dean Walter G. Muelder urged, there was need of discussing the meaning of the Responsible Society before examining its applications. And the content of the concept, most particularly its basis, has not been thought out, being irretrievably involved in the moot question of the social philosophy of the World Council's judgments on the social order.

Evanston represented an advance over Amsterdam, it can be said, in acknowledging the crucial importance of institutions in affecting social living and in achieving justice. Means must be devised to strengthen the family and other subordinate social groups, it was argued. 'No one form of government,' it was explained, 'has a universal claim on Christians. . . . The Church cannot uncritically support any particular form of [economic] organization as it exists in any particular country.' A more positive role was accorded to the State, though its 'action needs to be decentralized, limited and adaptable'. Examples of areas where State initiative was found warranted were: planning for urban development, stimulating industrial expansion and soil conservation, some types of large-scale industrial and agricultural research and guidance of the distribution of industry. On the other hand, concern was expressed in the Section discussions over allegedly totalitarian trends in the Welfare State. 'A status in society' was claimed for the worker, the justice of the farmers' demand for a reasonable measure of security was recognized. The interrelation of national and international policies was emphasized.

The problems of the underdeveloped areas of the world were given major attention in the Evanston Report, the issues mentioned following the lines of the Memorandum of the Preparatory Commission. Absentee landlordship and other unjust forms of land tenure and privilege were decried and positive measures fostering productive land use and community life endorsed. Thus, social and agricultural education, co-operatives, rural industry, facilities for credit and professional assistance were recommended. The possibility of finding capital for necessary industrial development within the country without depressing standards of consumption, or of obtaining foreign loans without endangering social objectives was discussed.

Focusing attention on the underdeveloped areas is an obvious consequence of the missionary concern of the Ecumenical Community throughout the world. Incorporating the findings of the Lucknow Study Conference, the Evanston Report questioned the attitude of Western Christians, particularly business men, towards Asia. It challenged, furthermore, the comprehension of the social implication of Christianity by the churches in former mission territories. For persistent effort to realize always more fully the ideals of the Responsible Society is the inescapable obligation of every Christian—such is the underlying conviction of the World Council of Churches—who must go beyond vain protest and cowardly surrender to bring stones for the building of a Temporal City which will manifest in its cultural life, economic practices and political institutions that the message of the gospel has at least been preached.

v. COMMUNISM AND CAPITALISM

Having termed the social situation best answering the demands of the Christian perspective 'The Responsible Society', the First Assembly of the World Council of Churches identified the forces opposed to the realization of this equilibrium of liberty and justice, this organized interplay of freedom and order, as communism and capitalism. It found points of conflict between Christianity and each, and condemned the ideologies of both.[1] The World Council's Second Assembly, held in 1954, renewed the earlier judgment on Marxist ideology and totalitarian practice; it found no occasion to reaffirm its censure of capitalism, noting that 'the capitalism of today is very different from the capitalism of even twenty or thirty years ago'.[2]

The debate on capitalism and communism seems pretty well adjourned in World Council circles. An analysis of its origins and implications reveals, however, the development of thought in the Ecumenical Community, the difficulties of ecumenical dialogue (as well as of comprehending its approach on the part of secular forces) and the differing points of view, not only between the years 1948 and 1954, but between Americans and

[1] In the rejection of the ideology of capitalism, the adjective 'laissez-faire' was added (by a Plenary Session considering the Report of Section II on Evangelism) under circumstances related earlier (cf. supra, p. 45 n.2). The adjective is italicized in the printed Report. The Secretary of the Amsterdam Section III denied that the addition of the words 'laissez-faire' radically changed the intention of the paragraph and felt that the 'actual sentences of the Report were not unfair to American capitalism'. John C. Bennett, 'Capitalism and Communism at Amsterdam', Christian Century LXV (December 15, 1948), 50, p. 1364.

[2] The editor of the Evanston documents states: 'The report [of the Section on Social Questions] does not reverse the Amsterdam criticisms of the ideology of "laissez-faire capitalism". However, it recognizes that the old dispute between "capitalism" and "socialism" has become more verbal than real.' Evanston Speaks, pp. 43–4. But the dispute at Amsterdam was between laissez-faire capitalism and communism.

Europeans in the same international organization.[1] An examination of the point is indicated.

The paragraphs on capitalism and communism proved to be the most controversial of all the statements issuing from the World Council's First Assembly. Complaints were undoubtedly inevitable: in the divided world of 1948, the repeated insistence that the Church stood above all economic systems, apart from all political blocs, could scarcely be expected to content the determined partisans of either camp. Part of the dissatisfaction, it must be added, flowed from the obscurity of the phrasing, reflecting an uncertainty as to what precisely was being analysed. Quite possibly the Drafting Committee preferred not to be concrete.

The choice of words was unfortunate. 'Capitalism', not least in Europe and Asia, is a term so charged with emotional connotations, so depreciated by demagogy, that its meaning is muddy. It is generally associated with the stereotype of callous manipulators of the financial markets, all-powerful, malign individuals, subject to no social sanction, who boss governments and public opinion and, by their control of the levers of industry and credit, ruthlessly exploit colonial peoples and the working class for their personal profit.[2] 'Communism', especially in America, is

---

[1] Professor Bennett declared as an indisputable fact that the thinking on economic questions in the churches of other countries 'is quite far to the left of most thinking in American Protestant circles', and, in consequence, without the paragraphs on capitalism and communism 'the Report would not be adequate as an ecumenical document as, in fact, it proved to be'. *Op. cit.*, p. 1362. Perhaps the difference of outlook can be glimpsed by recalling that the word *bourgeois* has no exact English equivalent, being employed (always in the pejorative sense) in the idiom of intellectuals. On the other hand, George Kennan has pointed out, 'The Russian language, in fact, never acquired a word comparable to our expression "business man"; it had only the word for "merchant" and this term did not always have a pleasant connotation.' 'America and the Russian Future', in *Foreign Affairs* XXIX (April 1951), 3, p. 363; reprinted in *American Diplomacy, 1900–1950*, p. 131.

[2] Professor Bennett indicated his awareness of the equivocal understanding of the term when he remarked that Europeans 'think of Capitalism as a spiritual phenomenon informed by the bourgeois mentality, as extreme individualism. In America we usually think of Capitalism in external and institutional terms—as a mechanism for producing and distributing goods that is capable of indefinite modification.' *Op. cit.* Fearing that if the term 'Capitalism' was employed at Evanston in any fashion, it would occasion misunderstanding, the same writer explained that: 'The word in this country points to a highly successful economic system which has proved it can be modified in the interests

a term evoking the phantasm of 180 Soviet divisions, poised for an invasion of the West, and of concealed traitors in high places.

Section III's terms of reference did not include a consideration of international problems. Unhappily 'communism' and 'capitalism' were the propaganda slogans of mutual recrimination current in the cold war. Whether they liked it or not, the Drafting Committee of Section III, charged with economic, political and cultural questions, seemed to be appraising the moral worth of the social systems of the United States and the Soviet Union. It might have been more satisfactory if it had done so forthrightly instead of analysing social categories in a historical vacuum.

1. 'Capitalism' as Economic Individualism

The strictures on 'capitalism' reveal that it was the complexus of political doctrines and economic practices accompanying and accelerating the Industrial Revolution of the nineteenth century which the Amsterdam Report judged. Historians and political scientists commonly call the first Liberalism and the second Economic Individualism. These nineteenth-century theorists and practitioners would have gladly pleaded guilty to the Amsterdam indictment of promising that 'justice will follow as a by-product of free enterprise'. Where did such doctrines and such practices prevail on the contemporary scene? What specific changes had occurred in modern times in the economic systems and political institutions of what the Oxford Conference of 1937 referred to as 'the so-called capitalist countries'?[1] Curiously enough, the question of which countries had corrected earlier

of justice against all the predictions of those who have been influenced by Marxism. But in most other countries Capitalism is a bad symbol. In Europe it suggests economic exploitation, a doctrinaire individualism and a middle-class form of materialism. In Asia it suggests imperialism above everything else.' 'The Responsible Society at Evanston' in *Christianity and Crisis* XIV (July 12, 1954), 12, p. 91.

[1] Amsterdam was disappointingly vague. The Report had earlier acknowledged that: 'In all parts of the world new controls have in various degrees been put upon the free play of economic forces,' adding: 'The developments of capitalism vary from country to country and often the exploitation of the workers that was characteristic of early capitalism has been corrected in considerable measure by the influence of trade unions, social legislation and responsible management. But . . .' *Amsterdam*, pp. 76, 80.

abuses and which had not seems not to have been asked. The Minutes of the six meetings of the Section contain no hint of such a point being raised in any of the discussions.

In the preparatory volume, comparing the American 'liberal capitalist society of free enterprise' and the British experiment of 'democratic socialism' with the situation in the Soviet Union, Dr. Joseph H. Oldham had argued: 'There is nothing which distinguishes the outlook that has been described from the ambition of state planners to shape history by means (in the phrase of Engels) of "a collective will according to an all-embracing plan".'[1] 'The outlook that has been described' is that diagnosed in a doctoral thesis studying the policies of the National Association of Manufacturers, a private organization of American industrialists, given to opposing trade unions, to publicity campaigns of self-adulation and to welfare grants to employers for their (alleged) ideological indoctrination.[2] On the other hand, a professional economist, in his contribution to the background volume, was under no illusions about the existence of a calcified capitalistic system rigidly controlled by business men. Dr. C. L. Patijn observed that economic structures are in rapid evolution, that the social crisis manifests itself precisely in the painful process of adaption to a new economic equilibrium, quoting with approbation the judgment: 'The age of "free enterprise", when the new vitalities of a technical civilisation

---

[1] *CDS*, p. 145.

[2] The source is given as *Business as a System of Power*, by Robert A. Brady. Whether the author accurately appraised the success of the NAM in influencing substantially American society, not to speak of controlling government decisions, was for Dr. Oldham (and presumably the university examiners) to determine. The book was published in a year when Franklin D. Roosevelt was nominated at a political convention where 'clear it with Sidney' (Sidney A. Hillman, a labour leader) was the cue for important decisions and was elected for the fourth time against the opposition, for the fourth time, of the NAM. The citation was put in evidence in a year when Harry S. Truman was elected despite the opposition of the NAM. Dr. Oldham should not have supposed that a study of the National Association of Manufacturers was a study of the outlook of even the business community of the United States. Paul G. Hoffman, President of the Committee for Economic Development, another organization of industrialists, was serving as head of the European Recovery Programme. As for the significance and effectiveness of pretentious public-relations programmes extolling the sanctities of economic liberalism, a *Fortune* magazine research study revealed that reactionary industrialists were wasting their time and money. The study was published as: *Is Anybody Listening?* ed. William H. Whyte, Jr.

were expected to regulate themselves, is over.'[1] A document issued by the World Council Study Department four years after Amsterdam, observing the necessity 'to be clear about the nature of the social changes which have taken place in recent decades', remarks: 'A strong case can be made for the idea that pure *laissez-faire* capitalism has disappeared.'[2] The case could have been suggested in 1948 by any delegate to the Assembly who asked himself if any contemporary government in the world was the political expression of such a viewpoint, owed its existence to such forces or was prepared to defend such practices before the electorate.[3]

Undefined and unidentified, capitalism was judged in the Report to be in conflict with Christianity on the following grounds:

1. Capitalism tends to subordinate what should be the primary task of any economy—the meeting of human needs—to the economic advantages of those who have most power over its institutions.

2. It tends to produce serious inequalities.

3. It has developed a practical form of materialism in western nations in spite of their Christian background, for it has placed the greatest emphasis upon success in making money.

4. It has also kept the people of capitalist countries subject to a kind of fate which has taken the form of such social catastrophes as mass unemployment.[4]

---

[1] *CDS*, p. 166. Dr. Patijn was quoting Reinhold Niebuhr's *Discerning the Signs of the Times*, p. 40.

[2] *The Responsible Society in a World Perspective* (Introductory Leaflet No. 3), p. 5.

[3] In 1954 Professor Bennett chided Americans for forgetting that Capitalism 'ever had a distinctive ideology, except for the libertarians of *Christian Economics* who are now reviving the doctrine of economic freedom in such extreme terms that they reject almost the whole development of the economic activities of government'. *Op. cit.* The reference is to a right-wing minority group of Protestants in the United States who equate Christianity with 'free enterprise', i.e. with economic liberalism.

[4] *Amsterdam*, p. 80. Reinhold Niebuhr, the key person of the Fellowship of Socialist Christians, a group accepting Marx's economic analysis, to which the writer of these paragraphs of the Amsterdam Report belonged, remarked on the irony involved in the customary condemnation of 'the profit motive' by clerics: 'Every parson who speaks grandly about supplanting [it] exemplifies it when he moves to a new charge because the old one did not give him . . . a salary adequate for his growing family. . . . The so-called "profit motive" can hardly be eliminated under any system.' *Christian Century* LXX (August 19, 1953), 33, p. 937. The comment might just possibly illumine the third of the points of the conflicts between capitalism and Christianity listed above.

Clearly, it is a philosophy of life (whatever its actuality) rather than an economic system (wherever existing) that is being here condemned.

The treatment of the subject of 'capitalism' at Amsterdam, because of its omissions and imprecision, must be deemed less than satisfactory. Considered as an economic order under which economic goods are used for the production of other goods rather than consumed for immediate enjoyment, capitalism is an innocent, even necessary technique of production. In a passing remark the economist, Patijn, characterized the Soviet system as 'State-Capitalism'. For capital in the form of savings or anticipated savings (as credit or slave labour) is essential to production, whatever the economic régime. The seed corn that is eaten cannot be harvested. Having earlier declared its incompetence to resolve the debate between the advocates of socialism and the defenders of a régime of private property, the Assembly of the World Council of Churches had disqualified itself from judging the economic systems of capitalism and communism.

The language of the indictment, moreover, makes it clear that the accusation was directed against the ideological engine of nineteenth-century liberalism which, shattering the brakes of social controls imposed by moral considerations outside its orbit, 'tended to'—and indeed did—drive the mechanism of production and trade roughshod over the defenceless and the downtrodden. That correctives, arising even from the intrinsic contradiction of that philosophy, its essentially anti-human character, could check and control these tendencies, had seemingly not occurred to Karl Marx. These might have been noted in 1948 by the Amsterdam delegates in connexion with point two on the 'serious inequalities' produced by capitalism. The daily Press supplied regular accounts of the effects of nationalization of industry, continuing war-time price controls, government supervision of credit terms, taxation planned designedly to distribute the national wealth, expanding social services including subsidies for higher education. Indeed the fear was widely expressed that the sources of risk capital were being dried up by confiscatory taxation and that incentive was being smothered by a programme of social egalitarianism that hailed 'The Century of the Common Man'. Political partisanship might cheer or view with alarm such policies; there was little doubt that they were permanent features of the societies of what the Oxford Conference had referred to as the 'so-called capitalist countries'.[1]

Certainly there are grave injustices in the distribution of income in 'the so-called capitalist countries' requiring radical correcting. By its omission of serious historical study, however, Amsterdam offered no hint as to how this situation had come about; by its looseness of language, its opting for a term of pejorative connotation, it had left the impression, moreover, that an economic order recognizing private property rather than a political doctrine, a cultural inheritance and a philosophy nullifying a sane functioning of that order, was responsible. The Oxford Conference of 1937 had also passed up the task of historical research. It had, on the other hand, escaped the confusion of seeming to assess the causes for the present state of the world by contenting itself with a listing of contemporary social evils which it identified with 'certain features of modern life in the so-called capitalist countries'.[2] Furthermore, noting that 'there is today no *one* economic order which œcumenical Christianity faces', the Oxford Conference observed that: 'The subordination of God's purpose for human life to the demands of the economic process seems in practice to be a tendency common to all existing kinds of economic organization.'[3]

2. *Communism or 'Stalinism'?*

When the Amsterdam Report came to discuss 'Communism'

---

[1] The candidate of the Conservative political group, Dwight D. Eisenhower, declared during the US Presidential election campaign of 1952 that the social gains achieved by the American people are 'not only here to stay but to be improved and extended'.

[2] *Oxford*, p. 88. The Main Report on 'Church, Community and State in Relation to the Economic Order' lists these evils as: (*a*) The Enhancement of Acquisitiveness, (*b*) Inequalities, (*c*) Irresponsible Possession of Economic Power, and (*d*) The Frustration of the Sense of Christian Vocation. The Report indicated, moreover, the positive achievements of this economic order.

[3] *Ibid.*

it seemed to have in mind what a later document[1] of the World
Council called simply 'Stalinism'—the political régime of the
Soviet Union, directing revolutionary groups in all countries
and pursuing policies of decisive international significance.
This—rather than a speculative philosophy or academic economic
order—is obviously the contemporary reality which 'makes a
strong appeal to the populations of Asia and Africa and to racial
minorities everywhere'. The Report confessed with contrition
to the involvement of many churches 'in the forms of economic
injustice and racial discrimination favouring [its] growth' and
acknowledged that '[its] atheism and the anti-religious teaching
are in part a reaction to the chequered record of a professedly
Christian society'.[2] It declared that this reality has filled 'a moral
and psychological vacuum' among youth who often fail to find
in church circles 'the appeal that can evoke a disciplined, purposeful and sacrificial response', and among the working class and
tenant farmers who 'came to believe that the churches were
against them or indifferent to their plight'.

The points of conflict between Christianity and 'the atheist
Marxian Communism[3] of our day' were listed as:

1. The Communist promise of what amounts to a complete
redemption of man in history.

2. The belief that a particular class by virtue of its role as the

[1] *The Second Report of the Advisory Commission on the Main Theme of the Second Assembly
of the World Council of Churches* (Geneva: World Council, 1952).

[2] Admitting 'the special importance of the absence of effective social idealism in any
of the Christian Churches' as a cause of the anti-religious character of the radical revolutionary movements of Europe, a church historian attributes this spirit also to 'the growth
of the scientific temper and of nineteenth-century materialism, to the prevalence of the
mechanistic conception of life which industrialism fosters, to the determinism of the
Hegelian philosophy in which Marx had been trained, to the bare fact that the leaders of
the movement were not religious men'. H. Richard Niebuhr, *The Social Sources of
Denominationalism*, p. 72.

[3] At the risk of seeming pedantic and even precious, the writer would observe that if
'Stalinism' is the reality under discussion the owner of the ideological franchise of that
system, Iosif Visarionovich Dzugashvili, employed the term 'Scientific Socialism'
and insisted that the transformation to communism was impossible before certain functional prerequisites were achieved, notably reducing the working day to six and then to
five hours, introducing 'universal obligatory polytechnical education' and improving
radically housing conditions. The real wages of workers must first be at least doubled
before the transition to communism can occur, Stalin claimed.

bearer of a new order is free from the sins and ambiguities that Christians believe to be characteristic of all human existence.

3. The materialistic and deterministic teachings, however they may be qualified, that are incompatible with belief in God and with the Christian view of man as a person, made in God's image and responsible to Him.

4. The ruthless methods of Communists in dealing with their opponents.

5. The demand of the party on its members for an exclusive and unqualified loyalty which belongs only to God, and the coercive policies of Communist dictatorship in controlling every aspect of life.[1]

The Report condemned the ideology of communism observing that it had made the false promise that freedom would come 'after the completion of the revolution'.

As in the paragraph on capitalism the imprecision of concept here is disconcerting. Neither the Amsterdam background volume nor the Minutes of the meetings of the Section manifest the desired clarity on the identity—much less the historical and philosophical origins and present policy—of this second menace to 'The Responsible Society' called 'Communism'. To be sure, in the key chapter of the preparatory study outlining the nature of a social order reverencing both freedom and order, Dr. Oldham had declared flatly: 'It has been our aim to show that the conflict between liberty and totalitarianism is not identical with the international tension between the Western democracies and the communist societies under the leadership of Russia.'[2] Yet apart from repeated references to unspecified pre-totalitarian tendencies in the Western democracies, the chapter—whatever its aim—had, by its illustrations, at least identified contemporary totalitarianism with the Soviet Union.

The questions transmitted unhappily involved almost a definition of the topic under discussion.[3] What precisely is 'communism',

---

[1] *Amsterdam*, p. 79.   [2] *CDS*, p. 153.

[3] A decisive instance of the ambiguity arising from the decision to omit any serious historical investigation is found in the same chapter: 'There is no space to consider here, important as the question is, what relative importance is to be attached to the present

this 'powerful ferment throughout the world'? Is it, as other references in the volume suggest, a popular preference for economic democracy paralleling Western emphasis on political democracy? Is it basically a manifestation of traditional Russian imperialism, exploiting local unrest for ancient Tsarist objectives? What connexion has the term with the meeting held in Poland on October 5, 1947, where representatives of nine European countries revived an organization known as a Communist International? A Soviet commissar, Andrei A. Zhdanov, presided at this meeting which established the Cominform.

Amsterdam's Section III devoted two-and-a-half hours on the morning of August 27, 1948, to a discussion on the nature and causes of communism, the responsibility and involvement of the churches in the problem, the conflict between communism and Christianity and the question of human rights. The Minutes reveal the same imprecision as in the use of the term 'capitalism'. Seemingly the word 'Soviet' was not employed during the entire discussion, whatever be the significance to be attached to that omission in a debate on 'Communism'. A delegate experienced in UN affairs observed that the greatest difficulty in dealing with Communists, 'especially with Russian Communists', in that organization was the uncertainty of their trustworthiness, suggesting by his remark the possibility of varieties of communism with, at least in the UN, different policies but with common human weaknesses. An Indonesian delegate attributed the strength of communism in his country to 'the clear line taken by Moscow' in the struggle for independence.

These are the only references recorded in the Secretary's Minutes indicating a connexion between the historical phenomenon

ascendancy of a communist ideology in comparison with the deeper and more enduring forces of the character, environment, tradition and historical experience of the Russian people; nor, in spite of its relevance to present political realities, the question how far the original purpose of Marxism to deliver the workers from economic exploitation has been replaced by a rigid system controlled by a relatively small political élite and directed to the expansion of Russian power. What we are concerned with in this chapter is the Christian attitude to the conception of life implied in communism, which is a powerful ferment throughout the world and aims at a complete transformation of human existence.'
Ibid., pp. 138–9.

called 'Communism' and the Soviet Union. The delegates present from the People's Democracies of Eastern Europe had no contributions to offer apparently. A delegate from Finland condemned communism utterly and recommended that Christians supporting it should join the Social Democratic Party; his reasoning, however, looked wholly to the relations of the two political parties to the Church and ignored the factor of extranational loyalties. The only speaker to suggest that communism had a conspiratorial character was a Manchurian who remarked that much of the appeal of communism lay in its secrecy, which offered excitement and interest particularly to the young. The view was expressed that communism was the specific fruit of Western injustice, a political totalitarianism making headway in creeping form in the United States and Switzerland. It should be fought, another delegate believed, by opposing centralization everywhere. The recognition of the obligation of the Church to interest itself in the people attracted by communism, to rid itself in Asia and Africa of all seeming association with Western interests, especially economic ones, to issue a challenging appeal for sacrificial service which alone could satisfy modern youth, were among the *desiderata* expressed. The final speaker underlined the necessity to formulate a Christian sociology and philosophy of law. Neither the discussions in the Section nor the words of the Report reveal any fear that the reality termed 'Communism' constituted a military menace. Yet six months before, on February 29, four days after the Communist *coup* in Czechoslovakia, the Premiers and Foreign Ministers of the Netherlands, Belgium and Luxemburg met in Brussels to accept the Anglo-French proposal for a union of Western Europe[1] which was formalized in the fifty-year security pact signed on March 17 and which was promptly used as the basis for energetic efforts to obtain the collaboration of the United States in a military defence programme.[2]

[1] The Chairman of Section III, an official of Holland's Foreign Ministry, can certainly not be accused of seeking to influence the Assembly in favour of his government's policy.

[2] As is clear from the *Diaries* of the US Secretary of Defence, James V. Forrestal.

3. *The Amsterdam Verdicts Explained*

The accusation was made[1] that Amsterdam had equated 'communism' and 'capitalism' as twin perils to a society satisfying Christian demands, had appraised their achievements as equally negative, had manifested a studied neutrality or, worse, a callous indifference to the over-riding issue of the times. There is no evidence that the charge particularly disturbed the World Council of Churches. The accusations were warranted at least in their assumption that Amsterdam expressed no preference as it confronted the realities of political institutions, economic practices and cultural values represented by the Liberal democracies and the Communist societies of the East. Such an attitude was the result of a policy, even if unformulated, of a decision, even if undiscussed, of an attitude, even if unanalysed. The year, it is important to remember, was 1948. How account for the position, lacking in realism when reviewed from the vantage-point of six years' further experience, adopted by the First Assembly of the World Council of Churches? Several reasons may be suggested.

1. The conviction that the Christian religion is above all political forms, is essentially uncommitted to a specific economic order. At Amsterdam the World Council of Churches did not consider itself 'the Church'—several changes to the plural were incorporated in the Reports (e.g. 'The Christian churches should . . .') to make that clear—but an association, a fellowship of ecclesiastical communions for stated purposes. As an expression of the qualified unity thus organizationally expressed, as well as to protect the independence of policy of its member churches, the World Council was determined to remain above the issues involved in the East-West debate.[2] In addition to the belief in

---

[1] By, among others, Stefan Osusky, former Czech Ambassador to France and England in *The Way of the Free*, pp. 163 ff., a book described by Sumner Welles as 'a major contribution to the political literature of our time'. Dr. Osusky is an ordained Lutheran minister. The Secretary of the World Council's Department on Church and Society acknowledged that the Amsterdam Report 'over-simplified the world's major political conflict by seeming to identify one side with Communism and the other with Capitalism'. Paul Abrecht, *ER* VI (October 1953), 1, p. 28.

[2] In the early months of the Second World War, during the Soviet invasion of Finland, 'a well-informed ecumenical source' (said to be the General Secretary who had just

the supra-temporal nature of the Christian religion, the World Council was conscious of the specific theological posture of some of its member churches towards *all* political developments.[1] An expression of this attitude is found in a pastoral letter of Bishop Ladislas Ravasz of the Reformed Church of Hungary, a delegate to the Amsterdam Assembly. Choosing the text (1 Thess. iv. 11) 'Study to be quiet and to do your own business and to work with your own hands,' the Bishop adverted: 'This word warns us that a pastor is not called upon to represent any secular ideology or to oppose such. The pastor's real task is to announce the evangelical conception of the world—the world which has, to its own misfortune, drawn away from God.'[2] This position of neutralism

returned from a meeting of the Administrative Committee) accounted for the 'silence [of the World Council of Churches in Process of Formation] in the face of the international situation', declaring: 'In answering this question we must start from the fact that the Œcumenical Movement does not exist apart from the churches which compose it, for it is a fellowship and not a monarchical institution. An œcumenical pronouncement can, therefore, be made only when there is substantial agreement among the churches.' Quoted in *EPS*, January 1940, p. 2.

[1] The Oxford Conference formulated this position as holding that 'there are no specifically Christian grounds and standards for the limitation of the State so long as the essential tasks of the Church itself are not involved. Christian freedom is an inner or eschatological freedom for which it is irrelevant how far the State extends its claims in the sphere of the social life. The freedom of the natural man and his subordination to the commands of the State is a matter of political responsibility. . . . The Church has no authority to demand in the name of the Gospel any rights either for individuals or for human associations. . . . The limits of its [the State] authority, however, have to be decided not from the standpoint of the Gospel or of the claims of the individual, but from that of the responsibility of the State to order and protect the common life. It is enough if, without presuming to interfere in the province of political authority, the Church makes it its concern to care for the oppressed and persecuted in compassionate love.' *Oxford*, pp. 268–9.

[2] *EPS*, January 1945, 3, p. 12. It is not to judge the attitude of any individual living under an alien occupation but because the metaphor employed intrigues the memory that the writer recalls the *bon mot* of Péguy: 'Ils ont les mains pures, mais ils n'ont pas de mains.' A pastoral letter of the Bishops of the Reformed Church in Hungary, issued on December 12, 1939, had a somewhat different accent. Archbishop Erkki Kaila of Finland had launched an appeal for spiritual and material aid at the moment of the Soviet invasion, stating: 'As we defend ourselves against the aggressor, we are also fighting against Bolshevism, the sworn enemy of Christianity. We feel that we are the advance guard of Western Christian civilization in the North. We have full confidence that the Christian Churches will not leave us to fight out this struggle alone.' In an answering pastoral the Hungarian Reformed Church expressed its sympathy and solidarity, announced services of public prayers of intercession 'for the Finnish people, and its Church, for the victory of its historically just cause' and arranged a special collection. Both documents are quoted in *EPS*, January 1940, 1, p. 3. When the German attack on the Soviet Union was under way, the Hungarian Reformed Mission Alliance declared: 'Now that the Crusade of Europe to wipe out Bolshevism is going on . . .' Quoted in *EPS*, October 1941, 34, p. 3.

was also the result of the absence of any serious, large-scale conflicts between Protestantism and the communist régimes of Eastern Europe up to that time.[1] The Protestant principle, with its emphasis on the individual who encounters a forgiving God in the solitariness of His saving Word, does not, of its nature, demand multiple ecclesiastical institutions and an international administrative apparatus whose very existence and normal functioning involve it inexorably in all the currents of history.[2]

2. The determination of the delegates to the Amsterdam Assembly, being in very large part clerics and thus professionally pledged to the ministry of reconciliation, to avoid any stand that would increase East-West tension or hot up the cold war.

3. The desire to achieve or express a solidarity with the working class and colonial peoples. Ecclesiastical leaders of all denominations in Europe are profoundly disturbed by the popular relegation of religion to the world of bourgeois culture; they are preoccupied with the loss[3] of the proletariat which they claim is a consequence of the alliance of the churches with reactionary forces in the nineteenth century; they are conscious that in mission lands national liberation movements have frequently identified Christianity with Western capitalism and have been supported by the Soviet Union. Whatever the ultimate allegiance of their local leaders, Communist Parties in many European countries have succeeded in attracting a popular protest vote of alarming proportions. At Amsterdam there was undoubtedly a proper concern lest any indication of even apparent partisanship should alienate the working class and colonial people further from the churches.

4. The tragic experiences of delegates at Amsterdam—including

[1] Except for the Lutheran Church in Hungary over the school question.

[2] Thus, Karl Barth: 'L'Eglise existe là, où l'homme écoute Dieu . . . Il n'y a aucune Eglise hors de cette relation.' Révélation, Eglise, Théologie, pp. 30–1.

[3] 'It is said that the Archbishop of Canterbury lamented to Disraeli, somewhere about 1860, that "the Church had lost the towns". "Your Grace is mistaken," replied Disraeli, "the Church never had the towns."' J. V. Langmead Casserley, The Retreat from Christianity in the Modern World, pp. 112–13. The working class was not 'lost'; it never had much connexion with organized religion from the time it came into existence between 1830 and 1880. Among other factors there were inadequate religious facilities in the new industrial agglomerations.

the Germans—at the hands of Nazism. 'Communism' evoked memories for some of collaboration in the Resistance, for all of the Soviet Union's 'Great Patriotic War' which had reduced the number of German bombers menacing European cities, withdrawn dozens of German divisions facing Allied armies and produced finally the common victory.

5. The political preferences of the authors of the Report. Section III, it can be fairly said, was inspired by the almost mystical appeal of *La Troisième Force*, its imagination caught up by the expectation of a dynamic, creative programme to be achieved mainly by Socialist political groups such as the British Labour Party. Socialism was favoured as a solution, if the political affiliation of the Chairman and the organizational allegiance of the Secretary are indicative. An Asian member of the Drafting Committee assured the Section that a rapid and thoroughgoing socialization in the West was the answer to communism and the means of creating conditions under which the message of the Church could be profitably heard in the non-Christian world. Marxist analysis offered for many an explanation of the disastrous instability of the world's economy between the two wars, years of widespread unemployment during which many of the Amsterdam delegates faced their early family or pastoral experiences. Disenchantment with the failure of the promises following 'a war to end war' was easily translated into a conviction that the pretensions of the Liberal society of the West were hypocritical, its basis a fraud. Such disillusionment tended to encourage a will to believe in the existence, if not of a Workers' Paradise in the Soviet Union, at least of a land of honest men bravely constructing a new society of equality and decency. Henry Wallace was by no means a solitary figure in 1948 in holding that, while political justice might characterize Western societies, economic justice was the achievement of the Soviets.[1]

[1] Thus, Reinhold Niebuhr: 'Those of us who used Marxist collectivism to counter liberal individualism, Marxist catastrophism to counter liberal optimism and Marxist determinism to challenge liberal moralism and idealism must admit that the "truths" which we used to challenge "error" turned out to be no more true (though also no less

6. The absence of accurate information on the nature and functioning of contemporary communist societies. Here, again, the lack of resources for historical inquiry (or the decision that such a method elicited tendentious themes) handicapped the Amsterdam analyses. The difficulties, to be sure, were major. The nature of the communist régimes newly installed in East Europe escaped the comprehension of an outstanding expert on the area, Hugh Seton-Watson.[1] If a specialist on an area could be deceived, it is perhaps not surprising that an editor of an American religious weekly, an alternate delegate to the Amsterdam Assembly, could make a rapid tour of East Europe and conclude that all was well.[2] The Secretary-General of the Hungarian Communist Party, Matyas Rakosi, had assured him in an interview that the régime had no malevolent dispositions towards religion, that it was, of course, having difficulties with one irascible prelate but that was because of his retrograde views and the support he was getting from fellow ecclesiastical conspirators abroad. Time and the flow of events would supply much information missing at Amsterdam.[3] There was, it should

true) than the liberal ones. But they were much more dangerous precisely because Marxism in its orthodox variety makes for a monopoly of political and economic power which is dangerous to justice, while a liberal society preserves the balance of power in the community which makes for justice, though there were and are some flagrant injustices as the result of a monopoly of economic power. Those of us who were critical of capitalism were in short too uncritical of the Marxist alternative even when we rejected the Communist version of Marxism and espoused democratic Marxism. The present writer is ready to confess to his complicity in these errors.' In *Christian Century* LXX (August 19, 1953), 33, p. 937.

[1] In a book reversing his former published opinions, the Oxford historian writes: 'In an earlier work somewhat hurriedly composed in 1942–3 and dealing with the period between the two world wars, I was, I hope, reasonably well supplied with the first qualification [personal experience of Eastern Europe and knowledge of its background] and to a lesser extent with the second [close attention to current events over the period concerned] but completely lacked the third [study of the theory and practice of Russian bolshevism and European communism]. I knew nothing of Russian history, the Soviet régime or the organization of Communist Parties. I had seen Communists in Eastern Europe only as martyrs of Fascist dictatorships, regarded with sympathy by many democratic intellectuals and discontented peasants.' *The East European Revolution*, p. lx.

[2] Clifford P. Morehouse in *The Living Church* CXVII (October 5, 1948), 10, pp. 6–13.

[3] Thus the same Matyas Rakosi in a speech as Premier on February 29, 1952, described with disarming cynicism how the Hungarian Communist Party feigned coalition tactics to dispose of its partners in the government one by one. Summarizing a seven-year history Rakosi referred to the gradual, day-by-day slicing off of allies and potential

be remembered, a fairly widespread disposition to regard Communists primarily if not exclusively as hardy social planners interested mainly in land reform with whom relations could be profitably conducted in the interest of a common effort at social amelioration.[1]

7. The aspirations of the Ecumenical Movement. Apart from the humane desire not to aggravate the difficulties of member churches living under (and in some cases co-operating with) Communist régimes, Amsterdam preferred to avoid an attitude which would impair the possibility of the future adherence to the World Council of the Russian Orthodox Church and the ecclesiastical communions owing allegiance to the Moscow Patriarchate, an adherence long desired in order to augment the geographical and confessional range of the Ecumenical Movement. This understandable sentiment was made explicit in the proposal by an English delegate during a plenary meeting that 'the Marxist Communism of our day', declared to be in conflict with Christianity in the Section III Report, should not be termed 'atheistic'.[2] Nor should the general resentment of the World Council constituency over the repressive restrictions imposed by the Spanish Government on a small Protestant minority be forgotten.

Whatever the intentions of the delegates to the World Council's

victims as 'salami tactics'. He frankly admitted that the success of these tactics was possible only because 'the presence in the country of the Soviet Army precluded any attempt at armed rebellion' and because the Soviet Government shielded local Communist Party leadership 'from diplomatic interference of the great Western powers'. Without this assistance, he concluded, 'the Hungarian People's Democracy— and we may well add, the others, too—would never have been born'. *New York Times*, March 1, 1952.

[1] This was the general attitude of the American people and certainly of its government up to 1947–8, argues former Ambassador John Leighton Stuart in his *My Fifty Years in China*. Nicolas Berdyaev, who at his death was a member of the Amsterdam Preparatory Commission III, had pointed out that 'Marxism in its Russian form proclaims the dominance of politics over economics' and this 'in spite of the doctrinaire understanding of Marxism' on the part of Russian revolutionary leaders. Berdyaev attributed this inversion (or subversion) of Marx's thought to Lenin who 'asserted the obvious primacy of politics over economics'. *The Origin of Russian Communism*, pp. 151, 170.

[2] 'It might prove detrimental to the relations of the World Council and of individual Christians with the Russian people and the Russian Church. It was wrong to think that Russian Communism was anti-God.' *Amsterdam*, p. 84. The suggestion was ignored.

First Assembly, whatever influences shaped their opinions,[1] they had found a double danger for the Responsible Society in two ideologies—*laissez-faire* capitalism and communism—which, by implication at least, they suggested were of equal menace and of equal actuality.

4. *Evanston Reassessments*

The counsel in the form of challenging questions which the Second Assembly of the World Council of Churches offered to Christians living either in a communist or a non-communist society will be considered later in the section on 'Corporate Christian Influence on Society'. By what it left unsaid, however, Evanston indicated that communism as an ideology and, more particularly, as a political reality is today generally recognized in ecumenical circles as a present danger to human freedom and religious liberty, while capitalism (which it termed 'the business system') is accorded a new respect. A larger experience, plus a determination to avoid abstractions of doubtful appositeness, explain in good part the change of focus.

In the six intervening years the Ecumenical Community encountered 'Communism' more as an historical reality than as an ideology. The results were disturbing. The developments in the World Council's member churches in China, for example, were the subject of a discussion *in camera* at the meeting of its Central Committee in 1951. No published accounts exist on the information received on the changes in the ecclesiastical structure of those churches nor on the reasons for their publicly deplored absence from Evanston but it may be assumed that the reports were disquieting. The attacks on the Evangelical Youth Movement in the Soviet Zone of Germany, the culmination of a series of interferences in church administration, shocked Karl Barth

---

[1] It is doubtful if any of the Amsterdam delegates were consciously reacting against the thesis first argued back in 1903 by Max Weber in his *Die Protestantische Ethik und der Geist des Kapitalismus*. Any delegate embarrassed by the charge that the capitalistic spirit derived from the Reformation would be aware of the subsequent revisions of the thesis in Professor R. H. Tawney's *Religion and the Rise of Capitalism* (1926) and Professor Amintore Fanfani's *Catholicism, Protestantism and Capitalism* (1938).

into a protest addressed to the Minister of Security of the German Democratic Republic.[1] The material for the Study Department's inquiry on 'The Witness of Christians in Communist Countries' was meagre enough but sufficient to reveal that, while religion might be purged of impure motivation and dubious associations under the experience of a communist régime, its possibilities of social action were non-existent.

The nature and function of the World Council of Churches, it need scarcely be remarked, debar it from any possibility of anathematizing any ideology or régime.

The Preparatory Commission's Memorandum on the Responsible Society acknowledged that in expressing alarm over the ideology or practice of *laissez-faire* capitalism it would be beating a dead horse.[2] Indeed the Memorandum pointed to the need for surveillance of trends towards excessive State intervention in the economic process with consequent dangers of centralization and rigidity. Both these cautions were adopted at Evanston. 'Capitalism' was accorded a measure of praise: 'At its best the business system has provided incentives for the responsible initiative and hard work which produce economic progress, and has embodied the wisdom of decentralized decisions and widely distributed power. These are virtues needed in any system.'[3]

A number of social evils were listed in the Evanston Report as making the delegates 'uneasy about the existing situation'.[4] In which type of society these abuses were found was not indicated. Since positive action to remedy these deficiencies and to guard against these dangers was demanded and since the Preparatory Commission had earlier acknowledged the impossibility of anyone 'exercising effective control over political

---

[1] *EPS*, April 29, 1953. Barth could hardly be considered a victim of sterile anti-communist hysteria. He had a little earlier characterized the Paris-Bonn Agreements, restoring sovereignty to the West German Federal Republic and providing for its representation in the European Defence Community, as 'the worst political error' since the Munich settlement of 1938. On the persecution in East Germany cf. Pasteur E. Ungerer's two articles in *Réforme*, May 9 and 23, 1953.

[2] 'Today, therefore, there is little support in countries with a democratic tradition either for consistent collectivism or a purely *laissez-faire* economy.' 'The Responsible Society in a World Perspective', *ER* VI (October 1953), 1, p. 78.

[3] *Evanston*, p. 118.   [4] *Ibid.*, pp. 118–20.

authority and economic power' under communist régimes,[1] it was manifestly the evils and failings of capitalist society which were being scrutinized. The tendencies to exploit human acquisitiveness, to create unlimited wants, to over-emphasize material values and to appeal to motives of social pride, envy, lust, through irresponsible salesmanship and advertising, were condemned as dangerous and in need of curbing. Conceding the place of incentive and the inevitability of a certain inequality if regimentation is to be avoided, the Report deplored the great contrasts between rich and poor as destructive of fellowship and the political institutions of a responsible society. Improved welfare legislation for the economically weak members of society was urged, together with resistance to any tendency on the part of the State to monopolize the social welfare field. Greater concern for the common good was looked for from trade unions and professional associations. A larger realization of the effect of national policies on the lives and welfare of people in other countries was desired.

The change of viewpoint was a result (and a reflection) of the rehabilitation of 'the business system' among thoughtful observers.[2] The news has broken through the Talmudic discussions of various schools of Marxists that, despite the alleged Iron Law announced by the Prophet, the real wages of the

---

[1] Cf. *supra*, p. 193 n.2.

[2] It is impossible to surmise to what extent delegates to World Council Assemblies share the prejudices against the business system and the capitalist social order ascribed to intellectuals and explained in these terms: 'Is all this not largely due to the fact that under capitalism, for the first time, due to the secular and "commercial" spirit that dominates it, the intellectual cannot find a place at the very centre of the system commensurate with his sense of charismatic importance? . . . In recent years, however, as a result of historical lessons that even the intellectual cannot escape, a marked change of attitude has taken place. Confrontation with Communist totalitarianism has well-nigh destroyed the ideological foundations of "progressivism" and has helped reconcile the intellectual with his society and culture, in which he has begun to discover hitherto unsuspected virtues. A new climate of opinion has come to prevail, very different from the orthodox "progressive" ideology of an earlier generation. The new anti-positivist emphasis on "values" in social philosophy, the new appreciation of the self-regulating mechanism of the market in economics, and the new appeal of a responsible Burkean conservatism in political thinking are marks of the spirit of our time.' Will Herberg in the *New Leader* xxxvii (June 28, 1954), 26, p. 25. Cf. also Raymond Aron, *L'Opium des Intellectuels* (Paris: Calmann-Lévy, 1955).

worker have steadily, if painfully, risen. This has not happened, to be sure, through the altruism of the employers but in part through the increased efficiency demanded by competition and in part through the success of 'countervailing powers' whose possibility Marx was incapable of foreseeing. For, as Professor John K. Galbraith pointed out to the meeting of the American Economic Association in 1952, an additional factor controlling the concentration of economic power has made its presence felt. Along with the force of competition and of State regulation, once deemed the only two conceivable shackles on monopoly, a series of elements—'countervailing powers'—have entered the scene to curb the excesses of *laissez-faire* capitalism'—labour federations and farm bureaux, organizations of large chain and department stores to offset the market power of great manufacturers. Political trends and, possibly, the success of the American economy in supplying material wants and a rising standard of living for its workers undoubtedly influenced Evanston in its 'fresh recognition of the importance of relative freedom in enterprise and of the regulating role of the price system'.[1]

The published reactions to the preliminary Memorandum on the Responsible Society offer assurance that the Evanston Report, which followed it closely, adequately represents the viewpoint of the World Council constituency on contemporary communism and capitalism. Its judicious balance of criticism and its appreciation of the benefits of 'the business system' express the average of the opinions held on the subject in the ecumenical world.[2]

vi.   CORPORATE CHRISTIAN INFLUENCE ON SOCIETY

The World Council of Churches has frequently asserted that the Church has a role to play in the right ordering of society, a

[1] *Evanston*, p. 117.

[2] The comments on the Memorandum appear in the June 1954 issue of *Church and Society*, a monthly bulletin published by the World Council's Department of the same name. One unidentified Professor of Economics in the United States regretted the absence of 'a unifying theme' and was struck by the number of times the Memorandum 'used the expressions "on the one hand" and "on the other hand", "in some countries", "in other countries", etc.'.

responsibility to fulfil in changing economic life. Both Assemblies described some modes of exercising an influence in the political and social spheres. Neither Assembly, however, defined in any detail the nature of this function; neither was very clear on what entity was to make this impact on society; neither indicated, in other words, in what sense the word 'Church' was to be taken.

1. Means of Influence

Is the Church merely to offer moral judgment on political trends and economic practices or has it in addition an action programme of its own—charitable, health and educational institutions, for example, paralleling State institutions but remaining independent of them—through which it makes its specific contribution to society? Is 'the Church' the composite of the ecclesiastical organizations found in the World Council constituency or is it the totality of individuals belonging to churches which are members of the Council? The latter question raises the possibility of the civic obligations of the Christian to the community and its political agencies apart from the fact of his membership in a church. To clarify these points, to illumine these questions, it is profitable to consider the discussions at other ecumenical encounters whose conclusions were used as foundations for continuing World Council study.[1]

(a) Thus the Oxford Conference of the Universal Christian Council for Life and Work of 1937 found 'The Basis for a Christian Concern for the Economic Order' in the scriptural commandment of love of the neighbour, obedience to which in the economic sphere implies the pursuit of justice by individual Christians and their energetic efforts 'to secure for all who are their neighbours such opportunities as are necessary for their full development as persons in body, mind and spirit'.[2] This

---

[1] 'The report from Evanston on Social Questions . . . is a continuation of the concern for social and political questions expressed in the ecumenical movement beginning with the Stockholm Conference (1925) and carried forward at Oxford (1937) and at the first Assembly of the World Council in Amsterdam (1948).' *Evanston Speaks*, p. 42.

[2] *Oxford*, p. 87.

concern for social justice was derived from a duty towards God who creates man in His image and proposes to restore that dignity through the redemption that is in Christ.[1]

By 'the Church' was understood a sociological phenomenon rather than an object of faith, 'organized Christianity rather than the Una Sancta', the sum of separate Christians in both their individual and corporate capacity. It also meant, in other contexts, the aggregate of those ecclesiastical institutions, denominations or societies, composing the total Church.[2] But the social function of the Church, as seen at Oxford, is primarily the fulfilment of the commandment to love one's neighbour by the millions of individual Christians who hear the Word of God and manifest in their actions their acceptance of its message. A semi-official preparatory volume, to be sure, considered possible lines of 'action of the Church through its ecclesiastical heads and leaders, through its synods, councils and assemblies and other official organs, and through the clergy and ministers, who are its office-bearers'.[3] It was from this more restricted grouping, called also 'the Church', that the Oxford Report expected guidance concerning economic life by way of the proclamation of principles and ends, the presentation of facts underlying social problems and the explication of the obstacles to social justice constituted by sin.[4]

(b) The Amsterdam Report of Section III judged that the social influence of the Church would result 'primarily from its influence upon its members through constant teaching and preaching of Christian truth in ways that illuminate the historical conditions in which men live and the problems which they face'.[5] Obviously, 'the Church' was here described as an ecclesiastical organization. The effectiveness of its influence was deemed proportioned to the *prises de conscience* of individual Christians confronting their responsibilities in the temporal realm. Furthermore, if the Church overcomes national and social barriers in its membership, the resulting solidarity would help to check, it was stated, the

---

[1] *Oxford*, p. 92.   [2] *Ibid.*, pp. 77–8.
[3] J. H. Oldham in *The Church and its Function in Society*, p. 207.
[4] *Oxford*, p. 90.   [5] *Amsterdam*, p. 81.

disintegration of contemporary society. Especially in the field of race-relations must the Church apply itself 'to eliminate these practices [of discrimination and segregation] from the Christian community, because they contradict all that it believes about God's love for all His children'.[1] On occasion, it was felt, the Churches must give concrete guidance, warning against specific forms of injustice or social idolatry; but Christian political parties, it was asserted, are instruments of dubious usefulness whatever their temporary justification. Finally, in an idea which shifted the meaning to emphasize the membership, the social influence of the Church was acknowledged to be conditioned by the situation in which Christians find themselves, their proportion in the total population and the attitude of the government in power. The lot of churches under contrasting conditions, their failures, achievements and sufferings, it was noted, have enriched ecumenical experience.

(c) The Evanston Assembly's Section III on 'The Responsible Society' reaffirmed the Ecumenical Community's conviction that 'the Churches . . . have a duty to society as part of their mission to the world'. The nature and sources of that duty were left unexamined.[2] The role of the Church in economic life, according to the Section on Social Questions, involves underscoring the moral implications of certain problems, issuing warnings against certain trends and practices and reminding Christians of some specific obligations. The Section, furthermore, indicated the lines of counsel the Church offers today 'in relation to Communist–non-Communist tension'.

It will be apposite, therefore, to review some fields where, in the judgment of the World Council, the Church may exercise a social role, and some of the problems connected with such activities.

---

[1] *Ibid.*

[2] 'Clearly, there were in the section many different theological explanations as to the way in which one proceeded from these theological premises to judgments about specific social issues as developed in the body of the report. It was agreed, however, that it was not necessary to resolve such theological differences in order to arrive at common judgments on the specific issues.' *Evanston Speaks*, pp. 42–3.

2. *Public Pronouncements*

One way in which 'the Church'—considered as an ecclesiastical organization rather than as a group of citizens composing its membership—exercises a social function is by expressing its judgment on political trends and economic proposals. As the formal expression of the Ecumenical Community, the World Council of Churches (its members would concede) has a duty to society in this regard, and one which it fulfils by issuing statements. The 'Appeal' addressed to the governments and the peoples of the world in the hope of relieving present international tensions, adopted in resolution form by the Evanston Assembly, would be an example. Concerning the public pronouncements of the World Council of Churches as an entity, the Amsterdam Assembly, as the constituting authority, approved the following declaration as Rule IX of the Constitution: 'In the performance of its functions, the Council through its Assembly or through its Central Committee may publish statements upon any situation or issue with which the Council or its constituent churches may be confronted.' Other sections of Rule IX state that such declarations do not imply that the Council has or can have constitutional authority over its member churches or the right to speak for them; furthermore, the Rule indicates under what circumstances and by what officers and organs statements may be published in the name of the World Council.

It is more than a little paradoxical that a generation which resents the enunciation of Christian principles of morality as an unwarranted interference, frequently demands that religious groups 'take a stand' on some issue of political import. Having been told to confine themselves to their own field, presumably the things of the next world, the churches are often pressed to favour one side or another on questions that are very much of this world. There is a very real and present danger, in democratic societies not least, that religion may be gradually adapted to fit secular aims, however worthy, that it may be used to serve as a social tonic spurring greater popular energy in a national cause. This is an example of the perversion of religion and the surrender by ecclesiastical officials described by T. S. Eliot, a participant in the Oxford Life and Work Conference, in his poetic dramatization of a Church-State conflict in the lines:

> The last temptation is the greatest treason
> To do the right deed for the wrong reason.[1]

The World Council of Churches does not live in an historical vacuum. It is subject to constant demand that it shore up the prestige of political groups by canonizing their objectives, that it pronounce a moral verdict on the manifold issues of the day— down to events as seemingly ephemeral as the Rosenberg case. It cannot take refuge in the fatuities of empty generalizations, of transcendental irrelevances.

In a paper contributed to the discussions preparatory to the Oxford Conference, Professor R. H. Tawney declared that if Christianity is normative, if it has a unique judgment to utter on contemporary conditions, then the leaders of the churches ought 'whatever the cost, to state fearlessly and in unmistakable terms what precisely they conceive that distinctive contribution to be. If they do not, then let them cease reiterating second-hand platitudes which disgust sincere men and bring Christianity into contempt.'[2] The Chairman of Amsterdam's Section III, Dr. C. L. Patijn, complained that Oxford's 'goals which represent the purpose of God for our time' were not specific enough and insisted that such abstractions do not come to grips with the applications of such norms to the problems of institutional life and structural reform.[3] The Secretary's Minutes of the Evanston Section on the Responsible Society contain similar demands for specification, for concrete instances of colonialism and the precise location of forced labour camps.

The eagerness for official moral guidance is understandable enough but it frequently does not take into account realistically the difficulties involved and the perplexity of the World Council's position. Some of these difficulties arise from its very nature: it

---

[1] From *Murder in the Cathedral*. Cf. also his *The Idea of a Christian Society*, p. 59 and the note on p. 85.

[2] Quoted in Oldham, *op. cit.*, p. 214. [3] *CDS*, p. 160.

can only voice a consensus of the opinion of its constituency. Some arise from its task: to maintain and enlarge the Ecumenical Community. Some arise from the intellectual climate of the day with its one-dimensional ceiling, blocking from view the Christian perspective and dulling the memory of Christian premises. Is even the grammar of the Christian discourse in general currency? The General Secretary was obviously adverting to this phase of the problem when he remarked at a gathering of the Commissions preparing for the Amsterdam programme: 'We must say something clear and definite also about the present world situation. How can that be done in such a way that it will be understood by a generation which has lost the ability to understand any Christian language? We must at least try.'[1] Nor do the World Council officials overestimate either the efficacy of public pronouncements or the actual influences of the churches today.[2]

Not the least of the difficulties involved in making public pronouncements on economic and political questions arises from the very complexity of the technical factors and historical facts upon which any responsible judgment must be based and from the limitations of the resources available to the World Council's Study Department and the Commission of the Churches on International Affairs. An adequate analysis of the technical factors and an efficient assembling of all the facts of contemporary social problems would demand funds not currently at hand for the Study Department. Moreover, the World Council is, by definition, to stimulate rather than to centralize ecumenical thinking; it may not impose answers.[3]

[1] At Bossey Conference, June 23, 1947. *Archives.*

[2] Thus, Dr. Visser 't Hooft: 'It [the Church] has long ceased to be the dominant factor of European life. It represents in many countries a small minority surrounded by paganized masses.' *The Kingship of Christ*, p. 8. And Stewart Winfield Herman who helped to initiate the World Council's relief and reconstruction programme: 'Despite the various degrees of influence prevailing in different countries, *at no point can it be said that Christian conviction—divorced from political pretension—is giving decisive direction to the trends in Europe.* This is the most serious thing that can be said about Europe today. But not about Europe only!' *Report from Christian Europe*, p. 198. Italics in the original.

[3] Thus Reinhold Niebuhr: 'The lack of a clear spiritual witness to the truth in Christ is aggravated by certain modern developments, among them the increasing complexity of

Basic and still unresolved, however, is the question of the World Council's social philosophy, its moral perspective (if the word 'philosophy' is deemed controversial), its criterion for appraising economic and political questions. Is an 'ethic of inspiration' to be favoured over an 'ethic of ends'? Such an option supposes norms not subject to rational scrutiny and produces conclusions that cannot be tested by human experience. Prophetic utterance raises the whole question of the credentials of the prophet[1] whereas the only authority assigned by the Constitution of the World Council to its public pronouncements is their intrinsic 'truth and wisdom'.[2]

3. Programmes for Action

As a fellowship of separate churches, organized to fulfil specified tasks assigned to it by its membership, the World Council of Churches has, obviously, no action programme of

moral problems and the increasing dominance of the group or collective over the life of the individual. The complexity of ethical problems makes an evangelical impulse to seek the good of the neighbour subordinate to the complicated questions about which of our neighbours has first claim upon us or what technical means are best suited to fulfil their need. The "Enlightenment" was wrong in expecting virtue to flow inevitably from rational enlightenment. But that does not change the fact that religiously inspired good-will, without intelligent analysis of the factors in a moral situation and of the proper means to gain desirable ends, is unavailing.' *Christian Century* LXX (July 22, 1953), p. 841.

[1] The conflicting views on rearmament expressed in German theological circles today do not appreciably clarify the basis of an 'ethic of inspiration'.

[2] Rule IX, 2. The difficulty of consensus is apparent from a consideration of a concrete political problem of historic concern to Christians. The Secretary of the International Mission Council 'in association with the World Council of Churches', Dr. Gloria Wymer, noted the 'deep and tragic' division within the Christian Church on the Palestine Question. Christians in the USA, she explained, on the whole support Israel while missionaries in the Near East support the Arabs. This rift 'frustrated it [the Church or the IMC?] in making any kind of commitment'. *EPS*, November 19, 1949. On December 10, 1949, the UN voted to organize Palestine in two states with Jerusalem and its environs an internationally administered enclave. The Commission of the Churches on International Affairs had addressed a letter to the members of the UN Political Committee calling for guarantees of human rights in the area and endorsing the principle of international responsibility but without indicating how it was to be exercised. When the Trusteeship Council was considering the mode of actualizing the settlement voted by the UN Assembly, Dr. Nolde, as Director of the CCIA, submitted a memorandum indicating the absence of agreement among the church groups involved on the political arrangements preferred for the Holy Land, though the Archbishop of Canterbury, in a separate memorandum, urged the internationalization of the Old City of Jerusalem. Cf. *ibid.*, December 5, 1949, and February 17, 1950.

its own, no mandate to express or implement its independent views on the social function of the Church. Its service to refugees, its relief and reconstruction programme constitute, to be sure, an exercise of charity with tangible social consequences—one need only think of the migration aspect of the work—but even here the World Council is an agent for the co-operative effort of its member churches. It is principally through the Study Department, through the discussions it inaugurates, through the encounters it arranges, through the thinking it stimulates, that the social influence of the World Council as an entity is exercised. With the Study Department can be equated, as having the same function, the Ecumenical Institute and its Graduate School of Ecumenical Studies. More direct is the influence on existing international institutions assigned to the Commission of the Churches on International Affairs, jointly sponsored by the World Council and the International Missionary Council, which represents the interests of the ecumenical constituency at the United Nations, studies trends as well as makes concrete proposals, and alerts its affiliated national committees as to the possibility of action in their several countries on issues of religious concern.

In preparation for the Amsterdam Assembly the Section III Study Commission conducted a survey of 'New Beginnings in the Relations of the Church with Society' to uncover evidence of the social influence of the churches. The summary appearing in the background volume noted efforts to allay enmity and ameliorate suffering connected with the war, citing the comfort and practical aid rendered by Protestant churches to the German minority expelled from Czechoslovakia, the *Volksdeutsche* driven from Eastern Europe, the displaced persons of all races; the proclamations of penitence for national sin by different churches seeking reconciliation with former enemy countries; the activity of *Cimade*[1] in sending teams of French Protestant young people to share the experience of prisoners of war, the refugees and the

---

[1] Another Section of the Amsterdam Assembly considered *Cimade* a specifically evangelizing effort, listing it among the instruments for spreading the Gospel. Cf. *The Church's Witness to God's Design*, pp. 152 ff.

inhabitants of bombed-out cities. Attention was called to programmes coping with the disintegration of the family such as the Christian Home Life Movement in China and India and the Home and Family Movement in Great Britain, said to have been the inspiration for the Central Marriage Guidance Council. The summary pointed to centres of study, such as Sigtuna in Sweden, Kerk en Wereld in Holland, Bossey in Switzerland and the Evangelical Academies at Bad Boll, Hofgeismar, Loccum and Tutzing in Germany,[1] where groups from the different professions and employments—doctors, politicians, social workers, journalists, representatives of labour and management—gather to discuss realistically how a Christian is to live out the implications of his faith in his vocational life. A similar purpose motivates the Christian Frontier Council in England, the Associations Professionelles Protestantes in France and the Layman's Movement in the United States. The collaboration of religious groups in the effort to transform the Dumbarton Oaks draft into a United Nations Charter that recognized the role of the smaller States, the existence of an order of justice and human rights, was hailed.

In the field of the reform of economic institutions, however, the summary acknowledged the absence of concrete achievement, remarking: 'The Church has not made up its mind finally what are the Christian incentives for industry in a world of economic change, nor on the claims of a collective society (distinct from anti-religious systems with which it is too often associated) as over against an individualist society, nor what ought to be the political alignments in which a Christian man will most effectively discharge his social and political responsibility.'[2]

The survey of recent ecumenical thought and activity in social

[1] One notes the absence of any mention of the Moral Rearmament Movement which proposes to transform society by changing individuals and wonders if MRA is considered not a specifically Christian Movement. Yet the preparatory volume on evangelism believed that Moral Rearmament 'rendered signal services to the Christian cause in the depressed period between the wars'. *Ibid.*, p. 139. Possibly MRA was not judged sufficiently formally related to any given church, but the same could be said for other movements noted, nor has the Salvation Army, which belongs to the World Council, a particularly pronounced ecclesiastical definition. [2] *CDS*, p. 119.

matters prepared for the Evanston Assembly delegates, reported a general acceptance of the idea of Christian responsibility for society. The present need, the replies to the questionnaires sent out by the Study Department revealed, is to think through clear Christian positions supporting a new set of specific objectives, a task made difficult by the very complexity of modern society and the lack of systematic contact between theologians and those immersed in political and economic life. A Swedish correspondent suggested an impediment to effective social action: 'The fundamental problem with all treatment of Christian social ethics seems to be to build a bridge that connects ideas formed on principles with a realistic programme of action.'[1]

With clearly no intention to offer more than an example of pressing problems the Evanston Report, in discussing 'The Role of the Church' in the Responsible Society, listed among its duties the promotion of 'adequate assistance on the national and international level for children, the sick, the old, refugees and other economically weak groups by means of church organizations, voluntary societies and local and national governments'. No effort was made to distinguish the relative spheres of voluntary as distinguished from government action in the social welfare field. An obligation on Christians, presumably as private citizens, to foster improved legislation for welfare and medical care while resisting tendencies of State monopoly, was asserted. The problems of making real the hopes of a Responsible Society in a World Perspective are recognized as prodigious.

4. Political Parties

One of the items in the 'Appeal' voted at Evanston directed 'the Churches to bid their members recognize their political responsibilities'. The Resolution went on to recommend that the churches 'ask Christian technicians and administrators to find a vocation in the service of United Nations Agencies engaged in meeting the needs of economically and technically under-developed countries'. Such careers, it was noted, would bring a

[1] *CHTC*, p. 30.

Christian temper of love and understanding to the programmes of mutual assistance. Given the nature of the United Nations and the posts indicated as deserving the dedicated service of Christians, a manifestly non-political activity was envisaged. However, in the national community, at least in democratic societies, programmes of assistance for the sick, for refugees and other economically weak groups, as well as legislation for improved social welfare and adequate medical care (to use examples drawn from the Evanston Section III Report) are inevitably matters of political action engaging the efforts of political parties.

How are the members of the churches to acquit themselves of these political responsibilities once recognized? And, to be more concrete, what should be their attitude towards political parties? The subject was not discussed at Evanston although it had been raised at a plenary session during the First Assembly where it was considered to constitute a problem.

The problem was occasioned specifically by the fact of political parties claiming to find their orientation and inspiration in Christian social principles, a supposition which had been rejected by the Reformed theologian, Karl Barth, and the Lutheran professor, L. Aalan.[1] The topic evoked small interest among those preparing the background volume for the guidance of the delegates to the Amsterdam Assembly. A conference of the Section III Study Commission, meeting just before the Assembly, concluded that, since all politics were morally rather dubious, such political groupings were undesirable. The Minutes of the Section discussion on the first draft of the Report reveal a negative judgment on 'Christian' political parties, delegates from Anglo-Saxon countries preferring the strategy of penetrating existing parties, others pointing out that semi-confessional political groupings invite the opposition of all other political

---

[1] In *Christengemeinde und Bürgergemeinde* and *Verkündigungstheokratie* respectively. Barth holds that sufficient political guidance is given the citizen through the preaching, petitions, publications and synodal resolutions of the Church. He recognizes, moreover, that the basis of such parties is the acceptance of the Natural Law which he rejects. For the Lutheran, Aalan, politics are 'worldly wisdom', the realm of this world.

parties to Christianity itself.[1] Seemingly the Drafting Committee decided to drop the topic.

During the discussion of the Report at a plenary session of the Assembly, the Chairman of Section III interrupted the debate to speak of an omitted paragraph concerning political parties and to ask for a public vote on its inclusion. As a result the Assembly agreed to accept a statement: (a) asserting that 'The Church as such should not be identified with any political party'; (b) warning that such groupings 'easily confuse Christianity with the inherent compromises of politics', deprive other parties of the leaven of Christian influence and may consolidate partisans of other groups against Christianity itself; but (c) conceding the possible usefulness in some situations for Christians to organize themselves into a political party for specific objectives, 'so long as they do not claim that it is the only possible expression of Christian loyalty in the situation'.[2]

What concrete situation was the paragraph concerned with, since it cannot be supposed that the delegates were indulging in an exercise of pure political theory? The Evangelical Church in Germany (EKiD) had expressed its pleasure two years earlier at the formation of a non-confessional party of Christian inspiration, a description which applied only to the Christian Democratic Union.[3] The Chairman of the Section told the present writer that the MRP group in France is not a confessional party in the sense discussed in the paragraph. There is no tradition of confessional parties in English-speaking lands and, probably because of the absence of religio-cultural conflicts, no thought of organizing such groups. The American and British delegates, therefore, can scarcely be supposed to have had much interest in the question.

[1] In a lone effort to be concrete an Italian pastor in the Section meeting claimed that the Christian Democrats in his country had not always given a great impression of integrity, with the result that most of his Evangelical members were Socialists or Communists.

[2] *Amsterdam*, p. 81.

[3] Cf. *EPS*, December 1945 (No. 46), p. 4. Later, difficulties arose with Chancellor Adenauer and Pastor Niemöller clashing bitterly over the rearmament question. Meetings were held between EKiD church leaders and CDU party leaders as well as with leaders of the Socialist Party. The Evangelical Church explained that every Christian should interest himself in political decisions but must decide for himself for which candidate to vote. Cf. *EPS*, April 7, 1950, p. 100.

Some Germans had viewed the establishment of the Federal Republic as an impediment to achieving national unity and a few irresponsibles had even suggested that the Christian Democratic Party was content to leave the preponderantly Protestant East Zone in Soviet hands. The partisan accusations of a 'Washington-Vatican-Bonn Axis', however, began to be heard considerably later and cannot be presumed to have had currency in the circles from which the delegates to the Amsterdam Assembly came.

By default, then, it would seem to be the situation in Holland that was principally envisaged. There a group of ministers and elders headed by Dr. Abraham Kuyper, on being expelled from the national Hervormde Kerk, had founded in 1885 the fundamentalist Gereformeerde Kerk and organized the conservative Anti-Revolutionary Party.[1] 'After the war,' to quote the Amsterdam preparatory volume, 'a number of prominent church members [including the Chairman of Section III] took action which resulted in the formation of a new Labour Party, to replace the old Social Democratic Party. Christians were included in the leadership of the new party, the previous Marxist outlook abandoned, and a positive attitude towards the Church and Christianity taken up.'[2] Was the World Council of Churches invited, in effect, to disapprove of Holland's Anti-Revolutionary Party by the inclusion of a paragraph in the Amsterdam Report? If so, the effort seems overzealous.

To examine the major issues scheduled for discussion at Evanston, especially in their relation to the situation in East Asia, an ecumenical conference was sponsored by the World Council's Study Department at Lucknow, India, during the last days of December 1952. With a number of members of the Council's Central Committee participating, the Study Conference, when considering the relevance of the idea of the Responsible Society, agreed that political action is a necessary means of promoting social justice. The fact, coupled with the obligation to change the structure of society, involves a duty: Christians 'must do

[1] Cf. Keller, *Church and State on the European Continent*, pp. 203 ff.
[2] *CDS*, p. 112.

everything possible to construct worthy instruments for responsible political action in order to realize the goal of the Responsible Society. This will mean in some cases the creation of healthy secular political movements.' The Lucknow Conference was more adamant, at least in language, than Amsterdam had been: 'under no circumstances,' it asserted, 'should Christians organize themselves into religious political parties'.[1] What a 'religious political party' particularly in the Asian context would be, is not clear. Conceivably, it would be the direct and unique expression in the political realm of some Christian ecclesiastical organization, thus paralleling the 'sects', say, in Vietnam. The danger is immediately obvious: such a tactic seems to submit the fate of the Kingdom of God to the electoral process.

The attitude of the World Council towards Europe's Christian Democratic Parties, then, seems to be one of reserve.[2] Liberty of choice of political allegiance, including the Communist Party, is upheld. Identification of the Church with the relativities of political action and the fate of political parties is feared. Each Christian is expected in the light of whatever norms of political wisdom he prefers, guided by either an 'ethic of inspiration' or an 'ethic of ends', to participate in the political life of the community and fulfil in his person the social function of the Church.

5. *Church and State*

Another area in which the Church, conceived as a concrete organization with religious purposes, exercises a social function is in its relations with the State, conceived as the political organ of the national community. Although the Evanston Assembly offered some observations on the Structure and Function of the State, the World Council of Churches has never systematically studied the problem of the relations of Church and State. Indeed an examination of the listing under that title in *Ecumenical Documents on Church and Society*, a symposium prepared by the

---

[1] *Christ—the Hope of Asia*, pp. 31–2.

[2] Yet Dr. H. Ehlers, a member of the Christian Democratic Union and President of the German Bundestag at the time of his death, was an active member of the Committee on the Christian Responsibility for European Co-operation.

Council's Study Department in preparation for the Evanston Assembly's discussions on the Responsible Society, reveals references only to conferences held before the World Council came formally into existence.

The Oxford Conference of 1937, meeting in the hour of the religious persecution in Germany, assigned to a separate Section, chaired by Professor Max Huber, the task of scrutinizing the relations of the two communities, one religious, the other secular. The Report was prefaced by a disclaimer: 'It is not the purpose of the following memorandum to set forth an abstract doctrine of the relation of Church and State either in sociological, legal or theological form.'[1] 'In any discussion of the relation of Church and State,' it was observed, 'the historical situation must always be considered.' It was the problems arising from the growing secularization of contemporary society and the growing power of the State, that the Oxford delegates chose to study.

Noting the distinctive functions of these two organizational entities[2] the Report listed the consequent obligations of the Church to the State, including prayer, conditioned obedience and fearless criticism.[3] The requirements of the freedom necessary as an essential condition for the Church to fulfil its primary purpose were specified;[4] it was indicated that these freedoms

[1] *Oxford*, p. 77.

[2] 'The Church [is] the trustee of God's redeeming Gospel and the State [is] the guarantor of order, justice and civil liberty.' *Ibid.*, p. 81.

[3] The duties for the churches and their members were listed as: '(i) That of praying for the State, its people and its government; (ii) That of loyalty and obedience to the State, disobedience becoming a duty only if obedience would be clearly contrary to the command of God; (iii) That of co-operation with the State in promoting the welfare of the citizens, and of lending moral support to the State when it upholds the standards of justice set forth in the Word of God; (iv) That of criticism of the State when it departs from those standards; (v) That of holding before men in all their legislation and administration those principles which make for the upholding of the dignity of man who is made in the image of God; (vi) That of permeating the public life with the spirit of Christ and of training up men and women who as Christians can contribute to this end.' It was added further that: 'In the interpretation of these duties it is important to keep constantly in mind that as the Church in its own sphere is a universal society, so to Christian faith the individual State is not itself the ultimate political unit, but a member of a family of nations with international relations and duties which it is the responsibility not only of the individual Christians but also of the Churches to affirm and to promote.' *Ibid.*, pp. 82–4.

[4] '(a) Freedom to determine its faith and creed; (b) Freedom of public and private worship, preaching and teaching; (c) Freedom from any imposition by the State of

could be present whether the churches are organized as free associations under the general laws of a country or whether, as Established Churches, they enjoy a special connexion with the State; should such an organic connexion impair the Church's freedom,[1] it was added, it would be the duty of ministers and members to secure that freedom even at the cost of disestablishment. The present tasks of the churches were indicated as repentance, co-operation, concern for religious freedom everywhere, sympathy for the oppressed and the renunciation of all forms of persecution.[2]

The duties of the State towards the Church were not specified beyond the recognition and protection of religious freedom. The Section on 'Church, Community and State in Relation to Education', however, called for co-operative action on the part

religious ceremonies and forms of worship; (d) Freedom to determine the nature of its government and the qualification of its ministers and members, and, conversely, the freedom of the individual to join the Church to which he feels called; (e) Freedom to control the education of its ministers, to give religious instruction to its youth, and to provide for adequate development of their religious life; (f) Freedom of Christian service and missionary activity, both home and foreign; (g) Freedom to co-operate with other Churches; (h) Freedom to use such facilities, open to all citizens or associations, as will make possible the accomplishment of these ends, as, e.g., the ownership of property and the collection of funds.' Oxford, pp. 84–5.

[1] The capitalization of 'Church' in the Oxford context would suggest that several churches (composing and corporately manifesting 'the Church') is meant, so that if the freedom of a minority church was seriously impaired, the established church should strive for general religious freedom even if it meant dissolving its organic connexion with the State.

[2] 'It is their duty: (a) To summon their own members to repentance, both as individuals and organized bodies, for their sins of omission and of commission and to pray for the spirit of consecration which shall make of them, both in their separate and in their united activities, agents which God may use for His purpose in the world; (b) To create within the local community, the nation, and the world such agencies of co-operative action as shall make it possible for them to discharge effectively such tasks as can be done in common; (c) To summon their individual members in their several callings, not only their clerical but also their lay members, men and women, to co-operate with the State in such constructive tasks as may be for the good of the whole; (d) To guard for all Churches, both as groups of witnessing Christians and in their organized capacity, the opportunity of worship, of witness, of service, and of education which is essential to their mission, and this not for their own sake only, but for the sake of the State; (e) To follow with sympathetic interest the fortunes of those, Christians and non-Christians, who are victims of cruelty and oppression, and to do what they can to secure for them a treatment compatible with the dignity of their human personality as children of God; (f) To renounce publicly and for ever the use of all forms of persecution, whether by Christians against other Christians, or by Christians against adherents of other religions.' Ibid., pp. 85–6.

of the government to make possible religious education for the nation's children.[1]

Advisedly, the Oxford Conference of 1937 abstained from any theological pronouncement on the knotty problem of the relations of Church and State. In a book published the previous year the Secretary of the Universal Christian Council on Life and Work, Professor Adolf Keller, had noted that the question was under serious study in the Ecumenical Community.[2] Positions have not changed substantially since that date: the World Council includes among its members established churches and free churches, each convinced of the value of the legal arrangement under which it lives. In general, the mind of the World Council would seem to favour the separation of Church and State[3] in the interest of greater religious liberty and more effective action towards constructing the Responsible Society.[4]

[1] 'If the majority of the population are in general sympathy with Christian standards and values, Church and State should find no difficulty in working together to assure a religious education to those who desire it. Obviously, freedom of conscience must be respected and no coercion exerted on those who do not wish religious training for themselves or their children. But the Christian or other religious elements in the population should not be deprived of their right to receive a completely religious education. Freedom of conscience in education has been too negatively conceived. There is both a liberty not to have religious training forced where it is objected to, and a liberty to have it provided where consciences feel it essential for the education of citizens of the State and of the Kingdom of God.' *Ibid.*, pp. 158–9. At Evanston the role of religion in public education was discussed in plenary session and it was voted, on the demand of the American delegates, to omit all references to the question whether God has significance for the educational process or not (as Dr. Van Dusen phrased the issue) and to refer the problem to the Central Committee. Cf. *Evanston*, pp. 109–12.

[2] 'The Ecumenical Movement is seriously seeking an answer to such questions. It is confronted with the tragic fact that the Reformation did not succeed in creating a spiritual unity among the Churches through a common re-discovery of the Gospel. Not only the conceptions of State and Church but even the interpretations of fundamental elements in the Gospel are different.' *Church and State on the European Continent*, p. 365.

[3] The term can have several meanings. It can mean (*a*) equal status for the Church with private societies; or (*b*) a position which allows the Church to order her own affairs according to common law; or (*c*) a situation in which the organization of the Church depends solely on the free will of its adherents; or (*d*) the reduction of the relations of the Church to a minimum. Or, as Professor Keller notes when describing the French legislation of 1905, it can mean 'the liberty to drown in unforeseen financial and other difficulties'. *Op. cit.*, p. 259.

[4] Thus, M. M. Thomas told a plenary session of the Evanston Assembly: 'The ideal of a secular State is basic to the ideal of a Responsible Society', quoted in Cecil Northcott's *Evanston World Assembly*, p. 39.

6. Race Relations

Possibly no problem is more pressing in the turbulent world of today than the manifold issues subsumed under the colourless caption—'race relations'. The upheavals in Asia, the unrest in Africa, the angry assertions of nationalism in all the former colonial areas of the world are rebellions against the nineteenth-century assumption of white supremacy and are resentful rejections of the political policies and social practices founded on that assumption. Sober scientific investigations by anthropologists and psychologists have exposed the myths invoked to justify fictitious essential human differences; their conclusions have been supported by the high authority of the United Nations' Educational, Scientific and Cultural Organization. The prestige of the Soviet Union in Asia and Africa is a result in no small degree of its constant claim of having achieved racial equality, of its boast of having outlawed in its Constitution racial discrimination.

On no question is the Christian conscience of the World Council's constituency more uneasy nor the evidence of the involvement of the churches in secular standards and practices more embarrassing.[1] It is not merely that distinctions based on race and colour retard the spread of the Christian Missions by reducing a universal religion to a provincial creed, nor that practices of racial segregation tolerated by Western church groups impair the desired harmonious fellowship with the 'younger' churches of Asia and Africa; it is recognized that such distinctions are a denial of the Gospel proclamation that God made all men of one blood to dwell upon the face of the earth and that the universal salvation wrought by the Cross has destroyed the man-made barriers between bond and free, Jew and Gentile,

[1] The Amsterdam preparatory volume noted that in the United States: 'Ninety per cent of the Negroes who belong to Protestant churches are to be found in purely Negro denominations. Most of the other ten per cent are to be found in local churches that are limited to their own race.' John C. Bennett in CDS, p. 100. The Evanston Inter-group Relations Commission put the figure of American Negro Christians customarily worshipping with white Christians at less than one-half of one per cent. Dr. Benjamin E. Mays told a plenary session: 'Local churches permit secular bodies such as the State and Federal courts, the United Nations, big-league baseball...colleges...and theatres to initiate change in the area of race...but local churches, Negro and white, follow slowly or not at all.'

black and white. The religious preaching of the churches is in danger of being outdistanced by the moral pretensions of the ideology of modern democracy, a secularized survival (in the Darwinian sense) of the Christian message.

Meeting in the day of the Nazi doctrine of the Aryan super-race and its untrammelled right, in virtue of its racial superiority, to dominate and even eliminate inferior peoples, the Oxford Life and Work Conference found racial differences fruitful and racial discrimination unwarranted.[1] The Amsterdam Assembly, as has been noted, listed as an exercise of the social function of the Church the 'call[ing of] society away from prejudice based upon race or colour and from the practices of discrimination and segregation as denials of justice and human dignity', adding that, if the Church's counsel is to be effective, it must 'take steps to eliminate these practices from the Christian community'. The suggestion made at a meeting of Section III to condemn segregation in principle and to deplore explicitly the toleration of the system in South African and American churches was not incorporated in the Report. The Minutes of the Section, however, show no consciousness of a distinction between the principle and the practice of segregation nor any disposition to defend such a dubious distinction. The Report of the visit of the World Council's General Secretary to South Africa, presented to the Lucknow Meeting of the Central Committee, revealed the tremendous complexity of the problem on that continent and the conflicting policies of the different church groups. Dr. Visser 't Hooft's Report occasioned a resolution condemning racial discrimination anew.[2]

---

[1] 'The existence of black races, white races, yellow races is to be accepted gladly and reverently as full of possibilities under God's purpose for the enrichment of human life. And there is no room for any differentiation between the races as to their intrinsic value. . . . The sin of man asserts itself in racial pride, racial hatreds and persecutions, and in the exploitation of other races. Against this in all its forms the Church is called by God to set its face implacably and to utter its word unequivocally, both within and without its own borders.' *Oxford*, p. 72.

[2] Lucknow *Minutes* (1953), p. 20. The resolution incorporates a quotation from the Amsterdam Report calling on the churches to eliminate practices of racial discrimination. One member abstained from the vote because of the omission of the phrase 'promptly brought to an end' which does not appear in the Amsterdam documents.

The Evanston Assembly broadened consideration of the topic to 'Inter-group Relations' and assigned the discussions to a separate Section. A preparatory brochure, issued by the World Council's Study Department introducing the topic, notes a difference of theological opinion. Some churches of the World Council constituency, it was reported, hold that the fellowship in Christ is 'a spiritual one, to be fully realized only in the final end of things in the future when Christ shall bring in His Kingdom [until which time] the divisions which God has created among men must continue even in the Church'.[1] Another view holds that 'the full unity of the Body of Christ presses constantly upon our imperfect churches, demanding that we enter into full unity at every opportunity ... to manifest in the churches a unity in which race and nation do not have separating significance'.

The Executive Committee of the World Council of Churches defined the task of the Inter-group Relations Section of the Evanston Assembly as an analysis and solution of the following questions: (a) How can the message of the Gospel be presented so as to affect the deep springs of race prejudice? (b) How should the Christian Church deal with it within its own membership? What import should the churches attach to questions affecting racial and ethnic homogeneity within the churches? How can the Church—in the congregation, in the nation, and in the world—so exemplify Christian conviction concerning race as to contribute towards the alleviation of injustice? (c) How may the

[1] *Inter-group Relations* (Geneva: World Council of Churches, 1952), p. 7. An Indian contributor to the Amsterdam preparatory volume mentioned 'two illustrations from the Protestant world devastating in their effects on the Asiatic nations and coloured races. There are many Dutch Christians in South Africa who find in the doctrines of calling and creation a justification for their policy of racial segregation; and Christian political parties in Holland take their stand on the doctrine of calling in defending the continuance of imperialism in Indonesia.' M. M. Thomas in *CDS*, p. 75. On the other hand there was the significant stand summarized by this 1946 statement: 'The Federal Council of the Churches of Christ in America hereby renounces the pattern of segregation in race relations as unnecessary and undesirable and a violation of the Gospel of love and human brotherhood. Having taken this action, the Federal Council requests its constituent communions to do likewise. As proof of their sincerity in this renunciation they will work for a non-segregated church and a non-segregated society.' Cited by John C. Bennett, *ibid.*, p. 100.

Christian community utilize and co-operate with government and other secular agencies in the alleviation of injustice?

The Evanston Section on Inter-group Relations was divided on the biblical and theological significance of racial differences but was firmly agreed that racial segregation is a sin and owes its origin to sin. Reconciliation, the Section averred, lies not in 'the economic and political reordering of society' but 'in the power of the Spirit' which overcomes racial pride and fear. Since all practices which maintain the physical separation of the races are a denial of the spiritual unity and brotherhood of man, the Church was summoned to put aside all excuses seeking to justify exclusion on the grounds of cultural differences or cultural mores. The Church was directed to educate its members on their responsibilities, support those who are challenging the conscience of society and withhold its approval of all discriminatory legislation affecting the educational, occupational, civic or marital opportunities based on race. Action to ameliorate racial tensions and injustice was recommended to every congregation, and co-operation where possible with agencies, international, governmental, private or civic working in the field, was suggested.[1]

The analysis and judgment of the Section was reinforced by Resolutions adopted by the entire Assembly, thus giving them greater authority. The World Council of Churches is thus on record as declaring that 'any form of segregation based on race, colour or ethnic origin is contrary to the gospel, and is incompatible with the Christian doctrine of man and with the nature of the Church of Christ'.[2] Moreover, the Council urged its member churches to work, despite manifest difficulties, for the ultimate abolition of all discriminatory practices both within their own life and within the societies in which they find themselves.[3]

---

[1] The Survey on *Inter-group Relations*, included in *CHTC*, listed some specific activities available to the churches themselves and calculated to reduce racial tensions.

[2] *Evanston*, p. 158.

[3] The fact that the Assembly had just voted to admit to membership in the World Council two segregated churches, the Dutch Reformed Church in Cape Province, South Africa, and the Bantu Presbyterian Church of South Africa, weakens in no sense its strictures on segregation but rather demonstrates the determination of the Council to leave questions of faith and ecclesiastical order to the decisions of its member churches.

A spokesman for the delegates from the South African churches, C. B. Brink, rose in the plenary meeting where the Report of Section V on Inter-group Relations was being voted to announce that, while the condemnation of segregation might make trouble for them at home, nevertheless they proposed to 'pledge ourselves personally to the task of urging our respective churches to apply themselves as urgently as possible to the study of the Report and to communicate their findings to the Central Committee as soon as possible'.

7. Christian Witness in Communist or Non-Communist Society

It was a member of the Drafting Committee of the Evanston Section on the Responsible Society, Canon H. G. G. Herklots, who provided a valuable explanation of the *status quaestionis*, the point of view, of the nine paragraphs in that Report sub-titled 'The Church in Relation to Communist–non-Communist Tension'. He explained: 'What was considered was not the Church and Communism, nor Christianity and Communism, but the task of the Church in relation to the tension between the two great systems which dominate the world.'[1] It was not, then, a judgment of the communist creed in the light of the Christian faith (on which there is a difference of opinion in the Ecumenical Community) that was sought. Rather, the discussion turned on the most effective strategy, the proper spiritual posture for Christians, pledged to the idea of the Responsible Society, living in either type of society. It was decided that the problem must be resolved by each Christian for himself in the perspective and with the aid of some questions raised by Evanston.

The issue, as Evanston acknowledged, has endemic political and economic consequences. Moreover, 'it creates divisions within the Church regarding the right attitude towards communism'. Some see in communism the way to a new order of material abundance and greater justice; others tend to rely on military measures, neglecting necessary social reform and forgetting the

[1] *Looking at Evanston*, p. 96.

menace to civil liberties. These are the errors, the Evanston delegates warned, which are connected with the reaction to the communist challenge. The task of the Church, the Report believed, was to point to the dangers inherent in the present situation.[1]

In its enumeration of the separate points of conflict between, on the one hand, 'the atheistic, Marxian communism of our day' and, on the other, 'capitalism', the Report of Amsterdam's Section III had inserted a paragraph calling for resistance to the spread of political systems of oppression.[2] Such systems were not further identified. It is not clear, therefore, whether a military dictatorship such as Spain, or a communist régime such as Rumania, was primarily under indictment nor whether by 'the Church'—to which is assigned an obligation of resistance—is meant citizens who are Christians or ecclesiastical groups corporately considered. The question has its interest in the light of the debate in theological, legal and military circles in Germany on *Widerstandsrecht* and the justification of the abortive revolt of July 20, 1944, against Hitler.[3] Reference to 'the extension of

[1] The dangers were described as: 'on the one hand the temptation to succumb to anti-communist hysteria and the danger of a self-righteous assurance concerning the political and social systems of the West; on the other hand the temptation to accept the false promises of communism and to overlook its threat to any responsible society'. *Evanston*, p. 122.

[2] 'The Church should seek to resist the extension of any system that not only includes oppressive elements but fails to provide any means by which the victims of oppression may criticise or act to correct it. It is part of the mission of the Church to raise its voice of protest wherever men are the victims of terror, wherever they are denied such fundamental human rights as the right to be secure against arbitrary arrest, and wherever governments use torture and cruel punishments to intimidate the consciences of men.' *Amsterdam*, p. 79.

[3] The issue arose in connexion with the speeches of the former commander of the Berlin garrison, Otto Ernst Remer, leader of the neo-Nazi Socialist Reich Party, attacking the memory of the generals involved in the July 20 revolt as traitors and oath-breakers. After hearing the expert testimony of historians, military specialists and moral theologians, a Brunswick court on March 15, 1952, sentenced Remer and exonerated the generals on the grounds that the Third Reich could be considered an 'illegal State'. Subsequently, Dr. Hermann Weinkauff, presiding justice of the German Federal Republic's highest court, wrote a personal memorandum as a contribution to the discussion of a study group headed by former Wehrmacht Maj.-Gen. Hermann J. W. von Witzleben who seeks to provide a 'clear moral compass' for the knotty questions of the limits of State sovereignty and the roots of civil obedience. Chief Justice Weinkauff blamed juridical positivism for leaving military men, politicians and jurists helpless and without counsel before the phenomenon of State power used for criminal ends.

such systems' and later writings of the author of the paragraph, Professor John C. Bennett, make it clear that Soviet-centred communism is the object, and that the resistance envisaged is that to be offered by ecclesiastical bodies in their support of UN collective security action on the political level and, on the spiritual level, in inculcating and demonstrating 'a positive witness to Christ in word and deed'.[1]

The problem was beyond the purview of the Stockholm Conference of 1925 with its optimistic expectation of a tranquil international order supervised by the League of Nations and of a steady amelioration of social conditions through the ministrations of the International Labour Office and programmes of progressive legislation. In Russia, to be sure, there was religious persecution and a government-promoted 'Living Church', but Russia was a distant land of closed frontiers, ostracized from the international community and preoccupied with its own radical transformation. The problem had arrived in all its inescapable acuity when the Oxford Conference convened in July 1937: in Germany the *Bekenntnisskirche* was making its protest while other Lutheran and Evangelical bodies were bewildered and stunned. Though *Mein Kampf* had announced the doctrine of *Lebensraum* for the Master Race, public opinion in Europe preferred to believe that Hitler sought only rectification of the Versailles settlement; he had not breached any frontiers, it was argued, in occupying the demilitarized Rhineland which, after all, was German territory. The topic of resistance seems not to have come up in the discussions of the Section on Church and State at Oxford. The Conference sent a strong message of sympathy and solidarity to the Evangelical Church in Germany (whose delegates had been refused visas to attend the Assembly) and voted to send a committee to communicate the conclusions of the Conference to the German churches. Three representatives of the German Free Churches who were present protested against the Message, extolled the achievements of the Hitler régime and declared that

---

[1] *Our Responsibilities as Christians in Face of the Challenge of Communism*, Geneva: World Council, March 1942 (mimeographed), Study Document 52E/332.

they had remained 'perfectly neutral' in the conflict between the government and the established churches.[1]

Such neutralism was loudly condemned by Protestantism's most powerful voice, that of Professor Karl Barth. 'A clear choice must be made between the policy of compromise and the policy of resistance' proclaimed the Swiss theologian who made his choice clear by writing his famous Letters urging greater effort in the war against Nazism.[2] Long before the religious crisis in Germany had become so plain, a Conference of the Ecumenical Youth Commission had bluntly urged the churches 'to dissociate themselves from every Church that does not affirm this universalism [of the Word of God], on the ground that it is not Christian'.[3] The General Secretary of the World Council of Churches in Process of Formation permitted himself some adequately unneutral observations during the war.[4] Dr. Visser 't Hooft was speaking at a meeting of a relief society working for the *Bekenntnisskirche*. His exaggeration was undoubtedly intended to underscore the bravery of that group of Christians in Germany and win them greater support in Switzerland. Few men were better informed about the determined resistance of the churches during the war.

Confronting communism, however, the mind of the ecumenical world does not discern the same sharp issues nor do its prophetic voices find material for similar utterance. Many reasons have been alleged for this difference of attitude and some have been suggested earlier when the Amsterdam judgment on 'Communism and Capitalism' was examined. A feeling that

[1] Commented Dr. Nils Ehrenström, Director of the World Council's Study Department, writing in 1952: 'It was a telling testimony—but in quite a different sense from that which the speaker had intended.' *History*, p. 588.

[2] Quoted in *EPS*, July 1941, 28, p. 6. Barth's 'Letter to American Christians' with comments by US ecumenical leaders appeared in *Christendom* VIII (Autumn, 1943), 4, pp. 441–72.

[3] *History*, p. 583.

[4] 'The distress of the Church is not the external pressure to which it is exposed today; the real distress of the Church is that the Church is not a Church. The frightful danger is not that the Churches in many countries are being outwardly crushed but that the Churches are not speaking and acting in this decisive hour as the Church of Jesus Christ ought to speak and act.' Quoted in *EPS*, November 1941, 41, p. 1.

communism's declared passion for social justice parallels the objectives of Christian social reform movements seems frequently behind the repeated remark that communism is a 'Christian heresy'.[1] The conviction that a sharpening of ideological tensions increases the likelihood of a general war which, in an age of nuclear weapons, would imperil civilization itself and, in any case, only breed worse disorders is another factor. Not to be discounted is a subtle anti-Americanism, endemic on the Continent, which sees the spiritual heritage of Christian Europe equally menaced by two materialist giants.[2]

Finally, the massive authority of Karl Barth has exercised a considerable influence in this difference of attitude in ecumenical circles.[3] Reporting on 'The Reformed Churches Behind the Iron Curtain' after a visit in early 1948 the doughty and indefatigable foe of Nazism declared that 'the Reformed Church in Hungary is on the right road'.[4] In an ensuing controversy with Emil Brunner who protested that Barth's views were 'incomprehensible to those who see no basic difference between the Communist or any other form of totalitarianism, for instance the National Socialist', the theologian of Basle answered that the

[1] Clarity was not helped by a similar paradox of Dante in placing Mohammed among the Christian 'sowers of schism' in *The Divine Comedy*, nor by R. H. Tawney terming Marx 'the last of the Schoolmen', i.e. Scholastic philosophers.

[2] Writing in a private capacity, an American who is a Secretary in the World Council Study Department asked: 'Is it too cynical to suggest that the lofty view which many Christians on the continent hold regarding the sins of the East and West is to be attributed not to the purity of their Christian witness but to an understandable reluctance to avoid having to take sides politically?' Paul R. Abrecht in *Christianity and Crisis* x (March 20, 1950), p. 28.

[3] Reinhold Niebuhr notes that the German, Pastor Martin Niemöller; the Czech, Professor Josef Hromadka; and the Hungarian, Bishop Albert Bereczky, are disciples of Barth who, 'despite explicit disavowal of secular ideologies, is influenced by a Marxist estimate of America as a "capitalist" country'. Niebuhr believes that Barth has 'a confidence in the "Socialist" economy of Russia which obscures the nature of her totalitarian régime'. 'Communism and the Clergy', *Christian Century* LXX (August 19, 1953), 33, p. 937.

[4] 'What carried conviction for me was this: that the Hungarian Reformed Protestants were not preoccupied with the undecided question of East versus West, nor with the memory of the Russian horror, nor with the question of the justice or injustice of their present government. They are trying to formulate the Word of God in fresh terms (which involves fundamental reconsideration on the theological side).' *Kirchenblatt für die reformierte Schweiz*, April 29, 1948, as quoted in *EPS*, May 7, 1948. The article is reprinted in Barth's *Against the Stream*, pp. 101 ff.

Church's concern is 'not with isms of this kind or that'.[1] Barth's definitive exposition of his counsel that a Christian should not 'take sides' was expounded in 1948 in a widely quoted conference, 'The Church Between East and West', which viewed the crisis primarily as another instance of the perennial struggle for power among nations occurring in history, a political issue of 'absolutely no concern to Christians'.[2] There is, he concedes, also a clash of ideologies, but an examination of American and Soviet societies produces the diagnosis that they have the same postulates, and the verdict of 'a plague on both your houses!'[3] Anticipating the

[1] Quoted in EPS, June 24, 1948. Brunner's Open Letter and Barth's Reply are both included in Against the Stream. His explanation: 'The Church must not concern itself eternally with various "isms" and systems but with historical realities as seen in the light of the Word of God and of the Faith. Its obligations lie not in the direction of any fulfilling of the law of nature but towards its living Lord. Therefore the Church never thinks, speaks or acts "on principle". Rather it judges spiritually and by individual cases. For that reason it rejects every attempt to systematize political history and its own part in that history. Therefore it preserves the freedom to judge each new event afresh. If yesterday it travelled along one path, it is not bound to keep to the same path today. If yesterday it spoke from its position of responsibility, then today it should be silent if in this position it considers silence to be the better course. The unity and continuity of theology will best be preserved if the Church does not let itself be discouraged from being up-to-date theologically.' Ibid., p. 114.

[2] In English translation the conference appeared in World Affairs (London), July and August issues of 1949, and in Cross Currents (New York), Winter 1951; it was published in French by Roulet (Paris, 1948), and included in the collection of Barth's post-war papers on political subjects, Against the Stream (1954). The General Secretary of the World Council agreed with Barth's emphasis, it would seem. Dr. Visser 't Hooft has declared: 'The Church is not to speak against the world as if it considers the world its enemy. It is precisely characteristic of the situation that whatever the world may do to the Church, however it may make war on its saints, the Church cannot forget that the world has been overcome, that its destiny has been decided and that, therefore, its denials and negations cannot change the ultimate outcome. The Church must, therefore, not fight back when it is attacked by the world. It should rather answer all opposition and all persecution by an even more joyous and certain affirmation that, in spite of all, its Lord reigns. . . . After all, the world is not half so dangerous for the Church as the Church is for itself.' The Kingship of Christ, p. 129.

[3] In an Open Letter on German Rearmament appearing in Esprit, January 1951, pp. 105–12, under the title, 'Ne Craignez Point', Barth wrote that American imperialism is not the only, nor even the chief cause of the present impasse and acknowledged that, were he an American or English statesman, he would not neglect military defence measures. Seemingly, however, that is the interest and task of the homo politicus, not that of the homo christianus; and never the twain shall meet. In the Open Letter Barth allies himself with Dr. Gustav Heinemann and Pastor Martin Niemöller. During the war Barth harshly upbraided Niemöller for his willingness to serve in Hitler's forces. As quoted in Christian Century LVII (March 6, 1940), 10, p. 301. Cf. supra, p. 11, n. 1.

objection that he proclaimed a Christian obligation to make war on Nazism, Barth explains that communism is different: its brutal hands are at least turned to a constructive task, the social problem; its honest avowal of atheism is infinitely preferable to the Nazi efforts to turn Christianity into a tribal religion and to the Nazi crime of anti-Semitism; it has no capacity to deceive Christians since there is nothing of the false prophet about it.

While sharing Barth's determination to keep the churches uncommitted on the East-West issue, other thinkers in the World Council constituency are disturbed precisely by the very messianism of communism which Barth denies; they are worried over the success of communism's insistence that it is the wave of the future in whose flux the Christian faith must navigate, if it is to survive and not be lost in the wreckage of a sunken bourgeois world. From first-hand contact with the communist system in Hungary and East Germany the Lutherans have concluded that neutrality is impossible on the question of communism.[1] At the Assembly of the Federation of Protestantism's largest denomination in July 1952, delegates, gathered at Hanover, Germany, heard Norway's Bishop Eivind Berggrav, a President of the World Council of Churches, call for active resistance to communism.[2] Bishop Berggrav had himself displayed uncompromising resistance during the Nazi occupation of his country.

Post-Amsterdam discussions, plus the experience of member churches in Eastern Europe, China and elsewhere, have contributed to a clarification of the issue. A study pamphlet on the Responsible Society theme, written by Professor John C. Bennett

[1] Declared the Executive Committee of the World Lutheran Federation in July 1949: 'Christians cannot escape the tumult of these days . . . the Church of God cannot keep silence when the liberty of men is endangered as it is today. There can be no compromise with any effort to organize a social order that infringes upon the individual freedom and the personal responsibility of human beings as created in the likeness of God and redeemed by His Christ.' Quoted in *EPS*, July 29, 1940, p. 219.

[2] 'Gullible stupidity is neither Christian nor Lutheran. . . . The most important of Luther's occasional utterances on this subject [obedience to rulers] is his statement that princes and Christian citizens need not obey emperors and kings who plainly violate the law. . . . Translated into modern terminology this means: active resistance.' *Ibid.*

and issued in November 1949, observed that, given the geographical spread of its membership, 'It is to be expected that within the constituency of the World Council there will be quite different views concerning the attitude which Christians should take towards Communism.' Considerations on which an answer should be based for 'one of the most difficult questions in the life of the World Council of Churches' appeared to the author to assume that communism as a faith must be resisted spiritually by Christians under all circumstances and that the extension of communist power must be resisted politically wherever there is a constructive alternative.[1] A later document by the same author, 'Our Responsibility as Christians in Face of the Challenge of Communism', circulated by the Study Department in March 1952, analysed the issue on four levels: the international conflict, the struggle for power between nations, particularly between Russia and America; the conflict between communism and capitalism as economic systems; the conflict between communism as totalitarian and a society that is open and pluralistic; and, finally, the conflict between communism as a faith and Christianity. While the Church must not offer the Gospel as a conservative anti-communist weapon or as a means of escape from social and political dilemmas, concluded Professor Bennett, it should inspire its members to resist the expansion of the political power-complex based on the Soviet Union, because communism is a faith that engenders a totalitarian system. Where political resistance to that system is impossible, spiritual resistance is always open to Christians, not least by presenting on every occasion the truths of religion as being different from the premises of the communist faith.

[1] Geneva: World Council Study Department, pp. 14–15. 'The conviction that is most widely held among the member churches is that Communism as a movement which has its base in the Soviet Union, and through Communist parties is seeking to extend its power throughout the world, should be resisted both politically and spiritually, and that the churches in the countries associated with "Western democracy" should give moral support to their governments in their efforts to check the extension of Communist power.... The whole ecumenical community, whatever differences there may be among its members about policies in particular nations, should recognize that it has a responsibility to do what is possible to prevent the world from coming under Communist domination.' *Ibid.*, p. 14.

The popular Introductory Leaflet on the Responsible Society theme prepared by the Study Department for the general membership of the churches pointed out that 'the churches must study some of the effects of the challenge of Communism on their own unity, especially as it affects their witness in society'. It noted that: 'There are some Christians who think they can co-operate with Communism because they see it as a short cut to a new order of greater material abundance and greater justice.' It pointed on the other hand to 'the temptation to engage in sterile anti-Communist hysteria and the danger of a self-righteous assurance concerning the political and social systems of the West'.[1] Whatever judgment recommended itself to observers in Geneva, the fact is that different attitudes have been adopted, different policies have been followed and different conceptions are held by member churches of the World Council living in communist-controlled countries on the means by which the social function of the Church can be fulfilled.[2]

In view of the complete autonomy left to each member church by the World Council's Constitution, there could be no question of the Assembly passing judgment on the choice of policy exercised by any ecclesiastical communion in this matter. To the Responsible Society Section it seemed best to alert its membership to the appeal of communism in underdeveloped countries and suggest some questions on the possible dangers facing Christians living in either communist or non-communist societies. The questions deemed urgent in a special way for Christians in communist lands turned on the means of manifesting effectively

[1] *The Responsible Society in a World Perspective*, pp. 7–8.

[2] The two views held within the World Council constituency by those living under communist régimes were stated thus in the Evanston Survey: 'The new economic society of communism is seen as the first step towards the classless society, which is a provisional hope which Christians can also affirm.' The other viewpoint 'sees in communism the attempt of another total ideology, a false faith, to press human beings into its mould and to wield total power in the world ... the task of Christians is to analyse the forces of society in the knowledge that God in Christ is their Lord and Judge, who has prescribed their true functions; to judge the policies of the government with sober empiricism, according to whether they serve the needs and preserve the freedoms of human beings; to act in whatever range God grants, in responsibility for one's neighbour in His Kingdom, without too much strategy, without too much hope for success or fear for the consequences'. *CHTC*, pp. 55, 57.

their faith in the presence of an official atheistic ideology and on the legitimacy of co-operating with the social programme of such a régime.[1]

The plight of Christians in such a situation is surely an agonizing one, undoubtedly more complicated than the Evanston Report succeeded in making clear. A certain amount of co-operation with the totalitarian system is inevitable on the part of every citizen living under such a régime.[2] To begin with, the right of non-participation, the freedom to be silent, to subtract oneself from the compulsory chorus of adulation, is not recognized in practice under such régimes. Surely the World Council would not consider such an attitude as succumbing to 'the temptations of a negative resistance' and, in consequence, blameworthy. (The moral legitimacy of active resistance seems ruled out by the Evanston Report.) The choice of the phrase 'prophetic witness' in the text was not particularly fortunate; its meaning escapes the general reader and obscures the understanding of the attitude of the World Council on a topic of universal interest. The question on 'the place of suffering in Christian social witness'

---

[1] '(1) What are the ways and what is the content of Christian witness in the face of atheistic ideologies? (2) What is the social significance of the existence of the Church as an inclusive worshipping and evangelistic community? How can the life of the congregation in all its forms, including its pastoral and social work, affect society? How does the Church's teaching ministry relate to state education under a communist régime? (3) What reforms are necessary in the life and structure of the Church? What are the values and dangers of agreements between Church and State? (4) At what points can the Church and Christians co-operate with governments in their plans for social reconstruction? What are the limits of this co-operation? How does Christian social responsibility avoid both surrender to communism and the temptations of a negative resistance? (5) What new forms of prophetic ministry are required? How far are public statements by the Church on social questions effective? (6) What Christian witness can church members bear in their daily work? What is the place of suffering in Christian social witness? (7) What, if any, is the Church's responsibility for standards of truth in all fields? For pre-communist social and cultural traditions? What is the relation between a Christian demand and a communist demand for repentance for past social injustices?' *Evanston*, pp. 122–3.

[2] 'If individual life is to go on at all within the totalitarian framework, it must go on by arrangement with the régime and to some extent in connivance with its purposes. Furthermore, there will always be areas in which the totalitarian government will succeed in identifying itself with popular feelings and aspirations. . . . These realities leave no room for our favoured conviction that the people of a totalitarian state can be neatly divided into collaborators and martyrs and that there will be none left over.' George F. Kennan, *American Diplomacy, 1900–1950*, p. 140.

suggests an awareness of the existence of compulsion and of psychological pressure in communist régimes, an allusion with interesting moral implications, particularly in view of the controversy in the United States occasioned by the admission of an American Protestant missionary that he had deliberately lied and had knowingly signed a false confession to win surcease from the 'brain-washing' inflicted on him by the Chinese communist police.

The questions of special urgency posed for Christians in non-communist lands involve attitudes towards the secularism of society, the responsibility of the churches by reason of their accommodation to bourgeois values and the function of the churches to defend traditions of freedom allegedly imperilled by social conformity.[1] The dangers of an over-emphasis on military defence in non-communist countries had been pointed out earlier; it can be assumed, therefore, that the Drafting Committee was prepared to concede that communism constituted in some fashion a threat of armed aggression.

The modes of expressing the social function of the Church in communist and non-communist societies were thus left to the prayerful decisions of the membership of the World Council of Churches. The approach adopted by the Evanston Assembly was publicly commended by Bishop János Péter, speaking for the Hungarian delegation.[2] The two views, of co-operation with

---

[1] '(1) What are the special temptations of the Church in a traditional "Christian society"? (2) Does secularism in the non-communist world differ from the materialism in the communist world? (3) What is the content of Christian witness towards the large mass of secularized people? How far is this secularization due to the class nature of the Church and the accommodation of its life and message to bourgeois interests and values? What reforms in the life of the Church are necessary to meet these challenges? (4) How far are the churches in non-communist lands genuinely prophetic in their relation to society and the state? (5) What is the responsibility of the churches in non-communist lands for the cultivation of traditions of freedom and community over against the growing pressure towards social conformity?' *Evanston*, p. 123.

[2] Security provisions of US immigration legislation presented difficulties for the delegates—some of them politically controversial personalities—travelling to the Evanston Assembly from East European countries. Thus it was that, when asked to explain the restricted visa given Bishop Peter, the State Department declared that the Hungarian delegate had not performed ecclesiastical functions or occupied a pulpit since he became a church official on December 8, 1949, that he receives 4,000 florints monthly known as a 'supplement of danger' from his government, a stipend generally paid to the police and

communist régimes in work of social reform or resistance at specific points with spiritual power, are equally valid, as the election of Professor Josef Hromadka to the World Council's Executive Committee made clear.

vii. THE INTERNATIONAL ORDER

The whole history of the Ecumenical Movement and indeed the definition of its organized form as a 'fellowship of churches' from all continents makes it inevitable that the international order will be one of the primary concerns of the World Council of Churches.

The advantages of co-ordinating the world-wide missionary enterprise of the churches suggested the summoning of the Edinburgh Conference of 1910, which set in motion events culminating in the Amsterdam Assembly of 1948 which constituted the World Council of Churches. The World Alliance for International Friendship through the Churches, an unofficial effort to pool the interest and influence of churchmen of many nations on behalf of greater international understanding, was one of the chief factors responsible for the Stockholm Conference of 1925 where the Universal Christian Conference on Life and Work, one of the parent organizations of the World Council of Churches, took shape.

The pace and direction of contemporary history, the unification of the globe through trade and especially by modern means of transport and communications accompanied by a sharpening of national rivalries and the rise of secular religions, undoubtedly hastened the search for church unity. 'The world is too strong for a divided Church,' declared the message of the Stockholm Conference.

When the representatives of the churches gathered at Amsterdam in August 1948 'to covenant together' to form the World Council of Churches a heavy menace hung over humanity, mocking the sanguine expectations which marked the origins of

soldiers on special missions, and that he had served as an 'informer' for the communist régime against anti-communist clergymen. Cf. *New York Times*, August 18, 1954, p. 6.

the Life and Work Movement.[1] 'To promote friendship between the nations' was one of the purposes listed in the Official Letter of Invitation for the Stockholm Conference. In 1925 the task of reconciling the Germans and making the war-guilt clause of the Versailles Treaty acceptable seemed the chief obstacle to a growing, general harmony of nations. Less than twenty-five years later, another ecumenical gathering noted, in a memorable euphemism: 'The World Council of Churches is met in its first Assembly at a time of critical international strain.' The Report of Amsterdam's Section IV, 'The Church and the International Disorder', declared: 'The hopes of the recent war years and the apparent dawn of peace have been dashed. . . . Men are asking in fear and dismay what the future holds.'

Had the Section pondered the significance of the Second Report of the UN Atomic Energy Commission, issued on May 28, less than three months before? An impasse had been reached in the effort to achieve international control of atomic energy, the Commission reported, the Soviet Government insisting that the plan involved an unwarranted invasion of national sovereignty, the majority opinion replying that the Soviet counter-proposals provided no protection against noncompliance. The month before the World Council came into being, the United Nations Military Staff Committee reported its utter failure, 'because of disagreement on general principles', to devise an acceptable plan for the armed forces to be available to the Security Council according to Article 42 of the UN Charter. That juridical instrument, devised 'to maintain the peace', had become the forum of unrestrained mutual recriminations. Were the Amsterdam delegates aware that General Lucius D. Clay had asked his government on July 10 to authorize the dispatch of an armed column into Berlin to break the blockade of that

[1] In his sermon opening the Stockholm Conference the Bishop of Winchester declared: 'We may sum it [the international situation] up, in fact, by saying that a new community-conscience is fast being formed and that this is already making itself felt as something to be reckoned with in the dealings of nations with one another, or groups and persons within those nations. A new bulwark has been built against every kind of tyranny, and this has been the result of centuries of personal influence and active propaganda on the part of those who believe in the Kingdom of God.' *Stockholm*, p. 43.

city?[1] If so, they might well have wondered if war would break in on their peaceful discussions as it had on the ecumenical gatherings at Constance in 1914 and at Apeldoorn, Holland, in January 1940.

Despite the manifest international disorder, the Amsterdam Assembly refused to be discouraged. The Report of Section IV proclaimed that the world is in God's hands, that war, a consequence of the disregard of God, 'is not inevitable if man will turn to Him in repentance and obey His law. . . . By accepting His Gospel, men will find forgiveness for all their sins and receive power to transform their relations with their fellow men.' The World Council of Churches found its own formation a factor in international affairs.[2]

Since the Amsterdam Assembly of 1948, observed the Survey prepared for the Evanston delegates, 'vast changes in the world scene have taken place'. Among the events and tendencies, noted in the summary review, are the entry of China into the communist camp, an intensification of the struggle between two great *blocs* of world powers which has affected the character of the United Nations as an impartial arbiter in international affairs, the strains resulting from the defence programme in the Western world, the fear of the use of atomic and other weapons of mass destruction, action on behalf of underdeveloped areas, efforts looking to the political and economic unification of Europe and a growing consciousness of the importance of basic human rights.

Against this disturbed and ever-changing background of events, the World Council of Churches fosters the concerns which earlier characterized the activity of the Universal Christian

---

[1] Cf. Lucius D. Clay, *Decision in Germany*, p. 374.

[2] 'It [the World Council] is a living expression of this fellowship, transcending race and nation, class and culture, knit together in faith, service and understanding. Its aim will be to hasten international reconciliation through its own members and through the co-operation of all Christian churches and of all men of goodwill. . . . It should not weary in the effort to state the Christian understanding of the will of God and to promote its application to national and international policy.' *Amsterdam*, p. 95. To achieve these purposes the World Council of Churches had joined with the International Missionary Council to form the Commission of the Churches on International Affairs.

Council on Life and Work and the World Alliance for Promoting International Friendship through the Churches. These primary preoccupations are (1) the prevention of war, (2) the establishment of a rule of law in international affairs protected by international institutions, and (3) the safeguarding of human rights, especially religious liberty. The CCIA and various national commissions are the official agencies charged to pursue these objectives formally in the spirit proclaimed at Evanston, 'ready to face situations that seem hopeless and yet to act in them as men whose hope is indestructible'.

1. *The Prevention of War and the Building of Peace*

Confronted by the idea of war the Ecumenical Community has no reservations in declaring: 'War as a method of settling disputes is incompatible with the teaching and example of our Lord Jesus Christ.'[1] This unqualified judgment of Amsterdam's Section IV echoed the mind of the Oxford Conference of 1937[2] and anticipated the verdict of Evanston that war's 'violence and destruction are inherently evil'.

Facing the fact of war, three broad positions are found among the World Council's membership, a trilemma of opinion expressed also at the Oxford Conference.[3] In the language of Amsterdam's Section IV Report:

> 1. There are those who hold that, even though entering a war may be a Christian's duty in particular circumstances, modern warfare, with its mass destruction, can never be an act of justice.
> 2. In the absence of impartial supra-national institutions, there are those who hold that military action is the ultimate sanction of the rule of law, and that citizens must be distinctly taught that it is their duty to defend the law by force if necessary.
> 3. Others, again, refuse military service of all kinds, convinced

---

[1] *Amsterdam*, p. 89.

[2] 'War is a particular demonstration of the power of sin in this world, and a defiance of the righteousness of God as revealed in Jesus Christ and Him crucified. No justification of war must be allowed to conceal or minimize this fact.' *Oxford*, p. 178.

[3] *Ibid.*, p. 179. Dr. Visser 't Hooft, now General Secretary of the World Council, was chairman at Oxford of the Committee considering 'The Christian Attitude to War'.

that an absolute witness against war and for peace is for them the will of God and they desire that the Church should speak to the same effect.[1]

Conceding the deep perplexity occasioned by these conflicting opinions, the Report urged upon all Christians the duty of wrestling continuously with these problems and of praying humbly for God's guidance. The Survey for Evanston, however, did not believe that these three opinions have been sufficiently re-examined and reformulated to warrant extensive discussion at the 1954 Assembly.[2]

As the event proved, in the face of the horrors of weapons of mass destruction, the delegates to the Second Assembly were prepared to accord the pacifists a more respectful and sympathetic hearing; in the face of threats to human freedom, the pacifists showed themselves at Evanston more realistic, less inclined to regard Gandhi as a Father of the Church. The theological debate in the Ecumenical Community on the legitimacy of recourse to arms and the circumstances conceivably justifying the use of force, if not adjourned, yields place to the consideration of the means of preventing war and creating an international community. World peace is the goal, declared Evanston, and the Christian approaches to peace must be studied afresh, 'taking into account both Christian pacificism as a mode of witness and the conviction of Christians that in certain circumstances military action is justifiable'.

The peace pursued by the World Council of Churches means far more than the absence of war. In the words of the Second Assembly, it 'is characterized positively by freedom, justice, truth and love'. It is a task making strong demands on Christian hope[3]

[1] *Amsterdam*, p. 89.

[2] 'Pacifist Christians have not faced sufficiently the charge that they make an absolute of peace at the expense of justice. Non-pacifist Christians who hold the conception of a "just war" have not sufficiently examined the implications of the new mass-destruction weapons for the idea of just means.' *CHTC*, p. 47.

[3] One ambiguous passage in the Evanston Report on International Affairs leaves the reader undecided whether the World Council believes that enduring peace is impossible (1) before the human race is converted to Christianity, or (2) without the help of God's

and, like every important goal, something to be worked for.[1]

The Stockholm Conference of 1925, reflecting doubtless the relatively untroubled international atmosphere and the optimism of the immediate post-war world, contented itself with generalities.[2] Amsterdam had a number of concrete suggestions: prompt completion of peace treaties with the defeated nations enabling them to rebuild their economic and political systems for peaceful purposes, the return of prisoners of war and the termination of purges and war crimes trials. Such precise demands were in addition to a declaration of the more general duties of the churches to safeguard their independence against all attempts to involve them in national and ideological causes, to teach unabashedly love of one's enemy and so 'withstand everything in the Press, radio or school which inflames hatred or hostility between nations', to promote the reduction of armaments, to resist the pretensions of imperialist power, to combat indifference and despair in the face of the threat of war. Denouncing all forms of tyranny, 'economic, political or religious', opposing 'aggressive imperialism—political, economic or cultural', the Amsterdam Section IV Report expressed its belief that 'the greatest threat to peace today comes from the division of the world into mutually suspicious and antagonistic *blocs*'. It concluded that 'a positive attempt must be made to ensure that the competing economic systems such as communism, socialism or free enterprise may co-exist without leading to war'.

The causes of war, it was pointed out, must be attacked 'by grace. Thus: 'The Assembly believes that an international order conformed to the will of God and established in His peace can be achieved only through the reconciliation which Christ makes possible. Only thus will those transformed attitudes and standards, agreements and practices which alone will ensure lasting peace become possible.' *Evanston*, p. 134.

[1] The Annual Reports of the Commission of the Churches on International Affairs indicate that this agency of the World Council, within the limits of its resources, considered as relevant to its responsibility almost the entire agenda of the United Nations Assembly, its Commissions and Specialized Agencies.

[2] 'We summon the Churches to share with us our sense of the horror of war and of its futility as a means of settling international disputes and to pray and work for the fulfilment of the promise that under the sceptre of the Prince of Peace "mercy and truth shall meet together, righteousness and peace shall kiss each other".' *Stockholm*, p. 713.

promoting peaceful change and the pursuit of justice'. The idea thus simply stated had been the principal preoccupation of out-standing lay leaders in the Ecumenical Movement, particularly those whose professional careers included experience in government ser-vice or teaching international law. In the absence of a superior political authority, noted the Oxford Conference, voluntary action, force or the threat of force were the only methods available to bring the international order into conformity with changing needs.[1]

Adequate factual knowledge of the international situation was indicated as essential in the exercise of the responsibility of Christians to work for a policy of peaceful change on the part of their governments. The support of juridical institutions making for international order—the League of Nations,[2] the Permanent Court of International Order, arbitration treaties, etc.—was strongly urged. The inevitability of change in human societies and the capital importance of channelling evolving forces and of registering new situations through instruments of free inter-national co-operation was the key concept of the paper prepared for the Amsterdam background volume on international affairs by John Foster Dulles.[3]

[1] 'It therefore particularly devolves upon Christians to devote themselves to securing by voluntary action of their nations such changes in the international order as are from time to time required to avoid injustice and to promote equality of opportunity for individuals throughout the world.' *Oxford*, p. 174. German repudiation of the Versailles Treaty and Italian demands for a place in the sun provided the context for this recognition of the need of provisions for change in the international order. Whether the Oxford delegates were aware of the ideological springs of the Nazi and Fascist régimes which accepted war as an instrument of public policy cannot be ascertained. Certainly the influence of the official ideologies was overtly minimized outside Germany and Italy. Did the Amsterdam delegates in 1948 similarly underestimate the importance of the official ideology of the Soviet Union as a complicating factor in effecting changes in the international order when they spoke (in the Section IV Report) of the co-existence of 'competing *economic* systems such as communism, socialism or free enterprise'? Once again, the decision to forego historical analysis, the policy of eschewing pronouncements on concrete political realities, the decision to remain 'beyond East and West', makes it impossible to know.

[2] *Ibid.*, p. 175. The Oxford Conference's characterization of the possibilities and weaknesses of the League of Nations bears a disconcerting resemblance to the statement, 'Christians Look at the United Nations', issued by the CCIA Executive Committee in August 1953. Cf. *CHTC*, p. 10.

[3] 'The Christian Citizen in a Changing World' in *The Church and the International Disorder*, pp. 73 ff. Mr. Dulles's mind and hand can be seen also in the Oxford emphasis on the need of provisions for peaceful change in the international order.

The possibility of peaceful change in the international order involves a multiplicity of factors all of which have claimed the attention of the World Council constituency in various degrees. A limited surrender of national sovereignty is considered a primary condition. This implies, first of all, recognition that dealings between nations no less than individual human conduct are subject to a rule of right and wrong, a moral order that is a consequence of God's sovereignty over nations as well as persons. The heart of the present evil, in its political expression, thought the Oxford Conference of 1937, was 'the claim of each nation State to be judge in its own cause'. The abandonment of that claim 'and the abrogation of absolute national sovereignty', at least to that extent, 'was judged a duty the Church should urge upon the nations'. By 1948 the experience of the United Nations had convinced the Amsterdam Section IV delegates that 'unless the nations surrender a greater measure of national sovereignty in the interest of the common good, they will be tempted to have recourse to war in order to enforce their claims'.[1]

It is not by reason of any advocacy of world government as an immediate objective that the World Council of Churches, through the Commission of the Churches on International Affairs, presses for a limitation of national sovereignty.[2] Effective international co-operation in some fields of traditional ecumenical concern supposes a certain pooling of political authority. Thus, by its charter the CCIA has among its objectives 'the international regulation of armaments'. To that end, its officers offered suggestions in February 1951 on the progressive reduction of national armaments, in view of the failure of the United Nations to organize an international military force. But any serious disarmament measure, it was pointed out, presupposes effective and continuous inspection and control on national territories under

---

[1] *Amsterdam*, p. 92.

[2] However, the Hungarian Ecumenical Study Commission, in the only statement from East Europe available for the pre-Evanston Survey, criticized any surrender of sovereignty, declaring: 'The end of this road ... would be that the smaller, weaker, poorer nations would come under the subjection of the richer, better-armed countries.' *CHTC*, p. 9.

the United Nations. 'The reduction of armaments is not an arithmetical proposition but a political and, above all, a moral problem,' the CCIA Director, Dr. O. Frederick Nolde, declared. Methods of peaceful change to rectify injustices in the international order and to limit national sovereignty, at least to the degree necessary for effective international inspection and control of armaments, are required for building a stable peace, the Evanston Assembly repeated.

Current efforts to reduce international tension and win time to allow the deeper and more creative influences of reconciliation to play their part were regarded as admittedly precarious but nevertheless morally imperative. The complexus of these efforts is popularly known as 'coexistence', a term avoided by the World Council 'because of its unhappy historical significance and some of its current political implications'.[1] The phrase preferred by the International Affairs Section of the Second Assembly was 'living together'.

Evanston had some concrete suggestions on how the nations might at least 'live together'. So basic were judged two points 'if catastrophe is to be avoided' that they were stated in a Resolution adopted by the Assembly at a plenary session. These were the prohibition of all weapons of mass destruction with provision for their international inspection and control and, secondly, the certain assurance that no country will engage in or support aggressive or subversive acts in other countries. As a point of departure for a more permanent concord between nations, the Report listed certain minimum conditions[2] to be met on both

---

[1] *Evanston*, p. 135. One of the implications of the term 'coexistence' was explicitly rejected: A 'willingness [on the part of Christians] to disguise from themselves or others the vast difference which lies between the search for an international order based on belief in Christ and His reconciling work, and the pursuit of aims which repudiate the Christian revelation'.

[2] '(a) A conviction that it is possible for nations and peoples to live together, at least for a considerable period of years; (b) A willingness not to use force as an instrument of policy beyond the existing frontiers. This would not mean the recognition and freezing of present injustices and the unnatural divisions of nations, but it would mean renouncing coercion as a means of securing or redressing them; (c) A vigorous effort to end social and other injustices which might lead to civil and, hence, international war; (d) A scrupulous respect for the pledged word; (e) A continuing effort to reach agreement on outstanding

sides, conditions which amounted to mutual acceptance by the two opposing political systems and their willingness to employ methods of peaceful change. Beyond this limited state of 'living together' Evanston foresaw the possibilities of positive co-operation through the free exchange of persons, culture, information and trade, common undertakings for relief and the growth of the United Nations. To promote such understanding the Assembly advocated visits between representatives of the churches in those countries between which tension exists in order to strengthen the bonds of fellowship and promote the reconciliation of the nations.

'The furtherance of international economic co-operation' is one of the objectives assigned to the Commission of the Churches on International Affairs, sponsored by the World Council. The topic raises questions of the right of access to raw materials in a given nation's territory or colonies, the freedom of international trade and even the legitimacy of unilateral fixing of national tariff policies. On these issues the Oxford Conference saw 'the unequal distribution of natural bounties' as one of the causes of war when control is used 'to create a monopoly of national advantages' and urged Christians to press their governments 'to provide a reasonable equality of economic opportunity'.[1] Amsterdam's Section IV was forthright on the ethical limitations of national economic practices and the obligation to subordinate particular programmes to universal needs.[2] The Second Assembly began its observations on 'What Nations Owe to One Another'[3] with the declaration: 'The world community has become interdependent.' From this fact, it rejoiced to see international responsibility as exemplified by the UN Trusteeship system replacing 'old colonialism', though it warned that a self-sufficient

issues, such as the peace treaties and disarmament, which are essential to a broader stabilization and pacification of relations; (f) Readiness to submit all unresolved questions of conflict to an impartial international organization and to carry out its decisions.' *Evanston*, p. 136.

[1] *Oxford*, p. 175.

[2] 'No nation has the moral right to determine its own economic policy without consideration for the economic needs of other nations and without recourse to international consultation.' *Amsterdam*, p. 91.

[3] *Evanston*, pp. 137–8.

attitude of nationalism, obvious in some of the newly independent countries, is an obstacle to international co-operation. A partnership between peoples hitherto 'subject' and 'ruling', with each side showing a readiness to learn from the other, was held out as the ideal. The participation of more developed countries in international programmes of technical assistance was praised as 'one of the brightest pages of recent history' but the effort was judged incommensurate with the resources available and the needs of the underdeveloped areas.

The sub-theme chosen for the discussions on international affairs at the Evanston Assembly, 'Christians in the Struggle for World Community', the increasing emphasis in CCIA thinking on the importance of Technical Assistance programmes, the appeal, in the concluding sentence of the Evanston Survey, for 'a larger ecumenical consensus on the present and future significance of the UN for the defence of peace and justice, the progressive development of international law and the building of a genuine world community', these are stray but significant signs of the international order which the World Council of Churches favours—one where the claims of narrow nationalism yield to the universal good of all men. The most effective action to prevent war is judged to be the constructing of a world community through the strengthening of existing instruments of international co-operation.[1]

2. International Law and the Need for Institutions

Introducing the volume prepared for the delegates to Amsterdam's Section on International Affairs, Sir Kenneth G. Grubb, Chairman of the CCIA, remarked: 'The Disorder of Man is to most men nowhere more painfully apparent than in international relations; the Design of God for the nations is difficult to perceive.'[2] The phrase, a play of words on the Assembly's general theme, 'Man's Disorder and God's Design', was a protestation that

[1] Thus, Baron F. M. Van Asbeck, President of the CCIA, in *The Church and the International Disorder*: 'We shall not have to fight *against* war and national sovereignty, but to arm ourselves *for* a legal order above the states, for an international law with binding force, for "peace".' p. 65.   [2] *Ibid.*, p. 13.

the World Council of Churches had no blue-print to offer for the proper functioning of the contemporary world of nations. Indeed, concluded Sir Kenneth, in discussing the intractable field of international relations, the World Council of Churches 'raised more questions than can readily be answered, and some that cannot be answered, and some that cannot be answered in print and only by a divine miracle in life'. There is, nevertheless, a broad consensus of opinion in the World Council constituency[1] on the desired direction of relations between people. It calls for a recognition of the sovereignty of God in the ordering of international affairs by the acceptance of international law administered by supranational institutions.[2]

The difficulties of achieving such an ideal are immediately obvious. 'Power politics and the attitude of mind it represents' was termed 'the root problem' of international conflict by the Oxford Conference. Certainly, the determination of each nation to fix its line of conduct exclusively in the light of its own interests is in disaccord with the 'rule of law' which the World Council constituency desires to see prevail in the world. Unhappily, however, international law manifests the weaknesses of contemporary international society. As Professor Max Huber explained to the group gathered at Bossey in April 1950 to discuss the problem, classical international law is by definition a complexus of contracts between sovereign national States. And Baron Van Asbeck, Professor of International Law at the University of Leyden, corrected any notion the Amsterdam delegates might have that contemporary international law is 'the expression by a superior authority of the common conscience of a community, as is national law in homogeneous states'; it is, rather, in its 'insincerities, inconsistencies and uncertainties . . . a compromise between group-interests determined by their

---

[1] The Hungarian Ecumenical Commission, however, according to the Evanston Survey, scorned reliance on institutional instruments of international order, insisting that the cross of Jesus Christ has provided all the necessary conditions of peace. *CHTC*, p. 8.

[2] The warnings against utopian illusions regarding the United Nations sounded by the CCIA, the seeming innocence of the nature of international law in some World Council circles, the ignoring of ideological factors affecting international tension, suggest that the difficulties are not universally obvious to the Ecumenical Community.

relative power'.[1] Distressing as the situation may be, it is inevitable in the absence of a genuine world community, bound
together by a pre-legal decision of a common conception of
justice, common convictions on the purpose of man and human
society. 'The *concordia* on which the *pax hominum* (Augustine)
must be based does not exist.'[2]

The Bossey Conference on the foundations of international
law, sponsored by the World Council of Churches, the CCIA
and the Ecumenical Institute in April 1950, urged the churches
to 'rouse the nations and their governments to a consciousness
of their duty to establish a just and lasting code of international
law'. The codification of a legal system drawing on radically
different conceptions of justice is a perplexing task. So is the
establishment of an international order in the absence of an
international ethos. Preparing for the Second Assembly, the
Survey for the Section on International Affairs declared flatly that
'the Christian obligation to seek the establishment of an international ethos as a common foundation of moral principles for
the world community has not been met'. Various reasons are
suggested: the lack of systematic study of 'the basic principles
of world order', the provincial outlook of Christians who 'do not
yet see international responsibility as part of the total field of
Christian witness', and the need of more effective ecumenical
organization, 'sound and active national commissions on international affairs—not names on paper but minds at work'.

[1] *The Church and the International Disorder*, p. 57. Involved is the conflict on the nature
of law underlined by Professor John H. Hallowell: law as 'the product of individual wills
and subjective interest' *versus* law as 'the embodiment of eternal truths and values discoverable by reason'. Cf. *The Moral Foundations of Democracy*, p. 72.

[2] *The Church and the International Disorder*, p. 64. 'In the world society of today various
religions, social conceptions, legal orders, ideologies, exist side by side, insulated or
inter-related, some of them politically or even fundamentally disunited, connected by no
common conviction; and inseparably bound up with that pluriformity is a difference of
economic systems and of standards of living.' *Ibid.*, p. 51. Continuing, Baron Van Asbeck
explained: 'When at the end of the Middle Ages the *corpus christianum* of Europe broke
up, the existing unity lost its common basis. That process went further and during the
nineteenth century the society of states came to be suspended in the air of relative power.
Since the nineteenth century we have been confronted with a new historical situation,
viz., the existence side by side of isolated states, between which there is no moral or
spiritual bond.'

An international ethos, however, will not come into existence by declaring its necessity nor by omitting consideration of its possible basis. Baron F. M. Van Asbeck believes that the *Oikumene*, the ecumenical fellowship expressed in the World Council of Churches, is uniquely designed to achieve this common ethos, to discover by investigation of divisions and search of points of contact the solidarity of spiritual and moral unity beneath different world conceptions. Such a mission, he wrote in a chapter contributed to the Amsterdam preparatory volume, 'is *the* task *par excellence* in the international world. . . . The ecumenical leaven should revolutionize the international world.'[1]

It is difficult to gauge how general are such hopes in World Council circles. In a chapter entitled 'The Churches' Approach to International Affairs' appearing in the same Amsterdam Assembly symposium two authors,[2] officially charged to influence public policy on behalf of the interests of the churches, reached a decidedly more modest view of such a possibility.[3] While they did not discuss the problem of working out 'the basic principles of world order' within the World Council constituency (resolving, in the process, the conflict between an 'ethic of inspiration' and an 'ethic of ends'), they did note in passing the question of collaboration, a methodology seemingly imperative in any effort to foster a common ethos harmonizing different world views.[4]

The strains put upon the *Oikumene* itself by contemporary ideological divisions makes dubious the possibility that 'an ecumenical fellowship, transcending all human divisions and groupings', could realize the goal the President of the Commission of the Churches on International Affairs set for it. Successive

[1] *The Church and the International Disorder*, pp. 67, 69.

[2] Roswell P. Barnes, Associate General Secretary, Federal Council of Churches, USA, and Kenneth G. Grubb, Chairman of the CCIA and of the International Department of the British Council of Churches.

[3] 'The execution of policy in international relations is, as is the case in politics generally, the art of the possible. Only in certain countries can the churches arouse popular interest, and then only over certain questions.' *Ibid.*, p. 28.

[4] 'The advisability of the churches correlating efforts with those of other faiths or of no fundamental faith in the struggle for standards and conditions rests upon considerations of prudence and convenience rather than of principle or conviction.' *Ibid.*, pp. 28–9.

attempts to produce papers on specific international problems and especially on the significance of Soviet Russia for the Amsterdam background volume proved unsatisfactory; ultimately, a projected omnibus chapter called 'Antagonisms and Alignments' was jettisoned.[1] Six months before the Assembly, Professor Josef Hromadka told the Conference of National Ecumenical Study Executives that the Section IV Commission 'had decided not to arrive at any synthesis which would be premature and futile' but proposed instead to put before the delegates analyses of the situation from two angles, the chapters of John Foster Dulles and himself.[2] The strain upon the *Oikumene* was aggravated by the endorsement by the World Council's Central Committee of the collective security action, under United Nations auspices, in Korea and was made public by the absence of World Council collaborators from East Europe and China from the preparatory conferences for the Evanston Assembly.

Finally, it must be conceded that the hope of building a common international ethos on what Baron Van Asbeck considers 'the sole foundation of world society',[3] the universal acceptance of the theological basis of the World Council of Churches, supposes a successful campaign of world evangelism whose beginnings are not discernible.

Nevertheless, the World Council's Second Assembly for the first time[4] addressed itself to the task of suggesting some general principles of international morality. It did so tentatively, noting

[1] With British humour the Chairman of Amsterdam's Section IV Study preparations explained to the final session of the World Council's Study Commission at Bossey on June 27, 1947, the difficulties encountered. His group, he noted, was 'composed of six professors, four clergymen and some bits and pieces and it has, I think, succeeded in producing results just above the level of the ghastly'. *Archives.*

[2] The two great issues to be emphasized were declared to be 'power without moral or spiritual leadership' and 'nationalism expressing the desire of subjugated masses for autonomy'. However, 'the attempt to deal with nationalism as such has been postponed until after the Assembly as it was too vast to be dealt with in a short time'. *Ibid.*

[3] 'viz., that God is the Lord of all nations; that Jesus Christ has been given full authority in heaven and on earth'. *The Church and the International Disorder*, p. 70.

[4] 'The ecumenical conferences under review did not attempt to spell out the responsibilities of the churches for the development of a common ethos.' Richard M. Fagley, 'Our Ecumenical Heritage in International Affairs', *ER* VI (October 1953), 1, p. 62.

that the task required 'sustained study'. Convinced, however, that 'the world of nations desperately needs an international ethos to provide a sound groundwork for the development of international law and institutions', the Evanston Section on International Affairs advanced nine relevant principles as 'considerations'.[1]

Whatever the understanding of the bases of an international ethos held by the different member churches of the World Council, they agreed at Amsterdam on the importance of 'that common foundation of moral conviction without which any system of law will break down' and on their obligation to foster a common set of guiding principles. They acknowledged that they had a significant contribution to make in supporting a series of manifest needs in the international field.[2] These fall largely within the function of the United Nations and concerning that institution the World Council pronouncements have been specific. While favouring a more comprehensive and more

---

[1] '(a) All power carries responsibility and all nations are trustees of power which should be used for the common good; (b) All nations are subject to moral law, and should strive to abide by the accepted principles of international law, to develop this law, and to enforce it through common actions; (c) All nations should honour their pledged word and international agreements into which they have entered; (d) No nation in an international dispute has the right to be sole judge in its own cause or to resort to war to advance its policies but should seek to settle disputes by direct negotiation or by submitting them to conciliation, arbitration or judicial settlement; (e) All nations have a moral obligation to ensure universal security and to this end should support measures designed to deny victory to a declared aggressor; (f) All nations should recognize and safeguard the inherent dignity, worth and essential rights of the human person without distinction as to race, sex, language or religion; (g) Each nation should recognize the rights of every other nation, which observes such standards, to live by and proclaim its own political and social beliefs, provided that it does not seek by coercion, threat, infiltration or deception to impose these on other nations; (h) All nations should recognize an obligation to share their scientific and technical skills with peoples in less developed regions, and to help the victims of disaster in other lands; (i) All nations should strive to develop cordial relations with their neighbours, encourage friendly cultural and commercial dealings and join in creative international efforts for human welfare.' *Evanston*, p. 142.

[2] 'They [the churches] should at present support immediate practical steps for fostering mutual understanding and goodwill among the nations, for promoting respect for international law and the establishment of the international institutions which are now possible. They should also support every effort to deal on a universal basis with the many specific questions of international concern which face mankind today, such as the use of atomic power, the multilateral reduction of armaments, and the provision of health services and food for all men.' *Amsterdam*, pp. 92–3.

authoritative world organization, it insists on the full use of the existing instrument of international collaboration.

Widespread disenchantment over the failure of the United Nations to fulfil the unrealistic hopes of many induced the Executive Committee of the CCIA to issue a Statement at the close of its meeting in August 1953. Acknowledging the handicaps under which the UN is forced to operate—the stubborn clinging to separate sovereignties, the abuse of the veto, the primacy of national and ideological interests—the Statement was a strong endorsement of the world organization and its related agencies and a solemn appeal for its support and development. As a world forum where diverse cultures meet, as an instrument for the growth of international law, as a regulator of the common interests of the nations and a mechanism for peaceful settlement of disputes, 'these institutions offer now an effective means of developing conditions essential to the rule of law in the world', the Statement argued.[1]

The Second Assembly reaffirmed the World Council's previous endorsements of the United Nations as having made significant contributions to order and justice despite the critical post-war tensions which have divided the international community. The General Assembly's serving as a 'forum of world public opinion' on major international problems, the international standard furnished in the Universal Declaration of Human Rights and the use of the Specialized Agencies as 'a centre for harmonizing the actions of States for human welfare', were listed as achievements. Continued growth of the United Nations was hoped for through more responsible use of present Charter provisions by members and by the evolution of powers inherent in the Charter or delegated to it by common consent. Consideration of the greater effectiveness of the UN Organization reminded the Assembly of the provision made for a periodical revision of the Charter. Should a conference for this purpose be convened, the Section believed it should try to determine the organic and structural requirements of the Organization 'for carrying out

[1] *ER* vi (October 1953), I, p. 57.

programmes dealing with universal, enforcible disarmament, human rights, greatly expanded technical assistance programmes and the more rapid development of self-government in colonial areas'.

Obviously such expectations suppose not only the abolition of the rule of unanimity which the Soviets, for one, consider an essential of the Organization, but also effective powers to investigate and punish serious violations of human rights and national sovereignties; the use of these powers would undoubtedly mean war. The Section on International Affairs at Evanston had no recommendations on the question of the Great Power 'veto' in the United Nations nor did it repeat earlier CCIA enthusiasm for Peace Observer Commissions. That meritorious mechanism for watching possible points of aggression, adopted by the General Assembly as part of its 'Uniting for Peace' Resolution on November 3, 1950, supposed the general acceptance of the United Nations as neutral. The arrangements to supervise the armistice concluded at Geneva in July 1954 and Thailand's subsequent withdrawal of its request for a Peace Observer team indicates that the supposition has small foundation.

The weakness of the United Nations has resulted in the formation of regional associations, notably the North Atlantic Treaty Organization, for common defence and the pursuit of mutual interests. Without identifying any of these groupings, the Evanston Section conceded them 'a valid place in a co-operative world order, despite [their] potential danger to international peace and security'; certain provisions, chiefly their subordination to the UN, were added.[1] Whichever regional organizations do pass these tests are judged to strengthen the United Nations 'by reducing threats to the peace and by lessening the number of international questions thrust before the world forum'. The principle involved resembles what economists call

---

[1] It is required of regional organizations that: '(a) They are clearly defensive in character and military actions are subject to collective decision; (b) They are subordinate to and reinforce the aims of the Charter of the United Nations; (c) They serve the genuine mutual interests and needs of the peoples of the region.' *Evanston*, pp. 139–40. It is doubtful if the Arab League was principally envisaged.

the division of labour. The same principle probably accounts for the demand made by the Section for a larger respect in the United Nations for the principle of the 'sovereign' equality of States, great and small.

In the CCIA statement, 'Christians Look at the United Nations',[1] the world organization was supported as offering 'the best means for co-ordinating the activities of the nations for human welfare'. The phrase reflects an outlook which recalls the missionary concerns of the ecumenical constituency. Protestantism's focus on world evangelism, an important factor in the history of the collaboration of the churches, dictates almost instinctively the interest of the World Council of Churches in the political and social advancement of dependent people and the UN programmes of Technical Assistance.

The struggle for political freedom in East Asia has been followed with particular attention by the World Council, for in this region are found most of the 'Younger Churches' which participate in the Ecumenical Movement. The Amsterdam Assembly declared itself against colonialism, against postponement of progress towards self-government for subject peoples. The revolutionary ferment in Asia has been on the agenda in one form or another of every meeting of the World Council's Central Committee since its formation. Obviously the effect of communist domination in missionary areas is a source of anxiety to the Ecumenical Community. This eventuality, the World Council has continuously counselled,[2] is best overcome by an unequivocal recognition of the right to self-determination for subject peoples, the abandonment of all pretensions of racial superiority and the fostering of technically aided programmes of self-help to raise the standards of living in economically backward areas. The CCIA follows the activities of the UN Trusteeship Council but its present 'major concern' is with inter-governmental efforts to conquer disease, hunger and poverty.

[1] *ER* VI (October 1953), 1, p. 57.
[2] A positive programme of justice, the Central Committee stated at its 1950 meeting, is 'the most important means of rendering the world morally impregnable to totalitarian penetration'.

Various studies have been made and graphs prepared to show the unequal conditions under which the world's population lives.[1] All such statistics are, given the proportions of the problem, approximations. They are cold attempts to express the situation more imaginatively summarized in the remark: 'Two out of three of God's children go to bed hungry every night.' The facts present a moral challenge which the World Council proposes to press on its constituency. The CCIA Executive at its mid-summer meeting in 1951 did not hesitate to declare: 'Perhaps the chief task of Christians and Christian agencies is to help create and sustain the favourable moral climate necessary for sound technical assistance programmes.' The World Council's Central Committee meeting at Lucknow in January 1953 added a strong endorsement.[2] The CCIA sees such programmes as a positive strategy for peace. Its annual Reports indicate that, beginning with a statement on seven requirements for international aid in economic and social self-development, this agency of the World Council has offered specific comment regularly on the developing UN Expanded Programme of Technical Assistance, calling particularly for better co-operation between governmental and non-governmental organizations at the field level. It is here, of course, that the co-operation of the missionaries with international institutions can be most effective.

Such regular consultation maintained by the Executive Secretary of the CCIA with the UN Technical Assistance Programme is calculated to remind these international civil

---

[1] A widely distributed poster of the World Health Organization indicates contrasting conditions, thus: 'Only one-fifth of the people of the world live in developed areas. . . . Average annual income $500 each. . . . Expectation of life 63 years. . . . two-thirds of the people of the world live in underdeveloped areas. . . . Average annual income $50 each. . . . Expectation of life 30 years.' An International Labour Organization poster notes as having a national income per head under $50 annually in 1949—Burma, China, Ecuador, Ethiopia, Haiti, Indonesia, South Korea, Liberia, the Philippines, Saudi Arabia, Thailand, Yemen; US average annual *per capita* income for the same year—$1,500.

[2] 'The Churches in the more developed countries must urge their peoples and governments to do everything possible to strengthen programmes of technical assistance, without which such efforts [to obtain a standard of living which meets basic human needs and to establish a more just social and economic order] in Asia cannot succeed.' Lucknow *Minutes*, p. 73.

servants of the existence and activities of these volunteers who are already on hand in the economically backward areas of the world. In the refugee field, at least, international organizations soon learned of the importance of the co-operation of private groups, particularly those under religious auspices. Even before its formal establishment the World Council of Churches was grappling with the spiritual and material problems of those uprooted by the war. Its interest has not abated. Through the CCIA it has supported moves to broaden the mandate of the UN High Commissioner for Refugees, to make permanent the UN International Children's Emergency Fund, to resettle and reintegrate those made homeless by the war in Palestine and to make possible civilian relief assistance in inter-governmental plans for Korean reconstruction. Through its Department of Inter-Church Aid and Service to Refugees, it has continued to find new homes for the uprooted. The Director General of the Inter-Governmental Committee for European Migration told the Seventh Session of that international body in April 1954 that of the 30,863 persons resettled by Voluntary Agencies the previous year, 42 per cent owed their chances for a new beginning in happier surroundings to the World Council of Churches and its closely allied associate, the Lutheran World Federation. The World Council of Churches, whose Central Committee has called the refugee problem 'a judgment upon our whole society', has not contented itself with merely piously deploring this manifestation of international disorder.

If on economic and social questions the mind of the World Council is found imprecise and reluctant to assay concrete institutions, in international affairs it is prepared to declare, in the words of Amsterdam's Section IV, 'International law clearly requires international institutions for its effectiveness.' The World Council of Churches, through the Commission of the Churches on International Affairs, seeks positively to influence the direction and decisions of existing international institutions and has no hesitation in participating in their activities.

3. *Human Rights*

'An essential element in a better international order is freedom of religion.'[1] This declaration of the Oxford Conference of 1937 is a summary expression of a permanent preoccupation of the Ecumenical Community; it was reaffirmed by the Amsterdam Assembly in its 'Declaration on Religious Liberty'.[2] Religious freedom was, moreover, recognized as finding its place among fundamental rights. On this issue there was none of the indefiniteness which characterized Section III's Report on economic and social questions. 'It is for the State,' Section IV asserted, 'to embody these rights in its own legal system and to ensure their observance in practice.'[3] The First Assembly went further in calling upon its constituent members 'to press for the adoption of an International Bill of Human Rights making provision for the recognition, and national and international enforcement, of all the essential freedoms of man, whether personal, political or social'.[4] Evanston called for the protection of 'God-given rights which are his Will for all men'.[5]

Whatever the differing theological views current in ecumenical circles on the origin and nature of the State and its role in human society, the World Council of Churches is clearly on record as assigning to the organized political authority the duty of condemning violations of human rights and of guaranteeing religious liberty. It believes, furthermore, that action by the international community should be invoked to enforce the protection of fundamental freedoms.

In widening the scope of its interests beyond the issue of religious liberty so as to include all fundamental freedoms, the World Council of Churches was undoubtedly encouraged by the successful effort of religious leaders to have the new world

---

[1] *Oxford*, p. 184.

[2] *Amsterdam*, p. 97. Amsterdam changed Oxford's 'a better international order' to read 'a good international order' to indicate, perhaps, that in practical political affairs the desirable 'better' is the enemy of the achievable 'good'.

[3] *Ibid.*, p. 93.　　　　　　　　　　　　[4] *Ibid.*, p. 96.

[5] *Evanston*, p. 140. The call was judged 'all the more insistent in this age when, in various parts of the world, totalitarianism—based on ideologies sometimes atheistic and sometimes under the guise of religion—oppresses the freedom of men and of institutions'.

organization, born of the war-time collaboration of the United Nations, include a formal recognition of human rights and a Commission charged to concern itself with their observance. Dr. O. Frederick Nolde, Director of the CCIA and the World Council's specialist on questions of human rights, played a by no means unimportant role in this phase of the San Francisco Conference of 1945.[1]

The Amsterdam Assembly summarized the requirements of freedom of religion and conscience, which had been enumerated by the Oxford Conference of the Universal Christian Council for Life and Work of 1937[2] and the World Meeting of the International Missionary Council, held at Madras in 1938.[3] 'The rights of all men to hold and change their faith, to express it in worship and practice, to teach and persuade others, and to decide on the religious education of their children' were listed as primary characteristics of genuine religious freedom. The Report of Section IV immediately indicated its awareness of other human rights, urging the churches to press also 'for freedom of speech and expression, of association and assembly, the rights of the family, of freedom from arbitrary arrest, as well as all those other rights which the true freedom of man requires'. The expulsion of minorities was denounced, and enforced segregation opposed. The concreteness of language stands in marked contrast to the indefiniteness of the Report of the Section on Social Questions which condemned merely 'any denial to man of an opportunity to participate in the shaping of society', without indicating whether this implied either the right of private property or the right to join a labour union.

Since Amsterdam the efforts to formulate human rights have

[1] *The Private Papers of Senator Vandenburg* supply warrant for Dr. Nolde's claim that 'an international Christian influence played a determining part in achieving the more extensive provisions for human rights and fundamental freedoms which ultimately found their way into the Charter'. *The Church and the International Disorder*, p. 151, where some of the details are recounted.

[2] *Oxford*, pp. 84–5.

[3] *The World Mission of the Church* (London: International Missionary Council, 1938), pp. 116–17.

become less prominent in World Council publications. The Questions for Discussion appended to the popular pamphlet prepared for the Evanston Assembly's consideration of International Affairs, for example, mentions fundamental freedoms only in passing, in connexion with the elements essential to the growth of an international ethos. The adoption by the UN General Assembly on December 10, 1948, of the Universal Declaration of Human Rights is clearly felt to have satisfactorily proclaimed the ideals of the Ecumenical Community.[1] Accepting the legal clothing of human rights, the World Council works for their recognition and application. In the phrasing of Article 18 of the UN Declaration on religious liberty the Director of the CCIA had collaborated, and the results won the support of that organization's Executive Committee which encouraged its constituency 'by processes of education and public opinion to seek to make the provisions of the Declaration effective in constitutions, in domestic laws, in court decisions and generally in practice'. Church leaders were urged to promote observance of Human Rights Day.

The announcement by the United States Government that, under the present circumstances, it would not ratify the two projected Covenants on Human Rights rather effectively adjourned hopes of translating the Declaration into treaty form, to be sure. The Director of the CCIA as a consultant had offered suggestions on the articles on religious liberty and religious education in the drafts of the Covenants which had received the general approval of the CCIA Executive in July 1952. The realities of the international situation, however, make the process of codifying rights, in the absence of any machinery to enforce their observance, seem fruitless. In the interest of human rights the World Council of Churches' General Secretary appeared before the UN Special Commission on Prisoners of War, an international effort doomed to failure in

[1] However, the Foreign Department of EKiD, whose chief, Dr. Martin Niemöller, is a member of the World Council's Central Committee, wants any Covenant on Human Rights to state explicitly that human rights are grounded in God's grace and that it is for secular authorities to recognize and protect them.

the absence of minimal co-operation by the Soviet Union. The work of the UN *ad hoc* Committee on Forced Labour, on the other hand, did not win the attention of the World Council or of the CCIA.

The Amsterdam pronouncement on religious liberty echoes an Anglo-Saxon accent. The overall approach of the Commission of the Churches on International Affairs on the question of human rights reveals especially the heritage of the political philosophy and experience of the Natural Law tradition. That is to say, liberty is claimed for religious groups in virtue of fundamental human rights possessed by the individual members as persons irrespective of their confessional allegiance. The World Council's constituency includes, of course, those who base human rights on the fact of an individual's faith as a Christian. For others the question of rights in the political order is of small interest, since the Church is concerned not with the menace of human ideologies but with the protection of the purity of doctrinal teaching and the independence of its ecclesiastical administration. Other opinion would vindicate religious liberty by appealing to the mission of the Church of Christ which gives it an absolute right to evangelize all men and a consequent claim on the protection of the State to guarantee that liberty of preaching. In a comprehensive monograph contributed to the Amsterdam Assembly Volume on International Affairs, Dr. O. Frederick Nolde observed: 'At the present time, there is immediate and urgent need for the development of the Christian view on human rights in terms which will apply to all men and which can be used in representations to national and international political authorities.'[1] The opportunity of collaborating with efforts to draft an International Bill of Rights, Dr. Nolde remarked, could not and should not be postponed pending the resolution of the theological debate on the basis of fundamental freedoms. Besides, as the Evanston Survey explained, the CCIA is not a theological commission.[2]

[1] 'Freedom of Religion and Related Human Rights' in *The Church and the International Disorder*, p. 148.
[2] Where, in the World Council framework, the bases of human rights would be discussed is not indicated. Once again, the problem raises the question of an 'ethic of

Its Director, therefore, in his analysis of human rights has had recourse to what he terms the 'juridical' considerations; in his dealings with relevant international bodies he has emphasized the functional approach.

Another aspect of the general topic of religious liberty, namely the question of the relations of the Church with the State, has not been discussed in World Council debates. Several members of the Council, it may be noted, are the Established Churches in their respective countries. With a telling quotation from Calvin, Adolf Keller argues: 'The Continental Reformation thought, therefore, not of a disestablished Church, but of the closest co-operation between State and Church, both being Divine orders in a fallen world to help the Christians to fulfil God's will.'[1] The Anglican Archbishop of York has more recently presented the case for an Established Church, asserting that the State 'has responsibility for the spiritual and moral welfare of its people, but as it cannot discharge this duty by itself, it should therefore hand it over to a Church'.[2] On the other hand, an American delegate to the World Council's Faith and Order meeting at Lund publicly rejected, as being opposed to political freedom and biblical theology, the views of Swedish theologians, headed by Anders Nygren, on a State Church.[3] The question is a knotty one, manifesting clearly the influence of political and social factors in theological traditions. Its appositeness in any discussion on religious liberty was shown in the announcement

inspiration' *versus* an 'ethic of ends', reason *versus* the Bible alone as a source of social philosophy, human nature *versus* divine election as the point of departure for a system of rights and duties in the political order.

[1] *Church and State on the European Continent*, p. 166.

[2] Cyril Garbett, *Church and State in England*, p. 24.

[3] Dr. Winfred E. Garrison was shocked at those who considered the thesis of the symposium *This is the Church*, that the entire population of a country is to be included within the State Church 'regardless of personal faith, repentance or commitment, as perfectly in harmony with the New Testament concept of the Church and with a sound theology of the Church'. Cf. *The Third World Conference on Faith and Order, Lund, 1952*, p. 187. Dr. Garrison should surely have heard of the settlement of the Peace of Augsburg —'jus reformandi, ubi unus dominus, ibi sit una religio'—if he had never come upon the definition of Bishop Nygren's predecessor in the see of Lund, Eduard Rodke: 'The Swedish people as a whole, considered from a religious angle, is the Swedish Church.' Quoted in Keller's *Church and State on the European Continent*, p. 169.

of the Greek Evangelical Church that it would not attend the Evanston Assembly of the World Council because it refused to associate in an ecumenical gathering with a member church, the Church of Greece, which, it alleged, was persecuting the Protestant minority of 6,000 in that country. The Church of Greece is an Established Church, the Greek Constitution providing for the union of Church and State. Ultimately through the mediation of the CCIA, the Synod of the Evangelical Church in Greece decided to send two delegates to the Second Assembly; the Church of Greece, for its part, announced it would send the Royal Chaplain and ten laymen, professors from the universities of Athens and Salonika, three Metropolitans who had previously been named being retained 'by pressure of official duties'.

There is a danger, as the CCIA undoubtedly realizes, that the promulgating of declarations of human rights, satisfying though the process may be to a rooted instinct for justice, may tend to blur the stubborn fact that their observance is conditioned by the structure and the historical evolution of any given society. 'The relativities of liberty depend in great part on the circumstances of the social reality and the degree of political maturity of a nation,' wrote Professor Claude Du Pasquier of the University of Neuchâtel in a symposium on the Swiss Constitution and civic rights.[1] The social realities of India are invoked to justify the Government's decision to interdict any increase of Christian missionaries entering that country, despite the liberty of religion clause in the Indian Constitution. It is certainly not a deficiency of political maturity among the Swiss but a differing estimate of the demands of public order that explains the judgment of the Confederation's Federal Tribunal that the propaganda of the Jehovah Witnesses exceeded the legal limit of freedom of conscience and belief. The United States Supreme Court, on the other hand, has on several occasions struck down all police limitations on the activities of this aggressive sect, invoking the freedom of speech and assembly guarantees of the American

---

[1] 'La Liberté et le Droit Suisse', in *Die Freiheit des Bürgers im Schweizerischen Recht*, p. 12.

Constitution rather than the religious liberty provisions. The need of information on, as well as of understanding of, the pattern of society is illustrated by the consultations reported in the Evanston Survey as being in progress 'with a view to establishing the facts regarding charges of violations of human rights in Colombia'.[1] In any case, as the Evanston Section on International Affairs noted: 'To build a strong defence of human rights requires vigorous, broad and persistent educational efforts. Christian education can make an important contribution here.'[2]

4. Problems of Practical Action

The common attitude of the Ecumenical Community, the general principles which guide its public pronouncements, were summarized in seven paragraphs in the statement, *Christians Stand for Peace*, issued by the Executive Committee of the CCIA at its Annual Meeting in 1951. Peace and justice were declared the twin goals to be prized and pursued, but not a peace purchased at the price of tyranny nor a justice achieved by means of war. These objectives, it was pointed out, suppose mutual trust between governments; they require international organs expressing the rule of law and order. The United Nations and its agencies represents at present the best means to develop this world community, it was held. General assistance by the wealthier to the poorer nations in their economic and social development, a common sharing of the responsibility for refugees and a respect for the rights of the individual because of his dignity as a child

[1] *CHTC*, p. 35. In its only specific condemnation of religious persecution, the Central Committee of the World Council of Churches at its Lucknow meeting protested against the violation of basic rights of Evangelical Christians in Colombia. The protest repeated that of the Executive Committee of the CCIA in July 1952. In its Annual Report for the same year, one notes: 'Every effort is made to determine the extent to which persecutions are attributable on the one hand to political conditions in Colombia and on the other to discrimination against the Protestant minority.' p. 30. The Annual Report for 1953–4 reveals: 'The CCIA has also followed with concern developments affecting religious liberty in a number of other countries, including Bulgaria, Czechoslovakia, the German Democratic Republic, Italy and Spain.' p. 35. Furthermore: 'Regret has been expressed that the governments of Bulgaria, Hungary and Rumania have refused to co-operate in the examination of charges against them of suppression of human rights contrary to the terms of the Peace Treaties.' *CHTC*, p. 33.

[2] *Evanston*, p. 141.

of God were claimed to be dictated by the goals of peace and justice which oblige Christians to put their loyalty to their common Lord above all other loyalties.

The implementation of these principles is the specific task of the CCIA in association with twenty-one National Commissions on International Affairs. In the selection of the particular issues engaging the attention of these ecumenical agencies, experience has shaped certain necessary criteria. As listed for the delegates in the Evanston Survey volume these are: (1) Is the problem urgent? (2) Is there a clear Christian concern about it? (3) Is there a substantial consensus of world-wide Christian opinion on the line to be followed? (4) Have those who have to handle the problem been able to acquire a real competence in it? (5) Is there a reasonable possibility that a contribution may be effective, or an over-riding imperative for Christian witness?

The necessity of 'a substantial consensus of world-wide Christian opinion on the line to be followed' is demanded by the very nature of the World Council of Churches which is only an instrument of the churches composing it. Such a necessity imposes certain inhibitions in the present circumstances of international politics. For opinion within the World Council is divided on the issues and even on the values involved in the current world tensions, not to speak of the concrete tactics required to deal with concrete manifestations of that tension.[1] As a result, the Survey prepared for the Evanston delegates listed with disconcerting imprecision two major goals of policy claiming

---

[1] A difference of opinion, involving perhaps the two best-known personalities in the Ecumenical Movement, on a crucial point of international relations is illustrated by this quotation from Reinhold Niebuhr: 'One hopes that the lessons of the Berlin Conference [of February 1954] will penetrate the illusions of Pastor Niemöller and his followers who have been engaged in some very fantastic political speculation prompted by the hatred of a Catholic régime at Bonn and presumably sanctified by Protestant theology.' *Christianity and Crisis* XIV (February 22, 1954), 2, p. 11. Professor John A. Mackay, President of the International Missionary Council, co-sponsor (with the World Council of Churches) of the CCIA, declared in 1953 that the only thing more dangerous than communism was anti-communism. The World Council constituency would probably be divided on that judgment of a member of its Central Committee. Certainly there is a marked difference of judgment within the small World Council inspired Committee on the Christian Responsibility for European Co-operation as represented by André Philip of France and Gustav Heinemann of Germany.

'immediate attention'. These goals are: 'to oppose the extension of tyranny and to restrain tendencies towards a "preventive" war'.[1] The location and springs and forms of the tyranny whose extension must be opposed were unidentified. The evidence of tendencies towards a preventive war was not indicated.[2] Nor was any description supplied of the forces fostering such tendencies.

To a degree not easily ascertainable, the positions on international affairs adopted by the World Council of Churches are influenced by its declared purposes and by its understanding of its own nature. As a fellowship of churches from different lands, composed of people subjected inevitably to different historical experiences, national aspirations and contemporary ideological pressures, it will be conscious of the diversity of opinion, political as well as theological, in its membership. As the organized expression of a common desire for an all-inclusive unity of the churches, it will be mindful of the tensions jeopardizing its hopes for ultimate ecclesiastical universality and the pressure imperilling even present collaboration. Writing on 'The Task and Attitude of the Church' in the Amsterdam Assembly volume, Baron F. M. Van Asbeck, President of the CCIA, explained: 'That new reality, the ecumenical fellowship, compels us to reconsider and re-think international relations.'[3]

In addition to the constitutional limitations interdicting any action not approved by all the member churches, the shapers of World Council policy cannot ignore strategic considerations.[4]

---

[1] *CHTC*, p. 47.

[2] A survey of US opinion, compiled at the same time as the pre-Evanston brochure was being edited, revealed that 6 per cent (of the 3,502 persons interviewed) were prepared to endorse a war with the Soviet Union, 4 per cent favouring a policy of appeasement with a unilateral abandonment of the armament programme. Cf. 'American Attitudes on World Organization', *Public Opinion Quarterly* XVII (Winter 1953–4), 4.

[3] *The Church and the International Disorder*, p. 47. The President of the World Council Agency noted further: 'In the words "the Church" we express our firm belief in a new reality, which is taking form and substance in the efforts of the different churches to reach, through all divergencies of opinions and attitudes, theological and ethical, a consensus concerning the central and vital problems of the present.' *Ibid.*

[4] In the only instance in the history of the Ecumenical Movement when the foreign policy of a specific nation was condemned, the Evanston Assembly accused the United States of strengthening reactionary political groups and weakening the forces of healthy

To be specific, they cannot forget that many Orthodox churches, following the lead of the Moscow Patriarchate, have stood aloof from the Ecumenical Movement, choosing to consider the World Council as an instrument of Western political interests. The associates of the World Council in East Europe undoubtedly believe that tendencies towards a preventive war are endemic in the United States: Bishop Albert Bereczky of Hungary endorsed the Soviet accusations in a protest charging the UN with 'bacteriological warfare in Korea'. On the other hand, the CCIA was obliged to issue a disclaimer against the misleading use of a quotation from the World Council's Central Committee appearing in the *Bulletin* of the World Peace Council. Indeed, as a result of the diverse reactions to the Toronto approval of UN intervention in Korea, Sir Kenneth Grubb, Chairman of the CCIA, opined that the first task of the World Council was to maintain its membership, not lose it by political stands. It is not the mission of the churches, he believed, to put themselves forward when a conflict has broken out but to interest themselves opportunely in menacing situations and to ponder and clarify preventive measures that will protect peace.[1]

More than most representatives of religious groups, the officials of the CCIA have cause to realize that the combined influence

social reform in East Asia. Cf. *Evanston*, p. 125. During the discussion of the Report at a plenary meeting, a delegate took exception to the passage. His protest was put to a vote and defeated, the Chairman explaining that 'the Section considered the matter to be of great importance in Asia'. *Ibid.*, p. 130.

[1] 'The Responsibilities of the Churches in Politics', *ER* III (January 1951), 2, p. 115. This issue of the *Ecumenical Review* offers several reactions to the World Council's stand on the UN action in Korea. The reluctance of the World Council to adopt positions likely to have a divisive effect on its membership is understandable. Endeavouring to avoid any action jeopardizing its membership, however, carries the risk of neglecting an issue which many think of substantial importance for a stable international order, the question of human rights and religious freedom in East Europe. Thus, the second-ranking prelate of Sir Kenneth's own Church, Dr. Cyril Foster Garbett, addressing the Convocation of his Province of York on May 7, 1953, called for a UN investigation of the anti-church policies in communist countries. In the opinion of His Grace of York, the opposing political and economic systems of East and West will continue to face one another for an indefinite period, their contradictions not necessarily standing in the way of peace. 'Religious persecution,' on the other hand, Dr. Garbett declared, 'is so detestable that, while it continues, it must be a fatal obstacle to good understanding between the democracies and the persecuting States.'

of the churches in international affairs is conditioned by their separate strength in the different countries. For it is with the functionaries of international organizations and with national political leaders that they must deal in explaining the point of view of the Ecumenical Community. And while the assistance of religious bodies is sought in caring for refugees and the counsel of experienced leaders is accepted in phrasing principles of human rights, the influence of the churches on issues involved in the basic power struggle being played on the world's stage today depends on the strength of public opinion behind the positions taken by spokesmen for the organized Ecumenical Movement. Stalin was more outspoken but not necessarily more cynical than the average contemporary political leader in inquiring about the number of divisions a religious leader possessed.

The question may be asked whether the Second Assembly provided helpful suggestions for achieving what one of its Preparatory Commissions termed 'two major goals of policy'— blocking the extension of tyranny and restraining a preventive war. Surely the demand for internationally controlled disarmament[1] and the renunciation of aggressive or subversive acts in the Evanston 'Appeal' would be universally acknowledged as the basis for any possible and permanent peaceful coexistence between nations. The cessation of hostile propaganda is certainly necessary for a climate of peace. The possibility of publicly criticizing the government and of peacefully practising one's religion are assuredly tests of freedom in any political community based on justice. Visits of ecclesiastics, supposing that they are not political agents, are calculated to promote mutual understanding between peoples. Aid to underdeveloped countries is at once an obligation of Christian charity and a policy calculated to ameliorate revolutionary unrest. The realization of all of these suggestions is indeed a consummation devoutly to be wished.

[1] Time alone will tell whether Raymond Aron was more knowledgeable or more cynical when he wrote: 'La recherche d'une convention internationale sur la limitation des armements est une distraction innocente pour les polytechniciens ou avocats en disponibilité.' *Le Figaro*, November 4, 1954, p. 16.

Progress along some of these lines is not impossible. In any case the World Council is confident that it has made its contribution towards a better international order. Closing its Survey of recent activities Preparatory Commission IV of the Evanston Assembly remarked: 'The road that has been traversed should provide some additional perspective of humility, courage, and hope as the road ahead is undertaken.'

V

CONCLUSIONS

THE General Secretary of the World Council of Churches, Dr. W. A. Visser 't Hooft, has described the Council as by nature having a 'pioneering programme', seeking to find a 'third way' that cuts across easily accepted dichotomies and deadlocks.[1] The concept is important for an understanding of the nature of its judgments on contemporary society.

1. Ecumenicism as a 'Third Way'

Ecumenicism by definition, Dr. 't Hooft indicated, transcends narrow denominationalism while prizing the peculiar heritage of its component ecclesiastical traditions and appreciating the distinct contributions each communion brings to the corporate whole. As the agent and the expression of the Ecumenical Community, the World Council has likened itself to a wheel in which the whole 'has value and importance over and above that of its parts'.[2] The World Council, it will be recalled, denies that it is *the* Church but conceives of itself as more than a federation of churches. It considers itself an ecclesiological Third Way in progress towards ultimate definition whose lineaments are not yet clearly seen.

Similarly, in the realm of social thought the World Council favours a Third Way, a position transcending, as Dr. 't Hooft pointed out, the dichotomies of capitalism *versus* other social systems and a mode of approach to international affairs that will clarify attitudes to Marxism as over against a purely sterile anti-communism. Convinced of 'the one simple idea that social

---

[1] *The Ecumenical Courier*, 12 (November–December 1953), 6, p. 1.
[2] In an information leaflet, 'Tell Us About the World Council of Churches'.

and economic systems are relative to time and place', the World Council seeks new and creative solutions whose ultimate formulation will merit the title of the Responsible Society, an ideal social organization whose concrete lineaments are not yet clearly known. In the elaboration of its social critique, moreover, it makes provision for the ethical insights deriving from different theological traditions and for the practical concerns of its members, since the World Council has also likened itself to a family whose 'members have a common loyalty and heritage, but they are not all alike and there is no reason to expect them to be'. It will be normal, then, that 'the many churches and nationalities each bring to the Ecumenical Movement their own historic, academic and spiritual gifts', not least in evaluating social questions and issues in the realm of international affairs.

Such an approach will not be lacking in negations, for the Third Way is a rejection of existing categories, a disavowal of choice between what are represented as current alternatives of social organization. It will be marked, too, by a certain tentativeness, since social and economic systems are deemed relative and because the method of inquiry must make allowance for points of view within the ecumenical family.

The approach produces on occasion statements whose indefiniteness has drawn the reproach of uncertainty.[1] Indeed the very aspiration to find a Third Way drew the suggestion of intellectual escapism or of timorousness.[2] Such an indictment

---

[1] Thus *Fortune*, the magazine of the American business community, observed in its comment on Amsterdam's Report on Social Questions: 'The fact that these questions [concerning the theological implications of economic actions] are not sharply posed and not fully answered suggests that the problem of whether the state or the individual is the agent of social goodness (as well as of social evil) is still a matter of religious quandary.' 'The Church Speaks to Business', xxxviii (December 1948), p. 122.

[2] The *Fortune* editorial continued: 'furthermore, the attempt of Amsterdam to find a middle ground between the extremes of Communism and Capitalism and the attempt of the Federal Council report ["Christianity and the Economic Order"] to find a middle ground between increased free enterprise and increased social control suggest that churchmen may be applying rather the law of compromise than the searing light of Truth. Are compromises, however loving they may be, the essence of Christianity?' As the *Fortune* writer should have remembered, compromises may be the essence of political wisdom in the practice of the celebrated 'art of the possible'. It was not absolute moral standards but a tolerable social order which was being discussed.

fails to recognize the intrinsic limitations of the ecumenical discourse. It ignorantly or short-sightedly refuses to acknowledge the importance of the specific contribution of the World Council's critique of the social order.

2. *Inherent Difficulties*

The difficulties of the ecumenical discourse on social topics are ample and obvious. Let us review some that this study has disclosed.

1. It is essential to recall that the World Council of Churches is, by definition, 'a fellowship of churches', an instrument enabling its members to consult together and give utterance to common convictions on the economic order and international affairs. It has no voice independent of that of its members. Its range of pronouncements, then, will be coextensive with the opinions winning the acceptance of its entire membership. Within that membership will be churches of different theological traditions, whose communicants are subject to different national loyalties, exposed to different social experiences, cultural prejudices and possibly political pressures.

Independence of judgment, freedom to dissent are more than charter rights of the member churches of the World Council; they are of the very genius of its constituent communions. F. Ernest Johnson, long-time Director of the Department of Research and Survey of the Federal Council of the Churches of Christ in the United States, has written: 'It is of the essence of the Protestant faith that the individual conscience is supreme. On all matters of political and social policy this means that the church may furnish guidance but no directives.'[1] Such freedom, as has been noted, is a consequence of the mode of apprehending moral truth: the individual discovering his present duty always in concrete circumstances by his personal contact with God's word. Such an approach explains undoubtedly the absence of any agreed definition of such terms as 'justice', 'the State', 'human rights' in

---

[1] 'Protestant Social Policy', *The Nation*, 177 (July 25, 1953), 4, p. 66.

World Council documents, although ecumenical discussions over the years invariably include the suggestion that agreement should be reached on the meaning of basic terms.

2. As an organization, the World Council is in a certain sense the culmination of a tradition. It is, in another sense, committed to establish a tradition, that of the permanent and official collaboration of many churches of differing traditions. Such a task imposes restraints in making pronouncements on international situations and social questions, restraints over and above the restrictions imposed by the Constitution of the World Council. The Council's Executive Committee adverted to these practical considerations in a letter to the member churches after the crisis provoked by the endorsement of UN intervention in Korea.[1] The determination of the member churches 'to stay together' does not annul differences of opinion[2] nor obviate organizational tensions.

3. The conviction that the ecumenical reality, organizationally represented by the World Council of Churches, is of a different order of existence from that of particular cultures and historical social systems explains further the refusal of the Council to identify Christianity with any political grouping or economic order. Such a conviction of the transcendence of religion,

---

[1] 'The chief task of the World Council is to maintain and develop the fellowship between the Christian Churches. But we recognize that the World Council has also the important task of giving concrete witness to the Lordship of Christ and to the implications of His Lordship for national and international life. We were all the time conscious of these two obligations which, things being as they are, often enter into conflict.' *ER* III (April 1951), 3, p. 267.

[2] At a meeting of the Australian Committee for the World Council, Anglican Bishop Ernest H. Burgmann termed John Foster Dulles, then a member of the Commission of the Churches on International Affairs sponsored by the World Council, 'a dangerous man'. The bishop conceded that 'probably Dulles is an honest Christian but we don't want to commit the World Council to anything he does. Nor should we commit this body to anything in the way of American international politics or we will get our fingers burned.' At the time Mr. Dulles was arranging the Japanese Peace Treaty which the Australian Government duly signed. In a special 'message to the nation' the meeting which the Bishop had addressed called for the admission of communist China to the United Nations 'because international justice demands such a step'. Cited in *Christianity and Crisis* XI (March 19, 1951), 4, p. 32. Differences of opinion on the obligations of international justice are obviously not impossible between Christians or even between segments of the World Council constituency. Mr. Dulles, of course, as an American diplomat, never pretended to represent World Council opinion.

however, risks nullifying in practice the ecumenical effort to
remake the Temporal City. When it is argued, as for example at
the Central Committee's Chichester Meeting, that the Church
should not make judgments on economic systems, the policy of
abstraction from political situations has stultifying implications.
For it would logically connote an ethical negativism in the face
of concrete problems of social justice and an attitude of abandonment, under the cloak of the transcendence of religion, an
attitude belying the obligation of social responsibility which the
World Council seeks to inculcate.

The uncertainty as to the nature of the World Council itself
introduces a complication at this point which would seem to
explain, indirectly at least, its hesitation to judge concrete
situations. That the Christian religion is not tied to any given
civilization is demonstrated by both theology and history: it has
survived the passing of established political structures and the
collapse of various systems of social organization; it has been at
home in widely different cultures.[1] But what *is* the relation
between the two realities, 'the Christian religion' and 'the World
Council of Churches', in this connexion?

Is 'the Christian religion' to be thought of primarily as a
message, a body of truth of divine origin, and 'the World Council
of Churches' to be here considered as the sum total of ecumenical
but still human appraisals of social problems in whose formulation
constant care must be exercised to keep the gospel message free
from political interpretations? This explanation of the World
Council's hesitation to deal with concrete social situations
contrasts the content of the gospel message with the defective
human understanding of any social problem and emphasizes the
importance of preserving the purity and integrity of 'the Christian
religion' understood as a body of superior truth. Or is 'the World

---

[1] Because the Christian religion cannot be identified with any political categories or
cultural forms, it does not follow that its institutions are uninfluenced by political changes
nor that the fate of Christians is unaffected by social revolutions. Hunneric, King of the
Vandals, exiled 464 bishops from North Africa. After the Arab invasion which followed,
three bishops could not be found in the eleventh century to consecrate an episcopal
nominee.

Council' to be thought of as a federation of churches, a form of ecclesiastical association, and 'the Christian religion' considered as the mission of the constituent communions, a ministry functioning in time which must not be compromised by identification with any given political or economic order? Such a distinction emphasizes the autonomy of the member churches in order to explain the reluctance of the World Council to make very precise pronouncements on concrete issues. Or is 'the World Council of Churches' an as yet undefined entity, to be equated with 'the Christian religion' itself as signifying the Christian community? Such a conception of its essential nature would certainly urge the World Council to guard its institutional entity[1] free of suspicion of pertaining to any particular political grouping and any definite system of economic organization; it would explain also the imprecision of its pronouncements, the tentativeness of the Third Way in social analysis and prescription. These possibilities recall the discussion in the chapter, 'The Nature and Authority of the World Council of Churches'.

It must not be forgotten, in any event, that while the Christian religion, as a divine revelation, neither derives from nor is tied to any civilization, the Christian, as an individual living in time and space, has obligations determined by his social situation. His faith does not exempt him from his civic duties but should, on the contrary, supply him with motives for their loyal and intelligent fulfilment. These call for the exercise of practical prudence estimating possibilities and proposals in the perspective of the Christian vision of man. A citizen who is a Christian has, for example, no special knowledge from his faith on how the almost universal housing shortage is to be solved, nor has he a claim on religious authorities for a legislative blue-print to remedy the situation. In the opinion of Dr. Patijn, the Christian citizen is entitled to 'pastoral guidance'. In the judgment of Archbishop Temple he needs a coherent social ethic enabling

---

[1] Some of the member churches of the Council, to be sure, do not hold that the Christian Message necessarily implies a definite institution to promulgate it.

him to deduce his present duty.[1] For without some means to make the insights of the Christian religion relevant in concrete circumstances, the separation, so generally deplored, between the spheres of public action and the inner world of the soul, between religion and life, becomes inevitable; Christian pronouncements on the social order tend towards fatuity; and ecclesiastics, in Reinhold Niebuhr's phrase, risk indulging the 'illusion of idealistic children of light [which is] to imagine that we can destroy evil merely by avowing ideals'.[2] Emil Brunner speaks of the 'borderland between technical action and ethics—in economics, in politics, in public life', as the area where 'the great decisions are made'. And he warns that 'if the Christian ethic fails at this point, it fails all along the line'.[3]

The problem is a phase of the ancient and abiding task of determining what belongs to Caesar and what to God, a task frequently escaped by refuge in 'political agnosticism'. Following its meeting in Brussels in October 1954, the Committee on the Christian Responsiblity for European Co-operation issued a statement deploring what it termed the 'Angelic Fallacy' in some Christian thinking about politics and indicting 'an incapacity to discuss and decide in terms of concrete historical alternatives'. It was in the context of the defeat by default of the European Defence Community that the Committee called 'upon the Churches for a thorough re-examination of the Christian's role

---

[1] In his address opening the war-time Malvern Conference, Archbishop Temple attributed the ineffectiveness of Anglicanism in the social sphere in part 'to a lack in the Church of England as a whole of any systematic grasp of the relevant principles. By "systematic grasp" I mean an apprehension of the various principles concerned in their due order and subordination—so that, if in any combination of circumstances it is impossible to give full expression to all, we know which should prevail and which should yield. We know the ultimate moral principle of all human relationships—"thou shalt love thy neighbour as thyself". But we do not know at all clearly how this is to find expression in the relations to one another of corporate groups such as Employers' Federations and Trade Unions, or different nations, nor how it bears on the action of Trustees such as the Directors of a Company or the Government of a country. We lack what one school of Greek moralists called "the middle axioms"—those subordinate maxims which connect the ultimate principles with the complexities of the actual historical situations in which action has to be taken.' *Malvern, 1941*, p. 10.

[2] *The Children of Light and the Children of Darkness*, p. 98.

[3] *The Divine Imperative*, p. 262.

in politics in order that the expression of his political concern shall not be dissipated but shall truly reflect the transforming mission of the fellowship of believers'.[1]

4. At present, as the chapter, 'The Social Philosophy of the World Council of Churches', has disclosed, the Council is not in possession of a coherent social ethic, though the beginnings may possibly be perceived in the inquiry being pursued under the general caption, 'The Responsible Society'. The need of such a body of principles to serve as an instrument of social analysis and a matrix of practical judgment in concrete problems is recognized in some circles of the Ecumenical Community. Thus, the Council's Study Department, preparing the Survey for the Evanston Assembly's Section on 'The Responsible Society' reminded the delegates of the declaration of the Oxford Conference in 1937 that the churches must develop 'a common body of Christian criteria and assumptions on social questions' to be able to meet the challenge confronting them in the modern world. Listed first among the 'Tasks for the Churches' was the need of developing 'a common ethos, common convictions concerning the destiny of man and his relation to society . . . convictions about the structure of political institutions, the function of the state in economic life, the goals of economic life and the Christian criteria for measuring the desirability of social policy at many levels'. These are categories with which an 'ethic of ends' alone can deal. An 'ethic of inspiration', by definition, has no relation to such abstract realities.

There is, however, no agreement within the Ecumenical Community on the necessity of an ethic of ends, much less an acceptance of a common basis for one. Possibly this is connected with a general falling off of interest today in theories about

[1] *European Issues* No. 5, p. 2. The statement further asserts: 'The Church is a pilgrim people, a people with a history and to whom history is meaningful. There is a certain sense in which the Church's obligation transcends historical demands and there may be moments in which the transcendent reference must take priority. But on the daily political level it is not the obligation of the Church to proclaim abstract values, but to help her people in obedience to God's will and in response to God's grace "to change what should be changed, to bear with what cannot be changed and to have the wisdom to know the difference".'

society noted by Professor Alfred Cobban.[1] The more likely explanation is the fear in many quarters of the World Council membership that such an approach supposes a static code of behaviour alien to the spirit of biblical charity, and, springing from this fear, a preference for the prophetic utterances. Being a personal perception of the proper course of moral action, such an approach can offer no counsel on general topics; it is perforce silent when questioned, for example, about the structure of political institutions. The proponents of an 'ethic of inspiration' would undoubtedly remonstrate that such questions are not 'interesting' and have no reference to Christian categories of thinking.[2]

It may well be a concession to such an outlook that the Survey speaks of the need of a 'common ethos' rather than a common ethic, the latter connoting in some ecumenical circles a code of human construction alien to the gospel. It is significant, moreover, that the phrases, 'civic duty' and 'the citizen', are not found in World Council literature on social questions, reflecting, perhaps, a fear that such concepts concede an autonomy to the natural order and imply a separation between the Lordship of Christ and the claims of the Temporal City. To raise such a question leads immediately into the field of strict theology which offers, in its different ecclesiastical traditions, various verdicts on the worth of the world and the condition of humanity after the blight of Original Sin. These theological preconceptions underlie discussions in the World Council constituency on the social order and international affairs; they are involved in such practical points as whether human reason is a dependable instrument of social

---

[1] 'The Decline of Political Theory', *Political Science Quarterly*, 68 (September 1953), pp. 221-37. Ominously, Professor Cobban finds this development 'a reflection of the feeling that ethical values have no place in the field of social dynamics and power politics'.

[2] An example of prophetic utterance is Karl Barth's judgment, 'speaking as a theologian', at the time of the Munich crisis that in the event of war Czech soldiers would be fighting for the Church of Jesus Christ. Cf. 'Brief an Hromadka in Prag', *Eine Schweizerstimme* (Zürich: Evangelischer Verlag, 1945), p. 58 as cited in Gill, *op. cit.*, p. 105. The warrant for such a verdict is found in a personal understanding of the meaning of God's Word in September 1938 and offers no basis for deducing the duty of the Czech Army in February 1948.

analysis, one capable of devising a more just Temporal City, whether non-Christians have political rights (and, if so, on what basis), whether co-operation for social objectives between men of different faiths is possible (and, if so, on what grounds).

The problem of ends, if a pun is permissible, comes first and would seem to be inescapable. There is as yet in the World Council of Churches no common conviction on ends; there has not been sufficient time (nor, perhaps, sufficient concentration) to establish a common tradition. Emil Brunner has pointed out that the absence of a theory of justice is stultifying.[1] And the Survey prepared for the Evanston Assembly's Section on International Affairs posed as one of the 'Underlying Questions for the Churches' the issue: 'Is there sufficient agreement on the principles of Christian action [in the international field] for any agency to act confidently in the name of the ecumenical fellowship?' The necessity of an 'ethic of ends', of a theory of justice, will be evident, for example, in considering possible modifications of the wage system. Are salaries to be measured by economic contribution, or is social need a factor to be included in a moral appraisal and provision made, consequently, for some form of family allowances? What, in fact, are the criteria to be invoked in calculating a just wage, a just price, a fair fiscal policy?

The first step in establishing the content of a common ethos would seem to be a routine problem of semantics, of compiling a common vocabulary for ecumenical discourse. The Faith and Order Commission has indicated that definitions are a primary

---

[1] 'Protestant Christianity has had none [a theory of justice] for some three hundred years past. That may sound a bold statement; it can, unfortunately, be proved. It is doubtless one of the main reasons why the Protestant church is so unsure of itself in questions of the social order, economics, law, politics and international law, and why its statements on these subjects are so haphazard and improvised that they fail to carry conviction.' *Justice and the Social Order*, p. 7. The lack of a common, coherent theory of justice which Brunner set himself to remedy was illustrated during a discussion of the World Council's Study Commission III, at a meeting at Bossey, June 24, 1947, preparing for the Amsterdam Section on economic, politics and cultural problems. During an inconclusive argument on the functions of the State, a member, Jacques Ellul, insisted that before the tasks of the State could be fixed, the nature of justice and the relation of the State to law must be settled.

necessity for the progress of its work. As a common acceptation of the word 'Church', for example, has its obvious relevance for discussions of theological problems, so a common understanding of the word 'State' would seem essential for ecumenical discussions on social questions. The request voiced by a delegate during a Sectional meeting at Evanston should not go indefinitely unanswered: he wanted the terms 'justice', 'democracy' and 'freedom' defined.

5. There is in the Protestant tradition of thought a deep-rooted suspicion of earthly power as contrary to the spirit of the gospel and a reluctant acceptance of force as a measure necessary to restrain the effects of sin. The collaboration of human wills towards a common goal calls for a unity of direction and thus implies authority (whatever its source) with the power of sanctions (else law is merely good advice); this, however, is an emphasis not altogether congenial to the genius of Protestantism which prizes personal independence and favours private responsibility. Such an outlook tends to expect that the solution of economic problems will follow if the moral climate of society is changed by the spiritual regeneration of individuals;[1] it tends to neglect the problem of the reform of structures, not least those of the State, as involved in achieving a greater measure of economic equity; it tends to subordinate the study of institutions. Both emphases are, to be sure, essential.[2] Unless selfishness in all its socially destructive forms—greed, callousness, exploitation of others, luxury, *incivisme*—is restrained by personal inner control, the most admirably arranged technical structures will prove ineffective. On the other hand, much of the imprecision of World Council pronouncements, it would appear, is a result of

---

[1] Moral Re-Armament is an example.

[2] Wilhelm Röpke's explanation of his social analysis is apposite here: 'Concentration on the moral and spiritual aspect with neglect of the institutional would be dangerously one-sided and in Theology would be condemned as supernaturalism or spiritualism; it would create the impression that we were mere dreamers being out of touch with the realities of life. The moral and the institutional are not subsidiary one to the other but stand in a relationship of mutual reciprocity like the Evangelists' seed and soil which must be familiar to every Christian. One cannot be separated from the other, the institutional is just as important as the moral and spiritual; fundamentally these can be conceived only as a unity.' *Civitas Humana*, p. xxii.

a failure to examine concrete political and economic institutions at close hand.

6. Clarification of the implications of the Third Way is hampered by the ecumenical methodology pursued by the World Council and by the meagreness of the resources at its command. From the description of its activity offered earlier, it will be recalled that the Council's Study Department conducts no independent research, maintains no organizational point of view on social problems, offers no solutions of its own. Even the topics it examines are designated by the Central Committee where official representatives of the member churches fix the policy and programme of the Council between Assemblies. The function of the Study Department, then, is exclusively one of service, encouraging the collaboration of interested groups in the churches, arranging ecumenical encounters on social questions, circulating material indicating opinion current in the World Council constituency.

In its endeavour to stimulate ecumenical interest in the social field and to formulate positions representative of the points of view of its entire constituency, the Study Department must rely (apart from its permanent, understaffed Secretariat) on volunteer collaborators. There is always the danger that collaborators will show more enthusiasm than competence.[1] Since the World Council is a fellowship of churches, these collaborators will be in large part ecclesiastics whose normal professional training will not have included much attention to economics, political

---

[1] The desire to hear the voices of the 'Younger Churches' is understandable, even if that is no guarantee of the wisdom, or even moderation of view, of the representatives from former mission lands. Thus, an Indian expressed his dissatisfaction with the summary of the Amsterdam studies for Section III as found in the introduction to the background volume because it did not opt for the Marxist solution. His political sagacity may be judged from his belief that 'the Communist Parties of Europe are standing for liberalism in Asiatic politics and as bearers of liberalism in world politics today. Socialism is all of the right, including Reinhold Niebuhr's Fellowship of Christian Socialists.' *Archives.* His engaging, if chauvinistic, assurance that, given fifty years, India will solve all the social problems under debate and his optimism, evidenced in the conviction that Asiatic Christians should co-operate with 'the bulwark of liberal ideas and liberal values, the revolutionary Communist Parties', make clearer the triumph of the Communist-directed coalition in Travancore-Cochin, India's most modern, most literate and most Christian State, in March 1954.

science, sociology and even history.[1] There is an awareness, expressed occasionally at ecumenical meetings, of the need of greater lay participation in the elaboration of Study Department inquiries, a recognition that realistic applications of the demands of justice in the concrete circumstances of modern social organization call for the co-operation of theologian, jurist and economist. One of the essential functions of the Ecumenical Institute at Bossey is to serve as a centre for such encounters. Such meetings are undoubtedly fruitful in forming friendships and introducing the participants to the problems and points of view of different intellectual disciplines.

Patience would seem to be the principal virtue demanded of the World Council Study Department as it prepares, for delegates to ecumenical meetings, background material which is often unexploited[2] and arranges the agenda for discussions which all too frequently is ignored because the speakers are arguing from different premises. Yet, in the absence of a common tradition, it is from the collaboration of dedicated volunteers and by means of ecumenical exchange over a period of years that the World Council must build the body of common convictions that will serve as its social philosophy, the rationale of its counsel for the bettering of the Temporal City.

In the course of its development, the World Council has had many questions to ask itself, the most primary and preoccupying being that of its own ecclesiastical significance. In the course of its growth (and in the process of organizing the common convictions underlying its criticism of the economic order) it will undoubtedly think through the rationale of its concern for social questions, an interest which seems sometimes confused with the

[1] An economist present once pointed out to World Council Study Committee members deploring the herding characteristic of modern cities that the phenomenon was not unconnected with the astonishing growth of the world's population in modern times and that this was in part due to the extension of life expectancy, a result of modern medicine and the reduction of famines by the division of labour. Technics, moreover, it was indicated, are necessary to feed the teeming population of the world today. *Archives*.

[2] After the Lund Meeting of Faith and Order, an observer suggested that delegates should be made to pass an examination on the background volumes, supplied as discussion aids, to guarantee that they would be read. Thirteen years had been devoted to preparing the material.

goal of evangelism.[1] An earnest concern that the gospel win a hearing among the economically underprivileged, a generous interest in the aspirations of the working man are understandable and surely praiseworthy on the part of religious leaders. Such apostolic interest sometimes seems, however, to identify the ambiguous political objectives, frequently proposed to the European 'proletariat', with the ethical good and to forget that the workers are subject to the same human moral frailties as their employers. Moreover, a surer notion of the audience envisaged for its appraisals of international affairs and economic conditions would aid the editorial point of view of ecumenical pronouncements.[2] Reports of World Council Assemblies are, to be sure, 'received and commended to the churches for their serious consideration and appropriate action', but manifestly it is hoped that the analyses and suggestions will be studied outside the member churches.

[1] During a meeting of the Study Department Commission at Cambridge in August 1946, Emil Brunner was led to remark: 'Our aim is not so much to convert the present world as to make Christianity relevant to it. That is only a first step. What interests people who are outside, what makes it relevant to them, is the message which the Church has for the present social problems in the widest sense of the word and, if we put that in the front, we shall have a chance to attract their attention, so that they say, after all the Church has a word for us. The difficulty is that in the Church on the Continent these two tasks are always mixed together. People want to speak of the essential message of Christ for reconciliation, and at the same time about the social message, but the two cannot be brought together in that way and our task seems to me to be to concentrate on our original purpose, which is the purpose of Life and Work and say what is the message of the church with regard to these problems of social life and not confuse them with the second part of the gospel.' *Minutes* (mimeographed) (Geneva: World Council, 1946), p. 9. Brunner's advice seems to have been ignored. The World Council official directing the inquiry on the Responsible Society writes: 'The concern of the Christian is not limited to that which is individual or that which is social but is for the whole of a man's life as included in the plan of God. . . . It is that evangelistic purpose, in its most realistic and inclusive sense, that is the motivation of the Christian thinking about society which underlies [the inquiry]. By our action in society we strive to ensure that the ground in which the seed of God's Word is planted will bring forth the largest harvest.' Paul Abrecht, 'Christian Action in Society', *ER* II (Winter 1950), 2, p. 151.

[2] Discussing the theme of the Evanston Assembly, Reinhold Niebuhr raised the question 'about the primary end and purpose of such a meeting', asking: 'Is it to "establish the brethren" and create the broadest and most satisfactory biblical basis for our ecumenical consensus? Or is the purpose of an ecumenical meeting to bear witness to our faith in the world? That can hardly be our primary purpose but no one can deny that what is said at the Assembly will be overheard in the world and will be meant to be overheard.' *ER*, v (July 1953), 4, p. 363.

3. Future Concerns

The World Council has no action programme of its own apart from the co-operative work for refugees attached to its Secretariat. The question of the audience envisaged for its pronouncements raises the more ultimate topic of its expectation of any possible implementing of its recommendations, of the grounds and possibility of co-operation, for example, with non-Christian organizations and groups. This last point repeats, but in different form, the question of the basis of the World Council's policy about temporal affairs. Is the Commission of the Churches on International Affairs, to be precise, to co-operate with United Nations agencies and specifically, is it to work for legal protection of human rights because the imperatives of the Christian religion seek the universal good of all men, or is its interest to be evoked by the particular organizational needs of its constituents?

Although it has no action programme of its own, an area which the World Council cannot permanently neglect is the field of education. The omission of the subject from the list of inquiries to date is somewhat surprising since the problems of education occupied the attention of an entire Section at the ecumenical assemblies at Stockholm and Oxford. Moreover, in his book on the State, the former Director of the Council's Study Department, Nils Ehrenström, recognized that it is on the cultural level that the lines between religion and the encroachments of the omnicompetent State are first drawn, that education is an especially sensitive area in the unending struggle for the protection of human freedom.[1] Subsequent history has furnished ample warrant for his fears. For the structure of a nation's educational system is an infallible barometer of the respect society is prepared to accord parental rights, and the CCIA's effort to have the principle written into the Declaration and Convention on Human Rights indicates that the Ecumenical Community is aware of this

---

[1] 'May it not be that the great conflict between the Church and the modern or neo-pagan State will be fought out in this sphere of the secondary functions of the State and within the sphere of education in particular?' *Christian Faith and the Modern State*, p. 228.

fact. Moreover, the availability of educational opportunities, even on the university level, reveals the acceptance of the claims of social justice in a society; the war-time campaign of the churches in England for an extension of these opportunities manifested an awareness of that fact.

In addition to serving as a test of cultural freedom and a symbol of social justice in the political order, the field of education has other angles of interest for the World Council. Obviously, secular disciplines must be drawn upon if its social analyses and prescriptions are to have any precision, not to mention accuracy. To elaborate the practical applications of justice in modern society, the theologian must collaborate with experts in apposite fields. That partnership has not been achieved,[1] probably because of the temper of contemporary education but, in any case, to the detriment of the World Council's hope to work out an intellectually acceptable and viable Third Way in social questions and international relations. More important still is the effect of education on the capacity of the modern mind to understand, not merely the language, but the point of view of World Council pronouncements.[2]

The situation is not remedied by establishing chairs of Social Ethics in the Faculties of Theology (though their absence in European universities does not facilitate the growth of common convictions to aid in furnishing the bases of the World Council's

[1] Emil Brunner describes the present situation thus: 'Firstly, theologians and other Christian teachers rest content with amateurish improvisations which have of late taken as their watchword: "The Church as Sentinel"; secondly, jurists, sociologists and economists entrench themselves behind the neutrality of a science which they allege to be free of philosophic bias.' *Justice and the Social Order*, p. 119.

[2] A Professor of Teachers' College, Columbia University, addressed himself to this problem which touches closely the work of the World Council. In the Rauschenbusch Lectures of 1940, Dr. F. Ernest Johnson argued: 'We are concerned throughout this whole discussion with the development of an adequate social ethic. My contention has been that in our tireless formulation of social creeds and framing of social resolutions we have overlooked the basic problem—the secularization of the modern mind. Before any ethical reconstruction can take place, there must be a widespread amenability to spiritual principles that have relevance to the common life. Otherwise religion inevitably becomes escapist. . . . Education is typically carried out without specific and continuous reference to the central spiritual values of our culture and without the reverent cultivation of those values which it is the function of religion to maintain.' *The Social Gospel Re-examined*, p. 169.

social criticism). There is need, to be sure, of persistent and systematized efforts to think out the implications for modern industrial society of the Christian message. The World Council's Study Department must be well aware of Professor R. H. Tawney's indictment, summarizing his impressive historical study: 'The social teaching of the Church had ceased to count, because the Church itself had ceased to think.'[1] The difficulties, however, are not confined to membership of the churches.

The task would appear to call for a realistic examination of the values which contemporary education assumes or avows, an appraisal of how these shape the popular mind and a prolonged consideration of the methods whereby the values, implicit in the Christian conception of man, values on which European civilization is built, can be reintroduced into the educational processes, whether formally through the official school systems, or by influencing the modern mass media of communication, the Press, the radio, opinion-forming literature, or in devising study circles on a large scale. For if public opinion rests ignorant of (or worse, instinctively prejudiced against) the premises of the World Council's social criticism, then the pessimistic prognosis of Ernst Troeltsch, expressed in 1911 on the effectiveness of Christian social action in the modern world, cannot be gainsaid.[2]

4. Summary of Achievements

But whatever its future influence (and he who would read the future today is a hardy spirit), the organized Ecumenical Movement has, by its pronouncements and its common action, made a

---

[1] *Religion and the Rise of Capitalism*, p. 185. 'In an age of impersonal finance, world-markets and a capitalist organization of industry, its [the Church's] traditional social doctrines had no specific to offer, and were merely repeated, when, in order to be effective, they should have been thought out again from the beginning and formulated in new and living terms.' *Ibid.*, p. 184.

[2] *Op. cit.*, II, p. 1012. The reasons Troeltsch adduced are two: 'Because the power of thought to overcome brutal reality is always an obscure and difficult question' and 'because the main historic forms of the Christian doctrine of society and of social development are today, for various reasons, impotent in face of the tasks by which they are confronted'.

distinct contribution to contemporary social thought whose importance should not be neglected. The World Council of Churches, it must never be forgotten, speaks for a constituency of different continents, races and nationalities. It has proclaimed truths whose significance for a human world of justice and peace cannot be measured.

1. It has indefatigably asserted the essential dignity of man, the object of a divine creating and redeeming love. On this dignity it grounds its demand for human rights and social justice for every person. For when any person is mistreated or disadvantaged, an incident of supreme importance has occurred, whether or not legal systems or political parties or a busy public condones the outrage. God has been mocked, and something sacred violated.

2. It has recalled a fundamental truth, that man cannot live for himself alone. In the Christian perspective he is his brother's keeper with responsibilities arising from God's love for all men. He may not wash his hands of the world, therefore, declaring that injustice is of no concern to him. This obligation of service is inescapable: it tests his love of God and by its fulfilment the quality of his life will ultimately be measured.

3. It has indicated that civic responsibilities are an intimate part of that obligation of service, responsibilities which are not limited to the mechanisms of national political systems but include interest in international organizations in view of the world community to be constructed.

4. It has, by its existence and activities, reminded national political authorities and international agencies of the motivation and the existence of programmes of social assistance of crucial importance which they are inclined to forget. The motivation is that of charity and the programmes are those in the fields of health, of education and of personal care, conducted by spiritually-motivated volunteers, under religious auspices, in mission territories as well as in the countries once called Christendom. Altruism is a social fact which international organizations tend to ignore until confronted with unrewarding chores such as

finding homes for refugees. Without charity—which, on the evidence of history, is inspired only by the Christian religion—the contours of the world of the future will be insupportably harsh.

5. It has proclaimed the spiritual solidarity of all mankind, thus challenging the pretensions of absolute national sovereignty, the myths of inevitable class conflict and the fears of irreconcilable regional rivalries. There are in these truths of the Christian religion political implications of incalculable consequence. Systems of legally enforced racial segregation, distracting ideologies, the division of the world into 'the haves' and 'the have-nots' stand under the condemnation of this principle.

6. It has taught the equality of all men in a common destiny and a divinely certified value. Such an announcement has nothing in common with any doctrine that would annul individual, native differences of talent, penalize the fruits of personal industry and sanctify the human instinct of envy in a destructive levelling of society to satisfy the politically inculcated aspirations of 'the common man'. It voices, rather, the irreducible claims of a common humanity to its common goods and bespeaks the rights of the individual to an equality of opportunity in providing himself and his family with the necessities for a truly human existence. It rejects, therefore, any claim to fix trade policies and immigration quotas without reference to the needs of other nations. It is unimpressed by the sacredness of any particular standard of living and its claim for protection in the face of hunger elsewhere in the world. Exclusive rights to the economic exploitation of territories by reason of colonial conquest strike it as a pettifogging justification of greed. Advances in technical knowledge that foster health and improve food production, it holds to be the heritage of all men. Opportunities of educational advancement, it insists, must not be determined by social status. And in potentially its most effective action the World Council's Second Assembly condemned any form of segregation and called on its member churches to work for its abolition everywhere.

7. It has declared that economic processes and international affairs are neither beyond human control nor are they self-regulatory. They are subject to norms outside their own sphere of operations, standards which are determined by their ultimate function which is to serve man in fulfilling his destiny. National prestige and private acquisitiveness stand under the judgment of these standards. For the activities of the market-place, the Parliaments and the councils of nations are answerable to an Ultimate Justice not of human contriving nor human perverting. To bring the mechanisms of man's dealings with his fellows into a clearer recognition of their subservience to God's Will and to frame more concretely the conditions for their equitable operation is a continuing task of the World Council in its search for a Third Way.

8. It has insisted that the world, despite the perplexities it presents, is not absurd, that human work, though humdrum and unrewarding, is not meaningless, that the life of the meanest individual, especially when forgotten or victimized, has significance. In announcing the reality of God and Christ's Lordship of His world, it speaks to a baffled generation a word of hope.

APPENDIX

The 'Catholic' and 'Protestant' Emphases

THE present work, as the Foreword declared, is not a theological study. In analysing the two principal attitudes and, indeed, approaches to the problem of a social philosophy current in the World Council constituency, reference was made to a distinction invoked at the First Assembly to represent the 'deepest differences' in the Ecumenical Community.[1] The difference 'to which, by many paths, we are constantly brought back', was attributed to two contrasting conceptions, each representing 'a whole corporate tradition of the understanding of Christian faith and life'. The two conceptions were acknowledged to be 'inconsistent with each other'.[2] The names used to denominate the twin tendencies, the contrasting emphases, the two conceptions, were 'Catholic', and 'Protestant'. The Amsterdam Report observed that the two categories were not co-extensive with confessional allegiances or ecclesiastical groupings: 'Clearly "Catholic" is not used here to mean Roman Catholic, and "Protestant" in most of Europe is better rendered by "Evangelical".' It added also that each category, while standing for distinct corporate traditions, 'contains within it a wide variety of emphasis and many "schools of thought"'.[3]

To categorize the two contrasting points of view in the field of social philosophy, each of them also standing for a whole corporate tradition, this study chose the captions: an 'ethic of ends' and an 'ethic of inspiration'. The captions, while not in general use, were employed by the editor of the Official Reports of the 1937 Oxford Conference of the Universal Christian Council on Life and Work, a predecessor of the World Council of Churches. It was feared that the use of the captions employed by the First Assembly to denominate the two

[1] Cf. supra, p. 93.
[2] Amsterdam, p. 52.
[3] The First Assembly averred, further, that the member churches of the World Council, despite the fundamental division between them, are able 'to speak in the common language of the divine revelation witnessed to in the Scriptures, about the points at which we find we meet'. They proclaimed that they intend 'to stay together'.

traditions would be distracting and might even appear tendentious. Besides, as the Amsterdam Report noted, within each conception there are differences of emphasis and separate schools of thought. Thus, Karl Barth and Emil Brunner, diverse though they be in their approach to the problems of social philosophy (and certainly in their political outlooks), are both members of the Swiss Protestant Church Federation.

There are, however, reasons beyond political preferences and individual temperaments accounting for the contrasting emphases in the field of ethics of the two chief corporate traditions of the understanding of Christian life and faith, as described by the First Assembly of the World Council of Churches. The roots of these differences between, to be precise, those opting for an 'ethic of ends' and those insisting on an 'ethic of inspiration' are found in opposing judgments on the human predicament, man's nature and capacities and, particularly, his relation to his Maker. They derive, then, from theology. The late Irving Babbitt noted some years ago that differences of opinion in economics (*translate:* social policy) were a manifestation of divergent ideas in ethics which were ultimately a reflection of contrasting conceptions in theology.

Some explanation, in summary and global fashion, may be expected of the twin theological traditions, 'Catholic' and 'Protestant', from which the two diverse approaches to social philosophy, the 'ethic of ends' and the 'ethic of inspiration', derive. Obviously, there is no intention of offering a supplement or commentary, or of suggesting a corrective, to the prodigious research of Ernst Troeltsch but rather of clarifying, perhaps, the doctrinal grounds on which some of the views expressed in World Council meetings are based.

It is of capital importance, at the outset, to recall that Christianity is not essentially a theology nor a moral system, much less a programme for the proper ordering of civilization. It is a gospel—an announcement—making definite affirmations about the nature and destiny of man, rather than a group of principles providing moral guidance for happy living and successful social relationships. As an interpretation of the human situation the complexus of the affirmations made by the Christian religion can, however, be called a philosophy; and, though this study is not a theological excursus, it may be useful to present a summary of that philosophy. The entire membership of the World Council would, I believe, accept without objection (beyond reservations on its completeness) the phrasing of V. A. Demant, a member of the Drafting Committee of Amsterdam's Section on Social Questions:

> This Christian philosophy contains three axioms. The first is that in the actual world things are not true to their essential nature. There has been a Fall. The second is that 'the good' of anything is a recovery of its true nature and that this recovery is made, not by any self-improvement, but by the act of God. There follows the third principle, that the true nature of any created thing is only sustained when it is held to its true end by supernatural direction and power. The good life is therefore in the Christian Faith something to be recovered rather than created by man. . . . Man's true nature is bought back with a price.[1]

The price was the death of Jesus Christ, God and Man.

The 'Catholic' tradition, interpreting these three assertions, maintains that mankind, impaired as a consequence of its primordial rebellion against its Maker, has been restored by the sacrificial obedience of its representative, Jesus Christ. This restoration is effected in the individual by his integration into the Christian Community, the Church, which communicates to him through special rites entrusted to it spiritual capacities (called grace) beyond all deserving. Grace does not annul nor supplant human nature but heals and perfects it, empowering the Christian to merit by his daily life the reward of eternity with his Creator, which he already possesses in germ. An adequate understanding of life's meaning comes only from hearing and accepting (by an adherence of the intellect) God's message to man preserved by the Community, the Church, to whom its proclamation and interpretation have been entrusted. Likewise, a faithful fulfilment of God's Will is possible only by reason of His assistance mediated through this Community; for human nature remains in precarious disequilibrium with pride and passion asserting themselves. By his reason, however, man may arrive at a knowledge of the basic truths of the human condition including the fact of the existence of God and the general rules of right and wrong. These norms are discoverable in the very structure of the universe, a hierarchy of created entities whose operations reveal their nature and whose nature reveals their ends, the whole a complex but co-ordinated order revealing the

---

[1] *Theology of Society*, p. 11. Admittedly, there is a 'Catholic' emphasis in this summary since Canon Demant is an Anglican. A certain disproportion is inevitable. If a single satisfactory comprehensive—and significant—statement, balancing both emphases justly, could be written, there would not be differing whole corporate traditions of the understanding of Christian faith and life—nor any World Council of Churches for that matter.

mind of God. The knowledge of this divine plan by human reason indicates duties, though supplying no power to fulfil them. The principles of moral conduct, deduced from a contemplation of the created scheme of things, known as the Natural Law, lends itself to more detailed deductions by further reasoning and to applications in concrete human situations. These more ultimate conclusions, specified generally in legal enactments, will be often fallible and fragmentary and frequently ambiguous, making severe demands upon the intellectual virtue of practical prudence.

The 'Catholic' tradition asserts, moreover, that the plan of God in creating man and humanity's admittedly imperfect comprehension of the plan are not in conflict with the effects of God's subsequent personal entrance on the human scene nor His direct communication of His will to men. The imperious thrust of man's nature to associate with his fellows has not been reversed by sin nor revoked by the forgiveness of sin. Thus, the family and society continue to answer the needs of man-as-man. Their purposes are permanent—the fulfilment of the individual's incompleteness—however ennobled by Christ's action and message. And since their essential purposes are stable, the general laws of their proper functioning can be established. To assure the steady co-operation of individual wills for the common good of the community, political authority is needed. The State, therefore, is demanded by essential human nature, and its purposes, the achieving of peace and the promotion of the temporal welfare, are dictated by human reason. In consequence, the wisdom of the philosophers, while of a subordinate level of truth, is not to be condemned: their discoveries of the laws of society's nature and functioning have not been cancelled. In some matters Alexandria *has* need of Athens.

The 'Catholic' emphasis, then, envisages articulated and integrated orders of reality, established in a hierarchy of values and purposes, fixed by God's knowledge of His infinite imitability and crowned by His gift to mankind of a new destiny beyond the deserts of human nature, a destiny disclosed in His messages and made possible by the work of His Son, one with man in all save sin, a destiny, finally, to be achieved by the individual in his toilsome fulfilment of God's will with the co-operation of His grace. Attaining his destiny for the Christian inescapably involves his conduct in the common life of communal activities and family responsibilities.

It will be evident that the 'Catholic' emphasis first locates the individual in the community. It is the community—mankind—that Christ rescued from its rebellion and re-established in God's favour. It is in the spiritual community—the Church—that the individual hears God's message; in the same community that he makes contact with God's grace. It is the secular community of his fellows—society—that is the scene where (in an old English phrase) he 'makes his soul', principally by his service to others. That human community—the Temporal City—is recognized as part of God's plan, with human reason reporting the general lines of the individual's proper place in that City. Specifically, the just laws of the community, whatever its political form, speak with the authority of God who fashioned man as an innately social being and are supported with sanctions beyond this world. The spiritual freedom of salvation does not excuse one from obedience to the just laws of the human community nor the obligation of engaging oneself in its legitimate tasks. Universal human sinlessness would not have obviated the need of a political order; nor did the primordial sin of mankind alone make legal direction an inevitable function of the political community. For the State has positive purposes (beyond the mere repression of anarchy), and the co-ordination of individual human wills, whatever their spiritual state, supposes the activity of political authority.

The 'Catholic' emphasis finds a basic order underlying natural social structures whose rules are discoverable by reason supplemented and clarified but never contradicted by God's direct message to mankind. Such a view strives to elaborate a coherent theory of social relations founded on a clear conception of human nature, a scaffolding of principles yielding judgments, sometimes ambiguous and fallible to be sure, on social questions.

The 'Protestant' emphasis finds this whole scheme a pretentious construction of human vanity, useless for the personal decisions of moral life and, in any case, too static to explain the religious experiences described in Reformation theology. It presents too benign a view of human nature, minimizes the demonic power of sin in the world and disregards the total transcendence of God.[1]

For the corporate tradition of the understanding of Christian life and faith termed 'Protestant' at Amsterdam states the religious problem

[1] Thus, at an early preparatory meeting for Amsterdam, Dr. Reinhold Niebuhr objected to the first formulation of the theme, 'The Order of God and the Present Disorder of Man', remarking: 'Order is too close to law to contain love, mercy, redemption as against the sin of man.' World Council Study Department Document: 20E/46, p. 5.

differently. Agreeing with the three assertions in Canon Demant's summary, the interpretation of the 'Protestant' emphasis centres its focus on the individual, his essential sinfulness and his solitary experience of his Saviour's forgiving embrace encountered through His saving Word in the Bible.[1] The sinfulness remains because essential rehabilitation is impossible; the redemption has happened because Christ's triumph is attributed to the individual; the restoration occurs because the trusting, sinful child has met his loving, heavenly Father.

In this theological conception the individual is irreparably corrupted in his essential nature by mankind's primordial rebellion against God, although restored to favour by the miracle of divine forgiveness. The paradox consists in the fact that the Christian is pardoned while continuing to be inextricably involved in sin. Within differing explanations of the modalities of that essential paradox, the leaders of the Reformation agreed that the merits of Christ's sacrificial death were substituted for the sin of humanity and are imputed to the individual when his will, in an act of trust, yields itself to God's mercy. Direct access to God is available to all who hear God's message as transcribed in the Bible and, relying on His faithfulness, answer the appeal by a proper attitude of confident acceptance of divinely proffered pardon. Despair, weakness, rebellion and impurity are not barriers to God's mercy; indeed, they may well serve to sharpen the consciousness of sin and heighten the sense of God's triumphant mercy.

The resolution of the problem proposed by the question, 'How shall I obtain a gracious God?' is presented as a dialogue carried on in the secret recesses of each human heart between a loving God and his trusting, sinful child. Human mediation is not merely superfluous, it is impossible in such an encounter. The reverent reading of the Bible provides the context of this saving confrontation of God's mercy and the individual's soul. The testimony of the Spirit, inwardly experienced, is the ineffable assurance of forgiveness as it is of the rightness of decisions of moral action taken under the guidance of

---

[1] The spokesman of the Swiss Delegation at the Stockholm Conference, Professor Hadorn, phrased this focus thus: 'For Protestantism, unlike the Catholicism of the Roman Church, does not proceed from the community to the individual, but from the individual to the community. In other words, the Protestant Church stands or falls according as the question, which so profoundly engrossed the mind of Luther, "How shall I obtain a gracious God?" becomes the foundation of a healthy life of Christian fellowship and of vigorous witness and propaganda in the world. . . . The salvation of the individual man through the Gospel of Jesus Christ by means of the grace of God grasped by faith (*sola fide*) is and remains the primary thing.' *Stockholm*, p. 439.

God's personal message disclosed to the Christian prayerfully consulting the Word.

There is, to be sure, a certain community of the saved—whose numbers are known only to God—a brotherhood of believers who have experienced God's pardon and trust in His promises. No one in the community has special spiritual powers; each individual makes contact with God in the privacy of his separate soul. Nor can the community as a social entity help him to obtain a gracious God beyond, of course, making available to him the printed record of God's Word and encouraging him to turn from sin and confide himself to God's loving mercy. Nothing stands between the individual and his pardoning Father Who has no authorized human agents empowered to perform certain rites as instruments of salvation, signs of grace. God has no need of men. The Christian Community will take visible, institutional form as a Church when a group of believers, following Christ's injunction, gather together to hear the pure preaching of God's Word, to strengthen one another in the faith and to be reminded, in the commemorative ceremony of the Lord's Supper, of Christ's redeeming death. 'The Church,' remarked Luther, 'is the company of people who believe in Christ', and 'belief', according to the Reformer, did not mean an intellectual acceptance 'that what is said of God is true' which he considered 'rather a form of knowledge than a faith'; it meant, instead, 'that I put my trust in Him, give myself up to thinking that I can have dealings with Him and believe without any doubt that He will be and do to me according to the things said of Him. Such faith, which throws itself upon God, whether in life or in death, alone makes a Christian man.'[1] Historical developments, political rivalries, the variety of national characteristics as well as personal vanity and group stubbornness, this tradition believes, account for the division of this Church into separate churches, a lamentable and sinful situation in manifest defiance of Christ's expressed will for unity.

In an effort to magnify the majesty of God and to high-light the malice of sin the Reformation fixed as irreducible antinomies Creator and creature, reason and faith, grace and good works. These elements, existing always in tension in the Christian *Weltanschauung*, had been elaborated in a synthesis of co-ordinating factors in the relations of

[1] Calvin, too, was forthright and exigent: 'Voici donc quel sacrifice il nous faut aujourd'hui offrir à Dieu, c'est que tout ce qui est de notre nature soit éteint et aboli et puis notre raison, car c'est le pire qui soit en nous.' *Oeuvres complètes* (Braunschweig edition), Vol. 23, p. 779; as quoted by Chenevière, *La Pensée Politique de Calvin*, p. 79.

God with His creation. Seeking a return to the simplicities of primitive Christianity, the Reformation suppressed as alien elements the categories of supernature, reason and good works in the account of God's dealing with men.[1] Human nature, essentially corrupted by sin, is incapable in this life of supporting the substantial ennoblement which St. Augustine had called a sharing of divinity; reason is an illusory instrument in the search for God's Will; good works a snare for human pride. The Natural Law, now identified with the Decalogue, is no longer a reflection in the structure of the universe of the infinitely imitable essence of its Creator but an arbitrary enactment of the divine Will having a provisional value to be obeyed in the spirit of faith. For, although annulled by the redemptive work of Christ, the Law yet remains in the new dispensation where all is grace and the saved are free of the bonds of legal systems and the burdens of compulsion. Its Two Tables divide the sphere of action of the faithful Christian, the Commandments concerned with specifically religious matters reminding him of his Saviour's forgiveness, those concerned with his relations with his neighbour inviting him to an outpouring of service in a spirit of love. A dualism is thus introduced by the division of the Two Tables but all is subsumed under the single, subjective religious attitude of faith. The Christian is to submit to the demands of the natural order in so far as these do not require him to deny the exigencies of the pure doctrine of the Gospel. Social institutions, the family, commerce, government, are provisionally permitted by God for the space 'between the times'; they serve the needs of material well-being and repress the ravages of sin. For there is no real contact between God and the natural order; Nature has been so corrupted by the Fall that not merely human nature but Nature in general only reveals God in exceptional circumstances.

The result is what Troeltsch terms an 'ethic of disposition' and a 'spiritual ethic', which is more a quality of living than a code of

---

[1] A celebrated sociologist of religion has described the verdict of the Reformers thus: 'Man does not ascend from the Primitive State to a supernatural perfection which has already been prepared by Nature; the universe and the earth do not evolve from Nature into the realm of Grace; Society is not linked with a natural basis in order that there may be a natural continuity between it and the supernatural fellowship of Grace. In the Protestant theory everything is completed in a moment and the Aristotelian doctrine of evolution disappears, as well as the Neo-platonic theory of emanations. The Fall does not mean a relapse into Nature, and Redemption is not the ascent from Nature to Grace; rather the idea is that the Fall means the removal of Nature, and Redemption is its restoration.' Troeltsch, *op. cit.*, II, p. 475.

conduct, a spirit of confidence based on the absolute religious values of love of God and love of one's neighbour rather than a set of obligations derived from an analysis of man's place in the created universe. Furthermore, in its concentration on the quest of the individual for a 'gracious God', this emphasis sees nothing organic in the social order, save human solidarity in sin.

In the 'Protestant' tradition the Christian looks backward with confidence in God's mercy to the work of his salvation accomplished on the Cross and forward with eager expectation to the day of Christ's return when this present world, spoiled by sin, will be no more and a new earth will be revealed and the Christian, glorified with Christ, will share His triumph. At present he lives 'between the times' and also between the conflicting claims of the Christ and the exigencies of the temporal order.

It is traditional to distinguish within the 'Protestant' emphasis the Calvinist from the Lutheran contribution, in the development of social attitudes. For both leaders of the Reformation, however, the religious problem was the central one. Ethics was inseparable from dogma and of interest only as involved in the preaching of the pure doctrine of the Gospel.[1] However, Luther's over-riding concern for a personal assurance of salvation in the blessedness of inner experience, his division of spheres of human activity into the Two Realms of the Heavenly Kingdom of love and forgiveness and the Earthly Kingdom of the sword and the law where power and coercion hold sway, his view that the world is the devil's inn and the human heart alone the sanctuary of God's grace, suggests a separation of the concerns of the soul from the contamination of mundane affairs.[2] The emphasis of the German

---

[1] 'This is why it is so mistaken to try to save the honour of early Protestantism by attempting to discover in it "theological moral philosophers". The people of that day neither desired nor needed any ethic alongside of dogma; this only became necessary after the upheaval of the Enlightenment.' *Ibid.*, II, p. 524n.

[2] Professor Ernst Wolf concedes the absence of a social ethic in contemporary Lutheranism with this explanation: 'Il n'existe pas encore, à proprement parler, d'éthique sociale du luthéranisme; cette lacune est due au fait que le luthéranisme, dans sa forme allemande, s'est considéré à tort comme "individualiste-quiétiste"; ou bien encore cette lacune est due à ce que le luthéranisme a faussé les idées de Luther au point de vue de l'éthique sociale sous la forme où Luther les avait exprimées conformément aux conceptions de son époque, et il en est résulté une théorie sociale chrétienne sans prise sur le présent.' *Une Enquête sur l'Ethique Sociale des Eglises*, p. 32. On the other hand, the impressive proportions of the activities of modern German Lutherans in the social field have been listed by Dr. F. Karrenberg in 'Church and Social Questions in Germany' WCC Study Department document, 53E/346 (mimeographed), scheduled as a chapter in the projected volume, *National Developments in Christian Social Thinking*.

Reformer produces a piety not unconnected with religious isolationism; it has been charged with producing a social defeatism, a spiritual *laissez-faire*, an abandonment of the tasks of the temporal order.[1]

In Calvinism the emphasis is other.[2] It is not the blessedness of the creature in the assurance of personal salvation that is sought but solely the glory of God; it is not a repose in the happiness of forgiveness and confidence but the service expected of the elect that is high-lighted. God is as remote from his fallen creation as in the teachings of Luther —*Finitum non capax infiniti!*—but He has, in His ineffable Will, permanently predestined some as His friends. Their establishment in His favour is manifested not in an inwardness and depth of feeling but in the energy by which the individual reveals the fact of his election as an instrument for the tasks of the Kingdom. As a result, Calvinism has shown itself a more influential and dynamic influence in politics and social action.[3]

There is a dualism in Calvin's teaching also, adumbrated in the Fourth Book of his *Institutes*. Two Kingdoms are opposed, Christ's and the State, with the latter inferior to the former. If the teaching of the Genevan Reformer viewed the universe as a single Christocracy (denying thereby any legitimacy or subordinate autonomy to the natural order), it did not for that reason fail to engender an integral vision of human society in the light of the Gospel.[4] This vision was

---

[1] For example, by Reinhold Niebuhr: 'How completely a certain type of orthodoxy is able to destroy every vestige of Christian tension upon the moral life may be illustrated by one of the criticisms of this paper submitted by a German Lutheran theologian. . . . It is perhaps a proof of the difficulty of the ecumenical task which faces the Christian Church if I bluntly declare that if I thought for a moment that the Christian gospel meant what is implied in these words [the critic's], I would prefer not to be a Christian. In such an interpretation Christian eschatology becomes a source of moral complacency. One accepts all the relative injustice of the world as justice, regarding it in the same breath as both God-ordained and as doomed to destruction. Many a secularist has truer instincts for the moral realities than this complacency.' *Christian Faith and the Common Life*, pp. 87-9.

[2] 'Le calvinisme organise la communauté; le luthéranisme n'organise que la vie individuelle du chrétien.' Jean-Marcel Lechner, *Le Christianisme Social de Jean Calvin*, p. 9.

[3] 'Calvinism, in spite of its harder and less tender side [than Lutheranism], has been the sower of richer and more social ideas, as far as the history of the world is concerned. For it has claimed for the New Law that it is to inspire, control, and train human existence as brought into Christ's visible kingdom and covenant; aiming at the mastery of man's whole life; at once discipline and propaganda; in its relation with the civil government insisting on liberty, a liberty, in the past at least, mounting up often to supremacy.' C. E. Osborne, *Christian Ideas in Political History*, p. 212.

[4] 'Thus we may sum up the Gospel of Calvin in the following terms: a new Israel has been born, a new holy city has been founded, established upon the Divine Law, which has been deepened by the spirit of the New Testament, directed by the Will and the Grace

communicated to the elect by the Holy Spirit through the independent and infallible authority of the Bible (as proclaimed by its preachers), enlightening them about those regulatory principles which lead to the realization of the Kingdom of Christ. The result was an ascetic and utilitarian ethic, demonstrating personal election in a spirit of sober resolution[1] and active engagement in political and social activities[2] which have imprinted a characteristic mark especially on the civilization of Anglo-Saxon lands.

Whether the particular emphasis in social philosophy associated with the 'Protestant' emphasis clarifies or obscures the task of constructing the Temporal City is an item of controversy. In the opinion of Karl Barth the Reformers failed to establish a relation between the transcendental level of God's justification of the sinner and the issues of the proximate ends of man's existence including the problems of human law and social justice.[3] The ingenious efforts of the theologian of Basle to use the principle of analogy in constructing a bridge between the order of the paramount religious issues and the order of the humanly important issues has been found radically unsatisfactory by his famous Swiss colleague and contemporary, Emil Brunner.[4]

of God which deals out punishments and rewards, elected to be the organ for the glorification of Christ, the God-man, in whom the hidden electing will has become flesh, with power to create the community of the Church.' Troeltsch, *op. cit.*, II, p. 586.

[1] 'The characteristic element is everywhere unlimited industry with solely spiritual recreation, the cutting down of the sense-life to the unavoidable minimum but without bodily injury or mortification, the purely utilitarian treatment of all secular things as mere means and the exclusion of all that is earthly from this aim, the methodical and systematic discipline and direction towards a final end in the other life.' *Ibid.*, II, p. 891.

[2] 'This peculiar combination of ideas [Calvinism] produces a keen interest in politics, but not for the sake of the State; it produces active industry within the economic sphere, but not for the sake of wealth; it produces an eager social organization, but its aim is not material happiness; it produces unceasing labour, ever disciplining the senses, but none of this effort is for the sake of the object of all this industry. The one main controlling idea and purpose of this ethic is to glorify God, to produce the Holy Community, to attain that salvation which in election is held up as the aim; to this one idea all the other formal peculiarities of Calvinism are subordinate.' *Ibid.*, II, p. 607.

[3] 'First of all I will state the question thus: is there a connection between justification of the sinner through faith alone, completed once for all through Jesus Christ, and the problem of justice, of human law? Is there an inward and vital connection by means of which in any sense human justice (or law) as well as divine justification becomes a concern of Christian faith and Christian responsibility and, therefore, also a matter which concerns the Christian Church? . . . To this question . . . we receive from the Reformers either no answer at all or, at best, a very inadequate answer.' *Church and State*, pp. 1–3.

[4] 'Anything and everything can be derived from the same principle of analogy; a monarchy just as much as a republic (Christ the King), the totalitarian State just as much

The problem is admittedly complicated. It is not merely a question of distinguishing which things belong to Caesar and which to God but of establishing what is the relation between the realities of the two categories. Conceivably, the problem was muddied when Luther announced that 'there is no greater enemy of grace than Aristotle's ethics'. The Greek political philosopher had offered a rational inquiry on the roots and range of human justice. On the origins and nature of human justice, as well as on the fashion of determining its claims, opinion in the constituency of the World Council of Churches is divided by conceptions as fundamentally different and as 'mutually inconsistent' (in the language of the Amsterdam Report) as its divergent views on the nature of the Church. Indeed the conflict of ideas on the two subjects is not unrelated, being a manifestation of differing corporate traditions of the understanding of Christian life and faith—a fact which makes a synthesis of the Social Thought of the World Council of Churches impossible and a summary of its positions on social questions and international affairs somewhat inconclusive.

as a state with civil liberties (Christ the Lord of all; man, a servant, indeed, a slave of Jesus Christ).' *Christianity and Civilization* (Gifford Lectures) I, p. 319 as quoted in Gill, *Recent Protestant Political Theory*, who adds: 'The Christological social ethics fails in practice. Either it claims too much for the areas of immediate activity, confusing Church and State, holy causes and good causes, love and justice. Or in reaction it resigns the proximate areas (which only borrow their significance) to the relative unimportance whence the essentials had lifted them by sharing with them their own ultimate importance.' p. 180.

BIBLIOGRAPHY

THE essential sources for this study are the Proceedings of the Assemblies of the World Council of Churches, the Minutes of the Secretaries of the Sections on Social Questions and International Affairs at Amsterdam and Evanston, the records of the meetings of the Study Department Commissions, the Minutes of the Meetings of the Central Committee and a few collections of official pronouncements. Among the published material are the following:

PRIMARY SOURCES

The First Assembly of the World Council of Churches: The Official Report, edited by W. A. Visser 't Hooft. New York: Harper & Bros., 1948. London: S.C.M. Press, 1949.

Evanston Speaks: Reports from the Second Assembly of the World Council of Churches, August 15–31, 1954. London: S.C.M. Press, 1954.

The Evanston Report: The Second Assembly of the World Council of Churches, 1954, edited by W. A. Visser 't Hooft. London: S.C.M. Press, 1955. New York: Harper & Bros., 1955.

Minutes and Reports of the Meeting of the Provisional Committee, Buck Hill Falls, Penn., April, 1947. Geneva: World Council of Churches, 1947.

Documents of the World Council of Churches. Geneva: World Council of Churches, 1948.

Minutes of the Meeting of the Central Committee of the World Council of Churches, Amsterdam and Woudschoten (mimeographed). Geneva: World Council of Churches, 1948.

Minutes and Reports of the Second Meeting of the Central Committee (Chichester). Geneva: World Council of Churches, 1949.

Minutes and Reports of the Third Meeting of the Central Committee (Toronto). Geneva: World Council of Churches, 1950.

Minutes and Reports of the Fourth Meeting of the Central Committee (Rolle). Geneva: World Council of Churches, 1951.

Minutes and Reports of the Fifth Meeting of the Central Committee (Lucknow). Geneva: World Council of Churches, 1953.

Assembly Work Book, Evanston, 1954. Geneva: World Council of Churches, 1954.

The Ecumenical Press Service. Weekly, 1933– . Geneva: World Council of Churches. Before January 1947, known as the International Christian Press and Information Service.

The Ecumenical Review. Quarterly, 1948– . Geneva: World Council of Churches.

Annual Report of the Officers of the Commission of the Churches on International Affairs established by the World Council of Churches and the International Missionary Council, 1947– .

SECONDARY SOURCES

(*a*) ECUMENICAL DISCUSSIONS

Une Enquête sur l'Ethique Sociale des Eglises. Geneva: Section des Recherches du Conseil Oecuménique du Christianisme Pratique, 1935.

From the Bible to the Modern World (mimeographed). Geneva: World Council Study Department, 1947.

Contributions to a Christian Social Ethic. Cahier de Bossey, No. 4. Geneva: Edition Oikumene, 1949.

Christian Action in Secular Society. Oxford, June 29–July 5, 1949 (mimeographed). Geneva: World Council of Churches, 1949.

The Christian Prospect in Eastern Asia. Papers and Minutes of the Eastern Asia Christian Conference, Bangkok, December 3–11, 1949. New York: Friendship Press, 1950.

The Treysa Conference on the Biblical Doctrine of Law and Justice. Geneva: World Council of Churches, 1951.

Christ—Hope of Asia. Madras: The Christian Literature Society, 1953.

(*b*) HISTORICAL SURVEYS

A History of the Ecumenical Movement, 1517–1948, edited by Ruth Rouse and Stephen C. Neill. London: S.P.C.K., 1954. Philadelphia: Westminster Press, 1954.

The Ten Formative Years, by W. A. Visser 't Hooft. Geneva: World Council of Churches, 1948.

The First Six Years, 1948–1954. A Report of the Central Committee of the World Council of Churches on the Activities of the Departments and Secretariats of the Council. Geneva: World Council of Churches, 1954.

(*c*) BACKGROUND MATERIAL FOR DELEGATES:

TO AMSTERDAM 1948

The Church and the Disorder of Society. London: S.C.M. Press, 1948. New York: Harper & Bros., 1948.

The Church and the International Disorder. London: S.C.M. Press, 1948. New York: Harper & Bros., 1948.

TO EVANSTON 1954

Christ—The Hope of the World: Report of the Advisory Commission on the Main Theme of the Second Assembly. Geneva: World Council of Churches, 1952.

The Second Report of the Advisory Commission on the Main Theme of the Second Assembly. Geneva: World Council of Churches, 1952.

Our Oneness in Christ and our Disunity as Churches. New York: Harper & Bros., 1954.

The Responsible Society in a World Perspective. New York: Harper & Bros., 1954.

The Christian in his Vocation. New York: Harper & Bros., 1954.

Christians in the Struggle for World Community. New York: Harper & Bros., 1954.

The Church amid Racial and Ethnic Tensions. New York: Harper & Bros., 1954.

The Christian Hope and the Task of the Churches. New York: Harper & Bros., 1954. An omnibus volume containing the foregoing Background Material for Evanston.

Ecumenical Documents on Church and Society (1925–1953), edited by John W. Turnbull (mimeographed). Geneva: World Council of Churches, 1954.

TO OXFORD 1937

The Christian Understanding of Man;
The Kingdom of God and History;
The Christian Faith and the Common Life;
Church and Community;
Church, Community and State in Relation to Education;
The Universal Church and the World of Nations;
all published in London by Allen & Unwin, 1937.

(*d*) PROCEEDINGS OF EARLIER ECUMENICAL CONFERENCES

The Stockholm Conference of 1925, edited by G. K. A. Bell. London: Humphrey Milford for the Oxford University Press, 1926.

Die Stockholmer Weltkirchenconferenz, edited by Adolf Deissmann. Berlin: Furche-Verlag, 1926.

La Conférence Universelle du Christianisme Pratique, Stockholm 19–29 Août, 1925. Saint-Etienne: Editions du 'Christianisme Social', 1926.

Faith and Order: Proceedings of the World Conference, Lausanne, August 1927, edited by H. N. Bate. London: S.C.M. Press, 1927. New York: Morehouse Publishing Co., 1927.

Le Christianisme Social. Tirage à part des numéros 4, 7, 8. Septembre-Decembre, 1935.

The Churches Survey Their Task: The Report of the Conference at Oxford, July 1937, on Church, Community and State, edited by J. H. Oldham. London: Allen and Unwin, 1937.

The Second World Conference on Faith and Order, edited by Leonard Hodgson. London: S.C.M. Press, 1938.

The Church and the State, edited by Kenneth G. Grubb. (Volume VI of the Reports of the Meeting of the International Missionary Council at Tambaram, India.) London: Humphrey Milford for the Oxford University Press, 1939.

Christus Victor: The Report of the World Conference of Christian Youth, Amsterdam, 1939, edited by Denzill G. M. Patrick. Geneva: Conference Headquarters, 1939.

(e) PERIODICALS OF CHRISTIAN SOCIAL THOUGHT

The Christian Century (Chicago).
Christianity and Crisis (New York).
The Christian Frontier (London).
Social Action (New York).
Revue du Christianisme Social (Paris).
Church and Society (Geneva).

GENERAL READING

(†cited in present work)

ALLEN, FREDERICK LEWIS. *The Big Change: America Transforms Itself, 1900–1950.* London: Hamish Hamilton, 1952. New York: Harper & Bros., 1952.

†ARON, RAYMOND. *L'Opium des Intellectuels.* Paris: Calmann-Lévy, 1955.

BAKER, A. E. *William Temple and His Message.* London and New York: Penguin, 1946. Out of print.

BAKER, A. E. *William Temple's Teaching.* London: James Clarke, 1949. Substantially a reproduction of the previous work.

†BARTH, KARL. *Parole de Dieu, Parole Humaine.* Paris: Editions 'Je Sers', 1933.

†BARTH, KARL. *Révélation, Eglise, Théologie.* Paris: Editions 'Je Sers', 1934.

†BARTH, KARL. *Church and State.* London: S.C.M. Press, 1939.

†BARTH, KARL. *Against the Stream.* London: S.C.M. Press, 1954.

†BELL, G. K. A. (ed.). *Documents on Christian Unity.* Oxford: University Press (First Series) 1924; (Second Series) 1930; (Third Series) 1948.

BELL, G. K. A. *The Kingship of Christ: The Story of the World Council of Churches.* London and New York: Penguin, 1954.

†BENNETT, JOHN C. *Christian Ethics and Social Policy.* New York: Scribner's Sons, 1946.

BENNETT, JOHN C. *Christianity and Communism.* London: S.C.M. Press, 1949; New York: Association Press, 1949.

†BERDYAEV, NICOLAS. *The Origin of Russian Communism.* London: Geoffrey Bles, 1937.

†BERGGRAV, E. *Der Staat und der Mensch.* Stockholm: Neuer Verlag, 1946. Eng. trans. *Man and State.* Philadelphia: Muhlenberg Press, 1951.

D'ENTREVES, A. P. *Natural Law*. London: Hutchinson, 1951.

†DEWEY, JOHN. *Democracy and Education*. New York: Macmillan, 1916.

DOORNKAAT, HANS TEN. *Die Oekumenischen Arbeiten aus Sozialen Fragen*. Zürich: Gotthelf-Verlag, 1953.

†DU PASQUIER, CLAUDE. 'La Liberté et le Droit Suisse' in *Die Freiheit des Bürgers im Schweizerischen Recht*. Zürich: Polygraphischer Verlag, 1948.

†EHRENSTRÖM, NILS. *Christian Faith and the Modern State*. London: S.C.M. Press, 1937. Chicago and New York: Willett Clark, 1937.

†ELIOT, T. S. *Murder in the Cathedral*. London: Faber and Faber, 1938. New York: Harcourt, Brace, 1940.

†ELIOT, T. S. *The Idea of a Christian Society*. London: Faber and Faber, 1939. New York: Harcourt, Brace, 1940.

ELLUL, JACQUES ET AL. *L'Homme, Mesure de Toute Chose*. Geneva: Centre Protestant d'Etudes, 1947.

†FANFANI, AMINTORE. *Catholicism, Protestantism and Capitalism*. London and New York: Sheed and Ward, 1938.

FENN, ERIC. *That They Go Forward*. London: S.C.M. Press, 1938.

†FLEW, R. NEWTON (ed.) *The Nature of the Church*. London: S.C.M. Press, 1952. New York: Harper & Bros., 1952.

†GABRIEL, RALPH HENRY. *The Course of American Democratic Thought*. New York: Ronald Press, 1940.

†GARBETT, CYRIL. *Church and State in England*. London: Hodder and Stoughton, 1950.

†GILL, THEODORE ALEXANDER. *Recent Protestant Political Theory*. (University of Zürich Thesis.) Privately printed.

GLOYN, CYRIL K. *The Church in the Social Order: A Study in Anglican Social Theory from Coleridge to Maurice*. Forest Grove, Oregon: Pacific University Press, 1942.

GREENSLADE, S. L. *The Church and the Social Order*. London: S.C.M. Press, 1948.

†HALLOWELL, JOHN H. *The Moral Foundations of Democracy*. Chicago: University Press, 1954.

†HERKLOTS, H. G. G. *Looking at Evanston*. London: S.C.M. Press, 1954.

HERMAN, STEWART WINFIELD. *The Rebirth of the German Church*. London: S.C.M. Press, 1946. New York: Harper & Bros., 1946.

†HERMAN, STEWART WINFIELD. *Report from Christian Europe*. New York: Friendship Press, 1953.

†HOCKING, W. E. (ed.) *Rethinking Missions: A Layman's Inquiry After One Hundred Years*. New York: Harper & Bros., 1932.

HOFFMANN, J. G. H. *N. Söderblom, Prophète de l'Oecuménisme*. Geneva: Editions Labor et Fides, 1948.

BIBLIOGRAPHY

†BERLE, ADOLF A., Jr. *The Twentieth Century Capitalist Re*
York: Harcourt, Brace, 1954.

BINGLE, E. J. and GRUBB, K. G. (eds.) *World Christian H*
London: World Dominion Press, 1953.

BINYON, GILBERT C. *The Christian Socialist Movement in Engl*
S.P.C.K., 1931.

†BOYD ORR, LORD. *The White Man's Dilemma.* London: All
1953. New York: British Book Centre, 1953.

†BRADY, ROBERT. *Business as a System of Power.* New Yor
University Press, 1943.

†BROGAN, DENIS. *The Price of Revolution.* London: Hamish Hami

†BROWN, WILLIAM ADAMS. *Toward a United Church.* New Yor
Sons, 1946.

†BRUNNER, EMIL. *Der Staat als Problem der Kirche.* Bern und Leipz
Verlag, 1923.

†BRUNNER, EMIL. *Die Kirche und das Staatsproblem.* Bern ui
Gotthelf-Verlag, 1923.

†BRUNNER, EMIL. *The Divine Imperative.* London: Lutterworth Pr

†BRUNNER, EMIL. *Justice and the Social Order.* London: Lutterw
1945. New York: Harper & Bros., 1945.

†BRUNNER, EMIL. *Christianity and Civilisation.* 2 vols. Londc
1948–9.

†CASSERLEY, J. V. L. *The Retreat from Christianity in the Modern Worla*
Longmans, 1952.

†CHENEVIÈRE, MARC-EDOUARD. *La Pensée Politique de Calvin*
de l'Université de Genève). Geneva: Editions Labor et Fi
Paris: Editions 'Je Sers', 1937.

†CLAY, LUCIUS D. *Decision in Germany.* New York: Doubleday, 19

†COCKBURN, J. HUTCHINSON. *Religious Freedom in Eastern Europe.* R
Va.: John Knox Press, 1951.

†COPEC, Proceedings of. London: Longmans, 1924.

†COURVOISIER, JACQUES. *Brève Histoire du Protestantisme.* Neuchâtel: D
et Niestlé, 1952.

DARK, SIDNEY (ed.) *Toward a Christian Social Order.* London: E
Spottiswoode, 1942.

†DAVIES, D. R. *Reinhold Niebuhr, Prophet from America.* Londor
Clarke, 1945. New York: Macmillan, 1948.

†DE DIÉTRICH, SUZANNE. *Cinquante Ans d'Histoire.* Paris: Editions du :
n.d.

†DEMANT, V. A. *Theology of Society.* London: Faber and Faber, 1947.

DEMANT, V. A. *Religion and the Decline of Capitalism.* London: Fal
Faber, 1952.

HOGG, WILLIAM R. *Ecumenical Foundations*. New York: Harper & Bros., 1951.

†HOPKINS, CHARLES HOWARD. *The Rise of the Social Gospel in American Protestantism, 1865–1915*. New Haven: Yale University Press, 1940. Oxford: University Press, 1941.

HORTON, WALTER MARSHALL. *Contemporary English Theology*. New York: Harper & Bros., 1936. London: S.C.M. Press, 1940.

HORTON, WALTER MARSHALL. *Contemporary Continental Theology*. New York: Harper & Bros., 1936. London: S.C.M. Press, 1938.

†HORTON, WALTER MARSHALL. *Towards a Reborn Church*. New York: Harper & Bros., 1949.

†HUBER, MAX. *Staatenpolitik und Evangelium*. Zürich: Schulthess, 1923.

†HUTCHINSON, JOHN A. *We Are Not Divided*. New York: Round Table Press, 1941.

†HUTCHINSON, JOHN A. (ed.) *Christian Faith and Social Action*. New York: Scribner's Sons, 1953.

IREMONGER, F. A. *William Temple, Archbishop of Canterbury: His Life and Letters*. Oxford: University Press, 1948.

†JOHNSON, F. ERNEST. *The Social Gospel Re-examined*. New York: Harper & Bros., 1940. London: James Clarke, 1942.

KARRENBERG, FRIEDRICH (ed.) *Evangelisches Soziallexikon*. Stuttgart: Kreuz-Verlag, 1954.

†KELLER, ADOLF. *Karl Barth and Christian Unity*. London: Lutterworth Press, 1933. New York: Macmillan, 1933.

†KELLER, ADOLF. *Church and State on the European Continent*. London: Epworth Press, 1936.

KELLER, ADOLF. *Christian Europe Today*. New York: Harper & Bros., 1942. London: Epworth Press, 1943.

†KENNAN, GEORGE F. *American Diplomacy, 1900–1950*. Chicago: University Press, 1951. London: Secker and Warburg, 1952.

KENNEDY, JAMES W. *Evanston Scrapbook*. Lebanon, Pa.: Sowers Printing Company, 1954.

KENYON, RUTH ET AL. *An Introduction to Christian Social Doctrine*. London: Church Literature Association, 1941. Out of print.

†KRAEMER, H. *The Christian Message in a Non-Christian World*. London: Edinburgh House Press (2nd edition), 1947.

†LATOURETTE, KENNETH SCOTT. *A History of the Expansion of Christianity*. New York: Harper & Bros., 1937–45. London: Eyre and Spottiswoode, 1938–46.

†LATREILLE, ANDRÉ and SIEGFRIED, ANDRÉ. *Les Forces Religieuses et la Vie Politique*. Paris: Armand Colin, 1951.

†LECHNER, JEAN-MARCEL. *Le Christianisme Social de Jean Calvin*. Geneva: Editions Labor et Fides, 1954.

LEIPER, HENRY SMITH. *Christ's Way and the World's in Church, State and Society.* New York: Association Press, 1936.

LEIPER, HENRY SMITH. *World Chaos or World Christianity.* Chicago and New York: Willett Clark, 1937.

†LIGIER, SIMON. *L'Adulte des Milieux Ouvriers.* 2 vols. Paris: Les Editions Ouvrières, 1951.

LIPPMAN, WALTER. *Essays in the Public Philosophy.* Boston: Little, Brown & Co., 1955. London: Hamish Hamilton, 1955.

LOCHER, GOTTFRIED W. *Der Eigentumsbegriff als Problem Evangelischer Theologie.* Zürich: Zwingli-Verlag, 1954.

McCONNACHIE, JOHN. *The Significance of Karl Barth.* London: Hodder and Stoughton, 1931.

McCONNACHIE, JOHN. *The Barthian Theology and the Man of Today.* London: Hodder and Stoughton, 1933.

†MACFARLAND, CHARLES S. *Christian Unity in Practice and Prophecy.* New York: Macmillan, 1933.

MACFARLAND, CHARLES S. *The New Church and the New Germany.* New York: Macmillan, 1934.

MACFARLAND, CHARLES S. *Across the Years.* New York: Macmillan, 1936.

†MACFARLAND, CHARLES S. *Steps Towards a United Church.* New York: Fleming H. Revell, 1937.

†McINTYRE, CARL. *The Rise of the Tyrant.* Collingswood, N.J.: Christian Beacon Press, 1945.

MACKINNON, D. M. (ed.) *Christian Faith and Communist Faith.* London: Macmillan, 1953. New York: St. Martin's Press, 1953.

McNEILL, JOHN T. *Modern Christian Movements.* Philadelphia: Westminster Press, 1954.

McNEILL, JOHN T. *The History and Character of Calvinism.* Oxford: University Press, 1954. New York: Oxford University Press, 1954.

†MALVERN, 1941. *The Life of the Church and the Order of Society.* Being the Proceedings of the Archbishop of York's Conference. London: Longmans, 1941.

MARSH, JOHN. *The Significance of Evanston.* London: Independent Press, 1954.

MARTIN, HUGH ET AL. *Christian Counter-Attack: Europe's Churches Against Nazism.* London: S.C.M. Press, 1943.

†MATHEWS, SHAILER. *The Social Teaching of Jesus.* New York: Macmillan, 1902.

MATTHEWS, BASIL. *John R. Mott: World Citizen.* London: S.C.M. Press, 1934. New York: Harper & Bros., 1934.

MUELDER, WALTER G. *The Meaning of the Responsible Society.* Boston: University Press, 1954.

MYERS, JAMES. *Religion Lends a Hand.* New York: Harper & Bros., 1929.

†NASH, ARNOLD S. (ed.) *Protestant Thought in the Twentieth Century.* New York: Macmillan, 1951.

†NEILL, STEPHEN C. *The Christian Society.* London: Nisbet, 1952. New York: Harper & Bros., 1953.

†NEILL, STEPHEN C. *Towards Church Union, 1937–1952.* London: S.C.M. Press, 1952.

†NELSON, J. ROBERT. *The Realm of Redemption.* London: Epworth Press, 1951.

†NICHOLS, JAMES HASTINGS. *Democracy and the Churches.* Philadelphia: Westminster Press, 1951.

†NICHOLS, JAMES HASTINGS. *Evanston: An Interpretation.* New York: Harper & Bros., 1955.

†NIEBUHR, H. RICHARD. *The Social Sources of Denominationalism.* New York: Harper & Bros., 1929.

†NIEBUHR, REINHOLD. *Moral Man and Immoral Society.* New York: Scribner's Sons, 1932. London: Scribner's Sons, 1933.

†NIEBUHR, REINHOLD. *Christianity and Power Politics.* New York: Scribner's Sons, 1940.

†NIEBUHR, REINHOLD. *The Children of Light and the Children of Darkness.* London: Nisbet, 1945. New York: Scribner's Sons, 1947.

NIEBUHR, REINHOLD. *Discerning the Signs of the Times.* London: S.C.M. Press, 1946. New York: Scribner's Sons, 1946.

†NIEBUHR, REINHOLD. *Faith and History.* London: Nisbet, 1949. New York: Scribner's Sons, 1949.

†NISBET, ROBERT A. *The Quest for Community.* Oxford: University Press, 1953. New York: Oxford University Press, 1953.

NORTHCOTT, CECIL. *Answer from Amsterdam.* London: Independent Press, 1949. Boston: Pilgrim Press, 1949.

†NORTHCOTT, CECIL. *Evanston World Assembly.* London: Lutterworth Press, 1954.

†OSBORNE, C. E. *Christian Ideas in Political History.* London: John Murray, 1929.

†OSUSKY, STEFAN. *The Way of the Free.* New York: Dutton, 1951. London: Benn, 1952.

†OUTERBRIDGE, LEONARD M. *The Lost Churches of China.* Philadelphia: Westminster Press, 1952.

PECK, W. G. *An Outline of Christian Sociology.* London: James Clarke, 1949.

†POLLOCK, SIR FREDERICK and MAITLAND, FREDERICK WILLIAM. *The History of English Law before the Time of Edward I.* 2 vols. Cambridge: University Press, 1895.

†RAPPARD, WILLIAM E. *A Quoi Tient la Supériorité Economique des Etats-Unis?* Paris: Librairie Médicis, 1954.

RAUSCHENBUSCH, W. *Christianity and the Social Crisis.* New York: Macmillan, 1911.

RAUSCHENBUSCH, W. *Christianizing the Social Order.* New York: Macmillan, 1921.

RAVEN, CHARLES E. *The Theological Basis of Christian Pacifism.* New York: Fellowship Publications, 1951. London: Fellowship of Reconciliation, 1952.

RECKITT, MAURICE B. *Faith and Society: A Study of the Structure, Outlook and Opportunity of the Christian Social Movement in Great Britain and the United States of America.* London and New York: Longmans, 1932.

RECKITT, MAURICE B. (ed.) *Prospect for Christendom.* London: Faber and Faber, 1945.

†RECKITT, MAURICE B. *Maurice to Temple.* London: Faber and Faber, 1947.

†RICHARDSON, ALAN and SCHWEITZER, WOLFGANG (eds.) *Biblical Authority for Today.* A World Council of Churches Symposium. London: S.C.M. Press, 1951.

†RIESMAN, DAVID. *The Lonely Crowd.* New Haven: Yale University Press, 1950. Oxford: University Press, 1951.

†RIESMAN, DAVID. *Faces in the Crowd.* Oxford: University Press, 1952. New Haven: Yale University Press, 1952.

†RIESMAN, DAVID. *Individualism Reconsidered.* Glencoe, Illinois: Free Press, 1954.

†RÖPKE, WILLIAM. *Civitas Humana.* London: Hodge, 1948. Chicago: University Press, 1953.

†ROWNTREE, B. SEEBOHM and LAVERS, G. R. *English Life and Leisure.* London: Longmans, 1951.

RUPP, J. C. C. *Die Sociaal-Economische Boodschap der Protestantse Kerken.* Den Haag: Uitgeverij Albani, n.d.

†SETON-WATSON, HUGH. *The East European Revolution.* London: Methuen, 1950.

†SHEDD, CLARENCE P. *Two Centuries of Student Christian Movements.* New York: Association Press, 1934.

SHILLITO, EDWARD. *Life and Work.* The Universal Christian Conference on Life and Work held in Stockholm 1925. London and New York: Longmans, 1926.

†SOMERVELL, D. C. *English Thought in the 19th Century.* London: Methuen, 1929.

†SOPER, DAVID WESLEY. *Major Voices in American Theology.* Philadelphia: Westminster Press, 1952.

†SPERRY, WILLARD L. *Religion in America.* Cambridge: University Press, 1945.

†STUART, JOHN LEIGHTON. *My Fifty Years in China.* New York: Random House, 1954.

†TATLOW, T. *The Story of the S.C.M. in Great Britain and Ireland.* London: S.C.M. Press, 1933.

†TAWNEY, R. H. *Religion and the Rise of Capitalism.* London: John Murray, 1926. New York: Harcourt, Brace, 1926.

TEMPLE, WILLIAM. *Essays in Christian Politics and Kindred Subjects*. London: Longmans, 1933.

†TEMPLE, WILLIAM. *Christianity and Social Order*. London: Penguin, 1942.

†TOMKINS, OLIVER S. (ed.) *The Third World Conference on Faith and Order, Lund, 1952*. London: S.C.M. Press, 1953.

†TRIBE, REGINALD. *The Christian Social Tradition*. London: S.P.C.K., 1935. New York: Macmillan, 1935.

†TROELTSCH, ERNST. *The Social Teaching of the Christian Churches*. Eng. trans. London: Allen and Unwin, 1931. New York: Macmillan, 1931.

†VAN DUSEN, H. P. and CAVERT, S. McC. *The Church Through Half a Century*. New York: Scribner's Sons, 1936.

VIDLER, A. R. and WHITEHOUSE, W. A. (eds.) *Natural Law: A Christian Re-consideration*. London: S.C.M. Press, 1946.

†VISSER 'T HOOFT, W. A. *The Background of the Social Gospel in America*. Haarlem: H. D. Tjeenk Willink, 1928.

†VISSER 'T HOOFT, W. A. *Introduction à Karl Barth*. Paris: Editions 'Je Sers', n.d.

†VISSER 'T HOOFT, W. A. *Le Conseil Oecuménique des Eglises: Sa Nature et ses Limites*. Geneva: Edition Oikumene, n.d. Tiré à part, extrait de *Hommage et Reconnaissance* (Neuchâtel: Delachaux et Niestlé, 1946).

†VISSER 'T HOOFT, W. A. *The Kingship of Christ*. London: S.C.M. Press, 1948. New York: Harper & Bros., 1948.

†VISSER 'T HOOFT, W. A. and OLDHAM, J. H. (eds.) *The Church and its Function in Society*. London: Allen and Unwin, 1937.

WARD, A. DUDLEY (ed.) *Goals for Economic Life*. New York: Harper & Bros., 1953.

†WHYTE, WILLIAM H., Jr. (ed.) *Is Anybody Listening?* New York: Simon and Schuster, 1952.

†WILLIAMS, DANIEL DAY. *Interpreting Theology, 1918–1952*. London: S.C.M. Press, 1953. Published in the USA under the title *What Present-Day Theologians are Thinking*. New York: Harper & Bros., 1952.

†WINSLOW JONES, ALFRED. *Life, Liberty and Property*. Philadelphia: Lippincott, 1941.

†ZABRISKIE, ALEXANDER C. *Bishop Brent*. Philadelphia: Westminster Press, 1948.

INDEX

AALAN, Prof. L., 233
Abrecht, Rev. Paul, v, 56 n., 95, 164 n., 248 n., 301 n.
Adenauer, Chancellor Konrad, 234 n.
Agriculture, 199, 201
Alexei, Patriarch of Moscow, 40 n., 132 n.
Amsterdam 1948, First Assembly of World Council, xii; absence of Orthodox, 17 n., 41 ff.; analysis of social disorder, 170–80; on bearing of arms, 258; on capitalism, 202 n., 206 ff., 219 n.; on causes of war, 257; on civic obligations, 224; on co-existence, 260; on communism, 45, 209–13; general reactions to, 46 ff., 289 n.; on human rights, 276 ff.; on international ethos, 270; on internatonal situation, 256 f.; on means of Christian influence, 224 f.; meeting of, 44–8; on national sovereignty, 262; on need of institutions, 188, 275; political orientation of delegates, 213–19; on political parties, 233 ff.; preparations for, 39 ff., 91 n., 133 n., 159 –64, 268 f., 297 n.; on property, 123 ff., 188; on race relations, 240 f.; on religious liberty, 277; reservations of Orthodox, 78; on resistance to totalitarianism, 245; on socialism, 188 f.; on the Responsible Society, 191 f.; on underdeveloped countries, 188 f.; on the United Nations, 189
Amsterdam–Woudschoten Meeting of Central Committee, xii, 48
Anglicanism, 12, 71 n.
Apartheid, 12, 51, 59, 306
Aron, Raymond, 221 n., 286 n.
Asmussen, Pastor Hans, 10
Associations Professionelles Protestantes, 231
Athenagoras, Archbishop (Metropolitan of Thyateira), 55 n.
Athenagoras, Patriarch of Constantinople, 79
Atkinson, Dr. Henry A., 26 n., 29 n.
Atom bomb, 2, 263
Augustine, St. (of Hippo), 120, 267, 316
Azariah, Bishop V. S., 23 n.

BABBITT, Prof. Irving, 310
Baillie, Prof. John, 61 n., 68
Banning, Prof. William, v, 122 n.
Baptist World Alliance, 18 n.
Barberi, Bishop Sante Uberto, 61 n.
Barker, Prof. Ernest, 36
Barmen Declaration, 84
Barnes, Rev. Roswell P., 268 n.
Barth, Prof. Karl, 8, 11 n., 34 n., 45, 63, 71 n., 84, 96 n., 104, 111 ff., 120, 142, 150–5, 197 n., 215 n., 219, 233, 248, 250 f., 296 n., 310, 319
Barth, Peter, 136 n.
Basis, The, 62, 72 n.
Bates, Prof. M. Searle, 162, 175 f.
Bednar, Prof. Frantisek, 12 n.
Bell, Bishop G. K. A., 50 n., 61 n.
Bennett, Prof. John C., v, 8, 23 n., 46, 157 f., 160 n., 162, 167 n., 179, 192, 197 n., 202 n., 203 n., 216, 240 n., 242 n.
Berdyaev, Nicolas A., 218 n.
Bereczky, Bishop Albert, 54 n., 248 n., 285
Berggrav, Bishop Eivind, 116, 142 n., 250
Biblical Insights, 94, 100–5, 110–15, 296, 314 f.
Bièvres Meeting of Executive Committee, xii, 53
Billing, Bishop Einar, 29 n., 32 n.
Blake, Dr. Eugene C., 167 n.
Bliss, Mrs. Kathleen, 173
Boegner, Pasteur Marc, 17, 39 n., 69
Bossey Conference on International Law, xii, 115–18
Bossey Conference on the Bible and Social Questions, xii, 111 f.
Boyd Orr, Lord, 2 n.
Brady, Robert A., 205 n.
Bratsiotis, Prof. Panayotis, v, 128 n., 133 n., 167 n.
Brent, Bishop Charles H., 26 f.
Brilioth, Yngve (Archbishop of Uppsala), 63 f.
Brink, Dr. C. B., 244
British Council of Churches, 18 n.
Brogan, Prof. Denis, 4, 11 n.
Brotherhood Councils, 84

Imprimi Potest

GULIELMUS E. FITZGERALD, S.J.
Praepositus Provincialis, Provinciae Novae Angliae
Die: 20 Martii, 1955

Nihil Obstat

REV. JAMES F. REDDING, Ph.D.
Diocesan Censor Deputatus

Imprimatur

RICHARD J. CUSHING
Archbishop of Boston
Die: 4 Aprilis, 1955